# Thinking
## Sociologically

# Thinking Sociologically

SECOND EDITION

**SHELDON GOLDENBERG**

Toronto   New York   Oxford
OXFORD UNIVERSITY PRESS
1997

Oxford University Press
70 Wynford Drive, Don Mills, Ontario M3C 1J9

*Oxford  New York*
*Athens  Auckland  Bangkok  Bombay*
*Calcutta  Cape Town  Dar es Salaam  Delhi*
*Florence  Hong Kong  Istanbul  Karachi*
*Kuala Lumpur  Madras  Madrid  Melbourne*
*Mexico City  Nairobi  Paris  Singapore*
*Taipei  Tokyo  Toronto*

and associated companies in
*Berlin  Ibadan*

*Oxford* is a trademark of Oxford University Press


**Canadian Cataloguing in Publication Data**

Goldenberg, Sheldon
    Thinking sociologically

2nd ed.
Includes bibliographical references and index.
ISBN 0-19-541201-X

1. Sociology.  2. Sociology – Methodology.   3. Thought
and thinking.  I. Title.

HM51.G625 1997      301      C96-932003-5


Design: Max Gabriel Izod
Compositor: Indelible Ink

1 2 3 4 - 00  99 98 97

This book is printed on permanent (acid-free) paper ∞.

Printed in Canada

To my late uncle Len, whose sense of humour never faltered.

# Contents

# Acknowledgements

It is, of course, impossible to thank or even name all those whose contributions have shaped this book in important ways. Still, some people contributed more than others, and I want to single them out for special mention here, in roughly chronological order:

My parents, Morris and Lillian, and my brothers, Syd and Barry, regularly and sympathetically challenged my ideas and provoked strident but constructive debate around the family dinner table. Perhaps my insistence on constructive criticism can be traced to these formative years.

Although many instructors played a role in teaching me what 'thinking sociologically' means, as I look back on my training four of my teachers—Allan Schnaiberg, Charles Tilly, Howard S. Becker, Jr, and Scott Greer—were particularly influential.

At the University of Calgary, Joe DiSanto, Jim Frideres, the late Sanford Labovitz, and Usher Fleising deserve to be acknowledged for the patience they showed in listening to my earlier ramblings; more recent discussions with Tullio Caputo and Val Haines have also shaped my understanding of what sociology is and how it might best be imparted to students. Diane Parsons Whitlow typed the first edition of this book and has continued to help in many ways in the preparation of this second edition.

The ideas in this book have evolved over some 20 years of teaching. During this time, all of my students have been subjected to these ideas, and their comments and criticisms have been essential, especially those of the graduate students who kindly volunteered to read and comment on the first draft and who have taken a proprietary interest in the manuscript throughout. Thanks to Ida, Cliff, and Margaret, and more recently to Michael, Warren, and Bill.

At Oxford University Press, Canada, I must thank Euan White and Ric Kitowski for their interest in helping me make this second edition a reality. Without their encouragement, it simply would not have happened.

Finally, thank you, Vikki, for all that you have continued to contribute, in so many ways so often taken for granted.

I thank all of you for your support and your help. It is our book, largely inspired by you and set to paper by me.

PETER L. BERGER. From *An Invitation to Sociology* by Peter Berger. Copyright © 1963 by Peter L. Berger. Used by permission of Doubleday, a division of Bantam Doubleday Dell Publishing Group, Inc. and Penguin Books USA Inc.

JESSIE BERNARD. From *The Future of Marriage*, Jessie Bernard, New York: Bantam, 1972, pp. 5–10.

MONICA BOYD and EDWARD T. PRYOR. 'Young adults living in their parents' homes' is reproduced by authority of the Minister of Industry, 1996, Statistics Canada, from *Canadian Social Trends*, 11–008, Summer 1989.

AUGUSTINE BRANNIGAN and SHELDON GOLDENBERG. 'The Study of Aggressive Pornography: The Vicissitudes of Relevance' from *Critical Studies in Mass Communication*, Speech Communication Association, Volume 4, September 1987, pp. 262–83.

JOEL CHARON. *Symbolic Interactionism: An Introduction, An Interpretation, An Integration*, 5/e © 1995. Reprinted by permission of Prentice-Hall, Inc., Upper Saddle River, NJ.

DAWN CURRIE. 'Re-thinking what we do and how we do it: a study of reproductive decisions', *CRSA/RCSA*, Volume 25:2 (1988), pp. 231–53. Reprinted by permission of the author and the Canadian Sociology and Anthropology Association.

WALTER DeKESEREDY and KATHARINE KELLY. 'The incidence and prevalence of woman abuse in Canadian university and college dating relationships' from *Canadian Journal of Sociology*, 18, 2, 1993, pp. 137–59. Reprinted by permission.

BONNIE J. FOX. 'On violent men and female victims: A comment on DeKeseredy and Kelly' from *Canadian Journal of Sociology*, 18, 3, 1993, pp. 321–4. Reprinted by permission.

ROSEMARY GARTNER. 'Studying woman abuse: A comment on DeKeseredy and Kelly' from *Canadian Journal of Sociology*, 18, 3, 1993, pp. 313–20. Reprinted by permission.

SHELDON GOLDENBERG. 'On Distinguishing Variables from Values and Hypotheses from Statements of Association' from *Teaching Sociology*, American Sociological Association, Volume 21, January 1993, pp. 100–4.

SHELDON GOLDENBERG and VALERIE A. HAINES. 'Social networks and institutional completeness: From territory to ties' from *Canadian Journal of Sociology*, 17, 3, 1992, pp. 301–12. Reprinted by permission.

RICHARD LaPIERE. From 'Attitudes and Actions' from *Social Forces*, University of North Carolina Press, Volume 13, 1934. Reprinted by permission of *Social Forces*.

STANLEY MILGRAM. 'The Experience of Living in Cities: A Psychological Analysis' reprinted with permission from *Science*, Volume 167, 13 March 1970, pp. 1461–8. Copyright 1970 American Association for the Advancement of Science.

D. PHILLIPS. From *Knowledge From What?*, D. Phillips, Chicago: Rand McNally, 1971, pp. 7–8.

NEIL POSTMAN and CHARLES WEINGARTNER. From *Teaching as a Subversive Activity* by Neil Postman and Charles Weingartner. Copyright © 1969 by Neil Postman and Charles Weingartner. Used by permission of Dell Books, a division of Bantam Doubleday Dell Publishing Group, Inc.

HYMAN RODMAN. *Journal of Marriage and the Family*, 'Marital Power in France, Greece, Yugoslavia, and the United States: A Cross-National Discussion', Hyman Rodman; 29:2 320–5. Copyrighted 1967 by the National Council on Family Relations, 3989 Central Avenue NE, Suite 550, Minneapolis, MN 55421. Reprinted by permission.

ALLAN SCHNAIBERG and SHELDON GOLDENBERG. 'From Empty Nest to Crowded Nest: The Dynamics of Incompletely-Launched Young Adults'. © 1989 by the Society for the Study of Social Problems. Reprinted from *Social Problems*, Vol. 36, No. 3, June 1989, pp. 251–8, by permission.

B. WELLMAN and S.D. BERKOWITZ. From *Social Structures: A Network Approach* by B. Wellman and S.D. Berkowitz (New York: Cambridge University Press, 1988). Reprinted with the permission of Cambridge University Press.

# Preface to the Second Edition

The first edition of this text came about as a result of an invitation to write an introductory text. In reply, I wrote a lengthy letter to the publisher in which I explained in some detail why I did *not* want to write another standard introductory book. Much to my surprise, the social science editor agreed and asked me to write the book I wanted to write. What you are reading is the second edition of that book. It has been significantly changed in response to my efforts to use it and make it more useful over the past decade.

Let me begin by sharing with you my concerns about standard texts, concerns that are not only clear throughout this volume but that have given me many worried nights during my teaching career.

## CRITIQUE OF STANDARD TEXTS

Standard texts seem to me to do the reader a great disservice, both in what they accomplish and in what they do not. They tend, from those written for elementary school children on, to be constructed as encyclopedias of facts, summarizing the current state of knowledge on each topic within a discipline. Such an orientation is misleading in several fundamental ways. Its main value is that students see part of the breadth of topics within a field. Yet curriculum-driven and fact-oriented coverage must remain partial, and it is almost always superficial as well. The most serious shortcoming of this orientation, though, is that *it fails abysmally even to attempt to teach students how to learn for themselves, since there is really no interaction with the student.*

This characteristic of standard texts has two elements, again in terms of what is and what is not taught. In the former category, students learn that the author's view is the only one that counts, that all questions have answers, and that the teacher's or text's are correct by fiat, and there is little point in, time for, or interest in, challenging them. At the same time, students are *not* taught how to think for themselves, how to assess evidence or even how to recognize what is relevant as evidence, how to read critically or sceptically or how to actually contribute their 'two cents' worth' to knowledge production. Standard texts abhor exploratory questions, whereas such questioning is the very core of education. They encourage a standardized transmission of information on the chapter-a-week formula.

## The Encyclopedia-of-Fact Fallacy

Textbook facts are often obsolete before the text appears; yet such books offer readers scant indication of this. Nor do they state that all claims to knowledge are, in fact, temporary in just that sense. From a standard text, one would certainly conclude—as most university students do—that knowledge is merely the accumulation of facts that dovetail neatly and that the work of scholars and their students is simply to add new facts to the storehouse. This is not so: claims to knowledge are made and challenged constantly. Some 'facts' stand up to evaluation better than others, but at times even the most basic ones are successfully challenged, and then our understanding of how the world works is radically revised. Such was the influence of Einstein or Darwin, for example. For just this reason contemporary social science has adopted a far more tentative and temporary regard for the status of all scientific claims to knowledge.

## The Denial-of-Disagreement Fallacy

Standard texts tend to be written in a simplistic and superficial manner, partly for the sake of coverage and partly to avoid 'confusing the student'. To read many of them, the 'facts' are clear and there is no disagreement among scientists. It is often not until fairly late in their careers that students realize that experts often disagree and that the 'facts' are anything but clear. I would argue that confusion and disagreement over the status of claims to knowledge are necessary parts of education and that oversimplification does not teach people how to deal with them intelligently. Standard texts deny the existence of confusion and disagreement, and so students learn as we have taught them—by demanding simple answers and running from complexity, by demanding that all questions be answered with no loose ends left behind. Such superficiality is both demeaning and counter-productive. In reality questions are never-ending, evidence is contested, disagreements flourish among 'experts', and loose ends both exist and are intriguing. Ignore this, and the challenge and much of the fun go too.

In contrast, standard texts teach hidden values, modes of non-thinking, obsolete knowledge claims—all things diametrically opposed to what education seems to me to be for and about. As a result, *students become more and more inept at handling their own further education*. They learn beyond doubt, but they learn things that are inappropriate and firmly rooted in the past even though we are speeding into the future.

This is a workbook. It is demanding of any reader, for in using this book one must go beyond it. Yet that is precisely what I believe the function of an introductory book to be—*it ought to encourage the reader to go beyond it*. It ought not to be a dead end, as so many introductory books seem to be. The impression from a standard introductory text is that the only reason to take advanced courses is to add more flesh—that is, facts—to the bones, but that in essence the text is a précis of the entire field. That is emphatically not the case with this book. *Thinking Sociologically* is only a limited introduction to a way of thinking, a way of practising sociology. It is not comprehensive, and I hope it is not superficial; introductory students still have much to learn even after reading this book. It simply tries to give them some idea of what the sociological imagination is and what sorts of things can be done with it.

## THE INTEGRATION OF THEORY, METHOD, AND SUBSTANCE

This book concentrates on the integration of theoretical and methodological or scientific concerns in its effort to help you develop an appreciation of, and some ability in using, a sociological perspective. Again this is in response to what I consider a gap that traditional books leave unfilled, a shortcoming that is often a source of great difficulty for students. Students rarely receive any help from their books in moving between the realms of theory and research. Though we may talk about the sociological imagination, we find it very difficult to convey any instruction in how to accomplish it. Standard texts tend to summarize and possibly to integrate findings, but they do not often teach how to develop an identifiably sociological hypothesis or translate it into a project that can be carried out in the real world. In chapter 6 of this text this problem is dealt with in the context of three illustrative research projects. In each of them, a problematic hypothesis is developed, and I describe several attempts to transform the hypothesis into a workable and defensible research project. Along the way, materials I mentioned in abstract form in chapters 2 to 5 are reintroduced in a far more applied context. It is my hope that this treatment will aid the reader in understanding the relationships between theory and research and in conducting his or her own research in an informed and thoughtful manner.

In addition, from the first chapter on, this second edition has been expanded by the inclusion of many more examples of sociological thinking, as problems are worked out with the reader, based on how students have dealt with them over the years and how I have found ways of explaining them more usefully to generations of those students. This text is now basically a workbook, a supplementary book with no substantive chapters as such. It is therefore a 'purer' attempt to teach the sociological perspective in use, and it relies on each instructor to teach the substantive materials he or she chooses to emphasize. In a sense, the illustrative articles now appended to most chapters have replaced what were once three substantive chapters. It is my hope that the inclusion of these articles will allow instructors to demonstrate, and readers to see, ways in which the arguments made in the chapters have been applied, even though few if any of the articles are themselves empirical hypothesis-testing papers. Though I have had a hand in most of these articles, they have not been selected for their quality but for their utility. Far from showcasing them, I ask for a critical assessment of them since I know them well, and of course, critical but open-minded assessment is what is emphasized throughout this book. I can think of no better skill to try to impart to those who would learn sociology.

I must admit, nonetheless, to some ambivalence in choosing to leave out all the substantive chapters from the first edition. It was my original intent to illustrate the ways in which perspective, theory, and methods have together influenced the kinds of questions asked and the interpretations of data collected in various substantive areas of interest to sociologists. I therefore included in the first edition of this text a critical and integrative review of some basic issues dealt with in each of the areas of the family, urban sociology, and identity. Disorganization perspectives were contrasted with network perspectives, and data were used to test propositions derived from both positions in an effort to let the student discover which made more sense of the phenomenon. This was an unconventional way of introducing students to substantive sociology, but it seemed appropriate within the context of this book.

I still think such an approach would be useful, but the choice of substantive areas is now completely in the hands of instructors and readers of this second edition. I expect that, along with this text, instructors will use a more substantive one, which will replace my original substantive chapters. It might still be useful to ask readers to do their own critical and integrative literature review of central questions in any area of substantive interest to them, concentrating on the chronological development of the treatment of their issues as they illustrate (if indeed they do) the movement from a disorganization perspective towards a more network-influenced perspective, or as they oscillate between macro-structural and micro-interpretive versions of the subject matter and between positivistic and interpretive attempts to come to terms with it. It might also be useful to provide several empirical papers in any area of interest to the instructor and to help students to take these apart and put them back together, having identified and assessed the central assumptions, hypotheses, design decisions, measurement choices, and data interpretation.

## WELL-INTENTIONED HINTS TO PROSPECTIVE READERS

As you can already tell, I have pulled no punches in this book. I do not talk down to the reader, nor is the book too difficult for most readers to understand. On the contrary, from my experience of teaching sociology from the introductory to the graduate level, I know that most readers at any level can handle this material, though not everyone equally well or without help. Some paragraphs, and perhaps even sections, may be hard to follow. At times you may feel lost or come across words that mean nothing to you. This is to be expected.

Pragmatically, I suggest you do what you might normally do in similar situations. Use a dictionary or ask for help from another person if you cannot understand a term or idea from its context, *and if* understanding it appears important. Where you find a section unclear, incomprehensible, or irrelevant, decide for yourself if it is worth working harder to grasp it. If you decide the section is of no real importance, skim or skip it. Most texts contain far more material than the reader can grasp the first time through. My experience has often been that a section of a book that made no sense to me at first suddenly acquired new meaning when I reread it later. This book is intended to speak to students at various levels with different interests or specializations.

Grasp what seem to you to be the central ideas of each chapter. The secondary ideas are less important. This is not a book in which the author assumes that each part is equally important, nor would I build tests on such an assumption. I have never found it necessary to ask for obscure or tangential material in order to 'catch' students. I believe it more reasonable to ask students only about the main idea in each section, and this is the orientation exemplified in the questions accompanying each chapter.

Use the structure of the book to guide you through the arguments and alternatives presented. That is the purpose of subtitles, headings, introductory sections, conclusions, and even paragraph leads. It has never been my intent to mislead you or to present ideas incoherently. Try to follow my logic by paying careful attention to the structural elements that are intended as guideposts.

Finally a word on theory. I mention, but do not take up in any detail, Marxism, ethnomethodology, structural functionalism, and other theories in sociology. Instead this book contrasts what one reviewer called the 'old warhorses' of the discipline with my view of the network approach. I do not mean to imply that discussing these other theories would be inappropriate; only that the way I have chosen strikes me as useful for my purposes. In an instructional setting, other materials can describe and introduce additional theoretical models used in the discipline. In other words—and I do not want to belabour the point—this book is truly intended to be introductory, and *it seeks to introduce not a body of knowledge but a mode of thinking*. In keeping with this goal, this is not a book to read, memorize, and regurgitate. It is a book to interact with, a book that asks you to read critically and imaginatively, a book that requires you to participate actively in your sociological education. It is my belief that if beginning sociology readers have learned how to think sociologically, they will make better use of the data presented in any course. They will use the studies they deem defensible and will not easily be persuaded by those that do not satisfy their critical evaluation. They will be far more intelligent consumers, and they will interact with the literature and with others far more critically and confidently than they otherwise might. In a real sense, in doing so they will be demonstrating their ability to think sociologically.

Much is accomplished in this book; more is mentioned, some directly and some indirectly. The reader may well be surprised at just how much one can learn while attending to so little, but there is much more. The measure of this book's success will be the number of readers who take up the invitation to enter further into the world of sociology and explore more of it, accepting the challenge to 'think sociologically'.

## TEACHING AND THINKING AS SUBVERSIVE ACTIVITIES

I can end this introduction in no more fitting a way than by telling the reader of my belief in teaching as a subversive activity, and I can do this no better than by quoting from the book with that title.[1] Thinking, whether sociologically or otherwise, is a critical skill. It will not endear you to everyone. It is risky and in a very real sense subversive. Even so, it is only by applying critical-thinking skills that we make what we read truly ours so we can claim to have actually learned.

The following statements are the authors' rather plaintive description of the premises of our existing system of education. I hope my book does not coincide with any of these principles.

Passive acceptance is a more desirable response to ideas than active criticism.

Discovering knowledge is beyond the power of students and is, in any case, none of their business.

Recall is the highest form of intellectual achievement, and the collection of unrelated 'facts' is the goal of education.

The voice of authority is to be trusted and valued more than independent judgment. Feelings are irrelevant in education.

There is always a single, unambiguous Right Answer to a question.

English is not History and History is not Science and Science is not Art and Art is not Music, and Art and Music are minor subjects, and English, History, and Science major subjects, and a subject is something you 'take' and, when you have taken it, you have 'had' it, and if you have 'had' it, you are immune and need not take it again. (The Vaccination Theory of Education?)

## NOTES

1  N. Postman and C. Weingartner, *Teaching as a Subversive Activity* (New York: Delacorte Press, 1969), pp. 20–1. Quotations copyright © 1969 by Neil Postman and Charles Weingartner.

# The Perspectives of Sociology and the Nature and Methods of Science

Part I has several purposes. Chapter 1 begins with a discussion of the kinds of questions that tend to be of interest to all of us and that, when dealt with systematically, begin to differentiate scientific treatments from others. I then suggest that these 'scientific' treatments tend to emphasize either nature or nurture and that such a distinction tends to separate natural scientists from social scientists, though only imperfectly. Narrowing the focus to social scientists, I suggest that each discipline tends to examine what may well be the same basic questions from a somewhat different perspective, and that sociology is characterized by two major perspectives. The elaboration of these perspectives completes the first chapter.

The second chapter goes on to discuss some of the concepts and processes that characterize science as an institution in general and to describe some essential characteristics of what could be termed the scientific way of thinking. Chapter 3 carries on in a narrower vein again, dealing specifically with competing treatments of the criteria usually used in the assessment and comparison of claims to knowledge by scientists. This chapter introduces a variety of methods employed by sociologists working from either of the two main perspectives introduced in chapter 1, and discusses their strengths as well as problematic aspects of each of them.

When you have finished part I, you should be able to imagine how you might conduct or at least design a sociological study of your own—one that seeks to explain variation in behaviour from either a macro-structural or a micro-interpretive perspective. You should also be able to evaluate scientific research more critically and knowledgeably. That is, you should be familiar with some fundamental criteria that social scientists use to judge the adequacy of claims to knowledge. Perhaps most important, you should have a sense of what defensible science, and credible sociology, look like and a clear idea of both how and why they can be produced.

# CHAPTER 1

# Social Science
# and the Perspectives
# of Sociology

I can't tell you the number of times I've been asked at parties what sociologists do or what sociology is. You may have experienced the same thing. If not, you will no doubt soon be asked if you continue to study sociology. Unfortunately there is no simple answer to this question, and most people at parties are not prepared to listen to a complex answer. They ask only as a matter of form, so you can tell them that sociology is the study of human behaviour as this is affected by the relationships among people. If your questioner shows real interest, you can go on to the kind of treatment provided here, if you find it persuasive.

In this chapter I try to provide you with a more sophisticated understanding of the ways in which and the degree to which sociology provides explanations of human behaviour that differ from natural science explanations and are even distinct from those of sociology's sister social sciences. There are two major perspectives in sociology, each with several variants. Since these two fundamental ways of explaining human behaviour differ in critical aspects, it makes a difference which way one adopts. Having read this chapter, the reader should have a sense of the main characteristics of these two competing perspectives, termed the social-structural and the micro-interpretive. He or she should also have some idea of how social science tends to differ from natural science and why these differences are important. Ideally readers should begin to be able to see how they could analyse aspects of their own lives in terms of the various perspectives introduced.

## THE ORIGINS OF SOCIAL SCIENCE

Social science emerges from the search for workable, useful explanations for variations in human behaviour. The questions we ask are not new, nor is our desire to make use of our knowledge. People have always wondered why other people behave as they do. In fact, attempts to make sense of such variation in behaviour are typically 'human' themselves. We want to know why revolutions occur in some countries and not in others, why some marriages end in divorce and others do not, why others like us or hate us, fight one another or love one another. We regularly use our knowledge of such things to try to affect the behaviour of others, whether in our capacities as politicians or voters, spouses or lovers, parents or children, students or teachers, friends or enemies.

We quickly learn that some explanations seem more useful than others. Good ones are reliable; poor ones do not work consistently. Science is simply the name we give to the evolving set of procedures that give us most often the most useful answers to the questions that interest us. Social science is the name we usually give these procedures when the questions concern human behaviour. Science is not the only means we have of attempting to answer questions, nor is science infallible. It is simply a set of guidelines that experience has shown to be productive. As we learn more, science too continues to change.

The search for something that works—and works consistently—expresses our belief that the universe is neither random nor whimsical. On the contrary we operate on the belief that people are alike in important ways and that they behave fairly consistently. In other words, we all more or less subscribe to a belief that human behaviour exhibits regularities and patterns and that a knowledge of the relevant patterns would allow us to anticipate, predict, and to an extent understand and perhaps even manipulate human behaviour. This belief in regularities or patterns in human behaviour is central to social science. If we did not believe that the study of an event, phenomenon or situation could tell us something about other instances of the same thing, since each was in principle unique, there would be nothing to be gained from study of the first, no general lesson to be learned from one and applied to others. Yet this is precisely the goal of science.

All social sciences then are systematic attempts to understand and explain variation in human behaviour, but not all such attempts are therefore social science. The characteristics of science are discussed more fully in the next chapter. For now I want to emphasize that, ideally, the scientific process is sceptical, systematic, evidentiary, and negativistic. Each of these general characteristics implies a host of procedures by which it can be implemented. Attempts to understand human behaviour that exhibit such procedures are more or less social scientific.

Perhaps the oldest and most basic distinction among scientific approaches to this question of why people act as they do is that between nature and nurture. This dichotomy emphasizes biological and hereditary factors on the one side as against learned and environmental ones on the other. Before discussing these, I have to note that these dichotomies, like all others, are exaggerations, and that although most real arguments may well tend to lean in one or the other direction, they do not fall neatly into so small a pigeonhole. The ends of the continuum are simplified and purified in the black and white of every dichotomy so that contrasts can most easily be understood.

In the broadest sense then, as illustrated in Figure 1.1, social scientists tend to believe in the primacy of learning and environmental explanations of behavioural variation, whereas natural scientists tend to rely first and foremost on biological explanations for the same behaviour. Thus, to social scientists deviance is primarily a learned response to a particular environmental condition, whereas natural scientists might emphasize the genetic or biological factors they think are the causes of deviance. Neither school necessarily believes that its own explanation is complete, but each does believe that its own explanation is primary or most powerful, and it is the one that occurs to them first when they consider the issue at hand.

**Figure 1.1** Basic Perspectives and Associated Disciplines

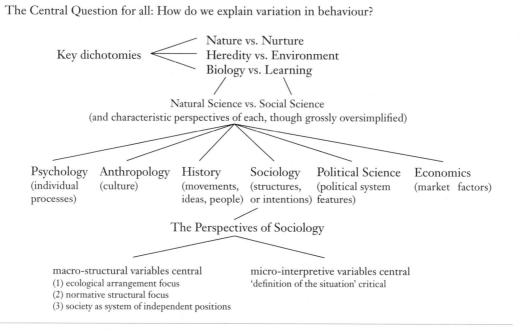

The Central Question for all: How do we explain variation in behaviour?

Key dichotomies
Nature vs. Nurture
Heredity vs. Environment
Biology vs. Learning

Natural Science vs. Social Science
(and characteristic perspectives of each, though grossly oversimplified)

Psychology (individual processes)  Anthropology (culture)  History (movements, ideas, people)  Sociology (structures, or intentions)  Political Science (political system features)  Economics (market factors)

The Perspectives of Sociology

macro-structural variables central
(1) ecological arrangement focus
(2) normative structural focus
(3) society as system of independent positions

micro-interpretive variables central
'definition of the situation' critical

For example, the image of the 'bad seed', captured in the book and movie of that name, may be useful here. To natural scientists, given their commitment to heredity, the root source of evil is the seed itself, and the title character was simply destined to be evil because she had inherited that quality from her parents. Although environmental conditions may affect its growth, the bad seed can only grow into a bad adult. It can no more change fundamentally than an apple can grow from the seed of an orange. A great many scientists have pursued the search for the biological sources of deviance, from studies of bumps on the head to morphological character (or body type) to chromosomal or genetic make-up and so on.

On the other hand, social scientists tend to begin from the premise that antisocial behaviour is learned in just the same way that conforming behaviour is, and this being so, anyone who has learned to behave in ways that are judged deviant can be resocialized, or taught, to unlearn one set of lessons and replace antisocial with social behaviour. At the very least, antisocial biological tendencies, if they exist, can be redirected into approved directions. Aggression can be displaced into athletic activity, into pounding nails, shouting, or even into watching sporting events. There is no simple and single outlet for biological drives, even if we grant that there are systematic differences in these drives. They can be sublimated, subordinated, repressed, or redirected even if they cannot be permanently replaced or eliminated. Culture overlays and often overrides any pre-existing inherited potential. In some societies, for example, women are the warriors and men the nurturers.

Very different policy formulas are derived from these contrasting perspectives. Those who hold the general 'nature' position would not likely favour a view of prison as an institution devoted to rehabilitation, since deviance is not a learned behaviour to be undone by teaching the deviant to act otherwise. By the same token it makes little sense to punish someone for doing what it is inevitable they must do; hence prisons make little sense as punitive institutions. Their only value is in segregating the offenders from the public, and presumably one must either do this permanently or intervene in the biological processes that generate deviance, since that is the true source of such acts. Thus the biochemist may believe that criminal behaviour is caused biologically by a chemical imbalance, an extra chromosome, or 'faulty wiring' in the brain. From such a position, no social science program will effectively reduce recidivism since social science is fundamentally on the wrong track. The effective treatment might be surgical 'rewiring', lobotomy, mind-altering drugs, or electric-shock aversive therapy. As a colleague puts it, it may involve administering 'Braino' to clear the clogged neural-chemical pathways—visions of *Clockwork Orange*, *Brave New World*, and *One Flew Over the Cuckoo's Nest*!

According to those who believe in the primacy of the environmental and learning factors, people have choices about how they act and can quite properly be held responsible for their actions, since they do not passively receive instructions and their behaviour is not predetermined. Humans participate in their own socialization, shaping its outcome by the choices they make. From such contrasting premises, prison can be advocated as an institution devoted to remaking the individual, replacing antisocial lessons and strategies with others more normatively appropriate. With time and attention, the controlled environment can transform criminals into law-abiding people who can behave responsibly when released. But, interesting as this example may be, and important as it may be in these days when governments are debating the privatization of prisons and the utility of various treatments that can be offered, we are getting a little ahead of ourselves.

## DIFFERENCES AMONG SOCIAL SCIENCE DISCIPLINES

Within the broad category of the social sciences there are many disciplines, though they all tend to fall closer to the environment, nurture, or learning side of the continuum than to the inherited, nature, and biological side of it, as explained above. Readers are often confused about the differences among these social sciences, particularly when the same issue is dealt with in classes on sociology, political science, economics, psychology, and anthropology. To add to the confusion, the same issue—be it the nature of one's identity or the origins of religion—may also be dealt with in biology, history, and philosophy. If these disciplines, many of which proceed in a scientific manner, ask the same questions, how do they differ? Where does sociology end, for example, and political science begin?

We can answer such boundary questions in several ways, though most introductory books try to define disciplines in terms of their substantive orientation or area of concentration. Thus historians tend to deal with past events, anthropologists with small-scale societies, psychologists with individual phenomena, and sociologists with phenomena not reducible to an individual level. Unfortunately such definitions oversimplify and mislead. The boundaries between disciplines are political artifacts. They are social products, created and altered over time through conflict and consensus. At any particular time, representatives of several disciplines may be struggling to make sense of the same question, each in a slightly different way or from a different viewpoint.

If one discipline generates what is widely accepted as the most useful information, that topic in question will tend in future to be considered part of the 'turf' of that discipline. Even in this case territory is not permanently owned. It is always subject to challenge from outside as advances are made in other fields. In recent years advances in biology have challenged much of the territory formerly held by the traditional social sciences. The most obvious current examples of this may well be the continuing debates over intelligence and criminal and sexual behaviour. In all cases biologists have presented evidence of an inherited biological basis of behaviour that social scientists have long tended to argue is very heavily if not exclusively learned. When competition produces no clear winner, several disciplines may continue to make territorial claims, doing research and teaching students what their perspective illuminates. This is true of social psychology for example. Both sociology and psychology continue to claim an interest in this area. Indeed the field lies in the area overlapped by sociology and psychology. It is taught in both departments, though usually somewhat differently. In fact there are so many specialists in social psychology that it has emerged as a separate discipline, often with its own departmental identity, artificially set off from both squabbling parents.

The fact that there is significant competition over a large number of issues makes it impossible to answer boundary questions solely by referring to each discipline's substantive areas of concern. Though it may often seem to the beginner, or indeed to the jaded cynic, that the only real difference is in the terminology or jargon of the discipline, a more useful distinction may be found in the discipline's perspective or point of view.

## DISCIPLINES AS PERSPECTIVES

Although social scientists share an emphasis on the environmental and perhaps more easily altered sources of behaviour, they none the less differ considerably among themselves in the perspectives they adopt for making sense of the particular variation in behaviour that they want to explain. As illustrated in Figure 1.1, economists tend to look for explanations in market factors, political scientists in the characteristics of political systems, psychologists in individual processes, and sociologists most often in the attributes of social systems. In other words, the disciplines are differentiated, not so much by where they want to go or by the manner in which they proceed, but by where they are coming from—the perspective or vantage point from which they see their subject matter.

As for how scientists actually operate in a discipline, it is the choice of key explanatory variables that characterizes the perspective of the discipline. This language of variables is the mother tongue of science. The basic idea is quite straightforward. In order to explain a difference or change, we must refer to another difference or change. The things that change are called *variables*. For the biologist, genetic factors are variables that differ from one population to another (i.e., genetic make-up varies), and they might therefore explain another difference, for example, in the behaviour of men and women. Political scientists use characteristics of political systems as variables. For example, political scientists may try to relate a population's varying state of morale to whether democratic or fascist governments are in power. In this instance, the nature of the government is the variable, and fascist, democratic, socialist, and various other types of government are the names of the kinds of values this variable can take, or the categories within the variable, or the ways the variable can change. Only variables can explain variables, and since variation in behaviour is what we wish to explain, we must do so by discovering another source of variation (in genes, markets, politics or personality) that is systematically related to the variation in behaviour.

Let me add one further refinement to this for now, that between independent and dependent variables. The variation in behaviour that we seek to explain can be thought of as an effect of a cause that we seek to identify. This effect is called the dependent variable because it depends on an earlier cause. This cause is called the independent variable. So from the beginning, we usually observe variation in a dependent variable and try to discover an independent variable to explain it. To this point, the argument has been that the various disciplines contend that different independent variables are of greatest importance or utility in accounting for what is often variation in the same dependent variable. An illustration will make this clearer.

Years ago I was asked to investigate possible reasons for the currently low level of student activity at a particular university (as evidenced in the voting for campus representation). (In other words, the dependent variable was variation in the level of student activity, which had been declining.) A brief literature review revealed that I was the first sociologist to accept this challenge. A psychologist had suggested that the students were apathetic; a management student, that the institution was run so well that there was no need for student input; a political scientist, that there were no divisive political issues to mobilize the students. My own analysis characterized a changing social structure that linked students to one another in ways that had been changing. More specifically I found that students on campus were less likely than in the past to know one another. The university was changing from a set of largely residential sectarian colleges toward a largely commuter and non-denominational multiversity. Instead of living in close contact with other students who were much like them and with whom they quickly developed close relationships, students were more and more likely to be commuters who lived at home and made few close friends in large classes of strangers. Formerly, friendships had been the basis for coalitions, loyalties, and mobilization of a large number of students. The current lack of these ties, in contrast, meant that students formed fewer coalitions, felt less loyalty to the college and university, and were not easily mobilized for any purpose. In other words, the change in the level of student activity seemed to be due to changes in the structure of the university and in the nature of the student population. In this analysis then, the independent variables for me were changes in the structure of the university and changes in the composition of the student body. These variables were held to explain the subsequent changes in the behaviour of interest, namely the level of student activity or participation. Conducting this exercise clarified for me what the sociological perspective meant as distinct from that of political science or psychology. I realized that I had also leaned toward one of several available sociological perspectives and had emphasized social-structural variables rather than others. Can you express as variables the explanations of the management student, the psychologist, and the political scientist?

Another illustration may give you a still clearer idea. When I was a confused under-graduate major in sociology, quite unsure how to distinguish my discipline from other social sciences, I had occasion to visit a doctor friend. He was a young man eager to help his patients, and we got into an interesting conversation about the problems he saw and the treatments he provided. It was his growing conviction that the physical ailments patients presented were in most cases caused by social arrangements they found stressful. Given some encouragement to talk about these, men attributed their ulcers to work stress, prob-lems with spouses or teenage children, and the like. Women explained weight problems or tension headaches or other symptoms in similar terms. I was pleasantly surprised to hear my doctor display such understanding of what I might have called the sociological or struc-tural underpinning of illness. At this point, however, our views diverged. He went on to tell me that his most common prescription was for tranquillizers to help his patients cope, and I objected that such treatment reminded me of Huxley's *Brave New World*, where the medi-cating of the population sustains a social system badly in need of overhaul.

Our argument is brought back to me quite often these days when Prozac and Rytalin and other drugs are extremely widely prescribed and quite likely overused. I suggested that if the problems were structural then genuine solutions must also be structural. If work rela-tions were problematic, it is they that needed changing and if communication patterns in the family were the source of friction it is there that change had to be made. I was adamant that 'papering over the cracks' was not a responsible solution. My doctor friend responded that I was naive and that his patients came for tranquillizers and could not be put off by recommendations that they seek family counselling or change jobs. If he didn't prescribe the tranquillizers they wanted, they would simply go elsewhere. At least as long as they came to him, he had the chance to discuss the 'real' issues with them, however gingerly.

Only when I was driving home did I realize that perhaps I had in fact become a sociol-ogist, naturally taking a structural view of illness and seeing it through to recommendations for structural change, whereas my doctor friend ultimately fell back on the medical model. The realization made me feel better than my visit to the doctor.

## THE TWO MAJOR SOCIOLOGICAL PERSPECTIVES

Sociology has two main classes of perspectives. One of these, the macro-structural perspec-tive, emphasizes explanatory variables that are social-structural. The other, the micro-inter-pretive perspective, emphasizes social-psychological explanations. This second perspective is far closer to the psychologist's perspective than is the first. In both cases what is to be explained—the dependent variable or effect—is the same. It is a particular variation in human behaviour. In the previous example, it was reduction in student activity or participa-tion that was to be explained. These two perspectives for explaining behaviour compete with one another as well as with non-sociological perspectives. Probably you will find one or the other more convincing. Just why one person will gravitate toward the macro-structural view and another to the micro-interpretive view we do not know. In fact, an explanation of this variation in human behaviour might produce an interesting sociological paper if the explanatory variables were those traditionally called sociological. For example, some of my students have suggested that the attractiveness of one or the other perspective may be related to sex: that is, men would find the structural perspective more attractive and women the interpretive perspective. Their rationale has been that men are still more likely than women to experience the coercive nature of the world of work and taxes and mortgages and laws, whereas women, to the extent that they are still buffered from this harsh environment, may be more in tune with the interpretive perspective and the voluntaristic nature of behaviour. By the same token, one could suggest that students from minority ethnic backgrounds might be more inclined to the structural perspective. But you may want to return to this question once you know a little more about the perspectives.

## The Macro-structural or Social-Structural Perspective

From the social-structural (or macro-structural) perspective, the cause of variation in human behaviour lies in the structure of the social system. Thus we explain people's actions by examining the forces that impinge on the positions they occupy in the system.

There are at least three basic variants of the macro-structural perspective, each emphasizing a somewhat different set of social-structural factors. The major variant emphasizes society as a set of interdependent positions. Another emphasizes the ecological arrangement of the system itself, and the third emphasizes the normative structure of society. By using the three variants, one might, for example, explain the conduct of an employee on the job in three different ways. The first might emphasize that employees are subject to dismissal by managers whose job it is to supervise. The second might emphasize the plant layout with particular reference to the proximity of such supervision. The third orientation might emphasize that the job contract spells out the employee's responsibilities.

*Society as Interdependent-Positions Variant* From this perspective the social system consists of interlocking positions, or statuses. Formal and informal rules of behaviour apply to these positions regardless of their temporary incumbent. Each position carries with it a set of powers and obligations in relation to other positions in the system. Each incumbent soon learns the rules for her or his particular position. These job descriptions spell out—though often only broadly, and sometimes in a contradictory way—the proper behaviour for those who occupy each position or status. Such proper behaviour is the 'role' attached to the status. It may be played well or poorly, to the hilt or well inside its limits. Though the role can sometimes be altered by the actor, in general most actors in a given position will act in about the same way, playing the role as called for in their 'script'.

Every individual occupies many positions in his or her various social systems. The same man may be a husband and father in his family of procreation, a sibling and son in his family of orientation, an engineer in the company he works for, and a board member at his country club. He is also a male in a male-dominated society; an Ontarian, a New Yorker, or an Albertan; a person with a particular educational background, income, and ethnicity; and so on. Each of these positions has its script, by which he will normally be constrained. This version of the structural perspective has a premise that *if* we could locate him according to all the positions he occupies and *if* we understood all the scripts for those positions as well as their relationships and hierarchical priorities, we would rarely err in predicting his behaviour in any particular circumstance. These 'ifs' are of course so large that you may doubt whether the man's behaviour would be predictable even if we knew him.

This perspective is a common one, one we all use every day. When we are introduced to someone, a traditional opening question is 'What do you do?' Most of the time, we read a great deal into the answer, interpreting it as an indicator of income and education and as a clue to political and social attitudes as well. In fact we often use information concerning occupation as a predictor of attitudes, such as when we expect police officers to favour law, order, and capital punishment, teachers to have liberal attitudes, and business people to favour less social welfare and a return to unrestricted free enterprise. It is a testament to the utility of this version of social structuralism that the expectations we derive from it are usually correct. Apparently strong patterns are easily discernible. Certainly knowing that our new acquaintance is a doctor improves our ability to predict her views on medicare.

***Society as Ecological-Arrangement Variant*** In this version of the social-structural perspective, the search for explanatory variables begins with the spatial or relational characteristics of the system itself. Ecology refers to the pattern of distribution of a population in space or over territory. Mapping is of great importance in this perspective. From such a perspective, for example, one might see leadership in locational terms; that is, the person at the hub of the communications system is thereby the effective leader regardless of the personal attributes he may have.

This perspective has been adopted by those who argue that the high population densities of cities cause suicide, homicide, or other antisocial behaviour. Density is a quality of the system; it is not an individual attribute. In the field of urban sociology, it was the ecological perspective that led researchers to relate rates of delinquency and mental illness, for example, to distance from the city centre or to the 'zone' of the city (Burgess 1925). The concept of growing up on the wrong side of the tracks is consistent with this ecological perspective. In the field of organizational sociology, this perspective tries to relate workers' productivity or morale to the physical character of the environment; that is, is it assembly-line or small-group work? Is the plant clean and quiet? Is supervision close by? The ecological perspective suggests that architecture and environmental design are significant considerations in urban planning, not merely for aesthetic reasons but also because people feel and act differently in different environments. You might take a few minutes to think about the kinds of social science 'knowledge' you might draw on if you were hired to advise a real estate developer planning a new development that was intended to become a true community.

This perspective also suggests that students who sit in the front row of a classroom are different in systematic ways from those in the back row. When freed from its territorial focus and concentrated only on the effects of the shape or form of the relationships among people, this ecological perspective merges into the network perspective described in chapter 5. For this reason the network perspective, too, is a clear example of the structural emphasis in sociology.

***The Normative Perspective*** Perhaps the most ambiguous version of the macro-structural perspective is the one that considers normative structure to be the major behavioural determinant. There is an apparent overlap with the interdependent-positions perspective in that again we expect that behaviour will follow from the rules attached to positions. The difference between these perspectives seems to be one of scale or degree rather than kind, in so far as the normative perspective is broader, and societal norms are far more general than the rules that apply to the specific statuses that are the crux of the interdependent-positions perspective. This version is ambiguous as well because the micro-interpretive or social-psychological perspective also deals with norms but in quite another way, which raises much more basic issues.

The underlying idea here is simply that people act as they do because the relevant rules tell them how to act and people usually know and obey these rules. It follows that it would be possible to explain people's actions if only we knew what rules govern the relevant situation in their society. Put even more simply, most people stop at red lights because the law says they must. Most students study for examinations because the informal rules or expectations tell them to do so. We call these rules or expectations the 'norms' of a society, and a description of them is a description of the normative structure of the society.

Not all norms are equally important, though, and a complete description would have to distinguish the more from the less important. The more important norms are usually institutionalized as laws, formal social-control agents being empowered to see that these are followed. Norms that are highly important and agreed upon are called mores, while the less important and less agreed upon are called fads or fashions. People use a system of positive and negative rewards called sanctions to maintain norms. In general the more important the norm, the stronger the sanction.

It is widely thought that people learn to repeat activities for which they are rewarded and avoid those for which they are punished. This principle underlies much learning theory. The law provides a range of formal negative sanctions to deal with those who violate our institutionalized norms. We may fine offenders, pardon them, jail them, or even execute them, depending on the social assessment of what they have done. But we also use informal sanctions in addition to formal sanctions. Here, too, a wide range of punishment and rewards comes into play. Perhaps the most serious negative sanction is invoked when someone is ostracized or shunned. Informal negative sanctions also include ridicule, negative criticism, gossip, and even a raised eyebrow. Positive sanctions include praise, the awarding of a medal, a smile, entering a person's name on an honour roll, and inviting someone to join a prestigious association. To the sociologist interested in this perspective then, behaviour is explained by relating it to the relevant norms and their associated sanctions. In the section dealing with the micro-interpretive view, I will return to the discussion of norms, there demonstrating the inadequacy of the structural-normative view as seen from this competing perspective.

***Overall Characteristics of the Macro-structural View*** As you can see, the macro-structural view of the determinants of behaviour emphasizes explanatory variables that lie outside the individual. No reference is made to the actor's intentions, motivations, or subjective states. In fact the overall impression is more of a puppet than an actor; people are pulled and pushed, moulded and constrained by forces they may well be unaware of and that are, in a sense, beyond them. Society is seen as a complex system that existed before the arrival of any individual and will exist after his or her departure. Though an individual may possibly affect it, society will surely affect the person. It is in this sense that the macro-structural view is commonly said to emphasize the *coercive* aspects of social behaviour rather than its voluntaristic aspects.

Peter Berger (1963: 73–92) suggests in his *An Invitation to Sociology* that one can appreciate this view by considering that each person stands at the centre (that is, at the point of maximum pressure) of a series of concentric circles, each representing a system of social control:

> The outer ring might well represent the legal and political system under which one is obligated to live. That is the system that, quite against one's will, will tax one, draft one into the military, make one obey its innumerable rules and regulations, if need be put one in prison, and in the last resort will kill one. . . .
>
> Another system of social control that exerts its pressures towards the solitary figure in the centre is that of morality, custom and manners. (74) . . .
>
> But in addition to these broad coercive systems that every individual shares with vast numbers of fellow controllees, there are other and less extensive circles of control to which he is subjected. His choice of an occupation (or, often more accurately, the occupation in which he happens to end up) inevitably subordinates the individual to a variety of controls, often stringent ones. (75) . . .
>
> One's other social involvements also entail control systems, many of them less unbending than the occupational one, but some even more so. (76) . . .
>
> Finally, the human group in which one's so-called private life occurs, that is, the circle of one's family and personal friends, also constitutes a control system. It would be a grave error to assume that this is necessarily the weakest of them all just because it does not possess the formal means of coercion of some of the other control systems. It is in this circle that an individual normally has his most important social ties. Disapproval, loss of prestige, ridicule or contempt in this intimate group has far more serious psychological weight than the same reactions encountered elsewhere. (77) . . .
>
> If we return once more to the picture of an individual located at the centre of a set of concentric circles, each one representing a system of social control, we can understand a little better that location in society means to locate oneself with regard to many forces that constrain and coerce one. The individual who, thinking consecutively of all the people he is in a position to have to please, from the Collector of Internal Revenue to his mother-in-law, gets the idea that all of society sits right on top of him had better not dismiss that idea as a momentary neurotic derangement. The sociologist, at any rate, is likely to strengthen him in this conception, no matter what other counsellors may tell him to snap out of it. (78) . . .

The approach to sociology that comes closest to expressing this sort of view of society is the approach associated with Émile Durkheim and his school. Durkheim emphasized that society is a phenomenon *sui generis*, that is, it confronts us with a massive reality that cannot be reduced to or translated into other terms. He then stated that social facts are 'things', having an objective existence outside of ourselves just like the phenomena of nature. He did this mainly to protect sociology from being swallowed by the imperialistically-minded psychologists, but his conception is significant beyond this methodological concern. A 'thing' is something like a rock, for example, that one comes up against, that one cannot move by wishing it out of existence or imagining it as having a different shape. A 'thing' is that against which one can throw oneself in vain, that which is there against all one's desires and hopes, that which can finally fall on one's head and kill one. This is the sense in which society is a collection of 'things'. The law, perhaps more clearly than any other social institution, illustrates this quality of society.

If we follow the Durkheimian conception, then, society confronts us as an objective facticity. It is *there*, something that cannot be denied and that must be reckoned with. Society is external to ourselves. It surrounds us, encompasses our life on all sides. We are *in* society, located in specific sectors of the social system. This location predetermines and predefines almost everything we do, from language to etiquette, from the religious beliefs we hold to the probability that we will commit suicide. Our wishes are not taken into consideration in this matter of social location, and our intellectual resistance to what society prescribes or proscribes avails very little at best, and frequently nothing. Society, as objective and external fact, confronts us especially in the form of coercion. Its institutions pattern our actions and even shape our expectations. They reward us to the extent that we stay within our assigned performances. If we step out of these assignments, society has at its disposal an almost infinite variety of controlling and coercing agencies. The sanctions of society are able, at each moment of existence, to isolate us among our fellow men, to subject us to ridicule, to deprive us of our sustenance and our liberty, and in the last resort to deprive us of life itself. The law and the morality of society can produce elaborate justifications for each one of these sanctions, and most of our fellow men will approve if they are used against us in punishment for our deviance. Finally, we are located in society not only in space but in time. Our society is a historical entity that extends temporally beyond any individual biography. Society antedates us and it will survive us. It was there before we were born and it will be there after we are dead. Our lives are but episodes in its majestic march through time. In sum, society is the walls of our imprisonment in history. (90–2)

This coercive view of an overwhelming and surrounding society that 'pulls our strings' is not quite accurate, though, for Berger also goes on to note that people 'want precisely that which society expects of them'. We are in fact born into a society and culture that mould us, give us identity, and teach us how to express ourselves. By and large we come to believe in the values of our culture, taking into ourselves its moral precepts and norms. The process by which this learning takes place is called *socialization*, and the related process by which we make society's standards our own is called *internalization*. So we are both coerced and taught. We usually do willingly what we have to do, but now and then we all rebel, for we are far from perfectly socialized, and our 'prison' has few guards.

In general the macro-structural perspective suggests that the key independent, or causal, variables are structural characteristics outside of and not reducible to individual characteristics. Ultimately if not usually, these tend to be coercive in so far as they are enforced by sanctions we may be unaware of until they are exposed. In practice, explanations from this perspective tend to make use of variables like age, sex, class, ethnicity, education, spatial location, and rules and associated sanctions. Émile Durkheim, the founder of sociology in France, is usually treated as the spiritual father of the macro-structural perspective. Durkheim created the discipline by defining as its unique concern those aspects of social behaviour that are 'social facts' as distinct from individual attributes and that must be treated in their own right since they cannot be reduced to characteristics of individuals.

### The Micro-interpretive or Social-Action Perspective

In contrast to the macro-structural perspective, the micro-interpretive, social-psychological, or social-action perspective emphasizes a much more individualistic and social-psychological explanation of the variation in human behaviour. The basic premise of this perspective is that behaviour is motivated and that each individual actively constructs a line of behaviour from the range of possibilities of which he or she is aware. It was the great German sociologist Max Weber who defined sociology as the study of *intentional* behaviour or social action. His emphasis on the subjective dimension makes him one of the founders of this perspective.

Behaviour selection is further based on each person's reading of the situation at hand, and different people will read the same situation differently and so respond differently. In other words the regularities that structuralists emphasize are far less predictable, stable, and enduring for these social-action theorists. In their view the social scientist can explain behaviour only by coming to share the individual's understanding of the circumstances, her so-called definition of the situation. It is this definition that is crucial, for people respond to what they think is going on, which is not always the same from person to person. W.I. Thomas (1928) coined the term 'definition of the situation'. Thomas's dictum is that 'a situation defined as real is real in its consequences'. This emphasis on subjective understanding is basic to the micro-interpretive perspective. For example, whereas we have said that age is a relatively non-problematic structural variable in terms of which a great deal of behaviour is often explained, from the micro-interpretive perspective it is not chronological age but the subjective sense of age that makes a difference. In other words, 'you are as old as you feel' in most important respects, rather than as old as your birth certificate says you are. It follows that chronological age will not explain why some 70-year-olds still seek out new thrills whereas some 20-year-olds avoid all risks and act as conservatively as possible. By the same token, although class can be measured 'objectively' (that is, by the detached scientist) and a score assigned on the basis of some combination of educational attainment, occupational prestige, and income, it may well be more useful to know what class people consider themselves to be in. Indeed, because of the potential difference between objective and subjective estimates of social class (among other variables), some sociologists explain that people sometimes exhibit 'false consciousness' in so far as they do not appreciate their true class interests. Needless to say, to the interpretivist there can be no false consciousness and it is access to consciousness (or definition of the situation) that is the critical independent variable.

Another example may be helpful. Many years ago, Orson Welles broadcast a radio adaptation of a story by H.G. Wells about a Martian invasion of Earth. The broadcast was so realistic that some people apparently thought the fictional events were actually occurring, and they committed suicide. Clearly we must understand their definition of the situation to explain their behaviour. This perspective then emphasizes the gap between what is in fact out there and what is understood to be out there.

The structural perspective tends to pay little attention to this issue. Accordingly what is solid ground to the structuralist becomes more shifting and less stable to the micro-interpretive sociologist. This issue of the 'fit' between subjective definitions of a situation and more objective characteristics of it is central to the debate between these major competing perspectives. To the structuralist, the fit is largely non-problematic, and both fit and lack of fit are interpreted in light of structural characteristics. Most situations are not that ambiguous. When there is no evidence of alien invasion, and growing evidence shows that it was just a radio play, it is difficult to continue believing that the invasion is real. To the interpretivist, on the other hand, the fit is always quite loose and problematic and can be made reasonable only by knowing what the actor thinks is going on. Thus, after all, only skinny people die of anorexia, considering themselves fat despite all the evidence to the contrary.

The interpretive or social-action perspective derives largely from the symbolic inter-actionist school of thought that originated in the work of G.H. Mead. In searching for key independent, or causal, variables, symbolic interactionism concentrates on the individual's understanding of the circumstances. In an interesting juxtaposition to Berger's concentric-circle analogy, Shibutani (1955: 567) too uses a geometric analogy, borrowed from Simmel, this time of humans each located uniquely at the point of intersection of multiple circles, each of which represents a social group in which they are members.

> One of the characteristics of life in modern mass societies is simultaneous participation in a variety of social worlds. Because of the ease with which the individual may expose himself to a number of communication channels, he may lead a segmentalized life, participating successively in a number of unrelated activities. Furthermore, the particular combination of social worlds differs from person to person; this is what led Simmel to declare that each stands at that point at which a unique combination of social circles intersects. The geometric analogy is a happy one, for it enables us to conceive the numerous possibilities of combinations and the different degrees of participation in each circle. To understand what a man does, we must get at his unique perspectives—what he takes for granted and how he defines the situation—but in mass societies we must learn in addition the social world in which he is participating in a given act.

The premises of the symbolic interaction perspective are particularly well explained by Joel Charon (1985: 29) in his *Symbolic Interactionism*:

> 1. The *individual* is not a consistent, structured personality as much as a dynamic, changing actor, never 'becoming' anything but always 'in the state of becoming', unfolding, acting. The individual is not socialized but is always in the process of socialization; the individual is not set or fixed but constantly undergoing change in the process of interaction.
> 2. *Society and the group* is conceptualized not as something static 'out there', influencing us, but entirely as an interaction process. Society is individuals in interaction, dynamic, with patterns emerging and constantly being changed or reaffirmed over time. What people call 'society' and 'the group' are patterns we infer from the interaction process.
> 3. The individual is characterized as possessing a *mind* and a *self*, but both are conceptualized as process, not as static entities. The person does not possess a mind so much as a minding process, meaning an ability to converse with self and an ability to pull out stimuli selectively from the environment, assess their significance, interpret the situation, judge the action of others and self, and so on. All of this means an active, dynamic conversation is taking place within the organism in interaction with others.
> 4. The human has many *selves*, each related to the interaction he or she is involved with, and each constantly being changed in the process of interaction. When the symbolic interactionist argues that the individual possesses a self, he or she is really saying that the individual has selfhood, that one treats oneself as an object, and that, as with other objects, a constant redefinition is taking place in interaction with others.
> 5. *Truths*, ideas, attitudes, perceptions, and perspectives are all conceptualized as process, being judged and changed dynamically by the organism in relation to what is being observed. People are

not brainwashed and conditioned so much as constantly testing and reassessing their truths. Truth is arrived at through interaction, and it is also transformed in the process of interaction.

Later, he elaborates on the idea of the definition of the situation (139):

Humans act in a world that they define. We enter a host of situations, most of them social, define those situations according to a perspective, pull out the objects in those situations that are important for our goals, and then act. It is a continuous process of defining and acting overtly. The central importance of this process is captured in a phrase that has become central to the symbolic interactionist perspective: definition of the situation. William and Dorothy Thomas capture the importance of this concept in their brilliant and simple pronouncement: 'If men define situations as real, they are real in their consequences' (1928: 572). Humans, this implies, do not respond to a world out there, but to a reality actively defined by them. In the end, it does not matter if you are a scoundrel or not; what matters is that I see you as a scoundrel and I act toward you as if you were one. And you, in turn, may not be a scoundrel, but you may accept my definition of you as one and then proceed to act that way. If I see a situation as threatening, then I will act accordingly, even if people in that situation did not mean to appear threatening. If I define school as hard or good or silly, then I will act toward school in that manner, no matter if others feel as I do and no matter if it is in reality harder, better, sillier than other schools. Our realities are our definitions of situations. Definitions of the situation may be influenced by others (indeed they usually are), but in the end, each individual must define the situation through engaging in mind activity. We each act in a world that we create through interaction with others and through interaction with our self.

Other variants of the micro-interpretive perspective include ethnomethodology and phenomenological sociology. All concentrate on the creation of meaning and meaning maintenance in the social world. From this perspective, reality is negotiated and renegotiated every day. It is not a given. Instead its fragile existence depends on a consensus from all relevant actors, and the processes by which this consensus is achieved or challenged is the proper subject of sociology. I have avoided a full introductory discussion of ethnomethodology or phenomenology only because these approaches are less common, particularly in North America, and are also philosophically too complex for a book of this level.

Before moving on to the next section, however, let me briefly return to the status of norms. Earlier I said it was somewhat ambiguous whether normative sociology would be structural or micro-interpretive. When one describes the rules and sanctions themselves and assumes that most individuals learn and obey them with no great difficulty, one operates in the macro-structural mode. Alternatively one could argue that knowledge of the rules is insufficient to explain behaviour. Rules are only broad outlines, with exceptions and details that are not spelled out. They are at most a resource used (differentially, like any other resource) by actors in arriving at their own definition of the situation and strategic thinking about how to accomplish their goals.

Rules are somewhat elastic; some actors can stretch them more than others, and certain circumstances allow for more stretching than others. Rules at least sometimes conflict with one another. Rules are made by people, and they reflect the interests and relative power of various groups who concern themselves with trying to create the rules. These groups and individuals are sometimes called 'moral entrepreneurs'; some sociologists have studied them quite extensively. Finally, rules must be known and understood, and their hierarchical arrangement must be clear before we can relate actions to them. Each of these statements could be elaborated at length, and a good deal of sociology of deviant behaviour concerns itself with doing just this, and with considering the implications.

To the micro-interpretive theorist then, no explanation that merely describes the set of rules can be sufficient. Social scientists must discover whether the actor *knows* the rules. The sociologist must discover *how important* they are to this actor, and *how they are understood to apply*. The search for this knowledge again forces the investigator to find a way to gain access to the actor's definition of the situation, for though the rules may be outside the actor, knowledge and evaluation of them are characteristics that exist only within the actor's mind.

## DIFFERENCES BETWEEN THE MAJOR PERSPECTIVES AND THEIR RELATIONSHIP TO PUBLIC POLICY

The two main perspectives by now must appear quite different and often contradictory. One is external, the other internal. One concentrates on action that is chosen and intentional and that could have been otherwise; the other concentrates on factors that mould our behaviour, often without either our awareness or choice. One perspective is individualistic (variation among the trees is its emphasis, one could say); the other has more of a large-scale or 'macro' emphasis (the broad patterns of the forest are its emphasis one could say), concentrating on regularities of behaviour as displayed by categories of people in similar circumstances. One perspective begins from the premise that reality is a 'hard' social fact with which we must learn to cope. The other arises from the premise that reality is a fragile construction depending on consensus and always subject to challenge.

It appears to many that both perspectives are valid. They express two sides of the coin of our existence in society and must then be complementary. To an extent this is true, but it is not easy to unify them, because they compete to answer the same questions and they assign different weights to the relevant factors, as explained in chapter 3.

Let us consider the ways in which both perspectives might deal with the problem of criminal recidivism, or repeat offenders. A great many people who have been jailed for a criminal offence return to jail for another similar offence not long after their release. So the question is, why do some offenders soon return to prison whereas others do not? Put another way, we have observed variation in a dependent variable or effect, that is, variation in reaction to imprisonment. We are seeking an explanation, cause, or independent variable with which to make sense of this.

A social-action or micro-interpretive theorist might well answer this question by discussing the situation as defined by the released offender. An important part of this definition of the situation would concern the self-definition and the influence of prison primarily as a socializing agent. In prisons inmates create and are assigned new conceptions of who and what they are. Inmates commonly support and confirm one another's identities as criminals who are different from those on the 'outside'. Having unintentionally provided the offender with a new 'reference group' of offenders against whose standards he can measure his own behaviour and with a new conception of self, prisons then release someone who thinks, acts, and identifies himself as a criminal. In such circumstances it is not surprising that many ex-prisoners soon return. They merely act as they expect themselves to and as others who are important to them expect. Variation in recidivism will thus be related to the variation in how thoroughly the criminals' identity was transformed.

A social structuralist, on the other hand, might explain the same recidivism in a different way, emphasizing the structural characteristics of the overall social system. Thus the emphasis might well be on the fact that most ex-prisoners return to their old job-poor environments with no more legitimate skills than they had before prison and even worse prospects of legal employment. In this environment they merely make once more what may be the only decision they can, gambling that this time they can get away with it. From this perspective variation in recidivism will be related primarily to variation in the availability of jobs suited to the ex-criminal's education and skills.

Now both positions contain an element of truth, but they have different policy implications. To the social-action theorist, the individual is where the action is, and policy must be addressed at this level. To the structuralist, it is the structure that must be dealt with. The action theorist may recommend pre- and post-release psychiatric treatment for all offenders in an attempt to change their self-image to that of a law-abiding citizen. The premise would be that those who consider themselves law-abiding will not even take advantage of easy opportunities, let alone create any. The structuralist might emphasize prison programs to give training and education to prisoners so they need not choose crime again. This position might also emphasize job creation in the neighbourhood so that released prisoners will have real alternatives to further crime. The structuralists' premise would be that the suitability of the offender's education or job skills to the available jobs is what distinguishes the potential recidivist from the ex-criminal who goes straight.

These two positions may coincide, though for different reasons, on some policies. For example, both perspectives could favour the idea of halfway houses. To the interpretivist, halfway houses represent the substitution of a new peer or reference group that could aid the former criminal's reconceptualization of him- or herself. To the structuralist, this could represent an important alteration of the environment, which would allow the former criminal to make new contacts and provide new opportunities for development in non-criminal directions.

It is at their extremes, as usual, that the contrast between competing perspectives is sharpest. The committed micro-interpretive theorist might argue that environmental changes, job-creation programs in the neighbourhood, retraining, and education will have no effect unless self-image is changed as well. In contrast, the committed structuralist might argue that whether the former criminal has a criminal or a law-abiding self-concept will make no difference if no way exists for her to survive other than through crime. How is the policy maker to deal with such a conflict among 'experts'? Where is public money to be spent most wisely: in psychiatric help or in altering the environment or opportunities?

In addition to this disagreement over effective policies supported by social-structural or micro-interpretive theorists are the competing explanations, diagnoses, and treatments of the natural scientists, which complicate the matter further. It is not my purpose to 'solve' this important theoretical conflict in this book. You can no doubt work out a position of your own. In this book, as in the field in general, you will find far more questions than answers. How *do* policy makers handle the issue in this and other instances? This, too, is a sociological question capable of analysis from both competing sociological perspectives.

## CONCLUSION

This chapter has dealt with the defining characteristics of social science in general and of sociology in particular. It is a dynamic picture of conflict—conflict over what is defined as the proper territory of social or natural science, conflict among the social sciences, and conflict within sociology between two major perspectives. Over time, proponents of each sociological position arise and then pass from the scene. With their passage a particular perspective that had been dominant for a term can fall to secondary status as another replaces it.

At present the two major perspectives, the macro-structural and the micro-interpretive, are quite different sociological ways of beginning to explain variation in human behaviour. The structural perspective involves an external point of view according to which the important causes of behaviour lie outside individuals in their environment. The interpretive perspective involves an internal point of view in which the principal causes of behaviour lie within the actor's mind.

These two basic perspectives in sociology are incompatible on certain crucial points. To illustrate both perspectives as used in a most contentious area, I used the illustration of how they explain recidivism. The two perspectives also tend to be associated with different views on the nature of science, as you will see in chapter 2. They certainly often suggest quite different methodologies for the investigation of the variables they consider crucial, as you will see in chapter 3. The following pairs of illustrative readings are intended to supplement this discussion by giving you examples and critiques of the two basic perspectives in substantive areas of interest. Instructors may well wish to provide other excerpts from substantive areas of particular interest to them.

## SELECTED QUESTIONS

1. 'Never trust anyone over 30.' Discuss this axiom of the younger generation as a structural statement about society. In other words, how might a structural perspective make sense of this statement? Why should you not trust anyone over 30?

2. Suppose you wanted to explain why some women become supporters of the women's liberation movement whereas others do not. How might a structural sociologist begin? How might a micro-interpretive sociologist approach this inquiry? What sorts of variables would each be likely to consider?

3. Discuss Thomas's dictum 'if a situation is defined as real, it is real in its consequences.' How might a structuralist reply?

4. Some students usually do well on tests, whereas others do not. How would you begin to explain such variation? That is, what sorts of independent variables strike you as most important? Are these primarily structural or micro-interpretive?

5. Suppose you wanted to improve the performance of those students in question 4 who do not do well. What sorts of recommendations would a structuralist make? What would a micro-interpretivist suggest?

## RECOMMENDED READING

Peter Berger, *An Invitation to Sociology: A Humanistic Perspective* (Garden City, NY: Double-day, Anchor Books, 1963).

Joel M. Charon, *Symbolic Interactionism* (Englewood Cliffs, NJ: Prentice-Hall, 1985).

## ILLUSTRATIVE READING 1

Jessie Bernard's book *The Future of Marriage* is an attempt to come to grips with the failure of a search for structural explanations of the variation in responses by husbands and wives to many questions about their relationship. This variation seems more easily understood from the point of view of the micro-interpretive perspective, though this is not really Bernard's perspective. The following illustrative excerpt comes from pp. 5–10 of this book.

### 'HIS' AND 'HER' MARRIAGES

*Jessie Bernard*

Under the jargon 'discrepant responses', the differences in the marriages of husbands and wives have come under the careful scrutiny of a score of research-ers. They have found that when they ask husbands and wives identical questions about the union, they often get quite different replies. There is usually agree-ment on the number of children they have and a few other such verifiable items, although not, for example, on length of premarital acquaintance and of engage-ment, on age at marriage and interval between marriage and birth of first child. Indeed, with respect to even such basic components of the marriage as frequency of sexual relations, social interaction, household tasks, and decision making, they seem to be reporting on different marriages. As, I think, they are.

In the area of sexual relations, for example, Kinsey and his associates found different responses in from one- to two-thirds of the couples they studied. Kinsey interpreted these differences in terms of selective perception. In the generation he was studying, husbands wanted sexual relations oftener than the wives did, thus 'the females may be overestimating the actual frequencies' and 'the husbands . . . are probably underestimating the frequencies.' The differ-ences might also have been vestiges of the probable situation earlier in the marriage when the desired frequency of sexual relations was about six to seven times greater among husbands than among wives. This difference may have become so impressed on the spouses that it remained in their minds even after the difference itself had disappeared or even been reversed. In a sample of happily married, middle-class couples a generation later, Harold Feldman found that both spouses attributed to their mates more influence in the area of sex than they did to themselves.

Companionship, as reflected in talking together, he found, was another area where differences showed up. Replies differed on three-fourths of all the items studied, including the topics talked about, the amount of time spent talking with each other, and which partner initiated conversation. Both partners claimed that whereas they talked more about topics of interest to their mates, their mates initiated conversations about topics primarily of interest to themselves. Harold Feldman concluded that projection in terms of needs was distorting even simple, everyday events, and lack of communication was permitting the distortions to continue. It seemed to him that 'if these sex differences can occur so often among these generally well satisfied couples, it would not be surprising to find even less consensus and more distortion in other less satisfied couples.'

Although, by and large, husbands and wives tend to become more alike with age, in this study of middle-class couples, differences increased with length of marriage rather than decreased, as one might logically have expected. More couples in the later than in the earlier years, for example, had differing pictures in their heads about how often they laughed together, discussed together, exchanged ideas, or worked together on projects, and about how well things were going between them.

The special nature of sex and the amorphousness of social interaction help to explain why differences in response might occur. But household tasks? They are fairly objective and clear-cut and not all that emotion-laden. Yet even here there are his-and-her versions. Since the division of labour in the household is becoming increasingly an issue in marriage, the uncovering of differing replies in this area is especially relevant. Hard as it to believe, Granbois and Willett tell us that more than half of the partners in one sample disagreed on who kept track of money and bills. On the question, who mows the lawn? more than a fourth disagreed. Even family income was not universally agreed on.

These differences about sexual relations, companionship, and domestic duties tell us a great deal about the two marriages. But power or decision making can cover all aspects of a relationship. The question of who makes decisions or who exercises power has therefore attracted a great deal of research attention. If we were interested in who really had the power or who really made the decisions, the research would be hopeless. Would it be possible to draw any conclusion from a situation in which both partners agree that the husband ordered the wife to make all the decisions? Still, an enormous literature documents the quest of researchers for answers to the question of marital power. The major contribution it has made has been to reveal the existence of differences in replies between husbands and wives.

The presence of such inconsistent replies did not at first cause much concern. The researchers apologized for them but interpreted them as due to methodological inadequacies; if only they could find a better way to approach the problem, the differences would disappear. Alternatively, the use of only the wife's responses, which were more easily available, was justified on the grounds that differences in one direction between the partners in one marriage compensated for differences in another direction between partners in another marriage and thus cancelled them out. As, indeed, they did. For when Granbois and Willett, two market researchers, analysed the replies of husbands and wives separately, the over-all picture was in fact the same for both wives and husbands. Such cancelling out of differences in the total sample, however, concealed almost as much as it revealed about the individual couples who composed it. Granbois and Willett concluded, as Kinsey had earlier, that the 'discrepancies . . . reflect differing perceptions on the part of responding partners.' And this was the heart of the matter.

Differing reactions to common situations, it should be noted, are not at all uncommon. They are recognized in the folk wisdom embedded in the story of the blind men all giving different replies to questions on the nature of the elephant. One of the oldest experiments in juridical psychology demonstrates how different the statements of witnesses of the same act can be. Even in laboratory studies, it takes intensive training of raters to make it possible for them to arrive at agreement on the behaviour they observe.

It has long been known that people with different backgrounds see things differently. We know, for example, that poor children perceive coins as larger than do children from more affluent homes. Boys and girls perceive differently. A good deal of the foundation for projective tests rests on the different ways in which individuals see identical stimuli. And this perception—or, as the sociologists put it, definition of the situation—is reality for them. In this sense, the realities of the husband's marriage are different from those of the wife's.

Finally, one of the most perceptive of the researchers, Constantina Safilios-Rothschild, asked the crucial question: Was what they were getting, even with the best research techniques, family sociology or wives' family sociology? She answered her own question: What the researchers who relied on wives' replies exclusively were reporting on was the wife's marriage. The husband's was not necessarily the same. There were, in fact, two marriages present:

> One explanation of discrepancies between the responses of husbands and wives may be the possibility of two 'realities', the husband's subjective reality and the wife's subjective reality—two perspectives which do not always coincide. Each spouse perceives 'facts' and situations differently according to his own needs, values, attitudes, and beliefs. An 'objective' reality could possibly exist only in the trained observer's evaluation, if it does exist at all.

Interpreting the different replies of husbands and wives in terms of selective perception, projection of needs, values, attitudes, and beliefs, or different definitions of the situation, by no means renders them trivial or incidental or justifies dismissing or ignoring them. They are, rather, fundamental for an understanding of the two marriages, his and hers, and we ignore them at the peril of serious misunderstanding of marriage, present as well as the future.

From J. Bernard, *The Future of Marriage* (New York: Bantam, 1972), 5–10.

Certainly my own wife believes that her contribution to the division of labour in our household is quite different from mine and from what I perceive hers to be. She often says, 'I know you think you do everything, but you don't. After you cook, you do the dishes so seldom that I am surprised when you do.' I, on the other hand, believe that I cook about 80 per cent of the time, do virtually all of the household shopping, and clean up quite often after I cook dinner for her. But then I also believe that the time I spend at the office is usually spent working, and this too she finds hard to believe. It would be difficult in the extreme, and actually not helpful in any case, to discover which of us is correct. The point, as the micro-interpretive perspective emphasizes, is that we act on the basis of our definitions of the situation, regardless of their accuracy. The sociologist must discover these and take them into account in trying to make sense of behaviour, and not only when the behaviour in question seems unusual.

## ILLUSTRATIVE READING 2

In the following reading, Rodman begins by recounting some of the ideas basic to Blood and Wolfe's theory of resources in marital power. This theory is structural and pays no apparent attention to the actors' definition of the situation. Essentially, attributes like education, income, and occupational status enhance the husband's power and explain why wives tend to have less say in marital decision making. To the extent that wives gain education, occupational prestige, and income, they will also gain a greater say in such decisions. The relative possession of resources predicts the relative power of each partner in the relationship. But there are many problems in this conceptualization and Rodman discusses a few of these. After the article I take up the discussion and extend the critique still further.

### MARITAL POWER IN FRANCE, GREECE, YUGOSLAVIA, AND THE UNITED STATES: A CROSS-NATIONAL DISCUSSION

*Hyman Rodman*

The amount of cross-national research is limited, and we are therefore highly fortunate to have access to comparable data on power structure in the marital relationship for four contemporary countries. The papers by Michel,[1] Safilios-Rothschild,[2] and Burić and Zečević[3] present data on an urban French, an urban Greek, and an urban Yugoslavian sample respectively, and they can all be contrasted with the data from an earlier study carried out in an urban area in the United States by Blood and Wolfe.[4] This provides an unusual opportunity to explore the comparative findings on Paris and Bordeaux, Athens, Kragujevac, and Detroit in detail. Only data collected from women are presently available.

### Resource Theory and Cultural Context

In presenting their data on Detroit, Blood and Wolfe found that a 'theory of resources' provided the best explanation for their findings.[5] For example, the husband's mean (average) authority score generally increased with increases in his education, income, and occupational status, and these variables were conceptualized as resources which the husband brought to the marital decision-making area and which gave him greater leverage in making decisions. Similarly, the husband's decision-making powers were enhanced, according to the theory of resources, if his wife did not work and when his wife had preschool-age children, because under these circumstances the wife was more dependent upon her husband. As stated by Blood and Wolfe:

> Having a young child creates needs for the wife which lead her to depend more on her husband for help, financial support, and making decisions. As children grow up, they shift from being burdens to being resources whom the wife draws upon in marital decision making. They also become resources in other ways, providing emotional support which makes the wife less dependent on her husband.[6]

In general, the data on Paris and Bordeaux provided by Michel lend support to the theory of resources. But Michel also sounds a note of warning about the possible differences to be found in developing countries where occupational and educational status may play a less important, or a different role. When we compare the data on Greece and Yugoslavia with those on the United States and France, Michel's cautions are shown to be well placed. The following are major differences:

1. In the United States and France, the husband's educational status and authority score are positively correlated. In Greece and Yugoslavia they are negatively correlated. For example, husbands at the highest educational level in the United States and France have the highest average authority score; in Greece and Yugoslavia, husbands at the highest educational level have the lowest average authority score.
2. In the United States and France, the husband's occupational status and authority score are positively correlated; in Greece and Yugoslavia they are negatively correlated.
3. In the United States and France, the husband's income and authority score are positively correlated; in Greece and Yugoslavia they are negatively correlated.
4. In Greece, the husband's authority declines through the various stages of the family life cycle; in France and the United States, however, it is not the newlywed

husband who has the highest authority score but the husband of the wife with preschool children.

In short, the Greek, and Yugoslavian data, in their sharp contrast to the French and United States data, present a theoretical challenge and opportunity. By pursuing the opportunity, one may possibly build upon the theory of resources in order to account for a wider range of findings.

The data on Detroit pointed to the importance of 'the comparative resource-fulness and competence of the two partners. . . . Once we know which partner has more education, more organizational experience, a higher status back-ground, etc., we will know who tends to make most of the decisions.'[7] From this perspective, variables such as education, income, and occupational status are resources, and the comparative amounts of such resources possessed by husband and wife are important in determining the outcomes of the distribution of power. But the reversal of the relationships for the Greek and Yugoslavian data forces us to reconsider our view of education, income, and occupational status. They are not merely resource variables in a power struggle, but are also positional variables in the social structure. The different positions of which they are indicative may involve differing patterns of socialization and may, for example, represent a greater or lesser likelihood of learning sentiments favourable toward the equalitarian distribution of power. This is particularly true for education: the more highly educated the Greek man, as pointed out by Safilios-Rothschild, the likelier is he to grant his wife a more equalitarian status within the marital relationship.

In Greece and Yugoslavia, therefore, we are not dealing so much with resources in a power struggle, but with the learning of a new role. The more education a man has, the likelier is he to grant his wife more authority, despite a traditional patriarchal culture.[8]

One issue that is at present difficult to resolve centres around the apparent lack of fit between the official norms and the behavioural data. It appears that traditional patriarchal norms are more stressed in Greece than in France or the United States. Yet the Greek women's responses, summed across all decisions, suggest that they have more actual power than women in the United States or France. Similarly, it appears that equalitarian norms are more stressed in the United States than in France or Greece; yet the behavioural data, summed across all decisions, suggest that the United States is more patriarchal than France or Greece. See Robert O. Blood, Jr, Reuben Hill, Andrée Michel, and Constantina Safilios-Rothschild, 'Comparative Analysis of Family Power Structure: Problems of Measurement in Interpretation', presented at the International Seminar for Family Research, Tokyo, Japan, September 1965.

Education may play its major role as a resource variable or as a cultural vari-able, depending upon the particular community or society under consideration. The stress placed here upon cultural differences stems from the attempt to deal simultaneously with apparently discrepant findings from four different societies. Blood and Wolfe also considered the possible influence of cultural factors in explaining the Detroit data, but found them wanting. They examined the influence of several variables that might indicate a greater acceptance of an authoritarian tradition—farm families, immigrant families, older couples, uneducated couples, and Catholic couples. But these families did not show a more patriarchal pattern of decision making. It was after testing for the influence of such cultural factors in Detroit that Blood and Wolfe turned to the theory of comparative resources. In the present discussion we have additional data that do indicate the importance of cultural expectations. Moreover, it seems that comparative resources play an influential role in the United States because of several underlying cultural factors: (1) the emphasis upon an equalitarian ethic; (2) a high degree of flexibility about the distribution of marital power; and (3) the importance that education, occupation, and income have in defining a man's status.

The French data are somewhat more difficult to interpret. The relationships between the authority score of the husband and variables such as family life cycle, husband's education, wife's employment status, and husband's income parallel the trends for the United States, but are weaker and frequently not statistically significant. It may be that lingering traditional patterns contribute toward a negative relationship between husband's educational level and husband's authority score while a developing flexible and equalitarian pattern contributes toward a positive relationship. Since these two trends tend to cancel each other out, the correlations are low. In addition, the family allowances that are paid to women provide an economic base of security for those in the lower classes, and the importance of education, occupation, and income are less stressed in defining the man's position than in the United States. These factors may also contribute toward the low correlations. It must also be remembered that there may be community and other differences within France and the other countries, so that the particular urban samples reported do not reflect all possible cultural authority patterns or family types.

To summarize, the following theoretical statement about marital power can be formulated: The balance of marital power is influenced by the interaction of (1) the comparative resources of husband and wife and (2) the cultural or subcultural expectations about the distribution of marital power. A similar statement, referring to the interaction of comparative resources and cultural expectations, can be made about the distribution of power in other areas.

## Exchange Theory and Cultural Context

The theory of exchange and reciprocity in social relationships has had a long history. Marcel Mauss, Howard Becker, Alvin W. Gouldner, John W. Thibaut and Harold H. Kelley, and George C. Homans, among others, have dealt with the idea of exchange and reciprocity in social interaction.[9] Heer has introduced exchange theory into the discussion of marital decision making.[10] According to this position, the balance of power is related to the comparative value of the resources obtained within the marital relationship to the value of the resources that could be obtained in an exchange outside the marital relationship. The theory of resources proposed by Blood and Wolfe and the theory of exchange proposed by Heer are closely related. The former emphasizes the comparative resources each person brings to the marital relationship: the more resources a person has in comparison to his spouse, the more power he will have. Heer's emphasis is upon a comparison of the value of the resources obtained within the marital relationship to that obtainable outside. Since he explicitly relates this to the resources each spouse has available for exchanging, it is similar to the theory of resources. The more resources a person is contributing to the marital relationship, the more he generally stands to gain from an alternative relationship and, therefore, the more power he will be able to exercise within the marital relationship.

The important contributions by Heer and by Blood and Wolfe were based upon data for the United States and helped to illuminate that data.[11] The Greek and Yugoslavian data, however, cannot be dealt with in strictly 'resource' or 'exchange' terms. They add a comparative perspective to the discussion of marital power and permit a modification of earlier theoretical statements that specifically takes the cultural component into account. The theory of resources in cultural context, as elaborated here, is still highly tentative, and much remains to be done in getting measures of the strength of cultural expectations about authority or of the nature of the interaction between cultural expectations and comparative resources as they influence the distribution of power. Nevertheless, the data on the United States, France, Greece, and Yugoslavia represent an important step in the accumulation of comparative findings and provide an excellent point of departure for further work.

## Situations, Norms, and Behaviour

In an ad hoc and inductive way, a 'theory of resources in cultural context' has been elaborated in order to place the findings on power structure in Detroit, Paris and Bordeaux, Athens, and Kragujevac into theoretical context. We found that the 'theory of resources' was adequate for the Detroit data and somewhat less adequate for the Paris and Bordeaux data. In modifying the theory to account for the Greek and Yugoslavian data we have expanded its explanatory power. The 'theory of resources in cultural context', inductively developed to account for the data from the United States, France, Greece, and Yugoslavia, requires further specification through testing on additional communities.

Now that we have developed the theory of resources in cultural context inductively, let us turn around and approach it deductively. A debate that once raged among psychologists had to do with whether behaviour was an automatic reaction to stimulus influences or whether there were certain mediating processes in the organism between the stimulus and the behaviour or response. A parallel debate among sociologists had to do with whether behaviour was an automatic outcome of situational influences or whether there were certain mediating cultural processes that provided normative guidelines for behaviour in particular environmental situations. Most psychologists realized that the naked stimulus was clothed in the prior experiential history of the organism, and in this sense the response was influenced by stimulus and organism interaction. Most sociologists realized that the naked environmental situation was draped with normative guidelines and that behaviour was influenced by the interaction between the situation and the norms. Similarly, to tie in the ad hoc theory we have developed, we might say that the naked theory of resources has to be set within a cultural context; in this way it is possible to state explicitly that decision-making behaviour is influenced by the interaction between resources and cultural definitions. In fact, of course, though the words and perspectives are different, the psychological S-O-R theory, the sociological theory of situation, norms, and behaviour, and the theory of resources in cultural context are all getting at the same general formula for predicting behavioural outcomes. There is a stimulus or a situation; there is an organism with prior experience which may include learned cultural or normative dispositions; and the response or behaviour that ensues is influenced by these factors in interaction with each other.

A restatement of the findings in terms of the theory of behaviour as a function of situation and norms summarizes several of the major arguments:

1. In the United States and France, the norms about marital decision making have two major characteristics that are of special relevance. They tend to favour, in general, an equalitarian ethic, and they tend to be flexible about the precise degree of decision making that should be exercised by husband or wife. As a result of this normative framework, the situation of interaction between husband and wife, including their comparative resources, comes into play and has an influence over the behavioural outcome.[12] As a result there are positive relationships between a husband's authority score and his occupation, and income.
2. In Greece and Yugoslavia the norms about marital decision making are more patriarchal in character and less flexible. As a result, the normative guidelines place constraints upon the possible influence of situational conditions or resources. It is, therefore, among those groups that have learned 'modern' norms regarding marital decision making—such as groups at the higher educational levels—that there is the greatest possibility for the increased participation of women.

## NOTES

Revised from a discussion of the papers dealing with 'Substantive Reports of Cross-National Family Research', at the Sixth World Congress of Sociology, Evian, France, September, 1966.

1 Andrée Michel, 'Comparative Data Concerning the Interaction in French and American Families', *Journal of Marriage and the Family*, 29, No. 2 (May, 1967).

2 Constantina Safilios-Rothschild, 'A Comparison of Power Structure and Marital Satisfaction in Urban Greek and French Families', *Journal of Marriage and the Family*, 29, No. 2 (May, 1967).

3 Olivera Burić and Andjelka Zečević, 'Family Authority, Marital Satisfaction and the Social Network in Yugoslavia', *Journal of Marriage and the Family*, 29, No. 2 (May, 1967).

4 Robert O. Blood, Jr and Donald M. Wolfe, *Husbands and Wives*, New York: The Free Press, Macmillan, 1960, pp. 11–46. This study, as well as research carried out in Belgium by Reuben Hill, was instrumental in encouraging the comparative research in France, Greece, and Yugoslavia.

5 Ibid.

6 Ibid., p. 42.

7 Ibid., p. 37.

8 A number of issues must remain clouded until further data are reported. For example, we do not have data on the distribution of responses for each decision in each country; we do not have data on men's responses; we are making assumptions about norms but we do not have normative data. Furthermore, in order to provide culturally equivalent decisions within each country it was not possible to use the same set of decisions. This makes it hazardous to compare the mean authority scores (summed for all decisions) of the different samples.

9 Marcel Mauss, *The Gift*, translated by Ian Cunnison, New York: The Free Press, Macmillan, 1954; Howard Becker, *Man in Reciprocity*, New York: Praeger, 1956; Alvin W. Gouldner, 'The Norm of Reciprocity: A Preliminary Statement', *American Sociological Review*, 25, No. 2 (April, 1960), 161–78; John W. Thibaut and Harold H. Kelley, *The Social Psychology of Groups*, New York: John Wiley, 1959; George C. Homans, *Social Behavior: Its Elementary Forms*, New York: Harcourt, Brace, 1961.

10 David M. Heer, 'The Measurement and Bases of Family Power: An Overview', *Marriage and Family Living*, 25, No. 2 (May, 1963), 133–9. See also Robert O. Blood, Jr, 'The Measurement and Bases of Family Power: A Rejoinder', *Marriage and Family Living*, 25, No. 4 (November, 1963), 475–7; David M. Heer, 'Reply', *Marriage and Family Living*, 25, No. 4 (November, 1963), 477–8.

11 For a discussion of some methodological issues in research on marital power structure and for additional references to data on the United States, see Heer, 'The Measurement and Bases of Family Power: An Overview', op. cit.

12 But the fit between norms and behaviour is not very good. See note 8. Cf. Irwin Deutscher, 'Words and Deeds: Social Science and Social Policy', *Social Problems*, 13: 3 (Winter, 1966), pp. 235–54; Irwin Deutscher, 'Public vs. Private Opinions: The "Real" and the "Unreal"', presented at the Eastern Sociological Society meetings, Philadelphia, April, 1966.

From *Journal of Marriage and the Family* 29 (2) (1967): 320–5.

From the perspective of the 1990s, it seems that resource theory was no more than a rationalization for the dominant role of men with respect to familial decision making. (This points to the rather discomforting possibility that even the claims of social science are ideological distortions that need to be analysed within a sociological context in themselves. And it is this task that is precisely what the sociology of knowledge is about. The possibly ideo-logical character of 'knowledge' is another reason why I am loath to subject you to a great many of the substantive knowledge claims now believed by sociologists, and have chosen to concentrate on trying to teach you how sociologists think, rather than exposing you to what they think.) In any case, critics were quick to point out that the designation of some things as resources and others as not was hard to justify theoretically. They also pointed out that education was more than a resource; it was confounded with attitudes acquired along with education, such that any differences in decision-making power might reflect either the differentials with respect to education as a resource or the new and more liberal attitudes that tend to be acquired along with education (Rodman 1967). There were two results of such criticisms: the first was to propose a challenger to resource theory—social-ization or attitude theory, which posited that relative power was best explained by attitudes rather than resources. The second result was a modification and extension of resource theory that added to the list of resources such additional factors as affection and, most recently, work commitment. The attempt to add new factors to resource theory seems to bring its old problems into clearer focus.

Blood and Wolfe conducted survey research attempting to identify those factors that explained the distribution of decision-making power between spouses. They found that husbands tended to have more education and income than their wives and that husbands reported more decision-making power than their wives. They inferred from this correla-tion that the possession of proportionately more resources *caused* proportionately more decision-making power and thus explained why men possessed this power. From the description above of the discovery of resource theory, it is clear that there may be several difficulties, not the least the possible spuriousness of the causal inference, an issue discussed in chapter 3. One might, even more abstractly, also question the meaning of the term 'explanation' in this style of research, since it can be argued that the correlation between resources and power *needs* explanation rather than *constitutes* an explanation.

But what is a resource, exactly, in this context? Can resources be identified in advance, from some theoretical assumptions? It seems that the only answer is that they cannot. Resources are those things that can be used in the dyad to negotiate the distribution of power, and different resources will be used and recognized by different dyads. If in the United States, income and education are usually highly valued and are therefore accorded this status as legitimate resources to be used in the negotiations, this is not because they are, in any absolute sense, resources, but because in the cultural context of that time and place, they have been widely accorded that status. Income is not always a valued resource. There are societies in which the possession of much material wealth is suspect and nega-tively sanctioned. The idea that material success is a resource that can be translated into other power seems likely to be a corollary of the Protestant ethic that Weber wrote of, in which Calvinists sought corroboration of their hopes for the next world by finding success in this one. But in India, for example, and in other times and places too, poverty was a resource that could be translated into power, for most holy men were itinerant paupers living only on alms from other people. Indeed, the association of holiness and poverty is common among many religious orders. In such circumstances, wealth is at least not a resource that tends to increase power. On the other hand, holiness, spirituality, and wisdom are widely considered to be valuable resources. Even in our own society, there is still a little ambivalence about great wealth, depending on how it is acquired, perhaps, that may lead us to resist giving political power to those who already possess wealth. There is a sense that such people do not share in enough of life's problems to be able to identify with the 'common man', as we would wish our politicians to do.

Education too is a culturally contexted resource that may or may not be considered legitimate as a basis for a claim to more decision-making power. Again, in our own society we display considerable ambivalence towards the educated, considering that education is at best a mixed bag, enabling people to do some academic things (which we tend not to think very valuable in their own right) but disqualifying them from perhaps even more of the pragmatic concerns of the workaday world. Certainly, if education were as valuable a resource as it appears from the early theorists, it seems hard to explain the rather shabby treatment often accorded to teachers and education in our society. The possession of higher education, far from being automatically translated into legitimate power in the real world, is as often used to disqualify a person from being taken seriously in just this pragmatic world.

Although there are then fundamental and radical arguments about what is to be considered a resource and why, there is another strong strain of criticism that simply wishes to augment existing resource theory by including additional factors. Certainly, to argue that resource theory needs to be augmented by the addition of factors like affection, attractiveness, occupational prestige, and work commitment is to argue that other resources, particularly women's resources, have been omitted until recently, for ideological reasons, and to force a reconsideration of the theory. In more complex fashion, arguments have been made that the very concept of resource must be re-examined with regard to *relative* resource holdings between spouses if it is to have any credibility. And yet this opens a terrible Pandora's box of issues, since, among other things, we have no way of understanding how couples actually assess the relative weights of those things they are willing to consider as legitimate factors in their negotiation for power. Is a salary differential of $5,000 worth as much as a stronger work commitment? How does one quantify one's affection relative to the other's occupational prestige? How much is attractiveness or sexual ability worth in this peculiar market? Not only is it clear that there is no standard for measuring the values of these items, but we have not the faintest idea how they compare. Yet if we are to use such knowledge to predict the outcome of such negotiations, we must know what is and is not a resource, and the market value of that resource compared to others. We need to understand the process by which couples actually negotiate the relative value of what they take to be relevant resources.

There appear to be no theoretical limits to what might be thrown into the resource model, since a resource seems to be anything for which a case can be made that it is useful in affecting the outcomes of negotiations of relative spousal power in decision making. Now this inductive way of identifying resources makes a great deal of sense, but one obviously cannot attempt to discover the factors that couples use in negotiating power by the use of a questionnaire that identifies some potential and plausible factors but not others. It seems that the inductive approach requires that one observe and intensively interview in as open-ended a fashion as possible, establishing generalizations only later.

And what might such an approach tell us? We begin from the premise that the only intelligent definition of a resource is that which is regarded as being of value in the negotiation of decision making. This inductive approach enjoins us to study decision making in the real world and decide what sorts of features real people construe as resources or assets in the course of their negotiation of who is to have how much power to make decisions that affect them both. In this situation, resources are ploys in the interaction. They are neither absolute nor constant; they must be legitimated by the other to be useful. Things must be seen as variables that emerge in the course of interaction and can be known only from and within that situation. This is a symbolic interactionist stance, and I suspect that Herbert Blumer (the father of symbolic interaction) would have been first to make similar critiques of resource theory had he been so inclined. Is the fact that the husband is stronger than his wife a legitimate resource? Will it be brought forward by him in an attempt to support his claim to more power? The answers to these questions depend on a great many factors, but it appears that it is currently widely thought to be illegitimate for a spouse to claim legitimate power on the basis of greater physical strength. Note that this does not mean that the illegitimate claim is not made. Clearly, in this as in other instances, it is made, the more so since these negotiations are usually conducted in private. Complicating the picture still more, battered wives may well accord some legitimacy to their beatings, agreeing they deserved them in some way.

In so far as we move towards a meritocracy, our ideology and values are such that only merit and fairness are considered legitimate resources to be called upon. Thus, to the extent that commitment to work is regarded as legitimate, what we seem to be saying is that since your work is so much more important to you than mine is to me, I will sacrifice my work and indeed my free time, to give you more time for your work. Interestingly enough, this means that the spouse who makes the sacrifice does so by taking on more, rather than less, decision making for the other spouse. Thus, some resources allow you to have a greater say and some allow you a lesser say, and either may be valuable. This points up still other basic problems with resource theory. The primary of these is that everything depends on what is ultimately of value. That is, if resource theory is correct, it presumably predicts that the spouse with the greater share of the resources will have the greater share of the power in the dyad. But will this mean greater or lesser share of any particular tasks? Clearly, it depends on whether these in turn are highly valued or not. If men value caring for infants and if they have greater resources, then they will use that power to increase the time they spend caring for infants. If they value housework, they will use their resources to purchase more time for doing what they value. If they value equality or the happiness of their spouse, things get truly messy when we try to predict any outcome of their greater resources. Guilt may lead them to sacrifice their time to allow their spouses some freedom from the constant demands of child rearing, for example. Does this mean that guilt is a resource that women have by which they increase their power to negotiate for a greater role in decision making? Each spouse's ideological commitment would seem critical, both in establishing the goals of each partner and in establishing what they will likely consider legitimate factors used in the negotiation of relative power.

A second issue raised is the longitudinal nature of such bargaining over power. Marriages may last many years, and spouses do their negotiating with that in mind. Thus, a husband may well allow his wife to decide what colour to paint the bedroom this time, fully intending to trade in an IOU for more power when it comes time to buy a new car. Thus, he may say, 'I'll let you decide this time' or 'I'll do this for you this time, but next time it is my turn'. If the other spouse has a commitment to fairness, such bargaining works, or is at least a factor in subsequent negotiations. Again, this is not to say that spouses must have any commitment to fairness, and it is certainly not to say that such a commitment guarantees any particular outcome. People are talented at reconstructing a situation, eliminating from it features they do not want to see. Typically, such instances begin with 'But that was different. . .', and the speaker goes on to explain why an apparent precedent should be given no weight in the negotiations under way at this time. Still another factor becomes evident from the illustration. A great deal would seem to depend on the ability of the spouses in question to anticipate the other's strategy and to offset it through superior rhetoric, logic, or appeals to emotion or raw strength.

## ILLUSTRATIVE READINGS 3 AND 4

Since this is the first chapter and the distinction is a pretty central one not immediately obvious, I would like to juxtapose the following two pieces and challenge you to decide which exemplifies which of the perspectives, and in what ways.

## READING 3

### YOUNG ADULTS LIVING IN THEIR PARENTS' HOMES

*Monica Boyd and Edward T. Pryor*

Recent decades have brought unanticipated turns in family composition and living arrangements among both the young and old. More elderly Canadians are living alone, while, until recently, the young have been leaving their parents' homes at increasingly early ages. In Canada, this latter tendency emerged as a growing trend for young adults to establish their own households, thus emptying the parental nest. Between 1971 and 1981, the percentages of unmarried adults who lived at home declined.

However, recent evidence from the Canadian Census has shown a reversal of this trend between 1981 and 1986. The percentage of unmarried young adults who were living with parents rose over the period 1981–1986.

This shift is particularly noteworthy for unmarried people aged 20–29 in respect to the choices they made between living as unattached individuals (that is, alone or with non-relatives) or living in a family household. As of 1986, six out of ten of these women aged 20–24 were living with one or both parents. Seven out of ten men aged 20–24 were still living with parents. Even by their late twenties, over four out of ten unattached or unmarried men and three out of ten women were living at home.

The increasing percentages of young adults in their twenties who are living at home have contributed to an aging of the entire population of children aged 15–34 living at home. In 1971, slightly more than one-quarter of the young women who lived at home and one-third of the young men were aged 20–29. By 1986, nearly 40 per cent of the unmarried women and nearly half of the unmarried men living with parents were aged 20–29. Not only is a higher percentage of the unattached or unmarried young adult population living at home, but they are also more likely to be older than young adults living at home in previous decades.

The reasons for interest in adult children living with parents are manifold, but two aspects are obvious: (1) recent trends in the living arrangements of young adults go against the grain of the previous long-term momentum of the young to make an early departure from their parents' homes, and (2) the underlying question of explaining such a reversal and its consequences for the understanding of contemporary family life.

In part, the reversal of the previous pattern has been masked by other changes in household formation patterns of Canadians, such as living alone, the increase in forms of cohabitation not based on a marriage, and increases in family breakdown.

While each has contributed to a proliferation of residential types and patterns, which taken together have tended to reduce average household size, delayed leaving of the family household and subsequent returns to it have apparently emerged as a countervailing tendency, possibly reflecting changes in marriage patterns and the economic conditions facing young adults today.

## Factors in leaving or staying in parental homes

Census data provide the overall pattern with respect to delayed marriage. The percentage of Canadians who had been married by a given age declined between 1976 and 1986, indicating a delay in the timing of marriages. Delayed marriage leaves the other residential options of (1) leaving the parental household for other independent living arrangements either alone or with others or (2) remaining in or returning to the parental home during the years that in previous decades might have been spent in a separate household in the married state.

It appears that an increasing number of unmarried young adults have chosen the second option. They remain in their parents' homes at a time in the family life cycle when parents might once have expected to be freed of direct parental responsibilities. The nest may still be emptying, but the process now extends over a longer transitional period.

Many other factors contribute to a decision to leave a parent's home and to establish a new household. Factors associated with the choice between living at home and establishing a separate household are: sex of the adult children, membership in particular ethnic groups, education level attained, labour force

Canadian Social Trends: Proportion of Unmarried Persons Aged 20–29 Living With Parents,[1] 1971–1986

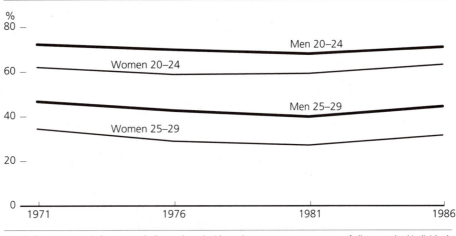

1 Includes never-married, separated, divorced, and widowed persons as a percentage of all unattached individuals living on their own plus unmarried children living at home.

Source: Statistics Canada, Census of Canada.

Unmarried[1] Persons Aged 15–34 Living With Parents, By Sex and Age, as a Percentage[2] of Unattached Individuals and Unmarried Persons Living in Families, 1971–1986

| | Men | | | | | Women | | | | |
|---|---|---|---|---|---|---|---|---|---|---|
| | 1971 | 1976 | 1981 | 1986 | DIFFERENCE 1986–81 | 1971 | 1976 | 1981 | 1986 | DIFFERENCE 1986–81 |
| Percentage of unmarried population living with parents | | | | | | | | | | |
| 15–19 | 93.3 | 92.7 | 91.9 | 92.0 | 0.1 | 91.5 | 90.6 | 90.5 | 91.4 | 0.9 |
| 20–24 | 72.4 | 70.0 | 68.1 | 71.2 | 3.1 | 62.1 | 58.9 | 59.3 | 63.3 | 4.0 |
| 25–29 | 46.8 | 42.8 | 40.0 | 44.6 | 4.6 | 34.5 | 29.0 | 27.2 | 31.6 | 4.4 |
| 30–34 | 35.1 | 32.7 | 27.8 | 28.8 | 1.0 | 24.7 | 20.0 | 17.1 | 17.7 | 0.6 |
| **Total 15–34** | **78.4** | **75.7** | **71.2** | **69.8** | **-1.4** | **74.4** | **70.2** | **66.1** | **63.9** | **-2.2** |
| Age profile of unmarried population living at home | | | | | | | | | | |
| 15–19 | 62.2 | 61.5 | 57.4 | 49.1 | -8.3 | 71.9 | 71.0 | 66.2 | 57.5 | -8.7 |
| 20–24 | 28.7 | 28.7 | 31.0 | 34.5 | 3.5 | 21.6 | 22.3 | 25.8 | 30.9 | 5.1 |
| 25–29 | 6.6 | 7.2 | 8.4 | 12.0 | 3.6 | 4.5 | 4.7 | 5.6 | 8.4 | 2.8 |
| 30–34 | 2.5 | 2.6 | 3.2 | 4.4 | 1.2 | 2.0 | 2.0 | 2.4 | 3.2 | 0.8 |
| **Total 15–34** | **100.0** | **100.0** | **100.0** | **100.0** | **–** | **100.0** | **100.0** | **100.0** | **100.0** | **–** |

1 Includes never married, separated, divorced, and widowed.
2 The population at risk (the denominator) consists of all unattached individuals and unmarried persons in economic families. Married people are excluded.

Source: Statistics Canada, Census of Canada.

Characteristics of Unmarried[1] Persons Aged 20–29 Living With Parent(s) and as
Unattached Individuals,[2] By Sex, 1981

|  | Unmarried living at home | | Unattached individuals | |
|---|---|---|---|---|
|  | Men | Women | Men | Women |
| *Rural/Urban* | | % | | |
| Rural . . . . . . . . . . . . . . . . . . . . . . . . . . | 24.9 | 20.0 | 11.2 | 6.2 |
| Urban . . . . . . . . . . . . . . . . . . . . . . . . | 75.1 | 80.0 | 88.8 | 93.8 |
| Total . . . . . . . . . . . . . . . . . . . . . . . . | 100.0 | 100.0 | 100.0 | 100.0 |
| *Home language* | | | | |
| English . . . . . . . . . . . . . . . . . . . . . . . | 63.8 | 63.7 | 77.4 | 76.9 |
| French . . . . . . . . . . . . . . . . . . . . . . . . . | 29.7 | 29.6 | 20.7 | 20.6 |
| Other . . . . . . . . . . . . . . . . . . . . . . . . . | 6.5 | 6.7 | 1.9 | 2.5 |
| Total . . . . . . . . . . . . . . . . . . . . . . . . | 100.0 | 100.0 | 100.0 | 100.0 |
| *Education* | | | | |
| Less than grade 9 . . . . . . . . . . . . . . . . . . | 5.9 | 4.2 | 3.3 | 2.2 |
| Grades 9–13 . . . . . . . . . . . . . . . . . . . . . | 41.6 | 35.7 | 35.5 | 30.6 |
| Non-university certificate or diploma . . . . | 27.7 | 30.8 | 29.4 | 32.7 |
| University . . . . . . . . . . . . . . . . . . . . . . | 24.8 | 29.3 | 31.8 | 34.6 |
| Total . . . . . . . . . . . . . . . . . . . . . . . . | 100.0 | 100.0 | 100.0 | 100.0 |
| *Attending school* | | | | |
| Not attending . . . . . . . . . . . . . . . . . . . . | 66.0 | 60.9 | 76.1 | 71.0 |
| Full-time . . . . . . . . . . . . . . . . . . . . . . . | 25.8 | 29.3 | 12.2 | 12.3 |
| Part-time . . . . . . . . . . . . . . . . . . . . . . . | 8.2 | 9.7 | 11.7 | 16.8 |
| Total . . . . . . . . . . . . . . . . . . . . . . . . | 100.0 | 100.0 | 100.0 | 100.0 |
| *Employment* | | | | |
| Employed . . . . . . . . . . . . . . . . . . . . . . | 74.3 | 72.8 | 87.3 | 88.2 |
| Unemployed . . . . . . . . . . . . . . . . . . . . . | 13.2 | 10.6 | 6.8 | 5.1 |
| Not in the labour force . . . . . . . . . . . . . | 12.5 | 16.6 | 5.9 | 6.7 |
| Total . . . . . . . . . . . . . . . . . . . . . . . . | 100.0 | 100.0 | 100.0 | 100.0 |
| *Income* | | | | |
| Less than $2,500 . . . . . . . . . . . . . . . . . . | 20.6 | 29.0 | 9.2 | 11.8 |
| $2,500–4,999 . . . . . . . . . . . . . . . . . . . . | 16.9 | 20.3 | 8.8 | 12.1 |
| $5,000–7,499 . . . . . . . . . . . . . . . . . . . . | 14.5 | 14.1 | 10.6 | 12.9 |
| $7,500–9,999 . . . . . . . . . . . . . . . . . . . . | 11.7 | 12.4 | 9.8 | 12.6 |
| $10,000–14,999 . . . . . . . . . . . . . . . . . . | 20.0 | 18.0 | 22.7 | 28.7 |
| $15,000 and over . . . . . . . . . . . . . . . . . | 16.3 | 6.2 | 38.9 | 21.9 |
| Total . . . . . . . . . . . . . . . . . . . . . . . . | 100.0 | 100.0 | 100.0 | 100.0 |

1 Includes never married, separated, divorced, and widowed.
2 Persons living alone or with non-relatives.

Source: Statistics Canada, 1981 Census of Canada.

participation, and individual income. Some factors are enabling (e.g., high
employment income makes household formation feasible, as does higher educational attainment, which often translates into desirable employment), while
other factors are retarding (full-time enrolment in higher education).

Compared with people in their twenties living unattached, unmarried persons in their twenties who were living at home in 1981 were more likely to live in a rural area, to have French as the home language, to have lower levels of educational attainment, to be attending school, to be unemployed or not in the labour force, and to have lower incomes. In 1981, nearly one-quarter of the young unmarried men in rural areas were residing with parents, compared with slightly over 11 per cent of unattached men aged 20–29. For young unmarried women living at home, nearly 30 per cent were in settings in which French was the home language, compared with slightly more than 20 per cent of the unattached population. Over one-third of unmarried people living with parents were attending school, in contrast to the lower school attendance of young adults living alone or with non-relatives. One-quarter of the unmarried-living-at-home population was unemployed or not in the labour force, compared with fewer than 15 per cent of unattached individuals in their twenties. Consistent with the patterns of school attendance and employment, over one-third of the unmarried men and nearly 50 per cent of the unmarried women living with parents had incomes of less than $5,000 in 1980. Approximately two out of ten unattached young women and men had incomes below $5,000.

## The cluttered nest

When all factors are considered together, there was an increased tendency in the mid-1980s for young adults in their twenties who were not currently married to live continuously in their parents' homes or to return to them. The increase occurred largely between 1981 and 1986, a period that encompassed a severe economic recession and increased time spent in pursuing higher education. The percentage of people in the age group 18–24 enrolled full-time in post-secondary education rose gradually from 19.8 per cent in 1976–77 to 24.5 per cent in 1985–86.

Using 1981 Census data, co-residency with parents rather than living as unattached individuals is seen to be related to low educational attainment, having French as a home language, being unemployed or not in the labour force, and with having a low income. School attendance was also an important factor. Some young adults may be effectively trapped in their parents' homes because of the high costs of establishing a separate household, particularly in large urban areas where the costs of accommodation are conspicuously higher than average.

What the effects on family life of delayed leaving, willing or unwilling, may ultimately prove to be are unknown. These findings do raise the possibility that contemporary young adults, unlike their predecessors in the late 1970s, will spend more time in a homelife over which they exert less than full control, possibly in the process adopting their parents' behaviour patterns more thoroughly. Whether as a by-product of pursuing higher education, or because of the relatively low salaries available to the young in the late 1980s, many seem destined to remain in their parents' homes considerably longer than was previously

Population Ever Married at Selected Ages, 1976, 1981, 1986

| Age | 1976 | 1981 | 1986 |
|-----|------|------|------|
| | | % | |
| 19 | 14 | 11 | 8 |
| 21 | 34 | 29 | 20 |
| 26 | 75 | 71 | 63 |
| 31 | 88 | 86 | 82 |
| 36 | 92 | 91 | 89 |

Source: Statistics Canada, Census of Canada.

expected. This possibility could indicate a fundamental alteration in the living arrangement patterns of young Canadians relative to previous generations.

But the permanence of this trend is questionable. Continued improvement in economic conditions, were it to be passed on to young adults, might again reverse the growing tendency to stay in one's parents' home; or alternatively, higher levels of enrolment in post-secondary education for longer programs of study could reinforce the existing trend by keeping children at home for even longer periods of time.

From C. McKie and K. Thompson (eds), *Canadian Social Trends* (Toronto: Thompson Educational Publishing, 1990), 188–91.

## READING 4

### FROM EMPTY NEST TO CROWDED NEST: THE DYNAMICS OF INCOMPLETELY-LAUNCHED YOUNG ADULTS

*Allan Schnaiberg*
*Sheldon Goldenberg*

This paper concerns problems in the successful transition to adulthood for young in middle-class American families. We call the most obvious symptom of this problem the returning young adult syndrome. We argue that this symptom points to broader questions of young adults' (YA) deviance from parental expectations of the YAs' autonomy, parental anomie, erratic performance by YAs in adult roles, and substantial intrafamilial conflict. We argue that the issue has emerged from separation-individuation tensions and the YAs' ambivalence about their capacity to play adult roles, coupled with more volatile causes, including postwar nurturance of children's rights, more recent legitimation of parents' rights to develop themselves, and the still more recent contraction in the opportunity structure for young adults. Two likely outcomes are increased YA capacity to play modified adult roles and decreases in parents' expectations about YAs' performance.

Our first goal in this paper is to draw sociologists' attention to the returning young adult syndrome (RYA), which we take to be the major symptom of certain recent changes in the American middle-class family system.[1] Our second objective is to outline some likely psycho-dynamic and sociological causes of these changes, and our final task is to suggest some consequences of this change in family structure and functioning for the development of the family and other institutions.

## Problems in the Transition to Adulthood:
### RYAs, ILYAs, and Their Parents

The general conditions associated with what has been termed the RYA syndrome (or the problem of a 'postponed generation') seem to include the following:

1. children's unanticipated economic *dependency* and/or failure(s) to 'launch careers' and become successfully autonomous adults;
2. *deviance* from parental expectations that children will physically separate from parents in 'young adulthood' (college years or post-college);
3. one or more 'attempts' by these children to fulfill these expectations, followed by a *return* to a parental home for varying periods of time; and
4. *anomic* context for household labour organization and allocation of family resources when there is a returning young adult in the household; anger of parents (and often of children), and substantial conflict over these issues.

The first factor is of critical importance; the others follow from it only in the case of co-residence. In consequence, we conceptualize the central issue as the 'incompletely-launched young adult' (ILYA). The other factors are problems only to the extent that they may follow from the first condition. Where children are arguably struggling to 'make it', even these other conditions can be tolerated, albeit with some strain, since these behaviours are not normative. Conversely, where the first condition exists, even without producing the phenomenon of the returning young adult, many of the same strains and adaptations we discuss will occur. However, these are not exacerbated by the additional stresses directly attributable to co-residence. In short, the unexpectedly-prolonged dependency (the first condition) is both necessary and sufficient to create many of the problems within the familial milieu that we treat below.

Although there are clearly quite different perspectives on this phenomenon among various family members, we focus in this paper on the perspective of parents.[2] Both media reports (e.g., Greenburg, 1985; Wilding, 1985; McCullogh, 1986; Sullivan, 1987; Sherrod, 1988; Rosemond, 1988; Kuttner, 1988; Cowan, 1989) and our own observations suggest there is a widespread concern about these matters among middle-class parents, especially those with professional, technical, or managerial occupations (Littwin, 1986; Okimoto and Stegall, 1987). Most commonly, this takes the form of anxiety about whether they have personally failed to adequately socialize their ILYAs for adulthood (including work and marriage) and anger/resentment at their ILYAs' violation of parental expectations (Hagestad, Smyer, and Stierman, 1984: 251).

Two features emerge in most accounts. First, parents are not enthusiastic about the 'failure' of their ILYAs to make a smooth transition to autonomous adulthood. Contrary to many social and psychological profiles of this life cycle stage as that of the 'empty nest', many modern parents find themselves instead in a 'crowded nest' (Greenberg, 1985) with an unexpectedly returned young adult. A second feature is the *personalizing* of the accounts, with a great deal of self-blame or blaming the victim (whether parent or child). In C. Wright Mills's (1959) classical conceptualization, the ILYA phenomenon seems at present to be stuck at the level of a personal trouble arising from the family milieu (Hagestad, Smyer, and Stierman, 1984) rather than having become a public issue, seen to arise from structural change in the society.

Sociologists are partly implicated in this absence of consciousness since we have largely ignored ILYAs as a social phenomenon. (Ironically, from our observations, sociologists at this stage of the family life cycle seem indistinguishable from other middle-aged, middle-class parents; they also struggle with ILYAs as personal troubles.) Yet a defining element of the ILYA phenomenon (and its frequent returning young adult adaptation) is a prior set of social norms about when young adults should separate physically, economically, and socio-emotionally from their parents (Cohler and Geyer, 1982; Hagestad, Smyer, and Stierman, 1984). Such norms have been grounded in structural contexts that have been changing for the middle class in recent decades. Institutional reinforcement of the norms, however, seems to be lagging substantially behind these changing conditions for ILYAs and their parents. Hence middle-class parents and children experience these socio-historical shifts as personal troubles, producing expressions of guilt, shame, and anger, rather than as public issues resulting from socio-economic forces, as Mills advocated.[3]

Toward defining this phenomenon as a social or public issue, we would like to focus attention on patterns that transcend the individual experience. We begin by noting that the phenomenon of relatively large numbers of ILYAs presents anomic conditions for parents (and ILYAs as well) with respect to both intrafamilial and extrafamilial roles and relationships. Both parties are confronted with questions of socially appropriate behaviour for themselves and their role reciprocals in dealing with such issues as failure/delay in achievement of middle class status, psychological tensions about being a 'good parent' or 'good child' and 'adult', and the additional stress of a rather anomic division of labour and resources in those households containing an incompletely-launched young adult (Hagestad, Smyer, and Stierman, 1984: 251).

There are, of course, anomic aspects of all parenting relationships. Dialectical *social* tensions between children's needs for support (dependency needs) and children's needs for freedom (autonomy needs) exist in all kinship systems. Likewise, at a *psychodynamic* or developmental level, parents struggle uniquely with each child at each developmental stage to achieve some balance between nurturance, control, and encouragement of self-development to facilitate the separation and individuation of the child (Cohler and Geyer, 1982). Nowhere has this tension been more acute and more attended to by various experts than in the American middle-class family in the post-Second World War period (Lasch, 1977; Hagestad, Smyer, and Stierman, 1984).

This paper elaborates this dialectic. It explores the heightened parental anomie produced by recent socio-economic transformations that have raised obstacles to fulfillment of previous developmental expectations (Elder, 1978). More abstractly, we suggest that the middle class norms about timing and success of children's adoption of adult roles that parents incorporated in the period of growth following the war may be increasingly difficult to achieve. Parents and their ILYAs (and other children) often confront a hiatus between the former's goals and the latter's insufficient means to attain such goals.

Following Merton (1957), we suggest that parents may display different behavioural adaptations to these conditions. Depending on their level of consciousness, resources, and personalities, parents may conform, innovate, retreat, ritualize or rebel in response to the strains experienced. They may alter their goals for their ILYAs and/or alter the means at their disposal by shifting the content of parental socialization, the allocation of resources to ILYAs, or by other behaviours. Alternatively, they may fail to recognize their own experience as exemplifying this particular public issue. Parents may remain stuck at the level of conflict within the family (without resolution) for some indefinite period. Yet another path is for parents to find some partial resolution through overt nego-tiation with their ILYAs. Finally, they may withdraw from their children, by emotionally or physically retreating from them.

We view the ILYA syndrome as consistent with Elder's (1978: 57) cautions about 'the complex meanings associated with age differentiation'. In particular, ILYA changes illustrate that 'observed variations in family patterns by stage . . . are subject to interpretations that are based on historical context and change . . . [and] may be due to historical trends and unique events, as well as to the constraints and requirements of particular role systems' (Elder, 1978: 56). We seek to extend Elder's insight by using a sociology of knowledge perspective to consider how the developmental ideologies and practices of the post-war middle-class family were shaped by historical trends and unique events that differ from those of the current 'crowded nests'. We stress, like Elder, that whether ILYAs are seen as a personal trouble or public issue depends as much on changing *interpretations* by parents as on changing *behaviours* of young adult children.

## Residence Patterns of Young Adults

One crude indicator of this changing behaviour is the demographic evidence of declining neolocal residence of many young adults, the phenomenon we label the returning young adult syndrome. Table 1 provides an overview of the recent turnabout in residence patterns of young adults. Interestingly, these recent increases in co-residence with parents are more striking for young males than females, which may be due to gender differences in several of the hypothesized ILYA causal factors we offer below. These gender differences run contrary to the expectations of high school seniors found in recent work (Goldscheider and Goldscheider, 1987), raising some questions about the launching process. While these RYA indicators in Table 1 are only partial surrogates for richer data on increases in incomplete launching, they do suggest that some recent shifts in relationships between young adults and their families of origin have occurred in the past 15 years. They are indirect evidence for a change in family milieus. We argue below that they are also consequences of public issues of changing opportunity structures for families (Knapp, 1987).

While Table 1 refers to co-residence increases across all family milieus, Riche's (1987) work suggests that these demographic changes most typify upper middle class families. Moreover, since expectations of launching are most prevalent in just this stratum, it strongly reinforces our sense that the level of personal troubles associated with incomplete launching should be greatest among these well-educated, middle-class parents (Hagestad, Smyer, and Stierman, 1984). Our contention that this is a problem of anomie is further reinforced by the fact that due partly to delays in marriage in recent cohorts, increases in RYA rates coexist with increases in rates of single young adults living apart from their parents (Goldscheider and LeBourdais, 1986; Goldscheider and Waite, 1987; Waite, Goldscheider, and Witsberger, 1986). Thus both parents and their ILYAs who are also RYAs confront evidence of the nonconventional nature of their circumstances, since at any given time most young adults are moving away from parents (albeit perhaps only to return to the nest at a later time).

Interestingly, our finding that male RYA rates are substantially higher than female rates may complement recent findings that living apart from parents has weaker effects on the attitudes and expectations of young men than on young women (Waite, Goldscheider, and Witsberger, 1986). The two sets of findings indicate that perhaps male RYAs are also less impacted by their co-residence than are female RYAs (though whether this is a result of selection or socialization factors is still unclear).

Finally, Table 1 understates the pervasiveness of returns to the 'crowded nest' because the data are cross-sectional indicators of a highly-fluid phenomenon. Waite, Goldscheider, and Witsberger (1986), as well as other research on YAs living apart from parents, note that this young adulthood period encompasses many frequent residential and role transitions. We believe this can be translated into a much higher frequency of incompleteness of launching than Table 1 indicates. As with unemployment or poverty statistics, a cross-sectional rate of seven or eight per cent can easily be congruent with perhaps one third of families experiencing some return of ILYAs during an elapsed one-year period. Even the longitudinal surveys to measure transitions to adult roles (e.g., Goldscheider and

**Table 1** Percentages[a] of Young Adults Living with Their Parent(s), by Age and Gender, United States, 1954–1988

| AGES | 1954 | 1964 | 1974 | 1984 | 1985 | 1986 | 1987 | 1988 |
|------|------|------|------|------|------|------|------|------|
| | | | | MALES | | | | |
| 18–19 | 88.3 | 89.9 | 82.4 | 84.3 | 83.6 | 84.0 | 82.5 | 84.1 |
| 20–24 | 53.4 | 52.4 | 40.5 | 52.5 | 50.1 | 48.8 | 52.2 | 50.7 |
| 25–29 | 23.9 | 17.4 | 11.3 | 16.0 | 16.6 | 17.6 | 18.8 | 19.1 |
| 30–34 | 12.0 | 9.5 | 5.5 | 8.3 | 8.3 | 9.2 | 8.9 | 9.6 |
| | | | | FEMALES | | | | |
| 18–19 | 72.3 | 73.3 | 64.3 | 70.1 | 69.9 | 71.7 | 70.5 | 70.9 |
| 20–24 | 35.0 | 29.8 | 26.1 | 32.1 | 33.6 | 32.2 | 33.0 | 33.6 |
| 25–29 | 15.3 | 10.0 | 5.4 | 7.8 | 7.8 | 8.1 | 7.6 | 8.6 |
| 30–34 | 10.9 | 5.8 | 2.1 | 2.8 | 3.1 | 3.0 | 3.1 | 3.1 |

Note:

a Percentages refer to data for all races combined, and for all children who are single and living with parents (married children are usually listed as 'subfamilies'). The Current Population Survey counts students in dormitories as living in their parents' household (Heer, Hodge, and Felson, 1985; Glick and Lin, 1986). However, this is a consistent bias across all these historical comparisons. Recent increases in educational indebtedness are likely to have produced lower levels of dormitory living among college students than in the pre-1974 period, suggesting that these observations may in fact underestimate the recent rise in RYAs. (That is, because of higher rates of dorm living in the era of greater federal support of higher education, the pre-1974 figures would be inflated by allocating too many dorm students in the category of 'living in parents' household'.)

Sources: US Bureau of the Census, Current Population Reports, 'Marital status and living arrangements', Series P-20, numbers 56, 135, 271, 399, 410, 418, 423, and 433.

DaVanzo, 1985; Goldscheider and Waite, 1987) are taken at broad intervals that underestimate returns to the parental household. The same caution is necessary in estimating the type and amount of other support from parents even if their ILYAs do not return to the household. This partly explains why these data fail to predict the nearly universal interests in this phenomenon expressed by our middle-aged colleagues, friends, and media audiences. They are responding to this in part *because* we are raising this as a quasi-public issue, while they have previously endured this only as a personal trouble.

## Parents' Expectations for Young Adults: Changes and Dilemmas

One way of grounding the ILYA phenomenon is to consider some idealized or ideal-typical expectations of white middle-class parents (among others) in recent decades. One way these parents dealt with the dialectics of parenting was to provide intensive support of children until 'young adulthood'. The influence of Spock and other experts on developmental guidelines for parents was pronounced (Lasch, 1977). We would note that this ideology of parenting styles and the concomitant idealized goal of raising *independent* children (Parsons, 1943; Parsons and Bales, 1955) was itself historically grounded in the expansions of opportunity for bureaucratic-professional employment for such children (Schnaiberg and Goldenberg, 1975; Kohn, 1959, 1963; Kotulak and Van, 1987).

This ideal typification logically led to the emergence of an isolated nuclear family norm to guide young adult offspring and their middle-class parents as the young adults reached a life-cycle stage of creating their own family of procreation.[4] In many of the dominant cultural institutions such as schools and mass media in American society in the 1950s and 1960s, social scientists and journalists thus both described and prescribed parental and children's roles as primarily separate in young adulthood (Skolnick, 1983: chs. 12–13; Lasch, 1977). They thus ignored the mutual dependencies present even in the American middle-class family system (Cohler and Geyer, 1982; Hagestad, Smyer, and Stierman, 1984).

The postwar American economic expansion of bureaucratic and technical jobs for a burgeoning middle class (Blumberg, 1980) helped ground the *ideology* of autonomous young adults and their 'isolated' nuclear families of procreation. Parents who produced the 1945–1959 baby boom were among the first to have some of the means to implement these goals with the expansion of post-secondary education and upper white collar jobs. But their parents did not fully share this ideology, leading to conflicts about 'ungrateful children'. In absorbing this ideology/goal and assuming an expansion of these means, parents of the baby boom often resolved to be more supportive of their own baby-boom children, to avoid the painful conflicts that these young parents had experienced as they often moved up the socio-economic ladder and away from their parents (Skolnick, 1983: ch. 12). The new ideology of the isolated nuclear family (Parsons, 1943; Parsons and Bales, 1955) helped firm up their resolve as it stressed the importance of self-orientation and need-achievement in the 'modern family'. In the classical formulation of Zimmerman (1947), the postwar middle-class American family represented a transition to atomism as part of a long-term cycle alternating with collectivism. We argue here that we may indeed have been experiencing another transition point in the past decade. Constricted opportunity structures for many young adults may be leading to greater and more prolonged reliance on families of orientation. Only for other middle class young adults in the 'yuppie' track is there heightened evidence of the growth of the earlier atomism (and narcissism; see Lasch, 1979).

The postwar model of parenting was one of heavy investment in children but with a time-limited commitment. Children were expected to leave the nest, either by going away to college and/or establishing considerable autonomy and separate residence soon after graduation. The postwar expansion of college enrolment rates as well as the rise in dormitory and off-campus housing was associated with this trend. By the 1960s, the concept of middle-class children's *rights* was dominant in parenting, perhaps one of the most diffused postwar increases in 'entitlement'. Along with the new material affluence, this was a core element of the emergent American 'youth culture'. Youth now had the right to a separate consumption agenda, to separate institutions, and to access to the material means to support these entitlements (Parsons, 1943; Coleman, 1960; Littwin, 1986).

**Table 2** Idealized Parental Expectations for Young Adults[a]

| Education | Living Arrangements | Family of Procreation |
|---|---|---|
| College attendance away from home[b] | Dorms or apartments or fraternity/sorority houses, away from home | Early marriage and early childbearing, in a context of a marriage expected to be permanent |
| Postgraduate or professional training away from home | Neolocal household, normatively and structurally *relatively* independent of kin utilization for utilitarian, instrumental purposes | |
| Entry-level position in a career, expected to lead to upward mobility and generally, sufficient income to provide independence | | |

Notes:

a There are almost certainly gender differences in these expectations, but we have neither the data nor the space to explore them in depth here. It is clear that this paper deals most closely with parental expectations for young males. We would welcome comparative study to examine relevant gender differences.

b Note that for many students the college experience is defined as a time for 'fun' or to 'find themselves'.

Table 2 provides a brief outline of the middle-class parents' idealized expectations about their own success as parents, reflected by their producing successfully independent young adults. In effect, these idealized arrangements constituted the social *goals* of parenting. Material and emotional support—recognized as children's 'rights'—were the *means* by which parents could express the separation-individuation of their children. As long as children were roughly 'on schedule' in achieving these conventional expressions of apparent separation-individuation, parents could feel that the heavy material and emotional investments in children had paid off. In contrast, Table 3 outlines a more contemporary constricted model of late adolescent achievement.

Table 3 points to multiple discrepancies in the achievements of young adults, in effect laying out three dimensions of the RYA syndrome. For parents who have expectations typical of Table 2, this is a condition of anomie; the old goals/expectations no longer apply. By the criteria of Table 2, these children are not successfully independent young adults. Parents are then confronted with the full range of potential responses to anomie. Do they reject Table 2's expectations or substitute them as targets and attempts to find new means of coping with the realities as described in Table 3? Do they simply continue their earlier parenting roles (conformity, ritualism)? Do they lower their expectations of their children, but continue supporting them (innovation)? Or do they emotionally or physically abandon ILYAs (retreatism, rebellion)? The fragmented media accounts of ILYA families have indicated parental responses in all of the Mertonian categories. Since every 'solution' of the ILYA 'problem' involves giving up some parental expectation and/or resource, it becomes clear that there are no cost-free technical solutions to this set of personal troubles.

**Table 3** Constricted Achievement Patterns of Young Adults[a]

| Education | Living Arrangements | Family of Procreation |
|---|---|---|
| Interrupted, postponed or intermittent college attendance[b]<br><br>Interrupted, postponed or intermittent post-baccalaureate attendance<br><br>Erratic job patterns, often remote from career path, and with no assurance of future upward mobility or even status maintenance. No assured income level for self-sufficiency. | Commuting from home daily, sporadic periods of household independence but with heavy reliance on parental home as base and resource pool.<br><br>'Home is the place you can always return', however unwillingly and uncomfortably. Unusual living arrangements (neither parental nor independent household of procreation). | Postponement of marriage and/or postponement of childbearing, or a decision to have children despite marital risks.<br><br>Expectations of instability and high marital pressure |

Notes:

a There are almost certainly gender differences in these achievement patterns, but we have neither the data nor the space to explore them in depth here (cf. table 1). It is clear that this paper deals most closely with the achievement patterns of young males. We would welcome comparative study to examine gender differences.

b For many students, the college experience is defined as strictly vocational.

Parental responses to the dialectical tensions of dependence/independence thus range from increased support for ILYAs to actual abandonment (Cohler and Geyer, 1982). The former synthesis increases opportunity costs for parents. Resources (time, money, emotional energy) that they had planned to invest in themselves after the children's departure are instead allocated to ILYAs. But they do maintain strong ties with children by this route (Granovetter, 1973, 1982). The opposite synthesis, cutting off support, permits parents to keep more of their resources but often entails a weakening of their ties to children. One way of reframing these shifts is to note the de facto change in extended familism connoted by the ILYA phenomenon, particularly in the returning young adult adaptation. As we have noted elsewhere (Schnaiberg and Goldenberg, 1975), strong postwar pressures were placed on *young* upwardly-mobile middle-class parents by their need to help support aging parents of lower status while they were also raising their own young children. These earlier strains may now have been replaced or augmented for ILYA families (Hagestad, Smyer, and Stierman, 1984). For parents at midlife, we can conceptualize the ILYA syndrome as a modern variant on extended familism, with subsidization of ILYA children rather than elderly parents. The less fortunate among these parents may have both burdens. Aging of the population implies greater presence of elderly parents, who may still need financial aid and personal services from their middle-aged children (Hagestad, 1986; Hagestad, Smyer, and Stierman, 1984).

From a psychodynamic development perspective, it is not clear which is the 'appropriate' parental response to facilitate their children's separation and individuation processes. As we note below, the emergence of the ILYA syndrome has both socio-economic and developmental roots and may be a complex mixture of different patterns. That is, some shifts may be due purely to changing opportunity structures. Some may be a consequence of children in this class having increasing problems meeting their parents' expectations of movement into adult roles. And some substantial portion of the rise in ILYA phenomenon may represent Elder's (1978) model of the interaction between developmental conflicts and historical-economic shifts. Given the paucity of systematic analysis, it is premature to partition the phenomenon in this paper.

## NOTES

1  Many studies are now appearing that deal with the socio-historical and demographic aspects of the returning young adult syndrome. They are for the most part descriptive rather than theoretical. They do not deal substantially with either reasons for the current increase of this phenomenon or with the implications of it as experienced specifically by the middle class (Glick, 1986; Goldscheider and LeBourdais, 1986; Goldscheider and DaVanzo, 1985; Goldscheider and Waite, 1987; Grigsby and McGowan, 1986; Heer, Hodge, and Felson, 1985; Riche, 1987; Waite, Goldscheider, and Witsberger, 1987; Boyd and Pryor, 1988). Our interest is primarily in the ILYA issue, which only overlaps partly with RYAs; many ILYAs are not RYAs and some RYAs may not be ILYAs, but only in transition to their next adult role set.

2  As noted, parents and/or children, along with other interested parties including social scientist 'experts', contest some definitions of social problems, depending on the norms of their culture. The same 'objective' phenomenon is certainly susceptible of conflicting interpretation, definition, and treatment.

3  We find it ironic that several reviewers have inadvertently reinforced our feeling about this in calling for further evidence on the breadth of this phenomenon. Our main point here is that the personal trouble perspective tends to be adopted because we do not know, or appreciate, the breadth of the phenomenon at hand. The social issue perspective we are suggesting requires us to demonstrate a broad structural pattern and link the phenomenon to other structural features of the society. It is this task that we have begun in this paper.

4  As the isolated nuclear family debate makes clear, the norm or ideology was not universal, and actual practice may well have been otherwise. Even for Parsons, it was in the white middle-class family that the transition to isolated nuclear familism was expected to be clearest and occur first.

From *Social Problems* 36 (3) (1989): 251–8.

**CHAPTER 2**

# Some Fundamental Characteristics
# of the Scientific Mode
# of Thinking

As an undergraduate I overheard the following conversation in the washroom one day at noon:

'Gee, Chuck, do you brush your teeth after every lunch too?' 'Yes, I do. I haven't had any dental problems in years. Still, while I'd like to think the brushing helped, I can't be sure, now, can I?'

Needless to say, as a budding social scientist, I found the conversation both amusing and enlightening. Methodological sensitivity is not turned on and off. Once acquired, it is permanent.

In the introduction to chapter l, I mentioned that I had been asked repeatedly what sociology is and what sociologists do. Sometimes the discussion did not end with my usual brief explanation of the nature of sociology, and I was called upon to elaborate. More often than not the conversation heated up considerably at this point, particularly if the audience contained doctors, chemists, or other natural scientists. The more I would say, the redder their faces would become until finally they were unable to restrain themselves. 'But what makes you think that what you do can legitimately be called science? Where are your contributions, your bridges and medicines, your cures for what ails us? You've just finished telling us that you disagree about how you practise your discipline, that is, that no firm rules of practice even exist, and that you have little confidence that your analysis can stand the test of time or be put into practice in different places with consistent results. Sociology may be fun; it even sounds interesting, but physics and chemistry, medicine, and geology are sciences. Sociology is not.'

Such objections are not uncommon, nor are they hard to understand. My imaginary critic seems to believe that in order to call itself a 'real science' a discipline must possess various attributes commonly associated with the natural or physical sciences and not clearly present in the social sciences. These characteristics include demonstrable practical significance or utility, at least a high level of consensus about the nature of the subject matter and also about acceptable methodology, consistency over time of results, and just plain unchanging 'truth'. Although many of us have learned to associate just such characteristics with the 'scientific method' in the course of our education, a thoughtful reconsideration of these characteristics is in order. In this chapter I attempt to present a more up-to-date view of the nature of science. Most of us have been exposed to a misleading view of science, and I seek to correct a few common misconceptions and replace this distorted view with a less ambitious and more defensible one.

Having completed this chapter, the reader should have a much better idea of what criteria are used in assessing and conducting scientific work, whether that work consists of experiments in the chemistry laboratory or the testing of sociological hypotheses. This chapter should lay several of the most common myths about science and its practice to rest and give the reader a rather more modest but realistic idea both of what science is and of how it is accomplished.

## SCIENCE AS A CREDIBILITY-ENHANCING METHOD

Using the sociological perspectives discussed in chapter l of this book, sociologists advance claims about how the social world works. These inferences and conclusions are claims that the sociologist 'knows' what is happening and why. They are claims that make sense of the world by connecting events to one another in ways that are judged to be meaningful. In sociology, they are statements linking one or more sociological independent variables to the dependent variables we are interested in; they are also claims beyond this, specifically that knowledge of this link can help us predict, understand, and explain the variation in behaviour that interests us. In this sense, just as all science seeks patterns, sociology seeks to discover and describe meaningful patterns of human behaviour.

Scientific methodology in general developed in an attempt to strengthen such assertions and make them more credible when challenged. Science gives its practitioners guidelines for conducting studies and presenting data so that even a critical audience, if open-minded, will be forced to agree that the scientist has dealt with all reasonable objections and that therefore the assertions must be at least temporarily accepted pending further attempts to invalidate or challenge them.

Note that science addresses itself only to the open-minded critic and stipulates that the would-be scientific critic must be open-minded as well. This criterion of open-mindedness is crucial. Scientific evidence and methods will not persuade the fanatic or 'true believer' (Hoffer, 1951). Science will not persuade the flat-earth society that the earth is round, nor will it persuade sophisticated paranoids that they are not being persecuted. Most of us have had unproductive discussions with friends who are so firmly wedded to an idea that there is little point in arguing it with them. Their minds are made up and no amount of evidence can change them. Science can succeed only where the critic has the potential to be persuaded. It can succeed only where statements and counter-claims can be tested and potentially falsified. If the claims of a paranoid or a true believer cannot be falsified by any evidence, they cannot be assessed scientifically and have no role to play in scientific discourse.

This emphasis on science as a credibility-enhancing method is probably different from what you have been taught. Most of us grow up learning that science is a body of knowledge or truths located in various substantive textbooks. These books are scientific encyclopedias of the *facts* about our universe, and we accumulate new facts as we learn them. Many teachers continue to emphasize such text learning and memorization rather than critical evaluation of evidence. Many texts do not encourage the reader to assess their evidence and examine plausible counter-claims. Most courses provide all too little guidance and instruction in the development and use of critical or sceptical thinking. They do not teach the careful use of criteria that enable competing knowledge claims to be evaluated. They do not teach students how to learn. Most classes emphasize the transmission of 'facts', and most examinations test the student's ability to recall rather than to evaluate the facts. This orientation, ironically and sadly, is clearly anti-scientific.

When my daughter was small, she believed that what her teachers said must be the truth or they would not be teachers. A few years later she believed that the 'answers' were in the textbooks and that the books were of course true—or they could not have been published. Only much later did it dawn on her that teachers and books can—and eventually will—disagree and that no convenient and permanent encyclopedia of truth exists, or is ever likely to. Her old rule was simple: what the teacher or book said was true. As we begin to study science more carefully, we must replace that rule. But if truth is not simply a matter of finding the right source, what is truth, and how are we to recognize it? For truth is what we seek, and all claims to truth can be challenged. Why, when I was in school, we were actually taught a little jingle to help us remember the 'fact' (rather strongly disputed since) that Columbus discovered America! And I won't even tell you how many elements there were in the periodic table of elements when I studied high school chemistry. At the time the teacher told us these were the basic building blocks of the universe and there simply were no more, nor was anybody making more so far as he knew. Like many of you, no doubt, when I got to university, the first advice given us by many professors was that we would do well to forget everything we had learned about the subject at hand in high school since now we were going to start from the beginning and get it right this time, and up to date as well! Obviously even these physical sciences are rebuilt constantly and there is at best only a weak and temporary consensus about what constitutes the facts. Why then do we spend so much time teaching students 'facts' that are obsolete by the time they are taught them? And what should we be doing in school instead?

Science is a set of procedures established by people who confronted this question about the identification of what is true. In facing it, they have developed criteria for evaluating various claims to truth. But science is not the only source of criteria; revelation and intuition are others, for example. What makes scientific claims to truth different is that they are supposed to be demonstrable to the sceptical critic. Nothing need be taken on faith alone. Science proceeds on the basis of evidence that is fully presented for assessment. This evidence consists of sensory or empirical data accessible to any observer and presented in considerable detail. We do this because, as scientists, we want our readers to agree with our conclusions—not because they are ours (and not out of some misplaced respect for us or our credentials) but *because their evaluation of the evidence itself forces them to agree with us*. We want them to be forced as open-minded readers to agree with us, however much they might wish not to. We want them to agree because they have no alternative and can think of no acceptable reason not to do so. Such a procedure embodies the fundamental rule of all scientific procedure, which is simple and yet challenging. This is the rule from which all else follows: be sceptical. Be the best critic you can be, of your own work and of others.

Take nothing for granted. Take nothing on faith. Do not accept a particular conclusion until you have examined every possible alternative and been able to discount or discredit them all. But do not phrase your claim in such a way as to make it non-falsifiable.

Even from this brief description, you should realize that the fundamentally sceptical orientation of science described here is at odds with the way it is often taught even at the secondary and post-secondary level. Science is not about findings but about procedures; it is not about what we know, but about how we make claims to know that are more or less defensible.

## SCIENCE AS A NEGATIVISTIC PROCESS

The view of science taught in school generally says little about the treatment of negative or disconfirmatory evidence. Our texts and articles also tend to give us findings rather than negated findings. Still less common is a presentation of the process used to reach the findings. Our emphasis on science as a set of findings or facts is incompatible with the view I present here that science as method proceeds negativistically, by systematically seeking disconfirmatory evidence or by what others have called falsification.

### Reconstructed Logic and Logic-in-Use

A. Kaplan (1964) distinguishes between 'reconstructed logic' and 'logic-in-use'. He suggests that scientific presentations in texts and articles almost always use the former, and that this tends to bring the latter into disrepute. Logic-in-use is chronological. It involves false starts, mistakes, revisions, serendipitous or accidental findings, modified expectations, changes in topic, new insights, and the like. It is process-oriented and a mixture of theorizing and testing, a mixture of deduction and induction. Usually though, scientists do not write up studies as they experience them, according to logic-in-use, 'warts and all'. Instead, they write up a 'pretend' experiment or study that makes them look omniscient *after* the real experiment or study is finished and the results are in. In the process of writing it up after the fact, the scientist does a certain amount of fine tuning: no longer are there any errors, false starts, or dead ends in the process. Thus science appears to begin with a clear and coherent theory and deduce from it testable propositions. It *looks as if* scientists always, and simply, formulate the appropriate research design, select the right method, collect the data, and confirm their hypotheses, thus lending credibility to their initial theory.

No wonder students have no idea of how actually to conduct a study when all they read is this reconstruction with the process cleaned up and the fuzzy edges sanded off. In the few instances where students actually try to follow this model of reconstructed logic as described, for example, in most physics texts, they may find themselves doing things for no apparent reason. They discover themselves forcing an experiment to create the sense the textbook says it should have, and they blame themselves if it fails to conform to the reported but also reconstructed logic.

Reconstructed logic then presents us only with successes, not failures. As a result students never find disconfirming evidence. They learn, instead, to illustrate theses rather than to test hypotheses. They believe they must be right in order to be scientific, and they gain no experience in dealing with faulty arguments or ambiguous findings. The common response is to ignore negative evidence, sweeping it under the rug when in fact this is precisely the crucial evidence.

Have you, for example, ever thought that if you handed in a paper stating you discovered that your original expectation was simply wrong you would get a poor grade? Have you ever ignored negative evidence on the grounds that considering it would weaken your argument by adding unnecessary complications to the argument you wanted to make? Yet learning from our mistakes is what science is all about, and such real 'working papers' are far more valuable than seamless reconstructions.

In the sociological literature, at least, there are exponents of logic-in-use. Hammond's *Sociologists at Work* (1968) is such an attempt, as is Glazer's *The Research Adventure* (1972). These books, and most good participant-observation studies, include examples from substantive research that detail each step, making it possible for the reader to see the interplay between theory and testing, between formulating expectations for behaviour and the analysis of it, between accidental discoveries and a change in the central questions of the study.

Such 'natural histories' of a research project give us many illustrations of how to treat disconfirmatory evidence. It is just this evidence that is crucial, as a closer look at the scientific process should make clear.

In a later chapter, you will find several examples of the process of moving 'from problem to paper'. In those sections I have tried to illustrate the steps in the scientific process used to transform a 'problem' into a scientific study. Here my purpose is a little different. The emphasis in the following section is not so much on providing a model of the process as on providing insight into the reasoning itself and the negativistic mode science uses to proceed.

### Formulating a Hypothesis

Suppose we are interested in explaining juvenile behaviour. More precisely, let us say that we have observed that rates of delinquency vary from place to place and we wonder why. Our purpose then is to explain variation in rates or incidence of juvenile delinquency. If we think of the dependent variable (or effect, or what we want to explain) in this way, it is clear that this is indeed a variable, that is, something that changes. Put still another way, we are asking why some populations display a higher incidence of juvenile delinquency than other populations. All such questions really seek the cause (or causes) of juvenile delinquency. In seeking an explanation, we move beyond describing differences in rates into the realm of causation. In human behaviour, causation is a particularly difficult area because humans can control their responses and change their behaviour as, or even because, we are studying it. In attempting to find cause, the scientist suggests possible relationships between a potential causal variable (the independent variable) and the effect (or dependent variable). The scientist puts this suggestion in the form of a *testable statement of the specific relationship between independent and dependent*. We call such a statement a hypothesis. In fact, you have already seen several of these earlier in our discussions.

We might hypothesize that variation in the amount smoked might explain to some degree the variation we find in rates of lung cancer. We might hypothesize that variation in the amount of exposure to television violence might account for or explain some of the variation in aggressive behaviour displayed by children. We might in this vein hypothesize that variation in exposure to violent pornography could be causally related to variation in incidence of aggression against women. We might hypothesize in the current instance that broken homes cause juvenile delinquency or more accurately that these two phenomena, *when considered as variables*, would be positively related. This means that as the incidence or frequency of the first rises the incidence or frequency of the second will also rise. (For those of you having difficulty grasping the concept of a hypothesis or what it really means to speak of a specific relationship among variables—and this is a hugely difficult way of thinking for many readers new to science—I have included a paper on the topic at the end of this chapter. It might be a good idea to read it now, since confusion between variables and their specific values is a very common problem for students at all levels, but is an essential part of the foundation of scientific thinking.)

**Creating an Operational Definition**
Now suppose that we were prepared to conduct a study in our home town to test this proposition linking broken homes and delinquency. We must first clearly and precisely define our two variables in a way that allows us to measure them. These two components (clarity or precision and measurability) are elements of an operational definition. What will we consider to be a 'broken home' and a 'juvenile delinquent'? How will we measure the incidence or frequency of these phenomena?

Any operational definition is a formula for measuring or consistently producing the phenomenon of interest. It does not answer the question 'what is X?' but rather 'how can I consistently and accurately measure X?' An operational definition then is not a synonym; thus it is not appropriate to consult a dictionary to find an operational definition of 'broken home'. One immediately obvious feature is that we can measure any term in several ways. The researcher must choose a definition that is as accurate as possible and useful enough that others can try to produce the same results.

With this in mind, we might suggest that a broken home could be defined as one that once had but no longer has two parents. If this is a useful operational definition, any investigator should be able to use it to distinguish the broken homes from those that are not among a set of households. If several investigators classify the families differently, the operating instructions provided by the measurement definition are not useful enough, which means the operational definition is weak. In addition to consistently sorting the data set in a prescribed manner, an operational definition should also be accurate. For example, though we could distinguish broken homes from others *consistently* by defining broken homes as those where the average height of the parent or parents is under five feet five inches, such a definition is not useful since it bears no obvious relationship to the concept we want to measure. That which is measured must be relevant.

With this in mind, we might identify juvenile delinquents by inspecting court records to see which young people aged from, for example, 13 to 17 had been convicted of an offence by a court in our home town. We could define those with court records as delinquents.

In combination then, the hypothesis we are testing now suggests that we examine a number of areas of our home town (this aspect not yet specified) to gather evidence (in some fashion as yet unspecified) concerning the incidence of homes that once had but no longer have two parents and also evidence from court records of any juveniles aged 13 to 17 who had been convicted of criminal offences under the Young Offenders Act or similar legislation. Specifically the hypothesis states that as the frequency or incidence of the first variable increases, the incidence of the second will also increase. But let us now consider how we must interpret the evidence once it is gathered, for it turns out that even with carefully stated hypotheses and clearly operationalized terms the data eventually gathered are not definitive.

**Responding to Positive or Confirmatory Evidence**
Suppose that we do find, as expected, that as the incidence of broken homes increases among areas of the city the incidence of delinquency also increases. Such evidence would be consistent with our hypothesis, but would it entitle us to draw the inference from it that, in fact, broken homes *cause* delinquency? Though such an interpretation is possible, it is not the only possible interpretation, and you must remember that science is about convincing the sceptical reader that the evidence forces them to agree with our conclusion because there is no alternative that is as plausible.

Perhaps the most famous saying in research methodology is 'Correlation is not causation.' Two variables may be correlated, as in the example, though causally unrelated. For example, a third variable could be related to both the incidence of broken homes and juvenile delinquency. In this case any change in the third variable—for example, ethnicity or race—would simultaneously change both our presumed independent and dependent variable. In other words, ethnicity or race may be related to the incidence of broken homes, and if ethnicity or race is also related to the incidence of juvenile delinquency, then a change in the ethnic or racial composition of city areas we are comparing would also mean a change in both other variables. Without knowing the change in ethnic or racial composition across the areas, one might interpret the correlation between broken homes and delinquency as causal. Knowledge of the relationship of ethnic or racial variation to both, though, might suggest that the original relationship is not causal but accidental—only a function of the fact that both variables are related to the same third. In other words, it is possible that broken homes do not cause juvenile delinquency, even though the two variables change together in the manner hypothesized.

Note, in addition, that it is not necessary to argue that ethnicity or race causes either broken homes or delinquency. As long as there is any systematic relationship among these variables, if ethnic or racial composition changes, so will both other variables.

This possibility of accidental co-variation is called *spuriousness*; I deal with it in some detail in chapter 3 in a general discussion of testing for causality. It is this possibility of spuriousness that makes positive evidence less powerful than we would like it to be. The sceptic must be convinced that there is no third variable that accounts for the relationship we intend to argue is a product of a causal connection between our independent and dependent variables.

There is a still more basic reason for our wariness about inferring causation from co-variation. This is called simply the problem of induction. When we move from a limited set of observations to the abstract formulation of a proposition positing 'laws', we do so most uncomfortably. Any set of observations is limited, and we cannot know in advance that the very next observation will not contradict every pattern we noted in all past observations. Thus, though every swan we have ever seen has been white, we cannot know that the next one will not be another colour. Though the sun has always risen in the east, we cannot be utterly certain that it will do so tomorrow. Inductive reasoning, or reasoning from observations to more abstract statements about the patterns among these, is inherently limited. Thus no amount of observation alone can provide the certainty that what we have seen is not about to be contradicted in the future.

The limitations of inductive reasoning and the possibility of spuriousness force us to try approaching issues from the opposite direction, that is, negativistically. Ironically, negative or disconfirmatory evidence is generally more useful to us than confirmatory evidence, though it too must be interpreted cautiously.

### Responding to Negative or Disconfirmatory Evidence

If we were to find that as the frequency of broken homes increased, the rate of juvenile delinquency was unchanged, how might we handle such apparently disconfirmatory evidence? What are the options available to us, as scientists, in such a case? We can, of course, decide that our original expectation was simply wrong and that broken homes do not cause delinquency. We could also deny the negative evidence or try to make it questionable enough to set aside. It might be more constructive to try to refine our hypothesis to take into account this particular negative evidence. To do this we might say, for example, that broken homes produce juvenile delinquency when the family income is drastically reduced. With such a revision we can handle—in fact we would predict—the cases where family income does not suffer and no relationship exists.

You can see that a range of possible responses is available, running from reaffirming our faith in the original hypothesis by eliminating the negative evidence to throwing out that hypothesis, having agreed that the evidence is clear and conclusive. In between are several options for making evidence and hypothesis more compatible.

### The Relevance of Evidence

It may be difficult for the newcomer to realize the full implications of the critical and cautious approach. For example, many of us are tempted in writing essays to find many illustrations of the thesis we wish to prove and to disregard any negative evidence we might come across. The scientist, however, knows that any thesis can be illustrated and that science proceeds by examining all the relevant evidence and going out of the way to seek particularly the negative cases.

Science is systematic and does not seek to prove or support hypotheses, but rather to test them dispassionately. Many, in fact, would argue that this systematic character of science is its essential characteristic and that most of its other characteristics are not strictly necessary. Such a view is particularly likely to be held by those who are inclined to the micro-interpretive perspective, since good work of this kind is systematic, though it may well fail to meet other criteria that a positivist would require if it were to be called scientific. In essence, systematic means that scientists do not select examples that illustrate their thesis or the case they wish to prove. They must confront all the relevant evidence and do so consistently and logically, ignoring none of it. They must also proceed in an organized manner, so that others could repeat their steps if they so desired.

One of our more serious difficulties is to decide just what all the relevant evidence is. This is far easier to say in principle than to put into practice. Scientists often disagree about what constitutes relevant evidence to any argument. Indeed *what is relevant really becomes known only after the fact*. For example, water boils at 212° F, but it 'turns out' that atmospheric pressure is a relevant condition affecting this simple proposition. Thus water boils at lower temperatures on mountain tops than at sea level. Atmospheric pressure is part of the relevant evidence affecting our proposition.

It is even more difficult to determine that we have examined *all* relevant evidence. This difficulty leads us to confront the inability of science to produce absolute, permanent laws. In principle we can never be sure we have *all* the relevant evidence since science is inductive and involves generalization to an unknown future that may at any time negate our expectation. It is this feature that makes science subject to constant retesting and revision. Scientific claims to know are permanently contestable, as previously unknown or unrecognized factors are argued to be relevant in accounting for them.

## The Importance of Replication

Every scientific proposition has attached to it, whether explicitly or implicitly, the phrase, *ceteris paribus*, which is Latin for 'other things being equal'. Our proposition that water boils at 212° F includes the idea of other things being equal. Similarly a sociological proposition that 'men behave more aggressively than women' must have the same attached rider. The importance of this rider cannot be stressed too much. Merely adding the qualifying phrase is to ask what the relevant conditions are; that is, which other things must be held equal? The boiling of pure water in the laboratory *under controlled atmospheric pressure* in a *sterilized* container may well produce repeated consistent findings as to the boiling point of water under specific conditions.

Repetition gives us more confidence in the proposition. This is the purpose of replication, which is what we call the process of repeated experiments in which each step is carefully duplicated to discover whether the same results consistently show up. Unfortunately, though, replication does not guarantee the validity or accuracy of our findings, and there is no rule for how many successful replications provide some security of interpretation.

The rule works only in reverse. Failure to replicate is informative; success is much less so. If the second attempt to establish the boiling point of water showed that the liquid boiled at 200° F, we would have to reconsider the truth of the original proposition. Such a reconsideration might promote careful examination of the studies to see whether the second was in fact a replication or whether the *ceteris paribus* qualifier had been violated. If we discovered, for example, that the water used in the second instance had more impurities, this might lead us to consider the effect of impurities. The proposition would have to specify, if necessary, that *pure* water boils at 212° F. The failed replication would have suggested that the addition of impurities of a certain type and amount seemed to lower the boiling point by 12° F. To the extent that we deem this important, we might well go on to develop a whole volume of chemistry concerning how the varying of certain conditions (atmospheric pressure, purity of liquid, and so on) affects the boiling points of liquids. If we can eventually replicate and subsume all these measurements under more general propositions about the effect of variation in atmospheric pressure or purity of liquid, we will have a fully developed set of theoretical propositions based on a more complete treatment of the model we suggested in our first experiment with boiling water. The temperature at which water boils will then constitute simply one case of the broader propositions in which variables are interrelated. Pure water is one type of liquid, and its boiling point only one value on the scale of boiling points.

A few years ago, there was a great deal of media coverage of the revolutionary discovery by two chemists who claimed to have produced cold fusion at little cost and in a novel manner. Their discovery would have been revolutionary, for physicists had been trying for years, at enormous expense, to produce cold fusion. As soon as their methodology was published, a great many scientists all over the world rushed to replicate the revolutionary findings. They all failed to do so, and what seemed a great discovery was quickly judged to have been something less. Failure to replicate reduces a finding to an 'accident'. Such findings cannot form the basis for generalizations or applications because they cannot be reproduced even with exactly the same methods used by the original scientists. They are usually quickly dismissed and regarded as error.

### Modified Replication and Constructive Criticism

If we created experiments in which the purity of water was intentionally and systematically varied in order to examine the effects of such variation under otherwise identical conditions, we would be engaging in 'modified replication', that is, replication where, for theoretical reasons, we tried to vary a single condition thought to be relevant in order to examine the consequences. This amounts to a constructive critic's claiming that the original proposition was at fault for being incompletely specified and going on to show that this criticism is warranted by providing evidence that the purity of the water does, in fact, affect its boiling point. Thus, in science the constructive critic does more than merely tear down arguments.

I have already said that each of us is our own most useful constructive critic. Science gains most in this way. The responsibility of the constructive critic is to help out by identifying weaknesses and at least suggesting how they might be important or be overcome, and by doing so where this is possible.

With this discussion of chemistry in mind, let us return to an analogous sociological proposition: Men behave more aggressively than women (other things being equal). How are we to replicate such a finding, and what other things must be equal for the same result to occur? Alternatively if we are interested in modified replication, what conditions will affect the proposition systematically so that varying them will systematically affect the results? This idea of modified replication emerges from our awareness that in a first study, usually only one value of what may well be a variable is examined and that recognition of this underlying variable amounts to developing a broader proposition base. Thus water was one liquid, and by modified replication we saw it to be only one 'value' of the variable 'type of liquid' (itself a host of other variables, like purity, density, chemical composition, colour, and so on). Here, again, we may suggest that a second study to measure the aggressiveness of men and women might not support the original proposition. Note that for the moment we are avoiding the issue of exactly what is to be done to replicate the finding. This issue will be dealt with more fully in chapter 3. For now, what would we do with such inconsistent findings?

You may note that we confronted this same issue of replication earlier in the discussion of negative or disconfirming evidence. One option is to reconsider the studies and try to see, as we did in the chemistry study, whether the repetition was a pure replication, that is, one with every attempt made to repeat the original study in every detail. If it was, we really have a contradiction to resolve. But perhaps the researcher accidentally or intentionally made a relevant condition different in the second study, in which case we have a modified replication. For example, the second study may have unwittingly or otherwise used men and women of different ages from those in the first study; it may have defined or measured aggressive behaviour differently, or it may have been done in a different culture. It was almost certainly done at a later time. Any of these changes (among others) could explain the change in results, at least tentatively, assuming the main proposition is correct. The 'failed' replication is then not so much a failure as a suggestion that a variation in one or more specific relevant conditions between the two studies affected the outcome. We might have to restate the original proposition to build in specific values of the variables as conditions under which the proposition will hold, as we do when we say that '*pure* water boils at 212° F *at sea level* atmospheric pressure'. Thus, analogously, '*adolescent* men *in North American culture will physically* attack one another *when challenged* more often than will women *of similar age*.' The implication in the proposition concerning the boiling point of water is that variation in the purity or the nature of the liquid and in the atmospheric pressure are recognized conditions that affect the boiling point (*cet. par.*). Similarly, conditions are set in the sociological proposition implying that variation from these will affect the outcome. In both cases, *cet. par.* is still understood since the possibility always exists that conditions we are unaware of may be essential to the effect we expect. Until someone tells us what these are and how they affect the outcome, they remain only potential and will not affect our belief in our proposition. As illustrated in these examples, we learn precisely from our mistakes, our false starts, and our failures to replicate.

## The Importance of Anticipating Criticism

In many ways science exhibits a peculiar negativistic logic or backward style. We do not prove; we disqualify alternatives until, we hope, only one explanation of a phenomenon remains, one that we cannot disprove. In our work we consistently try to anticipate the criticisms others might have. Thus we build into our studies attempts to avoid, address, and measure these criticisms. An example will be useful here. In a classic experiment done in 1930, Richard LaPiere sought to gather data on prejudicial behaviour directed against

Chinese Americans. One method of gathering data involved travelling across the United States with a young Chinese couple. He describes the study as follows:

Beginning in 1930 and continuing for two years thereafter, I had the good fortune to travel rather extensively with a young Chinese student and his wife. Both were personable, charming, and quick to win the admiration and respect of those they had the opportunity to become intimate with. But they were foreign-born Chinese, a fact that could not be disguised. Knowing the general 'attitude' of Americans towards the Chinese as indicated by the 'social distance' studies which have been made, it was with considerable trepidation that I first approached a hotel clerk in their company. Perhaps that clerk's eyebrows lifted slightly, but he accommodated us without a show of hesitation. And this is in the 'best' hotel in a small town noted for its narrow and bigoted 'attitude' towards Orientals. Two months later I passed that way again, phoned the hotel and asked if they would accommodate 'an important Chinese gentleman'. The reply was an unequivocal 'No.' That aroused my curiosity and led to this study.

In something like ten thousand miles of motor travel, twice across the United States, up and down the Pacific Coast, we met definite rejection from those asked to serve us just once. We were received at 66 hotels, auto camps, and 'Tourist Homes', refused at one. We were served in 184 restaurants and cafés scattered throughout the country and treated with what I judged to be more than ordinary consideration in 72 of them. Accurate and detailed records were kept of all these instances. An effort, necessarily subjective, was made to evaluate the overt response of hotel clerks, bell boys, elevator operators, and waitresses to the presence of my Chinese friends. The factors entering into the situations were varied as far and as often as possible. Control was not, of course, as exacting as that required by laboratory experimentation. But it was as rigid as is humanly possible in human situations. For example, I did not take the 'test' subjects into my confidence fearing that their behaviour might become self-conscious and thus abnormally affect the response of others towards them. Whenever possible I let my Chinese friend negotiate for accommodations (while I concerned myself with the car or luggage) or sent them into a restaurant ahead of me. In this way I attempted to 'factor' myself out. We sometimes patronized high-class establishments after a hard and dusty day on the road and stopped at inferior auto camps when in our most presentable condition.

To provide a comparison of symbolic reaction to symbolic social situations with actual reaction to real social situations, I 'questionnaired' the establishments which we patronized during the two-year period. Six months were permitted to lapse between the time I obtained the overt reaction and the symbolic. It was hoped that the effects of the actual experience with Chinese guests, adverse or otherwise, would have faded during the intervening time. To the hotel or restaurant a questionnaire was mailed with an accompanying letter purporting to be a special and personal plea for response. The questionnaires all asked the same question, 'Will you accept members of the Chinese race as guests in your establishment?' Two types of questionnaire were used. In one this question was inserted among similar queries concerning Germans, French, Japanese, Russians, Armenians, Jews, Negroes, Italians, and Indians. In the other the pertinent question was unencumbered. With persistence, completed replies were obtained from 128 of the establishments we had visited; 81 restaurants and cafés and 47 hotels, auto camps, and 'Tourist Homes'. In response to the relevant question 92 per cent of the former and 91 per cent of the latter replied 'No'. The remainder replied 'uncertain; depend upon circumstances'. From the woman proprietor of a small auto camp I received the only 'Yes', accompanied by a chatty letter describing the nice visit she had had with a Chinese gentleman and his sweet wife during the previous summer.

A rather unflattering interpretation might be put upon the fact that those establishments who had provided for our needs so graciously were, some months later, verbally antagonistic towards hypothetical Chinese. To factor this experience out responses were secured from 32 hotels and 96 restaurants located in approximately the same regions, but uninfluenced by this particular experience with

Oriental clients. In this, as in the former case, both types of questionnaires were used. The results indicate that neither the type of questionnaire nor the fact of previous experience had important bearing upon the symbolic response to symbolic social situations. (LaPiere, 1934, 230–7)

The point of the study is that what people say is at least sometimes, and possibly often, not a good indicator of how they actually act. Although this is an important point itself, and the one for which this study has justly become famous, our present concern is with the common sense examples of how LaPiere built into his study, in advance, reasonable safeguards to protect his conclusions from the criticism that they might be a product of something other than what he wished to suggest.

Thus, to begin with, one cannot object that the study was too short to gather useful data since it was carried out for two years. One cannot plausibly suggest that the findings are only a local phenomenon since LaPiere and the Chinese couple travelled 'twice across the United States, up and down the Pacific Coast'. One also cannot say that only inexpensive cafés or auto camps are the source of the data since they sampled a wide range of establishments. In addition LaPiere did not tell the subjects that they were subjects, fearing that this might affect their behaviour. He also did not often negotiate for the travellers since he did not wish to influence the results unduly. And so on. In the questionnaire portion, he allowed six months to elapse in the hope that 'the effects of the actual experience would have faded'. LaPiere even raises the possibility that it was as a result of their previous visit that the respondents now had negative views of Chinese. This he handles by being able to assure the potential critic that responses did not differ when obtained from similar hotels and restaurants they had not visited in the same areas. None of the objections he anticipates are profound, nor are the solutions he offers. The point I wish to stress is simply that the competent scientist anticipates possible criticism and takes account of it in conducting research, in all phases of research design, sampling, instrument development, measurement, analysis, and discussion. We believe LaPiere because he seems to have 'headed off' all possible criticisms. It is because no other plausible explanations for his data exist that we are forced to agree, at least until we think of some, that he is correct.

The point I make here is of great importance. In reading the research literature, one must be constantly demanding and critical. One must realize that there are usually many possible explanations for every result, and if the author wishes to promote a single one, she must do so by discounting and disqualifying all plausible competitors. If this task sounds overwhelming, let me assure you that, although difficult, it is possible. At least it is possible to a much greater degree than we often find it practised.

### Formulating Rival Hypotheses

Let us review this matter of rival explanations or hypotheses in more detail by considering another set of studies. Seymour Martin Lipset is a well-known American sociologist who has written widely on the topic of Canadian-American differences and their origins and explanations. His basic thesis has always been that Canada's counter-revolutionary history, as compared to the American Revolution, has produced a fundamental conservatism in Canada that underlies all Canadian-American behavioural differences. Thus, according to Lipset, Canadians behave differently because they are more conservative. In support of

Table 2.1 Rates of Marriage and Divorce in Canada and the United States per 1,000 Population for Selected Years

| Year | Canada | | United States | |
|---|---|---|---|---|
| | Marriage | Divorce | Marriage | Divorce |
| 1911 | | 0.001 | | 0.06 |
| 1936 | 7.4 | 0.14 | 10.4 | 1.7 |
| 1945 | 9.0 | 0.42 | 12.2 | 3.5 |
| 1950 | 9.1 | 0.39 | 11.1 | 2.6 |
| 1955 | 8.2 | 0.38 | 9.3 | 2.3 |
| 1960 | 7.3 | 0.39 | 8.5 | 2.2 |
| 1965 | 7.4 | 0.45 | 9.3 | 2.5 |
| 1968 | 8.3 | 0.54 | 10.4 | 2.9 |
| 1969 | 8.7 | 1.23 | 10.6 | 3.2 |
| 1970 | 8.8 | 1.36 | 10.7 | 3.5 |
| 1976 | | 2.36 | | 4.4 |
| 1980 | 7.8 | 2.59 | | 5.3 |

Source: *The World Almanac and Book of Facts 1972*; updated to 1980 from Canadian and United States census figures.

such an argument, he begins by demonstrating that Canadians have lower divorce rates, lower homicide rates, fewer police officers per capita, a lower proportion of the relevant age cohort in post-secondary education, less money invested in stocks and more in banks, and the like. But let us examine a version of just one of his tables more closely. Look at Table 2.1.

With reference to the divorce-rate columns in this table, Lipset makes the following argument:

> If Canadians were more conservative with regard to marriage than Americans (A), then the divorce rate in Canada would be lower than that in the United States (B). The divorce rate is lower in Canada than in the United States. Therefore, Canadians are more conservative than Americans.[1]

A critical logical flaw undermines this argument. Perhaps it would help to substitute A for the first phrase of the first sentence: 'If Canadians . . . Americans', and B for the second phrase of the sentence, following the 'then'. This substitution generates the following syllogism:

If A, then B

B

therefore A

This syllogism, as formal logicians term the structure of a logical argument, contains a logical error often seen in the social science literature. Again substituting clearer examples may make it more obvious.

1. If (A) students understand the material, then (B) they will ask no questions.
   (B) They ask no questions.
   Therefore (A) they understand the material.

2. If (A) this experimental drug works, then (B) the patient will recover.
   (B) The patient does recover.
   Therefore (A) this drug works!

3. If (A) the distributor cap is broken, then (B) the car will not start.
   (B) The car will not start.
   Therefore (A) the distributor cap is broken.

In all these cases, the flaw involves jumping to the conclusion that A caused B from observation of B alone. The logic here assumes that *only* A would result in B and therefore the occurrence of B proves A as the cause. But it is obvious to us all that students may fail to ask questions for a great many reasons, one of which is indeed that they understand the material, that patients do recover for reasons other than the drugs they take, and that cars fail to start for many reasons. It is equally clear that a lower divorce rate among Canadians is not sufficient to demonstrate that a difference in core values caused it. Before we go on to discuss other possible causes, please note that we are not arguing that the major premise in any case is wrong, though we *may* wish to disagree at this point. We may agree that if students understood they would not ask questions, or we may not agree with this major premise, feeling on the contrary that it is the students who do understand who ask the questions. We may agree (or not) that if the drug works, the patient would recover and that if there were a difference in values, the divorce rates would differ. At the moment, in the context of this fallacy, it is the argument back to the 'cause' from the effect with which we disagree. As noted, we may disagree with the major premise as well, arguing, for example, that differences in values do not in any simple way affect behaviour.[2] (See Valentine 1968, especially chapter 1.) In any event, the form of the present argument is logically fallacious, for it embodies what logicians call the 'fallacy of affirming the consequent'. The fact that other possible causes of B could exist is ignored, and we cannot ignore this possibility. The real argument is as follows:

If A (or C or D or E or . . . Z), then B.

B

therefore A (or C or D or E or . . . Z) where C, D, and
so forth stand for other possible causes of B.

In other words, the students may not ask questions because the professor is intimidating or because there does not appear to be time or because questions are supposed to be held for the tutorials. All are possible alternatives to the hypothesis that suggests that the only reason for them not to ask questions is that they do not understand the material. All of these (and more) might plausibly suggest why students may not ask questions in the absence of further evidence. Similarly, the patient may have recovered because patients usually do, or because he got lots of rest or good nursing care. These are competing plausible causes of recovery. They are the C . . . to Z in the above syllogism. Of course, the car may not start because of the distributor cap or because it is out of gas or because of a million and one mechanical complications. My mechanic, of course, will begin replacing parts with the most expensive first in an effort to get the car started again.

In the Lipset example my students can usually think of several plausible competing explanations for the difference in divorce rates. They have often suggested that the differences may be attributable to the different religious compositions of the two populations, Canada having a higher proportion of Roman Catholics than the United States. They sometimes suggest that differences in the severity of divorce legislation might produce such differences if Canadian divorce laws are stricter. They also suggest that rural-urban differences could be relevant if Canada is less urban (or has smaller cities or different compositions in them).

To the extent that these are plausible, they compete with Lipset's proposed explanation. All four hypotheses (his and the three competitors) are rival hypotheses predicting the same outcome. The outcome no more demonstrates that Lipset's explanation is correct than it demonstrates that any of the others are correct. But what then are we to do? Matters again appear hopelessly complicated. Surely an infinite number of rival hypotheses seem to exist. Can we say nothing? To begin with, only rarely do many plausible rival hypotheses make sense. Once the plausible ones have been identified, we can deal with them, negativistically seeking to disprove all of them, while hoping to fail to disprove the one we consider the most plausible (our working hypothesis). We operate very much like the doctor reasoning back from the symptoms she sees to the diagnosis of their cause, or like the good mechanic working backwards from the stalled car to the cause of the problem. In all cases, we eliminate wrong answers until we cannot eliminate one or more. This, or these, we believe to be true until one or more can be eliminated.

Let us return to Lipset and divorce rates. Would it be plausible to say that the cause of the difference in divorce rates is that Canada in general is colder than the United States? Though we could find a way of making this argument by suggesting essentially that Canadians stick together for warmth, the argument is not highly plausible. Simply put, no reason compels us to believe that the temperature difference would produce differences in divorce rates. Even more easily, we can discount differences in language as a cause, since the dominant language is English in both societies.

Plausible causes, then, will have to be differences between the two countries, but not all differences are equally plausible. To be plausible, the differences would have to be consistent with the direction of difference observed in the divorce rates. Differences that predict higher divorce rates for Canadians would not be plausible causes for the lower rates observed. Thus if Canada had fewer homogamous marriages (marriages between people similar in background, ethnicity, age, religion, or the like), this would seem likely to predict higher divorce rates and would not be judged as a plausible cause of lower rates of divorce. But more is still involved in assessing the plausibility that forms the first step in formulating rival hypotheses.

Consider differences in religious composition first. If we regard this as a plausible rival, we would first have to demonstrate two relationships. To begin, we would have to show that religious composition does in fact differ, with Roman Catholics constituting a higher proportion of the population in Canada than in the United States. Then we would have to show that the divorce rate among Roman Catholics is systematically lower than among people of other religions. Only if both conditions are met can we regard religious composition as a plausible rival to Lipset's or any other explanations of differences in divorce rates.

Similarly we would have to demonstrate both that Canada is less urban than the United States and that less urban places have lower divorce rates. Or we would have to demonstrate differences in divorce legislation, that Canadian legislation was stricter and that divorce rates are lower where legislation is more strict. Only if such demonstrations were possible would we have to go on to *assessing* these rival hypotheses.

## Eliminating Rival Hypotheses

As you can see, there is not an infinite number of equally plausible rival hypotheses to our main or working hypotheses. In fact, relatively few rivals have much plausibility, and the better our study, the fewer rivals there are. This is true for at least two reasons. First, certain rivals are related to methodology or measurement, and we can deal with these by anticipating problems when we design and conduct our study. In the LaPiere study, for example, we might object that his results could be the product of no more than the fact that his experimental subjects were naturally on their best behaviour if they knew what was being studied. He therefore did not tell them the nature of the study. The second reason why good studies do not produce as many rivals as poor studies is that a hypothesis is ideally related to a large body of theory, and this theory predicts not one outcome but a range of outcomes, sometimes of quite different kinds. Thus Campbell (1979: 21) sets out the following 'strong' premise.

> If Newton's Theory A is true, then it should be observed that the tides have period B, the path of Mars shape C, the trajectory of a cannonball form D.

In this case very few rivals are judged plausible in that they, too, predict these same outcomes in *all* these instances. Powerful theory is powerful because of just this simplicity, or parsimony, as it is sometimes called. Nor does it take a genius to work this way. Consider the following rather more mundane example.

> If the child has measles, then he would display symptoms a, b, c, and x, y, and z.
> He does display all such symptoms.
> Therefore he has measles.

In this instance, it is the joint occurrence of all the relevant symptoms that in combination are produced only by measles that gives us considerable confidence in the diagnosis. On the other hand, had the child displayed only one symptom and that so general as to be plausibly a product of many conditions, the case would be far more complicated and our hesitation in accepting a diagnosis of measles much better founded. In our language, there would be a great many plausible rivals that could account for the one symptom and that can be discounted when there are many specific symptoms present in a combination that suggests only one plausible cause.

Granted that several rival hypotheses are often plausible, then, how shall we proceed to discount them? In the Lipset example, we seem to have three legitimate rivals, which may not be equally plausible, plus his original hypothesis. Fortunately we can consider the effects of one of these rivals in a neat nearly experimental form from data collected since 1968 to augment his table. As you can see from Table 2.1, the Canadian divorce rate had

Table 2.2 Rates of Divorce in Canada and the United States per 1,000 Population

| Year | Canada | United States |
|------|--------|---------------|
| 1968 | 0.54 | 2.9 |
| 1969 | 1.23 | 3.2 |
| 1970 | 1.36 | 3.5 |
| 1971 | 1.37 | 3.7 |
| 1976 | 2.36 | 4.4 |
| 1980 | 2.59 | 5.3 |

Source: Canadian and American census statistics.

consistently been lower than the American rate up through 1968. Now if the real reason for this difference were a greater Canadian conservatism, embodied in greater respect for the sanctity of marriage, then it would seem to follow that changes in divorce legislation would not have any significant effect on the divorce rate. Canadians would not divorce more frequently even if it were legally possible to do so since the legal impediment would not have been the reason for the lower rate in the first place. Thus the law would not suppress would-be divorces as the desire for divorce would simply be lower in Canada, according to Lipset's cultural hypothesis.

In 1968 new legislation was, in fact, introduced by the then minister of justice, Pierre Trudeau. This legislation did, among other things, make a divorce decree significantly easier to obtain in Canada than it had been, which gives us a nice opportunity to test this rival hypothesis. If the divorce rate was being suppressed by legislation, we would expect an increase after the 1968 changes. But if legislation was essentially irrelevant, we would find no significant narrowing of the gap nor any significant jump in the Canadian divorce rate. Table 2.2 shows the divorce rates since 1968 only.

The Canadian rate jumps rather suddenly in 1969 and increases thereafter. The American rate also increases but not nearly by so much. Nor is this 1969 rate an anomaly easily dismissed as a 'backlog', for example. This seems to suggest that legislative differences did play a role either in addition to, instead of, or in interaction with cultural differences between Canadians and Americans.

My purpose here is not primarily to criticize Lipset's work but to examine the structure and operation of scientific argument. Let us continue considering how to test rival hypotheses by turning now to the rival hypothesis dealing with differences in religious composition between the two countries. The hypothesis states that the fact that Roman Catholics compose a higher proportion of the Canadian population accounts for the lower Canadian divorce rate. How would we discount or test this? How could we subject it to falsification? As in the previous instance, we are more concerned with the logic than the actual example. In fact, ideally, you should attempt to substitute other examples for those used here. Still, in this example, if it is because they are Catholic that they do not get divorced (rather than because they are Canadian), then the rate of divorce among Catholics should be about the same whether they are Canadian or American. Only if Canadian Catholics have a lower divorce rate than American Catholics is nationality still a plausible cause of the remaining difference. In this case, too, science gains no matter the outcome since we would have falsified the idea that religious differences fully account for differences in divorce rates.

Exactly the same logic obtains with regard to the use of urban-rural proportions as a plausible cause for the different divorce rates. If this, rather than national cultural differences is the cause, then comparisons of equally urban samples of Canadians and Americans will show no differences in divorce rates. If, on the other hand, differences persist even within these categories, they cannot be attributable to differences in what proportion is urban since this would be the same for the Canadians and Americans compared. They must, therefore, be explained by some other factor, and cultural differences are a factor that remains possible.

In the attempt to set up research to allow the falsification or disconfirmation of hypotheses, various research strategies are implied. The most fundamental strategy of all shows up in all these examples. It entails holding relevant variables constant so that they cannot be held responsible for any differences in outcome. This particular logic of holding variables constant, whether in your design or later in your analysis (where we do the same thing but through statistical manipulation) is the most basic feature of scientific research designs; it is a feel for this that I hope to have conveyed to you in the discussions about testing Lipset's rivals. Our basic premise was that only variables can explain variation in a dependent variable. That is, something that is constant cannot explain why something else varies. Thus, a good deal of design attempts to transform a variable into a constant so as temporarily to remove its potential effect while examining the remaining variables.

## CONCLUSION: THE CHARACTERISTICS OF SCIENCE

I have by now, although perhaps in a rather roundabout manner, suggested several characteristics of the scientific mode of investigation. Science is sceptical but open-minded. Scientists systematically test hypotheses against empirical evidence collected, in an attempt to falsify both the working (or expected) hypothesis and all plausible rival hypotheses. Scientists attempt to design studies with such care that interpretations of causal effect are more defensible; this involves carefully eliminating or otherwise treating as many potential criticisms as possible before collecting data. Scientists do, nonetheless, make mistakes, change their minds, and refine their hypotheses. They seek, not permanent and perfect studies, but better and improved—that is, more credible and defensible—studies. Since they place much importance on replication and critical assessment by others, science is really a 'community project' rather than an individual one. The scientific community includes all practitioners *and* consumers. It is only to the extent that a finding or claim to knowledge can withstand the sceptical scrutiny of all these others that we are forced to accept it as legitimate.

While some scientists describe or classify, most seek to explain, and most social scientists seek to explain variation in human behaviour. Seeking causes is difficult indeed and far more difficult with self-conscious subject matter able to react and change their behaviour even as we study it. In seeking explanations, scientists formulate hypotheses that are testable statements about the expected relationships among variables. In testing these various rival hypotheses, scientists must translate abstract concepts into measurable percepts, and they must defend and explain their particular translation and the particular research design they select to test the hypotheses. Not all such decisions are wise, but again they are made available to the scientific community so that unreasonable or faulty operational definitions and flawed studies will be discovered and corrected or not allowed to stand unchallenged. It is in this sense that science to a considerable extent is a self-correcting process. It is also true that this self-correction depends on a host of other sociological factors and that science does not always and everywhere practise what it preaches. Thus scientists do not scrutinize with equal care and caution the work of a neophyte and a distinguished expert. Work that challenges widely held conclusions is sometimes not given a fair hearing, or any hearing at all. Replications, though essential, are not highly valued in practice.

> At the present time, there are almost as many different measures utilized by sociologists as there are studies of social phenomena. Some indication of this can be seen from the results obtained by Bonjean et al. (1967) who—in examining every article and research note over a twelve-year period (1954–1965) in the *American Journal of Sociology*, the *American Sociological Review*, *Social Forces*, and *Sociometry*—found that (Bonjean et al., 1967: 9–10): 'there were 3,609 attempts to measure various phenomena by the use of scales or indices, and 2,080 different measures were used. Of the measures used, only 589 (28.3 per cent of the total number of scales and indices) were used more than once. . . . The lack of continuity in social research is reflected further by the observation that of the 2,080 scales and indices appearing in the journals over the twelve-year period covered by the analysis, only 47, or 2.26 per cent, were used more than five times.' For instance, eighteen different scales and indices were used in twenty-one different studies of 'cohesion'. Forty-seven measures of crime and delinquency were used in sixty-four different studies. (Phillips, 1971: 7–8)

Despite its flaws, science remains in practice our best guideline to defensible work, even if it—like all other human institutions—is imperfect and could be better.

## SAMPLE QUESTIONS AND AN ANSWER

In this section, I offer two questions I have used on tests in this course, and I discuss various aspects of answers given by students to the first of them. I hope the discussion may help you work out your own ideas for answering the question.

The second question asks about hypotheses in connection with data interpretation.

## Question 1

It is the author's hypothesis that Canadians are more law-abiding than Americans. Making reference to this hypothesis, how would you interpret the following data tables? Defend your position.

Table 1

| Country | No. of Police Personnel | Ratio per 100,000 Population |
|---|---|---|
| Canada (1961) | 26,189 | 143.2 |
| USA (1962) | 360,000 | 193.8 |

Table 2

| No. of Policemen Killed on Duty | | |
| --- | --- | --- |
| | 1961 | 1963 |
| Canada | 1 | 1 |
| USA | 37 | 55 |

## Discussion of Answer

To this point I have emphasized that science proceeds negativistically by disqualifying rival hypotheses or competing explanations; similarly, students are cautioned to proceed critically and sceptically when conducting their own work or evaluating others people's work. Nonetheless, most of us have a strong tendency to take data at face value and accept the interpretation of them offered by those with appropriate credentials. Still, learning to learn involves internalizing this critical style, and this question often catches students who are still unpractised in adopting a constructively critical and sceptical orientation that emphasizes such a negativistic approach.

This question gives the students an opportunity to exercise their critical imaginations, should they so desire. It is an ambush of sorts, in that most students when presented with a table of evidence assume that the author's conclusions are the only ones to be drawn. I have been emphasizing the constructively critical and negativisitic nature of science though, and the question asks for the *student's* interpretation of the evidence *in light of* the hypothesis that it is because Canadians are more law-abiding that there are differences between Canada and the United States. To begin with then, it would not be useful for the student to report what the differences in the tables look like and then conclude that the author is correct. Some students usually do this, and their reasoning in explaining their position is instructive. Putting it most clearly, they say that policing is a matter of supply and demand, and that since there are more police in the United States there must be a greater need for them to maintain order in that society. Since there are fewer police per 100,000 Canadians, it is clear that there must not be as great a need for policing. And indeed, the numbers of police personnel could be due to differences in need. The question is whether they might be due to differences in something other than need (or law-abidingness of the two populations). In other words, the real question is whether there are reasons other than need that might explain and predict such differences as are evident in the tables *even if Canadians were no more law-abiding* than Americans. Students who are sceptical and understand the question often begin by noting that the failure to provide and discount rival hypotheses to account for the data is to fall into the fallacy of affirming the consequent, since the syllogism would then be as follows:

If Canadians were more law-abiding than Americans, then there would be fewer police officers in Canada and fewer of them would be killed on duty.
There are fewer police officers in Canada and fewer of them are killed on duty.
Therefore Canadians are more law-abiding than Americans.

Having said this, one ought to remember that the way out of the fallacy of affirming the consequent was to identify and discount rival hypotheses that were as plausible as the working hypothesis. Some students account for the difference in police personnel by pointing out the difference in years in the two tables. This is a technical rival hypothesis in so far as it suggests that the apparent difference is an artifact of errors in measurement. Perhaps, they reason, many more police officers would be counted in Canada a year later, or many fewer were available in the United States a year earlier, and the particular pair of years chosen creates the impression of a difference in policing that is really an artifact of the arbitrary years chosen for presentation. But this objection, though possible, is not very strong. It seems unlikely that a particular event in 1961 or 1962 would have so altered the number of police in either society as to bring the ratio of police to population into balance. By the same token, some students object that the term 'police personnel' is vague and might be interpreted differently in Canada and the United States; that is, the American numbers might count as among police personnel people in clerical, secretarial, or support positions who might not be so counted in Canada. Though this too is possible, it does not on the face of it seem very plausible that discrepancies in what jobs are counted could explain the differences in numbers. On the other hand, it is hazardous to generalize about Canadians and Americans forever on the basis of data collected 30 years ago, since various things may well have altered the numbers and ratios since then, though of course this is an empirical question.

Some students, recognizing their responsibility to identify rival hypotheses, suggest, substantively, that the real reason there are fewer police personnel in Canada is just that there are roughly 10 times as many Americans as Canadians. They do not realize that this rival is taken into account by the author, who presents the ratios of police personnel per 100,000 population. Although simple population size is thereby eliminated (assuming that by standardizing we really can eliminate the effect of size, which is an assumption with which some people are uncomfortable—for example, see Lieberson, 1987) many students go on to tell me that even if size does not explain the differences, there are still many other variables related to population. These include density, since it is suggested that American cities are considerably denser than Canadian cities, and if density is related to crime this could explain why there are more American police. By the same token, Canada is said to be more rural and small-town compared to a bigger, more urban United States. Note by the way that this could be construed as a reason why Americans need more police, but the argument from this need is different from that based on individual motivations of the people. This version of 'need' says that density produces pathology and thereby a requirement for policing. It is not that Americans are by nature or culture less law-abiding or Canadians more, as in the working hypothesis. On the contrary, if there were the same numbers in cities there would presumably be no differences in behaviour requiring policing. Density is a structural ecological feature of the environment, not a cultural attribute, as law-abiding is. Other students concentrate on racial differences and tensions, arguing that such tensions might produce more trouble in American cities, where they are clear and common, than in Canadian, where they are neither. By the same token, class differences are greater in American than in Canadian cities and that might explain differences in need for policing.

But some students realize that arguments from a presumed need fail to recognize that even if we were to grant differences in some sort of need, it may still not follow that in either society the need is met! That is, there may simply not be enough police in Canada to meet the needs of the society. Or there may be more police in the United States than are needed. Knowing how many there are is not the same as knowing that the needs are being met, nor is it legitimate to infer the latter from the former. Needs are socially constructed, and some students argue that political and economic considerations probably explain how many police personnel there are in any jurisdiction. Perhaps American cities are simply able to devote a larger proportion of their budgets to policing than are Canadian cities. This could be an accounting phenomenon or a matter of pork-barrelling. And perhaps it is every American youth's dream to become a police officer, whereas Canadians aspire to other occupations and professions. Some students have even suggested that the better training of Canadian police personnel allows Canada to have fewer of them, even though Canadians are no more law-abiding than Americans! In all of these and subsequent cases, there are implicit theories of deviance, social stratification, socialization, and social control that underlie each proposition. It soon becomes clear that these are often opposing theories, and that students operating from various theoretical perspectives can make sense of the data in various and competing ways. Clearly, one could develop this insight further by asking them to devise more defensible tests of hypotheses drawn from various competing models.

Returning to the interpretation of the data at hand, and turning now to the second table, many students see this one as being more relevant and the conclusion inescapable that indeed Americans are less law-abiding than Canadians. How else explain the enormous differences in the number of police killed on duty? Again some students explain the difference as due to simple population size differences between the two countries, but the ratios given of police to population do not translate into expectations of ratios this size in the number of police killed on duty. Since the years of data collection are in this table the same, the conclusion seems warranted that the police are more highly respected and less often killed in the line of duty in Canada than in the United States. There are some sceptical students who suggest that since the manner of their deaths is not specified it is possible that American police are choking on their doughnuts or dying of heart attacks more often than Canadians. This goes to the thesis concerning differential selection, recruitment, and training of police in the two countries. There are others who suggest that American police may be killed in traffic accidents while on duty, and that we do not know that their deaths are a direct result of contact with armed criminals. Though these are possible, they are not very plausible rivals, and there are better.

For example, most students inclined to be sceptical of this table quickly realize that the fact that guns are more numerous and more easily available in the United States could account for the differences in police personnel killed on duty since criminals are more likely to be armed and dangerous in the United States. Other students have similarly suggested that perhaps Canadians are more likely to injure or beat up policemen than to kill them, and differences in death rates need not be the same as differences in injuries.

Most students have been able to point out that the two tables provide no evidence of law-abiding behaviour or attitudes at all, only the relative number of police and police killed on duty. They would prefer to see evidence on national rates for crime and arrest, and not simply for violent crimes, but for all categories of offence. They would also like to see direct evidence concerning attitudes to law officers in the two countries, since data on crime reflect differences in legislation and enforcement in addition to possible differences in attitudes of Canadians and Americans.

Clearly, there is more than meets the eye to the assessment of 'facts', and the sceptical and constructive orientation of social science is a challenge to all who would adopt it. Now try your hand on the following question. Think sceptically.

## Question 2

Using the materials introduced in this chapter, write an essay answer to the following question. Remember to address each part explicitly, to be critical, and to be specific. When asked for several examples or factors involved in a question, students often mention two or three and then add 'etc.' or 'and so on'. Please avoid this, since instructors cannot be expected to read your minds.

> What sociological factors might systematically distinguish between adolescents particularly vulnerable to the pressures of the 'adolescent subculture', and those less vulnerable? From which sociological perspective does each factor emerge? Put three of these factors into properly phrased hypotheses, in which the degree of vulnerability is the dependent variable. Include in your answer an explanation of why these independent variables may be relevant. That is, how do they operate?

## SELECTED QUESTIONS

1. 'There is less loss of life in car accidents in summer than in winter. I think this is because people are more likely to wear seat belts in summer.' Assuming that, in fact, people are more likely to wear seat belts in summer, how would a negativistically inclined sociologist reply? In other words, what other potential explanations would you have to consider before accepting this conclusion?

2. Why is the idea of operational definition considered basic to a scientific sociology?

3. What is the function of modified replications? That is, what do we learn from them?

4. How is the logic of the 'fallacy of affirming the consequent' rectified in 'proper' scientific treatments?

5. Why is confirming evidence never completely persuasive? What of disconfirming evidence?

6. What sorts of possible responses are there for the investigator who encounters apparent disconfirming evidence?

## NOTES TO THE CHAPTER

1  The argument Lipset makes is a little more sophisticated than its presentation here, but the logical error still exists. I have merely simplified it for presentation in the present context. Nor is Lipset the only author to make such logical errors, as I will demonstrate shortly.

2  As you will see in chapter 3, this is a point of some importance. The idea of spuriousness involves the incorrect inference of causality from an association that is actually accidental rather than causal. Put more simply, we may want to suggest in the examples here that the major premises are incorrect. We may not believe that throwing a rock will break the window; we may not believe that if the drug works the patient will recover or even that if Canadians were more conservative they would have lower divorce rates. The test of spuriousness requires that plausible rivals be related to both the alleged independent and dependent variable. However, it is also possible that though we are prepared to accept the causal role of the independent variable we believe that other independents are equally or more important. In this case, we are not involved in testing for spuriousness, and we need simply relate our rival independents to the dependent variable (and not to the independent as well) and then compare the abilities of the rival independents as competing explanations of change in the dependent.

## ILLUSTRATIVE READING

Many students have trouble with the concept of variable and with the part of the sociological imagination that requires you to think of things in terms of variation. Variables change values; they have within them variability, at least potential. Sex varies from male to female; age varies by years, months, and days; social class varies from upper to lower (through as many categories as you want to create or recognize); wealth varies through as many dollar categories as you want to deal with, and so on. On the other hand, plumber is a value or attribute of the variable occupation; rich is one value of the variable wealth; Protestant is one value of the variable religious denomination. This is not to say that plumbers do not themselves vary with respect to other attributes; they may vary by sex, wealth, and religion, but they are all plumbers and so do not vary by occupation. Indeed, we say that for them, occupation is a constant, an invariant.

Hypotheses relate variables to one another in systematic ways. As one changes in a specific manner, the second changes systematically with it, often as a result of it, though this is not strictly necessary. That is to say, not all hypotheses are causal, but all involve a specific relationship between change in two (or more) variables. Hypotheses must also be testable in order to be useful, and this further narrows how they can be stated. Essentially you have to imagine what data can be brought to bear that will allow you to decide whether your hypothesis is supported by the data or falsified by it. Remember, scientists learn from their mistakes; they do not have to be correct. In fact, it is often argued that we can learn far more from our mistakes than from tests that confirm our hypotheses. All of this means that it is misguided to try to state your hypothesis in such a way that it cannot easily be falsified or tested. You should seek the contrary; say it as simply, concisely, and testably as you can.

Generally there are several formats that are suggested for hypotheses. The easiest is of the form: *As x changes* (specifically increases, decreases, changes in a more complicated non-linear manner, or changes from one category to another) *y changes* (specifically increases, decreases, changes in a more complicated non-linear manner, or changes from one category to another). This is the form that most clearly specifies the changes in each variable and virtually directs you to measure them in terms of that variation. Any hypothesis can be restated in this form, and doing so goes a long way to spelling out what your operational definitions will have to capture and what your research design will have to produce if the hypothesis is to be tested (aside from identifying those rivals that will also have to be tested).

Consider the following, more or less progressively closer examples of attempts at hypothesis construction:

1. 'Rich people are intolerant.' This is not a hypothesis, since there are no variables in this statement. It is only a statement of association between values (of potential variables that are not stated as such). Both rich and intolerant are values only.
2. Rich people are likely to be intolerant. This is still not a hypothesis, but a weaker statement of association than the first attempt. Note that the dependent variable now is *likelihood* of being intolerant, not intolerance. Students often phrase hypotheses with 'likelihoods' or 'tendencies' or 'chances of' as the dependent variable. They are unwilling to go so far out on the limb as simply to state that level or degree of intolerance will be a function (of some kind) of wealth; they seem to think they can hedge their bet, as it were, by saying only that the tendency to be intolerant will change with wealth. This is fine, except that tendencies are difficult to measure, and this makes the hypothesis far more difficult to test empirically. It is generally possible to rephrase the hypothesis to avoid such phrasing, and it is advisable, in the interests of hypothesis testing, to do so.
3. 'Rich people are more likely to be intolerant.' Although the addition of 'more' helps, since it suggests variation in at least one variable (though the variable is likelihood), this is still not a hypothesis because there is no explicit group with which to compare the rich people (and the hypothesis would be better if likelihood was left out).
4. 'Rich people are more likely to be intolerant than tolerant.' This is still not a hypothesis because, though you now have a fully specified dependent variable (that is, likelihood of tolerance) there is still no independent variable that clearly varies.
5. 'Rich people are more intolerant than poorer people.' Since wealth varies from rich to poorer and tolerance varies from more to less, you now have a hypothesis.

The following article attempts to elaborate these points still more clearly.

### On Distinguishing Variables from Values and Hypotheses from Statements of Association

*Sheldon Goldenberg*

Scientists generally find it useful to think in terms of relating variation in one phenomenon to variation in another, though Blumer's (1956) critique of variable analysis stands out as one indicator that this position has long been contentious among sociologists. Nonetheless, most of us try to teach students to conceptualize variation in behaviour and the factors related to that variation systematically in terms of variable relations.

Year after year I have been frustrated in all such attempts to help students to think in terms of variables. They persist in confusing categories, attributes, or values of variables with variables themselves, and until recently my best attempts have met with very little success. I have had many students try to explain positive attitudes toward abortion by reference to one feature and then suggest quite another feature to account for those displaying negative attitudes toward abortion. They do not seem to realize that attitudes toward abortion *vary* from positive to negative and that finding an explanation *for the variation* in the distribution, or among those expressing opinions, would require that they find another variable that is systematically related to the entire range of attitudes toward abortion (that is, related to both positive and negative attitudes and, therefore, related to *change* in attitude). They seem to focus determinedly on each possible outcome rather than on the process or variation itself.

I think I understand the source of some of their confusion. In everyday argument, after all, we frequently and perhaps usually look for a common denominator to account for the phenomenon of interest to us. We reason that if we look carefully at thin people, or successful ones, we will be able to find out why they are thin or successful. Newspaper and magazine articles and self-help books often are based on just this premise. Even in some versions of social science research we appear to have reasoned that if we examine all those who are criminals, for example, and find that all possess peculiar bumps on their heads, an extra chromosome, or a common denominator of some other kind, this common denominator must account for their criminal status. Explaining why others are not criminal calls for the search for another factor common to this other and distinct category of people. Criminal and other-than-criminal are not viewed as categories or values of the same variable, but as nominal and distinct job classifications, not unlike plumber and farmer. They are not typically juxtaposed or treated in relation to one another any more than one might try to explain why people become farmers by reference to why they do not become plumbers.

This search for common denominators is what J.S. Mill called the method of agreement, and it is methodologically suspect since the most it can produce is association, which may well be spurious. Another way to put the objection is that we ought to be wary if in fact we have no dependent variable, but only one attribute, category, or value of that variable; such is the case in the examples mentioned. We simply cannot *explain* a constant. We must have a comparison case of non-criminals among whom there is a *different* frequency of bumps, chromosomal make-ups, or whatever for us to be able to explain variation in outcome.[1]

When asked to carry the discussion of variables further, by linking them in the form of a hypothesis, my students often further confuse matters by simply asserting that there is no difference between a statement of association between values and a hypothesis. Thus they might suggest, for example, that 'old people drive slowly' is a hypothesis. At this point, I might remind them that we have agreed, at least for the sake of simplicity, to confine ourselves to hypotheses that are testable statements of specific relationships between two or more variables.[2] When asked, accordingly, to identify the alleged variables in their hypothesis, the students may identify 'age' and 'driving speed', and when pressed, they may admit that neither of these is specifically mentioned. They often argue nonetheless that both variables are present but *implicit*, suggesting that 'if old people drive slowly, *it follows* that young people drive faster than old people'. Of course it is clear that once you have *supplied* variation in speed of driving and in age, the so-called implicit variables can be easily identified. The resultant statement is a hypothesis: 'Young people drive faster than old people'. But I regularly point out that this allegedly minor 'reading between the lines' is simply not a legitimate option. As I begin to explain my rather unsympathetic position, the students quite often come to appreciate much more clearly the distinction with which this paper is centrally concerned.

## Contrasting the Cases

I begin by putting on the blackboard that portion of Figure 1 that appears above the dotted line. Here example A states an empirical association between the values of two unstated variables. It temporarily postpones consideration of the kind of conceptual relationship that may underlie the association—a point of great importance and one to which we will return shortly. In the empirical association, then, 'old' is one value (in the generic sense) of a variable that might be called age. Very crudely 'old' might be simply one value or category of a dichotomy in which the other value or category would be 'young'. Or one could trichotomize the variable into categories corresponding to 'old', 'middle-aged', and 'young'. Or age could be measured in years (or finer gradations) and treated as a ratio variable. Explanation of the range of values of the variable allows the interested instructor to introduce the idea of nominal, ordinal, and interval levels of measurement, as well as clarifying the distinction between values and the variable that encompasses their variation. This introduction of levels of measurement is presupposed to some extent when we turn to the bottom half of Figure 1.

The other value or category in the statement of association in example A is 'conservative', and it is usually treated as one category of the variable 'political ideology'. That is, one variety of political ideology is conservatism, and one could distinguish other ideological positions ranging from fascist through varieties of conservative to varieties of liberal, radical, socialist, or communist. One might conceptualize such values as nominal categories or perhaps as ordinal values if indeed they imply a relationship to one another in which one might move from more conservative to less conservative, for example. If one were to use a numerical

Figure 1  Association Between Values as Contrasted to a Hypothesized Relationship
Between Variables

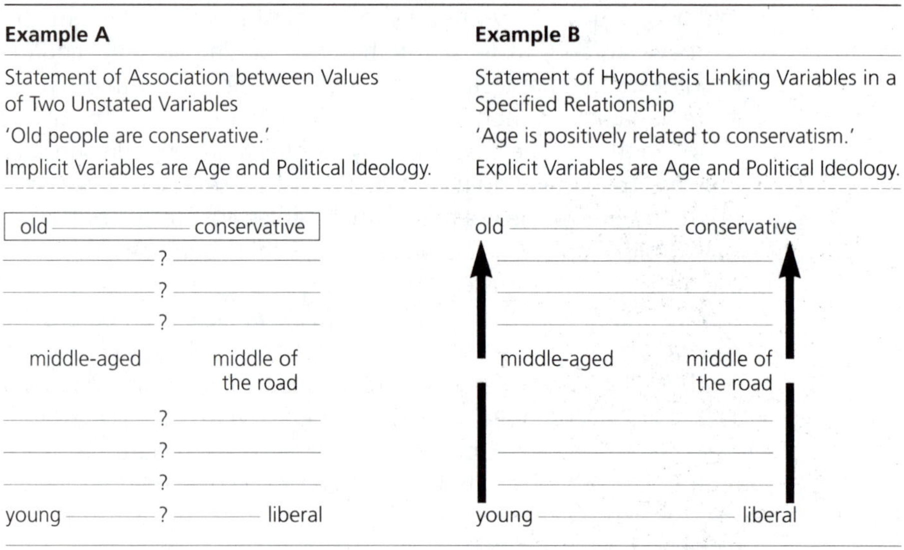

| Example A | Example B |
|---|---|
| Statement of Association between Values of Two Unstated Variables | Statement of Hypothesis Linking Variables in a Specified Relationship |
| 'Old people are conservative.' | 'Age is positively related to conservatism.' |
| Implicit Variables are Age and Political Ideology. | Explicit Variables are Age and Political Ideology. |

Example A:

old ———————— conservative
——————— ? ———————
——————— ? ———————
——————— ? ———————
middle-aged            middle of
                       the road
——————— ? ———————
——————— ? ———————
——————— ? ———————
young ———— ? ———— liberal

Example B:

old ———————— conservative

middle-aged            middle of
                       the road

young ———————— liberal

scale of conservatism, it might even be argued that this measure could be interval-ratio in nature.

The point of the discussion of the various values of the hidden variables is to point out to students that a statement of association between particular values *implies nothing, by itself, about the relationship between any other values of either of the variables.* That is, claiming that old people are conservative in no way tells us anything at all about what younger people's political ideological position might be. They might indeed be more liberal, but they might also be more conservative or at least as conservative. We simply do not know and cannot guess *from the information contained in the association only.*

With this introduction, it is sometimes tempting to launch into discussion of the use of the theory and relevant literature in suggesting fruitful conceptual linkages between constructs. The general question of whether hypotheses are arrived at deductively or inductively could be addressed here as well. Indeed at this point the whole set of relationships among theory, hypotheses, operational definitions, and empirical data could be addressed. However, in my experience such an invitation to abstraction is best postponed since this still-too-abstract explanation of why you cannot simply 'fill in the gaps' in the hypothesis has little concrete meaning as yet for students. I find it most useful to return to Figure 1, elaborating by adding a few more lines—those below the dotted line—that seem to help make the point more clearly.

The solid lines indicate associations. In example A the box around the one association further emphasizes that *it is the only association of which we have knowledge from the statement that 'old people are conservative.'* In example B, because we are relating all values of each variable to all values of the other variable, all the associations are explicit in the statement of the hypothesis. We have stated that the two variables are related positively to one another; thus each variable has an arrowhead on the end of the line pointed in the same direction (up), and the two arrows stand parallel to one another. This indicates that all values within each variable's range will be associated with parallel values in the range specified by the other variable. Each horizontal solid line in the figure thus represents an association between categories or attributes of the two variables while the overall pattern represents the correlation between the variables. In example B, we *do* know that old people are conservative *and also* that middle-aged people are less conservative and that young people are least conservative. None of these associations is either explicit or implicit in example A, devoid as it is of theoretical underpinning. Indeed it is worth noting that we might have suggested initially, had we in fact worked from theory to hypothesis, that as people get older we would expect them to become *less* conservative, rather than more. In this case, the arrow in example B from conservative to liberal would be turned upside down. Given such a hypothesis, we would be suggesting that as values shift along the age dimension from younger to older, the shift in the parallel political ideology dimension would be from conservative to liberal. This would mean that old people would be expected to be more liberal than middle-aged people who would in turn be expected to be more liberal than young people. We might even have suggested that the relationship is not a linear one at all, but curvilinear, such that as people grow older they become more conservative to a point, and then as they continue to age they tend to become less conservative again. Such a curvilinear expectation still relates changes in age, through all its values, to systematic changes in political ideology. It still allows us to predict the entire range of associations that correspond to all values of both variables as they are related to one another. The point is that various empirical relationships could have been predicted in our hypotheses had we begun from differing theoretical positions.[3] Statistically we might even have begun by testing the null hypothesis that there is no difference between young and old people with respect to political ideology. Disqualification of this null, however, tells us nothing about the shape of the actual relationship—only that there is one of some sort.

To this point we have depicted only one variable at a time and tried to describe what it means for them to vary together in some manner. There is, of course, a more conventional and informative manner of representing cases with respect to their position on two or more variables simultaneously.

This requires that we rotate one of the dimensions that we have looked at, setting it at a right angle to the other. This gives us two axes, the vertical axis in this case representing political ideology and running from least conservative (or most liberal) to most conservative, and the horizontal depicting age and categorized crudely as extending from younger to older. For present purposes it is immaterial whether these variables are more than ordinally arrayed. The point is that if we were to calculate a group mean for the people we decide are to occupy the 'young' category, it might be represented by the point labelled A on Figure 2. Point A now simultaneously refers to both young people and to their conservatism scores. One might read Point A as saying that 'young people have a relatively low score on the conservatism scale represented by the vertical axis.' Having said this much, it is also clear that this alone provides us with absolutely no evidence as to where a point B, representing the average views of the 'older' category, might fall in the same figure. B could fall at B1, B2, or even B3, where B1 could be read as saying that 'older people have views as conservative as the younger category'; B2 could be read as saying that 'the views of the older category are more conservative than those of the younger category'; and B3 could be read as saying that 'the views of the older category are less conservative than those of the younger category'. Note that even had we graphed the actual position of the older category as well as the younger, it would still not be legitimate to draw a line connecting those two points (A and B) interpolating from them the position on this graph of the intermediate age category or categories. Two points define a linear relationship, but we do not know that this relationship between age and political leaning is linear. It is possible, for example, that the middle-aged category might be most conservative, as depicted by C in Figure 2 (if both the younger and the older categories were to score appreciably lower on conservatism than the middle category).

Reference to theory, familiarity with relevant literature, and skill at sociological thinking allow us to formulate hypotheses linking variables to one another in useful ways. While statements of association between values, attributes, or categories have their place, they cannot by themselves generate, and certainly do not by themselves constitute, hypotheses.

I have found these graphic presentations of the differences between thinking in terms of associations and thinking in terms of relationships between variables to be an effective teaching tool for making this point. Students exposed to these graphic presentations have performed better on their papers (which require them to conceptualize and test a hypothesis) and on examination questions in which they are asked to identify hypotheses and distinguish between variables and categories or values. They seem less inclined to look for common denominators that fit a category or value and more inclined to search for other values of the often hidden but encompassing variable. They often try to imagine or discover another variable that is systematically related to the first.

To the extent that they can take this first step, it becomes far easier to introduce them to the application of the sociological imagination as they are encouraged to find and use appropriate sociological theory and relevant literature in

Figure 2 Depiction of Several Possible Hypothesized Relationships Between Age and Political Ideology, Including Curvilinear

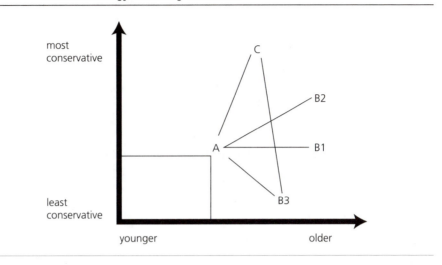

generating ideas of how theoretical constructs might be related to one another. For example, rather than 'discovering' that the common denominator among those who are 'conservative' is their age, students might try to suggest sociological factors that could explain, at least in part, why some people espouse totalitarian political ideologies, while others support socialist, and still others liberal or conservative belief systems. Having read a little bit of the literature relevant to this topic (a topic they would otherwise never even have discovered), students might consider that an argument could be made that would link variation in social class position to variation in ideology in a plausible manner. From here, they might be led to consider the exact nature of the linking mechanism or the component of social class most responsible for the relationship. Whatever direction they might choose would certainly involve improving and demonstrating their ability to think sociologically.

## NOTES

1 Discussion with the class of some conditions necessary for what we are prepared to consider a *defensible* explanation may well lead to consideration of the varying and various criteria used by positivists, interpretive social scientists, and critical social scientists. In no case does a common denominator constitute such an explanation, nor must a factor be common to all instances for it to play an explanatory role (Hirschi and Selving, 1973).

2 Consideration of null hypotheses and associational but nondirectional hypotheses is postponed because they may be addressed better in other contexts.

3 The relationship between these variables is not stated in causal terms, and for this reason there are no arrowheads linking the values of 'age' with those of 'political

ideology'. While it is most likely that this is a true causal relationship, the issue of causality and its assessment can be separated from that addressed more narrowly here.

## REFERENCES

Blumer, Herbert
1956  'Sociological Analysis and the "Variable"', *American Sociological Review* 21: 683–90.

Hirschi, Travis, and Hanan Selvin
1973  *Principles of Survey Analysis*. New York: The Free Press.

From *Teaching Sociology* 21 (1) (1993): 100–4.

# CHAPTER 3

# Premises, Evaluation Criteria,
# and Principal Methods
# of Sociology

Chapter 1 introduced the perspectives of sociology and gave some indication of what kinds of explanations sociologists might suggest for why people act as they do. Chapter 2 introduced some of the major characteristics of science to show what kinds of very general attributes a study would have to possess in order to be considered scientific. Chapter 3 tries to illustrate how one might put the two perspectives of chapter l into practice in a way that would satisfy some of the general requirements of science discussed in chapter 2. In other words, this is a more applied and practical chapter. Since all scientific research, whatever position it takes with respect to these issues, must confront the same issues of validity, reliability, generalizability, and demonstration of causality, it is important to deal with these first. After reading this chapter, you should have a fairly good idea of the nature of the debate around these issues between proponents of so-called hard (or positivistic) and soft (or qualitative) methods, and you should have become acquainted with the most common methods practised by sociologists in each of these scientific camps and with the different positions they take with respect to methods and criteria for evaluating the credibility of scientific claims to knowledge.

Social scientists are concerned with describing, predicting, and understanding, but mostly with explaining variation in human behaviour. Not all these goals, however, are subscribed to equally by all social scientists; in fact there are systematic differences between proponents of the two major perspectives. Macro-structural positivists are generally more concerned with predicting and at least potentially altering this behaviour, whereas micro-interpretivists are more likely to be satisfied with understanding or describing it, as you have seen in the excerpts included in chapter 1. This difference, as you should expect by now, has many implications as well for the methods favoured by each of the perspectives.

The further fact that our dependent variable is human behaviour is another complication for both schools of thought. Although humans can explain their own behaviour if you ask them why they did something, they can also lie or rationalize, they may not know, or they may tell you what they think you want to hear. Furthermore, humans are self-conscious or reflexive—that is, they reconstruct the past as they look back on it—and that gives them some freedom to adjust their behaviour as you watch, for any number of reasons. In spite of all these difficulties, it is human behaviour where our interest lies, and we must look to methodologies that help us overcome the difficulties of studying it.

## METHODOLOGICAL IMPLICATIONS OF THE MICRO-INTERPRETIVE AND MACRO-STRUCTURAL PERSPECTIVES

There is fairly wide, though not unanimous, agreement in the social sciences that our goal is to explain variation in human behaviour. Regardless of our selection of an independent variable, our dependent is generally the same: variation in human behaviour. In chapter 1 I suggested that social-structurally inclined scientists seek to explain this variation by reference to social-structural independent variables, whether ecological, normative, structural, or other. For micro-interpretive or social-action theorists, the key independent variables lie inside the actor's head in his or her *definition of the situation*, motivations, and intentions.

It should be noted, however, that there are some, particularly in the interpretive camp, who do not subscribe to this search for explanations. For them, social science can only produce descriptions: concrete, richly detailed attempts to recreate the specific situations and cultures in which actors find themselves, so that the reader can vicariously experience what it might feel like to be a patient in a mental institution, a native of a foreign culture, a shop worker in an automotive plant, a pool hustler, or a juvenile delinquent. The goal of such a version of social science is to understand rather than to explain, and the search for generalizations or theories that cross cultures or situations is viewed sceptically. The general position adopted here, which concentrates on the historical and cultural specificity of behaviour, is called *historicism*. There has always been vigorous debate between those who believe that human behaviour can be compared across situations, epochs, and cultures in an effort to generate broad theories of human behaviour and those who opt for a historicist position. Indeed, this debate was discussed briefly at the beginning of chapter 2, where the premises of science were introduced, including the premise that behaviour was sufficiently patterned that what we learn from observation of one case can be applied to others not yet observed. Since historicists do not grant this premise, they must practise their discipline for another purpose, that being to understand each case in its uniqueness.

Obviously the methods of the social sciences will reflect these two basic beliefs about our purposes and goals, and indeed arguments very like those of historicism have strongly influenced the interpretive camp. Still, I believe that for most sociologists in both the interpretive and the macro-structural camps, the goal remains explanation rather than description, however rich the latter may be. A descriptive goal based on historicist principles seems considerably more common among historians, clinical psychologists, and anthropologists than among sociologists. This goal leads to descriptive 'case studies' of particular events, people, situations, cultures, or structural arrangements rather than to the search for a common denominator among diverse cases. Of course, some historians, psychologists, and anthropologists do adopt a comparative perspective, and their work is much more difficult to distinguish from that of sociologists. And some sociologists conduct case studies only, producing work that is almost indistinguishable from that typically done by historians or anthropologists. But I suggested in chapter 1 that the differences among sister social science disciplines are better understood as artifacts of their historical development than as matters of substance or even method.

With respect to the majority of sociologists, then—those who seek to explain why people act as they do—the biggest difference between the two primary sociological perspectives lies in their choice of independent variable, again as noted in chapter 1. Schematically one might contrast the structuralist's position or model or paradigm (I) with the social-action or interpretive theorist's (II) as follows:

Figure 3.1 The Two Prevailing Models of Sociological Explanation

I   Variable characteristics       ————————————————————▶       Variation in behaviour
    of social structure

II  Variable definitions           ————————————————————▶       Variation in behaviour
    of the situation

The social-action theorist's methods require the researcher to gain access to the actor's thought. The methods of the structuralist will concentrate on aspects that are externally observable. We can put the two perspectives together as shown in Figure 3.2, but some basic points of incompatibility remain.

Figure 3.2 Composite Model of Structural and Social-Action Explanations of Behaviour

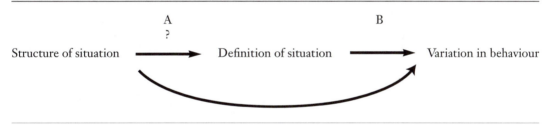

Interpretive theorists look no further for independent variables than the definition of the situation because their premise is that different situations may be defined similarly and that the same situation may be defined differently by different actors. In other words, there is no systematic relationship between the 'objective' situation and its definition. Hence the question mark at A. People react differently. Situations do not simply produce corresponding and self-evident definitions of themselves.

Structuralists, on the other hand, are struck by the regularities in all forms of behaviour, by the patterns seen in behaviour, including people's definitions of the same situation. They simply do not believe that as much variability exists as the action theorists posit. Hence the arrow at A. For them there is no question mark. Furthermore, structuralists might say that the conditions under which variability might be higher can also be analysed by structural methods. In other words, situations where people define what is happening differently from one another are *unusual* situations. They are ambiguous in structural ways. Another way of expressing this idea would be to say that in any situation the micro-interpretive theorist

Figure 3.3a The Micro-interpretive Perspective: Wide Range of Definitions of the Situation or Variation in Behaviour as Related to Structural Circumstances

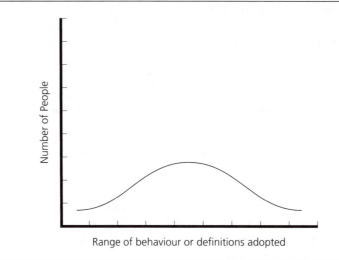

Range of behaviour or definitions adopted

Figure 3.3b The Macro-structuralist Perspective: Narrow Range of Definitions or Behaviours

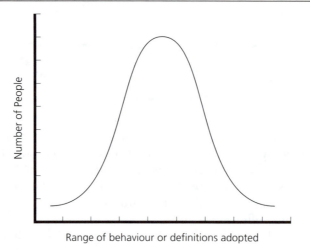

Range of behaviour or definitions adopted

sees a wide range of possible definitions of it and a correspondingly wide range of actual behaviours. In any situation there will be many definitions and many ways of behaving and not many people will behave in the same way (or define the situation the same way). (See Figure 3.3a.) The structuralist sees a relatively narrow range of definitions of the situation, except in unusual circumstances, and a correspondingly narrow range of actual behaviours. That is, there will be a fairly strong consensus about what is going on and only a few kinds of behaviour will result. There will be many people who agree and therefore behave similarly. (See Figure 3.3b.) These two perspectives represent long-standing alternatives, each with its champions. In this text I raise the questions and challenge you to find your own answers. *How much variation is there in how people respond to the same circumstances?*

Before we leave this point, let me return to our composite model (Figure 3.2). Extreme structuralists will go even further than we have. They will assert that since the definition of the situation normally corresponds so closely to what the structural characteristics of the situation demand, there is no need to find out how people define the situation at all. One can move directly from analysis of the 'objective' situation to the behaviour it produces without bothering to try to discover something as ephemeral as actors' definitions of the situation. This is the looping arrow. Micro-interpretivists, who do not believe that situations are ever so unambiguous that you can assume the actors' definitions will correspond to them, insist that the *only* way to get to the dependent variable is by knowing the definitions of the situation. Now perhaps you can see why those who champion the two perspectives rarely get along well. They really hold positions that are contradictory in many fundamental ways.

## Positivist versus Interpretive Premises

Most sociology still follows a *positivistic* paradigm or model, though there is a wide variety of kinds of sociology and at various times and places it has been practised quite differently. For positivists, the model of science is found in the physical sciences, and the social sciences will succeed to the extent they are able to emulate the physical sciences. In other words, science is science and there is only one way to do it. All science, including the social sciences, is about seeking patterns, generalities, or laws of the way the world works. They all proceed by systematically observing and manipulating and by recording the results of such study. The accuracy of scientific claims is measured ultimately against the external reality that it seeks to apprehend, and over time we generally approach ever more closely to a correct apprehension of the way the universe really is. Positivists also hold that scientists should be objective in the sense that they must do their best to ensure that their own characteristics, values, and desires do not distort their findings or claims. Scientific methods have been developed in an effort to be able to defend the claims of scientists when challenged by critics, and the use of well-established methods is deemed a sufficient defence of the credibility of the scientist's conclusion. Science then is systematic, empirical, and impartial, and the goal of science is to uncover the basic universal laws according to which the universe functions.

Of course there are additional characteristics of positivism and in fact many varieties of this epistemological position. Some positivists, who believe in all of these premises, model their work closely on that of physical scientists, whereas others, who agree less strongly and perhaps with only some of these premises, work accordingly. Among those who disagree with these premises, again there are a variety of positions taken, from those who work from a completely different model of science to those who use less stringent forms of most of the same criteria. This same battle is fought in all the scientific disciplines, though it may be particularly evident among social scientists and is quite clear (and often vitriolic, *ad hominem*, and divisive) among sociologists. In a later chapter, you will be able to read some samples of these debates.

To some interpretive sociologists a basically positivistic epistemological position would be acceptable, but a majority would require at least that the criteria of science be 'softened' to take into account the unique character of human behaviour. After all, when humans are able to choose how they behave, it is hard to take the position that such behaviour is govern-ed by 'laws'. Many micro-interpretivists would therefore argue that at least some positivistic criteria (like reliability, for example) are fundamentally misguided and unattainable, given the fragility, reflexivity, and volatility of human behaviour. Their position is that social reality is not some Durkheimian 'social fact' but is constructed and negotiated every day, in ways described well in the Charon excerpt quoted in chapter 1. They would likely opt for qualitative methods as primary ways of coming to know the world. Feminists and critical sociologists again might have different views of the acceptability and rank ordering of these criteria and might well substitute others, including authenticity and utility. Post-modernists reject not only positivistic criteria but all criteria, believing that science is only one way of apprehending reality and that it is no more privileged, legitimate, or inherently credible than any other. They seem curiously untroubled by the contradiction in claiming that their position is correct, while arguing in principle that no position can be any more defensible than another. For post-modernists there is little point in making methodological arguments or defending a conclusion as methodologically warranted, since for them methodology is no more than the expression of power through the medium of science as ideology.

In this book, I take the position that a sceptical critic, if not obliged to demand to be persuaded that a scientific position is defensible, is at least entitled to be offered such a defence, and at the same time is obliged to accept at least tentatively any position that satis-factorily answers his or her criticism. Furthermore, though the criteria for assessing scien-tific claims do change, at any one time some criteria seem fairly well established, and these are the ones used by both critic and scientist in struggling to evaluate the many claims that bombard us daily. It is these to which you will shortly be introduced.

The dominance of these competing perspectives (that is, positivist and interpretive) has led to a parallel debate in methodology, as mentioned above, and as you might well have expected. In general the micro-interpretive or social-action theorist uses methods that differ greatly from those used by the macro-structuralist. The structural perspective mini-mizes the differences between studying human and animal behaviour, for example. Even more generally the structuralist most often favours, with as little change as possible, the traditional methods of the so-called hard sciences. These methods include systematic observation, surveys, experiment, and the judicious use of indicators of various kinds. Careful measurement is usually emphasized, as is reliability. This version of science sees social science as essentially a complex branch of the main trunk of science as represented most clearly in the more mature physical sciences such as chemistry, biology, or physics. It is strongly positivistic.

In contrast, the social-action theorist usually views the human sciences as qualitatively different from the other sciences, as a tree of a different species and not an offshoot. Since humans are self-conscious, the methods for studying such subjects must be capable of delving into the actors' minds. No models from physics suffice. Much 'softer' methods, such as introspection, detailed ethnographic case studies, participant observation, *verstehen* (empathy leading to understanding through identification), and interpretive life histories are called for. The emphasis is not so much on measurement or reliability but on validity and even empathy. This perspective, which is definitely not positivistic, is sometimes said to favour qualitative approaches to the study of human behaviour. Most often, this debate is framed as one between 'hard' positivists and practitioners of 'soft' qualitative methods.

At one extreme, the 'hard' scientists accuse their opposite numbers of losing sight of reliability in their efforts to attain validity. At the other extreme, the 'soft' scientists accuse their counterparts of an overemphasis on reliability to the point of losing validity. Unfortunately there is some justification for both claims, though they are also overstatements and gross oversimplifications that fail to do justice to either side. As argued earlier, it is wise to remember at all times that scientists are first and foremost men and women, who, like people in every walk of life, are sometimes caught up in politics.

## THE CENTRAL METHODOLOGICAL CONCERNS OF SCIENCE

Research in all sciences, including the social sciences, must somehow come to grips with the same fundamental problems that challenge any claims to truth, whatever positions they take in abstract with respect to epistemology. We can therefore compare research in all sciences as to how and how adequately in our view they tackle the following key problem areas as they strive to defend themselves against our criticism and to explain why we, as critical but open-minded readers, must accept their claims. Although no research is perfect, some claims are clearly more defensible and others less defensible, and you should be able to compare scientific claims intelligently and capably with reference to these problem areas, among others. In each case, you should be familiar with the interpretation and use of each criterion from both positivist and non-positivist positions.

These, then, are some central methodological concerns of science:

1. Validity (or 'truth value' or accuracy)
2. The translation of concepts into percepts: operational definition or empirical measurement
3. Reliability (repeatability, consistency)
4. Generalizability (utility)
5. Demonstration of causality (non-spuriousness, control)

Whether the research in question deals with molecular or social structures, with human behaviour and attitudes or with the behaviour of molten metals, the same issues must be addressed. Work that is defensible addresses these issues in ways that make sense in light of what else we think we know. Let's take a closer look at these fundamental issues, first from a positivistic perspective and then from that of the non-positivist interpretive researcher.

## Validity

For science the accuracy, or 'truth value', of the study or measurement at hand is fundamental. That seemingly simple statement grows complex, however, when one inquires into
the demonstration of accuracy. How does one prove a study or a measurement used in a
study to be true? The short answer is that we do not prove studies to be absolutely 'true'; we
only lend them credibility to the extent that their main hypotheses cannot yet be falsified.
The more consistent a finding, the more credible it becomes. Yet some findings are true
only under specifiable conditions, and thus neither consistency nor inconsistency is enough
to allow us to judge a conclusion to be true. The stronger we can show a relationship to be,
the better; but again strong relationships may be spurious, and weak ones may be of great
theoretical importance. Even while acknowledging such problems, we still attempt
somehow to assess the validity of measurements, studies, and conclusions or interpretations.
And so we must since validity in this broad sense of truth is the elusive goal of science.

Though many terms apply to specific aspects of validity, there are only two basic categories of such terms. The first category is conceptual or theoretical, the second empirical
or measurement-oriented. An assessment of the validity of a study or knowledge claim
depends on judging how well the claim or finding fits with the literature. Such assessments
are of the *construct*, *face*, or *convergent* validity of the claim. This basic idea of convergent
validity is easy to illustrate. Suppose the literature contained a well-documented finding
that workers on assembly lines were more alienated than those who had personal control
over their tasks. If a new claim were made that assembly-line workers were the less alienated, such a claim would run counter to what we would expect. It would not be a good fit.
Given some confidence in the existing literature, we would have to examine the study in
question cautiously. A particular *measurement* is also said to display convergent validity
when it correlates with other *measures* of the same thing, particularly when we have some
confidence in these other measures; but, for obvious reasons, convergence among measures
is better understood as an example of measurement-oriented validity.

Consequently, assessments of theoretical or conceptual validity tend to be biased against
revolutionary findings. Studies that corroborate what is considered well established are
judged to have higher validity than those that contradict such material, other things being
equal. For obvious reasons many scientists are uneasy with this attitude because, if science
is, by definition, an exploration of frontiers, new and contradictory findings must not be set
aside simply because they lack consistency with the received science. If so, where would
revolutionary findings come from? But such questions take us into the sociology of science,
which is not our current concern.

The second type of validity, being empirical or measurement-oriented, is easier to grasp
and use. It is also far more likely to be stressed by scientists who take a positivistic point of
view. Measurement-oriented concepts of validity involve assessing our ability to *use* in a
fruitful way the measurement we have made. Thus if we have a valid measure of 'liberated
women', we ought to be able to discriminate between them and non-liberated women, both
now (*concurrent* validity) and in relation to some future activity (*predictive* validity), such as
a willingness to support equal rights legislation or to strike for equal pay for work of equal

value. If we have an invalid measure or scale of female liberation, someone's score on it will not help us predict a woman's attitude towards these issues.

The main reason that measurement-oriented conceptions of validity are less problematic is that they use a fairly clear *criterion*, a yardstick against which we can measure the accuracy of our measure or claim. *Assuming* that the criterion is, in fact, a good yardstick, then we can regard any measurement or statement that is inconsistent with it as invalid or less valid than a competitor. In this same vein, social scientists use the phrase 'validation against outside criteria'. This notion suggests that if I am trying to measure the excellence of students, others will assess my measurement as more valid if it identifies as excellent students those who are also nominated by teachers and other students as such, who regularly appear on the school's honour roll, and who regularly receive A's. If my measurement is consistent with these *outside* criteria, one could say mine is fairly valid.

Since the real question in using these criterion-related measurements of validity is the appropriateness of the yardstick selected, measurement-oriented scales of validity are related to theoretical measures. After all, who says that being on the honour roll is itself a good criterion of excellence among students? Perhaps this status is only a measure of their popularity. And if my identification of liberated women does not, in fact, predict accurately who will strike, perhaps my measure is none the less valid, but the need for income is an even stronger factor in predictions of who will strike. Thus, in both cases—theoretical validity issues and measurement validity issues—it is simply unclear that validity can actually be demonstrated, at least unambiguously. Nonetheless, we can all agree that some arguments are far less convincing than others. Scientists do operate within fairly strong constraints, as do the critics they must legitimately satisfy.

Those social scientists who are uncomfortable with a positivistic position concerning validity consider it a matter perhaps best established by those most immediately involved and in the natural environment of those actors. That is, they often take the position that only the actors themselves can tell us if our studies are accurate and that we ought to evaluate our claims by seeking validation from the community, group, or situation we are trying to understand. This is referred to as *member or host validation*. It amounts to little more than being able to claim to have discussed our analysis with the actors, who in turn acknowledged its accuracy. A still more practical, though perhaps crude, way in which accuracy is assessed by those of a more qualitative bent is simply to try to put into practice what the sociologist has claimed to be so. For example, if a study of hobos is accurate, it would seem to follow that a competent and careful student of that study should be able to 'pass' successfully as a hobo, speaking their language, and displaying enough familiarity with their culture to be able to survive in their environment. Short of this rather risky criterion, we may simply take the position that a claim will be judged to be valid to the extent that no one can suggest plausible criticisms or alternative interpretations. Or we may evaluate it as displaying validity to the extent that when the claim is set out in the public domain (through publication or the circulation of an unpublished paper) readers do not suggest exceptions but on the contrary can support it from their own experiences. Thus, if it matches the experiences of others, it can be said, albeit tentatively, to be valid. Finally, the validity of such claims is assessed in the light of the description of the data provided by the author, and the internal consistency and progressive refinement of the description and explanation testify to the accuracy of both. Data gathered in this manner are claimed to be accurate because they are gathered in the natural environment over a long enough time that one can have considerable confidence that the behaviour described is fairly typical of what occurs in the environment and was not produced for the researcher or by the artificiality of the data collection situation, as sometimes appears to be the case in discussions of experiments or survey research. Later in this chapter, when participant observation is discussed, we will see that it is by these kinds of qualitative assessments of validity that micro-interpretivists would usually evaluate the validity of a study. In experiments or surveys, it is the earlier more measurement-oriented notions of validity that will be used most often.

## The Translation of Concepts into Percepts:
## Operational Definition or Measurement

The translation of theoretical concepts like excellence into empirically observable referents, such as having one's name on the honour roll, cannot succeed fully because our percepts are simply not equivalent to our concepts. For this reason, theory—which is purely conceptual—is never really tested and can never be either verified or falsified by empirical testing alone. What allows us to translate concepts into percepts, is operational definitions, which we can assess in terms of both validity and reliability.

In terms of validity, an ideal operational definition is a measurement rule that captures everything we mean by a given concept and no more than that. Ideally it would be completely equivalent to, or isomorphic with, the concept. Though such complete equivalence is impossible, we can still compare attempts along this dimension. In other words, how well do operational definitions capture the meaning of the concept? How clearly do they succeed in measuring only what we want to measure and not something else? For instance, as we discussed earlier, one could propose to measure juvenile delinquency by examining court records of the cases tried under, for example, the Young Offenders Act where the defendant was found guilty. Although such an operational definition bears a relationship to the concept we want to measure, it is not the only or necessarily the most effective or most valid operational definition. Someone else might operationally define juvenile delinquency from self-report data gathered in a large-scale survey of adolescents asking about violations of the law they had been involved in, regardless of whether they were arrested. This definition would delineate a different group of people from those defined in the first instance. Which is more valid?

Depending on our purposes, either could be more valid, but both are surely more valid than a third definition of juvenile delinquents as adolescents who wear leather jackets, ride motorcycles, and have strange haircuts. This last definition clearly has less validity than either of the former. It covers only a fragment of what we mean by the concept *juvenile delinquent* (thus displaying low construct validity) and may identify punk rockers better than juvenile delinquents. In other words, this operational definition has little of what social scientists call *discriminant* validity because it does not discriminate between motorcycle gang members, punk rockers, and juvenile delinquents.

That is still another of the many meanings of validity, and it is important in terms of measurement-oriented validity. The famous study by Adorno et al. (1950), *The Authoritarian Personality*, is sometimes accused of having low discriminant validity because its central measuring instrument could have simultaneously measured several things as well as the target concept of authoritarian leanings. In our earlier discussion, the question of whether being on the honour roll measures excellence or popularity or both is an issue of discriminant validity.

The better an instrument or operational definition or study is, the more precisely and accurately it measures only what we wish it to, no more and no less. Validity, after all, means accuracy. Valid measures succeed in measuring true differences in the variable that interests us and only those differences.

Operational definitions are less important to qualitatively oriented researchers, whose research style is more open-ended and unstructured and who are less likely to set out to test hypotheses that are themselves arrived at deductively from well-established theories. They usually conduct exploratory research, arriving inductively at general propositions by inspecting concrete cases only. They often build theory at the same time as they select and analyse cases. In fact, qualitative researchers often hold that it is impossible and unwise to begin with some theoretically derived operational definition since flexibility is the key to their research style. They begin instead with what Blumer called 'sensitizing concepts', which function like guidelines for their exploration. These concepts change and are refined in the course of the study. Of course that makes it much harder to replicate qualitative research of this kind, but these researchers value validity more than reliability in any case, and replication is only one of many ways of adding credibility to a study.

## Reliability

The idea of operational definition indicates a linking or transitional procedure that joins concepts to empirically measurable percepts. To this point I have emphasized that there can be several operational definitions of any concept, but the one we want is the one with the greatest evidence of validity. We must assess evidence of validity both in conceptual and empirical terms. It is not possible to make such assessments exclusively on an empirical basis because we must also judge the appropriateness of the criterion variable, and these judgements are fundamentally theoretical. In simpler words, the use of their legal record as a criterion against which to assess our instrument for identifying delinquents assumes that delinquents will have records and that non-delinquents will not. This theoretical position is debatable.

Perhaps because the issues of validity are so debatable and apparently unresolvable for many social scientists, the emphasis seems to have shifted to the reliability or repeatability of measures. At least here scientists feel on firmer ground. Thus operational definitions are most commonly compared, not in terms of validity, but in terms of reliability. 'Good' operational definitions are formulas for measurement that produce consistent results. A measurement of intelligence that consistently results in the same distinctions among the same people is said to be reliable. The reliability of an operational definition or of a study refers then to its repeatability or replicability. Measurements that are highly reliable consistently yield the same results. Measurements with low reliability vary greatly from one measurement to the next. Most commonly, reliability is considered to be the degree of correlation among simultaneous measurements or observations of an event. High reliability simply means that several judges, observers, or measurements agree in their reports of what occurred. Think of the skating judges at an Olympic event. All have been trained to use more or less the same criteria in evaluating a performance, and after the performance is over, their scores are flashed to the audience. Usually their scores will be quite close, though they do their assessments independently. Agreement among judges is known as *inter-observer* or *inter-rater* reliability. In like manner, *inter-item* reliability refers to the extent of agreement among several different items (such as on a questionnaire, for example) designed to measure the same phenomenon.

Inter-item reliability is usually measured by a *split-half* technique. In this procedure, an instrument with 20 separate items on the same area of interest will be split in half, and the investigator can measure the correlation between scores on each half. Because all measures are attempts to get at the same thing, there should be a strong correlation between the two subscores. Social scientists generally interpret such a correlation as evidence of the inter-item reliability of the scale as a whole. We sometimes also look at the correlation between each single item and the score for the entire test (*the item-to-total correlation*), the reasoning again being that good items should correlate strongly with the overall scores and that items that do not probably do not measure whatever the test as a whole is designed to measure.

Reliability over time is also a goal and, though problematic, is probably the most critical aspect of reliability. For example, two different studies using the identical measurement instrument in exactly the same way but at different times may not agree as to the level of alienation of your class. The difference could be due either to a measurement error or to a true change in alienation. Unfortunately it is difficult to say which interpretation is correct, and we do not want either to reject a true hypothesis or to accept a false one. Therefore if a study done at one time suggests one conclusion and a careful replication at another time suggests another, we are unable to decide if one, neither, or both are valid. Lack of reliability therefore opens a virtual Pandora's box of problems.

On the other hand, reliability by itself is no guarantee of validity. Even if both studies produce the same scores on alienation, both may be wrong if, for example, the measurement instrument consistently understates or fails to capture certain elements of alienation. It is therefore never enough to know that a given operational definition consistently divides the world in the same way whenever it is used. Indeed it is for this reason that we generally view the relationship between validity and reliability as asymmetrical. It is often said that validity presupposes reliability but not vice versa. With demonstrable reliability, we can discuss possible validity; but without demonstrable reliability, we have no foothold and cannot begin to decide whether any finding is valid.

As already explained, practitioners of qualitative methods do not believe that reliability is so important. How could they, given their belief in the malleability and fragility of the socially constructed world? Since reliability over time is simply unrealistic and reliability among coders or observers does not guarantee validity in any case, why make so much of it? Of course the crucial question for them is whether validity can be established in the absence of demonstrable reliability (in opposition to the positivistic position), and to that question they must be able to give a persuasive positive answer. As indicated earlier, they try to do so in terms of member validation, 'passing', ability to discount plausible rival explanations, internal consistency, and other such criteria.

## Generalizability

In order for valid and reliable findings to be useful, they must be generalizable to similar events, situations, or groups of people as yet unstudied. Science gives us knowledge that we can use to make sense of the unknown. Clearly a valid study of a unique phenomenon would not aid us at all in this way. Historicists might value such knowledge for its own sake, but it would have little utility. Generalizability requires that the researcher convince the sceptical critic that there is a reason to allow knowledge claims to be extended beyond the data from which they were generated. Most often this is considered to be a sampling issue in which the scientist must demonstrate that her conclusions are based on study of a representative sample of the population to which generalization is desired. With this in mind, positivistically inclined scientists have developed a number of probability sampling methods that, when used properly, will produce samples that are representative of the populations from which they are drawn. In this vein, you may have heard of random samples, systematic samples, stratified samples, cluster samples, or multi-stage probability samples. Where these sampling strategies are followed faithfully, we can confidently generalize to the population from which the samples have been drawn. On the other hand, even with the best design and intentions, we often have achieved samples that are based on response rates of 30 per cent or so, and in these circumstances it seems legitimate to wonder if the respondents are a biased sample of those originally contacted. If so, of course, one cannot legitimately generalize from the sample to the entire population.

In practice the issue is most often one of political negotiation, since we generalize from non-representative samples as well as those that are demonstrably representative. In reality the scientist can generalize as widely as her critics, including herself, will allow her to, though confidence in such generalizability depends on our assessment of the likelihood that the sample is in fact representative of the relevant population. Some psychologists have been known to generalize to all humanity from an introspective study of the workings of their own minds. Their rationale is that in fundamentals at least all minds are the same. Hence, if they are, a sample of one is truly representative and is a perfectly adequate basis for generalization. Freud generalized to all human beings from a small sample of neurotic Viennese women. Piaget developed generalized models of development and learning among all human beings from the study of a small sample of children. Only recently have such generalizations come under critical scrutiny.

Suppose I were to study the relationship between gender and attitudes to marriage in your own class. Would you allow me to generalize to this relationship among people your age everywhere in the world, in the Western world, in North America, in university in North America, in your college or university, or in your class? The decision is yours.

Reasons might be brought to bear favouring each alternative, but the outcome would be negotiated between the scientist and his or her scientific critics. Certainly the more widely generalizable the findings, the more powerful they are.

Interpretivists working in a qualitative tradition may well not be interested in generalizing at all, as noted earlier in the discussion of historicism. They may be satisfied with producing a 'thick description', a richly evocative account of the group or situation they are studying, with alternative interpretations provided along with theirs, so that the reader can see all the relevant evidence and assess it for themselves. Or they may take the position that they do wish to generalize and can do so in several ways. Most simply, qualitative researchers justify generalizations to the real world on the grounds that their studies are generated in that real world, rather than in the artificial environment of the laboratory experiment or survey. Since their behaviour specimens are more typical of the real world, generalization to that world is warranted.

Sometimes they justify generalizability by analysing the specifics of their topic for what it reveals about something more generic. That is, every specific interaction, actor, or situation can be seen as an example of a category or type of interaction, actor, or situation, and the qualitative researcher displays his or her sociological imagination in using the topical or specific to provide insight into the generic or more categorical (see Lofland, 1976). Just how one moves from the topical to the generic is not clear; the relationship between the two is not that of a sample drawn from a population, but more like finding the generality of which any particular can be seen as an example if only we have the imagination. In other words, again it is more inductive. Such researchers are in any case quite happy to allow the audience to decide whether the claims they make are generalizable. The factor by which generalization is usually limited is the description of a negative (or disconfirming) case. The negative case at least sets an outside limit on the generic in that it does not extend so far as this.

## Causality

When we move beyond classification, description, and prediction into explanation, we encounter difficulties in demonstrating causality. Indeed many scientists try to avoid causal language by speaking only of correlations, but if we are interested in explaining why something happens, we are interested in its cause, call it what you will. Causal relationships are extremely difficult to demonstrate, and the adequacy of explanation rests heavily on the adequacy of just this demonstration. Causality is a key dimension in terms of which we can compare explanatory studies.

Four criteria must be satisfied before we accept the claim that one variable is the cause of change in another. These are (1) association, (2) time priority, (3) non-spuriousness, and (4) rationale.[1]

*Association* In order for one variable to be the cause of the other, they must vary together (or 'co-vary'); if they did not, it would make no sense to claim that one caused the other. Although this appears simple enough, it is not always clear which things co-vary. Researchers must recognize association before any causal argument can begin. For example, many novice marijuana smokers have to learn that their increased desire to eat is, in fact, associated with use of the drug. The association is present but often goes unrecognized until pointed out.

*Time Priority* Causes occur before effects. Independent variables must occur or change before the dependent variable occurs or changes if a causal connection exists between the two. This seems simple enough, but it is not always clear in our data which variable occurs first. Since we usually gather data on all variables at the same time we do not have the first-hand opportunity of seeing which comes first. Thus going away to school may well lead to increased psychological independence, but it is also possible that increased psychological independence leads to going away to school. As suggested in the previous chapter, broken homes may produce juvenile delinquency, but the co-variation could also indicate that the presence of juvenile delinquents produces broken homes.

*Non-spuriousness* Spuriousness or non-spuriousness refers to the inference one may make from the association between two variables that their relationship is causal. If the relationship is truly causal, it is also non-spurious. If the relationship is really only accidental, we say the inference of causality is spurious. In this instance the correlation is real, but it is not causal. It is really the reasoning to causality from it that is spurious. Remember our discussion in chapter 2 of the relationship between broken homes and delinquency and particularly of our conclusion that a third variable might account for the correlation between them.

The non-spuriousness requirement could well be the most exacting criterion of causality. A great deal of methodology consists of advice about designing studies to provide reasonable assurance that the relationships we interpret as causal are not accidental (or spurious). Our discussion of rival hypotheses, such as in the Lipset example, dealt with the possible spuriousness of inferring a causal connection from the association between national differences in culture and differences in divorce rates. In that argument I raised the possibility that the relationship between those variables might have been accidental and due only to the fact that another variable was related to both the alleged independent and dependent variables. Any change in it alone would then result in simultaneous change in both independent and dependent variables, not because they were causally connected but because each was related to this third variable.

Schematically what I am proposing is the contrast between Lipset's proposed causal sequence (I) and the rival (II), as shown in Figure 3.4. In the schema, A is correlated with B. Lipset's reasoning is that A causes B. But C also exists and is related to both A and B such that change in C could explain why A and B co-vary. Such co-variance between A and B might then be considered accidental rather than causal, an accidental effect caused by the fact that both A and B are related to C. As illustrated further in that discussion, there might be more than one so-called third variable. In order for a scientist to term a relationship causal, then, he or she must convince us that there are no such third variables that might plausibly explain away what seems to be a causal connection. Careful attention to research design and methodology is what allows us to exercise sufficient control over our studies that

Figure 3.4 A Causal and a Spurious Relationship Illustrated

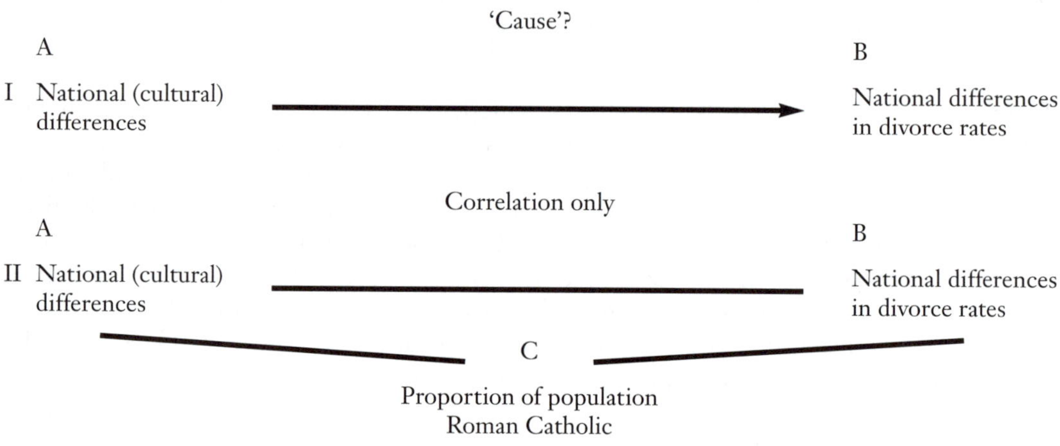

'Cause'?

A                                                                          B

I  National (cultural)                                             National differences
   differences        ─────────────────────────►      in divorce rates

Correlation only

A                                                                          B

II National (cultural)                                            National differences
   differences        ────────────────────────────      in divorce rates

                                        C
                        Proportion of population
                            Roman Catholic

third variables are anticipated and either eliminated in advance so that they can have no effect or measured so that we can see exactly what effect they do have.[2]

*Rationale* The most basic of all criteria for assessing causality is rationale. We must, above all, have good reason to believe that a relationship is causal. No amount of statistical expertise can replace rationale. Rationale is based on the findings already reported in the relevant literature and on the theory that underlies these findings. If an association exists where theoretically it makes little sense to expect to find a causal relationship, we ought to be suspicious, expecting to be able to find that it is only spurious. If no relationship exists where theory and literature review have convinced us that it ought to, we ought again to be suspicious that some related factor has distorted the real relationship or suppressed the causal association. The upshot of this is that statistical findings are insufficient by themselves, for positive findings may be spurious, and negative findings could be evidence of a suppressor variable. The crucial element is rationale: it allows or tells us how to interpret what the statistical outcome shows.

Only if an argument can meet all four criteria do we normally grant it causal status. Since causation is the crucial element of explanation, that is what we must have, and it is in those terms that we can most readily evaluate arguments.

Non-positivists also make causal arguments and are concerned with these same criteria. They often conduct studies that carry on over a longer period (called longitudinal studies) than the snapshot surveys usually conducted by positivists. For that reason, at least in the context of these kinds of studies, they might argue that their knowledge of time priority is far stronger than what can be provided in many positivistic methods. They are also in a position to test for non-spuriousness by carefully collecting and assessing the evidence needed to test alternatives as they arise. For such reasons, among others, non-positivists frequently suggest that such qualitative methods are even stronger with respect to the demonstration of causality than are most positivistic methods.

In point of fact, the methods of the 'soft' scientists do have a hard time when a critic examines their reliability, and the methods of the 'hard' scientists do not easily satisfy a critic who stresses validity. A closer look at the methods themselves should clarify this debate.[3] In the following sections I will introduce first the major methods of the soft social scientists and then the major methods of the hard scientists. I note potential problems and advantages of these methods and encourage the reader to try to assess the adequacy with which the various methods address the issues introduced throughout this book.

## THE SOFT METHODS OF THE MICRO-INTERPRETIVE SCHOOL

### Participant Observation

Participant observation (PO) is the method favoured by most sociologists who want to get an insider's view of the world. Though, technically, participant observation describes any field method where the scientist is simultaneously a member of a group studied and student of it—regardless of the extent of participation—the term generally refers to social scientists' attempts to participate without influencing the group or organization they are trying to understand. If one thinks of PO as occurring along a theoretical continuum, the reasons become more obvious. (See Gold, 1958: 217–23.)

At the complete-observer end of the continuum (as in voyeurism or watching through a one-way mirror), the scientist must infer the meaning of the behaviour observed. Since he may well err in such inference, this position is sometimes called that of the 'Martian observer'. The suggestion is that such an observer is as unlikely as a Martian to make the correct inferences about the actors' behaviour. At the other end of the continuum, the scientist is no longer scientist, but convert. He has lost any ability to analyse the behaviour as an outsider; this is termed 'going native'. Reports produced (*if* produced) by 'natives' are not usually given much credence. For these reasons the participant observer normally makes every effort to keep at a distance from the actors yet close enough to them and active enough in sharing their world to be able eventually to understand them as much as possible the way a native does—while keeping one foot in the other camp that is science. Since great pressures push one to move along the continuum in response to the demands and expectations of others in the situation (both 'natives' and researchers), participant observation is like walking a tightrope in a high wind. It is a risky methodology, potentially rewarding but equally demanding.

Figure 3.5  The PO Continuum (following Gold)

| Complete observer | Participant as observer | Observer as participant | Complete participant |
| --- | --- | --- | --- |

Participant observation confronts the researcher with ethical problems that are more dramatic if not more frequent than those of other methods. These may occur at the outset of the project, as a result of the strategy chosen to gain access to the subjects or during the project, as a result of participating in the subjects' lives.

Participant observers do not always introduce themselves as social scientists to those whose worlds they wish to enter. Sometimes such a declaration would invalidate any subsequent study. More often, the study would not be allowed, as in a case where the sociologist wishes to study a cult, a wealthy or powerful élite, or a deviant group of some kind. By pretending to be an authentic participant he or she may sometimes gain access but there are obvious ethical and practical problems. Ethically such pretence automatically violates the rights of subjects to know that they are subjects of study and makes it impossible for them to give informed consent. In practical terms such pretence restricts the researcher to what is normal for participants in similar positions in the group. In other words, pretending to be a prisoner may allow you access to the world of the prisoners, but it will not enable you to examine prison records or to interview the warden. Pretending to be a mental patient may allow you to talk with other patients, but it will not allow you to interview their doctors. You may be able to understand the actors' definitions of the situation since you are one, but often you cannot ask others the questions a sociologist might. For these reasons most experts in participant observation recommend that the covert, or disguised, kind be avoided and that, if at all possible, you let others know you want to study their world by participating in it to some extent.

Since participant observation involves the researcher personally in the world of the actors, other ethical problems occur as well. Some result from particular knowledge the researcher has that is potentially harmful to the subjects. Unlike most surveys, in participant observation the subjects are not anonymous. Their attributes, attitudes, explanations, and the like can be associated with the particular individuals involved. The social scientist may well know who is sleeping with whom, who is cheating on their income tax, or who is feeling guilty about how they have treated others. Since more often than not participant observation studies deal with the 'deviant', the subject's vulnerability and the social scientist's potential power are increased. The threat to subjects is increased still more since social-science knowledge is not accorded the status of privileged communication such as that between client and lawyer. Taken all together these considerations have often created serious ethical dilemmas for the participant observer.

Participant observers take part in the real world of their subjects. Though they may wish to stay on the outskirts, they can also be urged to participate more fully in the way of life being studied. In the course of studying juvenile delinquents, athletes, executives, or criminals, participant observers could be asked to help their subjects commit illegal acts; at the very least they may well have prior knowledge of such acts. The actors will interpret the behaviour of the social scientists in such instances as a measure of how much they can be trusted; if researchers lose this trust, their study will be of little value. In other words, because they are participants, they are accountable not only to their academic advisers but also to their subjects. The fact that they are not safely ensconced in the laboratory or library thus creates ethical problems for the participant observer that, though not peculiar to this method, are more common and often more severe than with other research methods.

If the subjects can sometimes affect the social scientist's behaviour, the reverse can also happen. The presence of a social scientist might affect the behaviour of the subjects. This phenomenon is called *reactivity*. There is reactivity in all research where the subjects know they are being studied. It is variable in so far as some circumstances make it both reasonable and possible for some actors, but not others to alter their behaviour. Remember those days in elementary school when the principal sat in on your classroom or looked in through a window? Did the principal's presence result in unnatural behaviour from the students? Such reactivity is important to us because, as social scientists, our interest lies primarily in generalizing to cases as yet unstudied that resemble the ones being examined. To the extent that reactivity distorts the behaviour under study, that behaviour is no longer natural and hence no longer generalizable to like cases where no observer is present.

Participant observation deals with the possibility of reactivity in several ways. First, participant observers try to remain marginal to the group. They certainly would not wish to be in a position analogous to that of the principal. Second, participant observers are committed to longitudinal research, and it is their experience that the reactive effects of an observer tend to wear off over a short time. Third, it is the premise of participant observation that in the real world it is not possible to maintain a false front for any length of time. The day-to-day constraints of the situation force the subjects to revert quickly to their usual behaviour. In point of fact it is sometimes argued that reactivity is a more serious problem in methods that involve data collection at only one point in time. For example reactivity is greater when interviews are conducted by people considered (by the respondents) to be of higher status than they are. Reactivity is increased when the topic of the interview is a sensitive one. It is increased still more when the interview is conducted in a place not part of the subject's normal world. Experiments too are accused of reactivity in so far as the subjects often try to guess the nature of the study and act as they think the researcher expects. Such 'expectancy effects' or 'demand characteristics of the situation', as they are often called, are reactive effects that make you wonder what is really being studied and how characteristic of natural behaviour that displayed in the experiment actually is.

To the participant observer, problems of validity and reliability are additional important concerns. It is highly unusual to have two participant observers simultaneously conduct a single study. More often it is a method employed by an individual scientist, and a method in which the perceptiveness of the individual researcher is crucial to what he is able to see and to how he interprets it. In fact, it is widely acknowledged that in participant observation, as in most qualitative research methods, the investigator *is* the tool. That being the case, reliability simply cannot be demonstrated to the sceptical critic after the report has been completed, nor is the study replicable in the sense that a different researcher can believe that he or she would have produced the same analysis. Without demonstrable reliability, validity becomes most problematic to those who are positivistically inclined. Of course with either significant reactivity or over-identification, any wary audience might well doubt the validity or accuracy of the data. Ultimately participant-observation studies are filtered through the interpretations of the single observer. While strategies have been devised to control for possible errors in sampling, data gathering, presentation and interpretation of data, claims to validity and reliability rest finally on the ability and willingness of the sociology community to compare the participant observation reports with what they have read elsewhere or experienced themselves.

If ethics, reliability, and validity are the central problematic aspects of participant observation, the major advantage of participant observation is that it is a temporally sensitive methodology more capable than most others of chronicling change over time. Participant observation is a longitudinal method, and all such methods can, in addition to their capacity to describe change, generate clearer information on time priority than any cross-sectional case study or survey done at a single point in time. Perhaps the principal advantage of participant observation is that, alone of all methodologies available, it allows the successful practitioner to enter the actor's world of meaning and share and understand their definitions of the situation and their own culture. This can give participant observation accounts a sense of depth, sensitivity, and validity rarely attained in experiments or social surveys. In well-done accounts, the researcher's analysis has the ring of truth.

## Other Soft Methods

The interpretive position has encouraged social scientists to develop other methods in an effort to share the definition of the situation of actors. Whether through life histories, qualitative content analysis, thick (intensive) description, introspection, historical study, or discourse analysis, for example, the goal of these efforts is to get inside the minds of the actors and to learn from them what 'makes them tick'. The researcher's purpose may be situationally specific and descriptive; it may be to develop grounded theory through constant comparison and a systematic search for negative cases; it may be to emancipate those with whom the research deals. It may seek to be defensible by the standard criteria discussed earlier; it may eschew such standards, claiming to be more art than science; or it may fall anywhere between these extremes. As noted much earlier, there are a wide variety of methods and a wide variety of purposes held by the researchers who employ them.

Many of the so-called soft methods generally produce qualitative research of a case-study variety in which intensive analysis of a single case is treated as a representative slice of life. Some practitioners of such methods avoid the issue of generalization by claiming to be interested only in understanding the single case in its own right and exhaustively. Others claim that a deep understanding of a single group, organization, or even individual can produce legitimately generalizable knowledge about human behaviour to the extent that, at a deep enough level, we are all alike. Thus we can take information on how one couple adapts to divorce, for example, and legitimately extend it not merely to other divorced couples but also to all people undergoing stress. We can take an insightful self-analysis or introspection and from it develop insight into the development of identity in general and for everyone, or into the process by which moral standards are acquired. The question of the external validity of such claims is not easy to resolve, but you may recall that I suggested earlier that generalizability was not primarily a technical issue of sampling but one of negotiation—whether as consumer or producer, *you* participate in that negotiation.

## SOCIAL-STRUCTURAL THEORISTS AND HARD METHODS

Two primary hard (or positivistic) quantitative methods predominate: experiment and survey. Both are hard in that they are centrally concerned with demonstrable reliability and careful quantitative measurement throughout. Both are also hard in the sense that their emphasis on reliability leads to careful operational definitions of terms and considerable emphasis on identifying and measuring the independent effects of each variable present. Finally both are hard in the sense meant by robustness, which means anyone can replicate them fairly easily, at least in modified form. That is not so clear with most qualitative methods, which depend more on the talent of the particular investigator involved. Either in research design or analysis, the emphasis here is on control of variables and picking apart the intricately interwoven complex of attitudes, values, and structural circumstances that produces a given behaviour. By contrast, the qualitative methodologist tends to emphasize a comprehensive and sensitive description of behaviour in all its natural complexity.

### Experiment

Experimental methods are widely respected and regarded as the scientific method par excellence because they give the scientist maximum control over the variables at hand. The fundamental idea of experiment is that only the independent variable—as administered, altered, and measured by the investigator—will distinguish between the experimental and control group. The scientist who can accomplish this can be certain that differences in the effect or dependent variable, as measured at time two, must be a function of the independent variable.

Figure 3.6 The Classic Pre-Test/Post-Test Control Group Design

| | *Time One* | | *Time Two* |
|---|---|---|---|
| R (random assignment to the experimental group) | 01 (observation of the dependent variable, e.g., attitudes to pornography) | X (exposure to experimental stimulus, e.g., film on effects of pornography) | 02 (remeasure attitudes to pornography) |
| R (random assignment to the control group) | 03 (observation of the scores of the control group— same instrument) | | 04 (remeasure) |

The difference measured at time two minus the initial small difference that may be present at time one, even with random assignment, is attributable to X or, to be very careful, possibly to the effects of X on a group already observed at time one. Since there are no other differences between the groups or their experiences, there are no other plausible ways of accounting for the time-two difference. It is randomization, or the random assignment of subjects to the control and experimental group, that accomplishes this equivalence between the two groups. All variables, both known and unknown, are distributed approximately equally in the two (or more) groups in the design. That being the case, most of what Campbell and Stanley (1963) refer to as threats to internal validity no longer apply since they do not systematically differentiate between the groups of the design. Thus, for example, the two groups will display about the same age distribution, the same proportion of males and females, about the same ethnic composition, the same average intelligence, and the same motivation. In both groups, the subjects will be equally likely to drop out of the study (this phenomenon is called experimental mortality) or mature or get tired or become sensitized, and both groups will be equally affected by other time-related variables like the historical events that take place during the study. Randomization is the feature by which experimental designs eliminate all other rival hypotheses.

Experimental methodology is quantitative and precise. It is easy to see that with careful operationalization this method generally satisfies the scientific demand for reliability and demonstration of causality.[4] Its validity depends to some extent on operationalization. If experiments often have to transform the stimulus from its form in the real world to one more appropriate to the laboratory, or allow expression of its effects only in specific ways not natural to the real world, the critic can suggest that the experiment is incapable of informing us about the phenomenon at hand. Thus, experiments concerning the possible relationship between exposure to pornography and assaults against women—a real-world problem of enormous importance—have been criticized for both their operationalization of exposure to pornography and their measures of the dependent variable as well. Critics claim that in both cases the experiment simply fails to represent the real world closely enough to be able to tell us anything about what goes on there. (See the article appended to this chapter for an example.)

One of the most severe potential problems of experiments, as was true of most qualitative methods, has to do with generalizability. Experiments are usually contrived or artificial and conducted in the unnatural environment of the laboratory. Questions arise about the resemblance of behaviour produced under laboratory conditions to natural behaviour in the real world. Thus the results may be internally valid in the laboratory but not generalizable elsewhere. Of course the other major limitation of experimental designs is that they require a great deal of control over the circumstances, control that is not always possible. Social scientists are often not able to assign subjects to an experimental or control group and measure their responses. We do not assign children to families that will experience a divorce and others that will not. We do not decide which societies will industrialize or go to war.

At the same time social scientists can sometimes approximate the ideal conditions of a true experiment by engaging in what Donald Campbell (1969) calls 'quasi-experiments'. These are real-world situations the scientist can take advantage of by selecting cases to fit the requirements of a valid experiment. The most important requirements are repeated measurement and comparison to similar cases that differ only in strategic ways, that is, in ways the scientist thinks relevant and informative. For instance the sociologist often knows in advance that a law will be changed; for example, the speed limit may be lowered in one of two similar provinces or states. Knowing this gives her the opportunity to gather data on the type and number of accidents before the new speeding limit is imposed and after. If the two provinces or states are nearly identical in all other relevant ways (that is, in ways relevant to the production of accidents, such as climate or number of police but not necessarily in population or average height), the conclusion that differences at time two are attributable to the legal change is relatively credible. This design relies on a strategy of *matching* characteristics in the comparison groups in order to translate other rival hypotheses into constants. Matching, however, is not as effective as randomization (and hence quasi-experiments are not as effective or persuasive as true experiments), because the researcher can never be certain that all relevant variables have been matched or that the matching is precise enough.

In the example above, the interpretation that a change in the accident rate is due to a legal change would not be certain if—as I have emphasized repeatedly—the change might have been due to other plausible independent variables. Thus any other relevant differences between the provinces or states in question—for example in age distributions, policing, or education—could have produced the observed differences. Hence the quasi-experiment is more credible than studies done where there are more rival hypotheses but less credible than a perfect experiment would have been if that had been possible. Unfortunately, perfection is rarely attainable. In the social sciences we are usually content if we can improve our work, making it more credible than it might have been, and more defensible against its critics.

### Survey Research

The experimental design seeks control by eliminating all sources of potential variation other than the scientist's variables of interest. Thus one obtains control but only by substantially narrowing the focus. The experimenter is often accused of helping us to learn more and more about less and less. The variables that are held constant have no differential effect on the dependent variable, and this is what experimentalists want; but since they are excluded or held constant, we cannot see what effect they might have had, either by themselves, in interaction with, or in relation to, other variables of interest.

In that regard the strategy of survey research is quite different. Whereas experiments are usually done with only a few subjects, the strength of survey research lies in the large numbers of subjects. Survey research does not often eliminate many rival hypotheses in advance during the design stage of a research project. In surveys the researcher often asks a great many questions and measures a great many variables. The investigator carefully operationalizes all plausible rival hypotheses as well as the major or working hypothesis and makes the measurements necessary to test each of them. Rather than experimental control by which rivals are excluded or not allowed to vary, the survey researcher employs statistical control after the data are collected to isolate and analyse the effects of each variable of interest.

For example, suppose the researcher were interested in how attitudes toward pornography are affected by watching a film dealing with the effects of pornography. The simplest experimental design has no provision for looking at the effects of sex or education or marital status on this issue. The researcher may well hold these variables constant since they could otherwise be confused with the effects of the movie *per se*. To eliminate their effects the experimenter may decide to allow only single males in the first year of university to participate. Or the experimenter might randomly assign subjects to the experimental and control groups in the belief that if the groups are identical, the effects of all these variables will be the same, though unknown, in both groups. Hence these variables will not explain any difference in group average scores found at time two.

In the survey these and most other variables will be allowed to vary, and they will be tapped in the interview or questionnaire used to gather data, for example, from a large number of all kinds of people who come out of a theatre, having seen the film in question. With such data on a large sample of subjects, the survey researcher will be able to divide the subjects by sex or education or marital status, analyse the effects of exposure to the film separately for men and women, for the well and the not-so-well educated, and for the single and the married.

Surveys usually have no pre-test measurement. They are one-shot cross-sectional studies done at only one point in time. They could be done with a pre-test, but cost usually makes this prohibitive. Instead the survey researcher usually asks retrospective questions concerning earlier attitudes or events. In this example, he might well try to find out what the respondents' attitudes were before seeing the film. Of course respondents may not give valid information for any number of reasons, but survey researchers must live with such limitations, minimizing and measuring them as best they can.

The advantages of survey research are generalizability, efficiency in the sense of data generated per unit of cost, and the ability to handle more variables than are common in experimental designs. The weaknesses of surveys include the difficulties they frequently have in demonstrating causality (since all data are usually gathered at one time) and their reliance on verbal reports. They depend on the willingness and ability of respondents to give accurate information, and they must assume a strong correlation between what people say and what they do. This assumption is seriously problematic (Deutscher, 1973).

## CONCLUSION

For those who, whether micro-interpretive or macro-structural in perspective, accept it, the challenge of explaining variation in human behaviour remains the same. In some manner we must be able to gather the information we deem relevant to the behaviour in question to see if our proposed pattern, regularity, or hypothesis is consistent with what is, in fact, observed. We must exercise great care that alternative explanations are also considered since our working hypothesis gains credibility only if it cannot be discounted and if other rivals can. Doing the job credibly and defensibly requires attention to validity, reliability, causality, and generalizability, though how social scientists deal with these issues will depend on whether they are positivistically inclined or otherwise and on exactly what criteria they think are legitimate and important.

The actual methods used to collect data may vary depending on our orientation. Researchers interested in interpretive independent variables tend to collect data by participant observation or other intensive field methods designed to get inside the actors' minds. Researchers interested in structural independent variables often adhere as closely as possible to the methods of the natural sciences, conducting experiments and surveys to gather data on structural patterns. Both kinds of methodologies have advantages and disadvantages. The researcher must be prepared to defend her or his choice and use of either methodological strategy in any particular case and in all of its particulars. Several illustrations of some of the complex decisions social scientists must make when conducting empirical studies will be considered in a later chapter.

## SAMPLE QUESTION AND AN ANSWER

In the previous chapter, dealing with the general nature of science, you learned what hypotheses are, where they come from, and what they look like. The following question asks you to identify variables, decide whether they are independent or dependent, and then, using resources introduced in chapter 3, provide the theoretical reasoning by which you might make the case that they are linked causally to one another. This reasoning may well lead you to consider additional variables and the possible role they might play in the relationship. It could even lead you to reconsider the nature or direction of the relationship. That is no more than we would expect from the open-minded consideration of the issues that become evident when the statement is systematically explored and considered. Before reading the discussion of the question that follows it, take a few minutes to think about how you might answer this question if it were on an examination in this course.

### Question
'The residential segregation of different social classes and ethnic groups is one factor producing ethnic and class cultures'. What are the variables in this statement? What is the hypothesis, rephrased in your own words? What other factors might be interesting to examine in light of this hypothesis, and why, in each case?

### Discussion of Answer
Perhaps the first advice for students confronting this kind of question for the first time is to examine all parts of the question and then organize their answers so that each part is addressed. Instructors usually assign a certain number of marks to each part of the question. In this example, students receive one point each for stating the correct independent and dependent variable, three for restating the hypothesis correctly, and the remaining five for referring to two or three other variables of interest, in each case explaining why each might be interesting. Failure to address a part of the question means losing the points set aside for that portion. It is not a wise decision. Even if time is short, it is probably wiser to answer each part of the question briefly than to answer one part thoroughly.

In this statement, students are expected to identify the variables correctly and to recognize which are independent and dependent. The independent variable (the cause) is residential segregation. The dependent variable, or effect, is some feature of ethnic and class cultures. You can tell which is independent and which is dependent in the statement if you remember that independent refers to the cause and dependent refers to the effect. The quotation says that 'residential segregation is one factor *producing* ethnic and class cultures'; remember that causes produce effects. Though it may strike you that in real life it is culture that leads to or produces residential segregation, in this statement, segregation is the independent variable, though you could mention this opposite interpretation of a cross-sectional correlation (if that is how you envision the situation) in a later part of the question.

Since hypotheses are 'testable statements of specific relationships between variables', we need to state the specific relationship (not merely direction) between residential segregation and the production of culture. That is, we have to explain how, according to the hypothesis, specific change in the independent variable is expected to cause specific changes in the value of the dependent variable. Perhaps the simplest way to do that in this case would be to suggest that where segregation occurs, classes are produced (whereas where segregation does not occur, classes will not be produced). Thus, the presence of one causes the presence of the other. Or, as the value of the independent changes from absent to present, the value of the dependent does likewise. But this is a rather crude dichotomous measure of the values of variables that could be thought of as varying not merely categorically or nominally, but ordinally or even more precisely. One might suggest that the more intense, the more widespread, or the stronger the residential segregation, the more vital the cultures or the sooner they will be produced or the faster they will occur, though here we are beginning to reach somewhat in order to spell out the details of a relationship that is left rather unspecified in the existing statement of relationship.

Given that the statement says that segregation is *one* factor producing cultures, the most natural way of introducing other interesting factors would be to name *other* factors that also have a role to play in the production of cultures, in other words, other independent variables also related to the same dependent. So you might argue that the size of the (class or ethnic) group or its resources might be positively related to whether a culture will develop; or you might suggest that the more visibly different from the mainstream the class or ethnic group, the more likely it would be that a culture will develop. You could suggest that a different language might be a contributing factor or that the proportion of new immigrants in the group could be relevant. You might suggest that the in-group ideology might play a role or that the ideology (and discriminatory behaviour) of the surrounding society might be part of the story. These and many other factors could be interesting to examine as additional independent variables. Some students also have suggested that income and education could be relevant, but I remind them that since both these variables are themselves constituents of social class they are already in the mix. You could argue, of course, that income or education *per se*, aside from the way these are expressed through residential segregation, could contribute to the development of cultures, though a mechanism other than residential segregation would need to be specified. Again, students have sometimes suggested that preferences and values (living with others of the same heritage, background, religion, beliefs about children, ritual, or whatever) would be another variable accounting for the production of culture. Again I hesitate since such preferences and values are the constituent elements of what culture is, and we do not want to explain the development of culture as an effect of culture, or we would be guilty of arguing a tautology (in which the independent variable and the dependent are really the same thing. Tautologies are true by definition, and hence usually not very informative.)

You could also ignore the strategy by which one seeks additional independent variables, since this is not specifically required in the question, and suggest instead that one could focus on intervening or conditional variables that are interesting in light of the hypothesis. For example, residential segregation may create ethnic or class cultures only where there is a critical mass of residents (a conditional relationship), or it may do so by providing a market for services of all kinds that can be specifically tailored to that ethnic group or class (an intervening relationship). These are not additional independent variables, but they could nevertheless be interesting in light of the hypothesis.

Finally, you could in this context come back to the comment earlier that perhaps the hypothesis as stated (if based on the correlation observed between the two variables) has the causal direction backward, and that it makes more sense theoretically and empirically to examine culture as the independent variable that leads to residential segregation. This objection to the causal interpretation of the correlation on the grounds that time priority has not been demonstrated could lead the student to question the adequacy with which the other criteria for making causal statements have been met in this question. Although the statement provides a correlation, it gives no rationale for the causal nature of the relationship, it fails to address the plausibility of a reversal of the time priority requirement, and it does not address issues of non-spuriousness. Though it is fairly easy to provide a rationale by which residential segregation could influence the development of cultures, a particularly sceptical critic might want to conceptualize at least some of our additional independent variables as extraneous and capable of explaining the correlation as accidental rather than causal.

Thinking in this vein, the critic might suggest that residential segregation is not necessary for the development of culture; to argue this would be to make ecological factors more important than they are in a society increasingly characterized by networks of common interest that are not territorially located or bounded. There is considerable evidence in fact that widely dispersed ethnic populations may develop viable ethnic cultures without residential segregation (see, for example, Goldenberg and Haines, 1992, appended to chapter 5 of this text). Therefore one could argue that discriminatory practices by the surrounding society cause both segregation and the development of ethnic cultures but that any inference of a causal relationship between these two could well be at least partially spurious, based as it is on the outmoded notion that communities can spring up only in shared neighbourhoods. It would be appropriate only to note once again that arguments about spuriousness need to be tested to find out whether the relationship withstands the charge. Simply identifying a more or less plausible extraneous variable does not make the charge of spuriousness correct.

## SELECTED QUESTIONS

1. Reliability and validity are two central concepts in methodology. Explain what each of these terms means, and discuss the relationship between them.

2. How might one best choose among equally reliable operational definitions of a concept?

3. What are the basic issues in demonstrating causality? What sorts of evidence must one present to deal with causality successfully?

4. It is often said that investigators must view human behaviour from the point of view of the actors. What is the basis of such an assertion? How might a macro-structuralist reply?

5. How much variation do you think there is in how people respond to a given set of circumstances? In answering, are you adopting a micro-interpretive or a macro-structural position?

6. If you were to engage in a quasi-experiment comparing two fairly similar classes in the same subject and with the same teacher in an effort to see what difference a change in text-book alone makes, what sorts of rival hypotheses might arise to compete with your desire to attribute differences in average achievement to the difference in text?

## NOTES TO THE CHAPTER

1  This discussion draws from several sources, the most succinct of which is Labovitz and Hagedorn, *Introduction to Social Research*, 3rd edn (New York: McGraw-Hill, 1981).
2  But see chapter 2, note 2.
3  Let me make it clear that not all social-action theorists favour soft methods, though most structuralists do favour hard methods. The ideology of science has led most scientists to try to copy the methods that have been so successful in dealing with the non-human world. Thus the bias and emphasis, regardless of theoretical orientation, have been toward the use of hard methods—quantitative analysis and the like.
4  The pre-test/post-test control group design is only one of many experimental designs. The best discussion of these and related issues is in T.D. Cook and D.T. Campbell, *Quasi-Experimentation* (Boston: Houghton Mifflin, 1979).

## ILLUSTRATIVE READING

The following article is principally a methodological critique of experimental studies linking exposure to pornography with aggression. It displays the same kind of critical and sceptical thinking emphasized thus far in this text. You may well wish to investigate and debate further the substantive and methodological issues raised here.

### THE STUDY OF AGGRESSIVE PORNOGRAPHY: THE VICISSITUDES OF RELEVANCE

*Augustine Brannigan and Sheldon Goldenberg*

This paper reviews some crucial experimental studies of the behavioural consequences of exposure to violent or aggressive pornography and evaluates their validity and relevance as support for censoring pornography in the aftermath of the Meese Commission. We find this research deficient on a number of grounds.

Many designs confound the effects of the stimuli with the anger of the subjects. The theoretical models consistently do not explain the results, and, to the extent that they do, such models do not offer support for censorship policies. The evidence of aggression is ambiguous and subject to contradictory interpretations. Means in factorial designs are reported incompletely, scales constructed incredibly (particularly the Likelihood to Rape Scale), and the experimental procedures relate only questionably to everyday realities. Consequently, while censorship policies might have a sound basis on moral and ideological grounds, this particular strain of research does not constitute a scientific basis for such policies.

It is commonplace for political interests to enforce morality through use of the criminal law. Many examples suggest themselves. The temperance movement quickly comes to mind (Gusfield, 1963), but many others follow, including sundry legislation concerning homosexuality and other 'crimes without victims' like prostitution, gambling, suicide, and abortion (see Becker, 1963; Geis, 1974; Schur, 1965). Sunday or 'blue laws' are another such example, and it can be argued that legislation concerning most criminal offenses and many civil matters also embodies a strong commitment to upholding morality (see Erikson, 1966).

## Social Science and Policy

While we have institutionalized a morality and criminalized deviations from it, we also have enshrined various constitutional guarantees of freedom, freedom of speech and freedom of the press among these. The limits of such freedoms, however, are conditional. The determination of these limits is a social process, and governments respond to public pressures to act when they can be convinced that there is enough sentiment in favour of doing so. As a political product, legislation is not always justified scientifically. When moral constituencies are divided, however, we increasingly insist that governments provide a sound scientific basis for legislation to show that identifiable harm to others is resulting from a specific behaviour. Upon the presentation of such evidence, we consider legislation to prohibit or limit our freedom to behave as we might wish. Thus we justify intervention only when there is harm to innocent third parties. For example, smoking control bylaws stem from some concern for physical harm to third parties attributable to tobacco use, and legislation controlling environmental pollution similarly follows some demonstrable physical harms attributable to it. The criminal sanctioning of drinking and driving is even more obvious. Whether similar harms arise from pornography is consequently a politically relevant question pressed by moralists with the backing of social science (see Fagan, 1984, for an illustration of this collusion; see also Vance, 1986).

In this rationalistic and scientific age, it is not surprising that behavioural scientists respond to what they perceive to be important issues to which their research could contribute. Research funding is more easily available in support of what is defined as important and socially relevant. In the instance of obscenity, since the President's Commission (Commission on Obscenity and Pornography, 1970), there has been a wave of research on the effects of aggressive or violent pornography that contradicts the conclusions of that commission. This research has been cited by the Meese Commission (Attorney General's Commission, 1986) as proof of pornography's harmfulness and forms the backbone of current attempts to stimulate legislative reform and extended regulation on pornography.[1] This scientific rationale is also the common foundation for the unlikely feminist-fundamentalist alliance against pornography. The scientific research has transformed morality into an issue of public safety as psychologists self-consciously seek to influence legal change on the strength of their work (Brannigan and Goldenberg, 1986; Linz, Turner, Hess, and Penrod, 1984; Penrod and Linz, 1984).

The scientific writings of concern in this review are summarized by Donnerstein (1980a; 1980b), Donnerstein and Berkowitz (1981), Malamuth and Donnerstein (1982; 1984), and Zillman (1984), some of the chief investigators in research on aggressive or violent pornography. In addition, there are several critiques of this research (Amoroso and Brown, 1973; Gray, 1982; McCormack, 1985a; McKay and Dolff, 1985). This essay focuses on several elements that merit close attention in weighing the importance of the research. Though this discussion does not touch on all the relevant studies, nor even on the most recent work, it does focus on what we find to be the most important studies. Our criticisms of these studies apply, however, to the entire corpus.

Before analysing these studies, we want to stress that the psychological laboratory experiments we focus on are defended by their proponents as the strongest available methodology for the assessments of treatment effects, stronger than the uncontrolled correlational studies that characterize criminology. Most scientists acknowledge, however, that the price of this potentially heightened internal validity is paid in reduced external validity or generalizability to other subjects in other less artificial settings. The authors of these studies also acknowledge their limitations and are cautious in generalizing from their conclusions. They, nonetheless, have loaned their professional credibility to renewed controls under consideration by various governmental inquiries (the Meese Commission in the United States; the Fraser Commission in Canada; the Klugman Committee in Australia). Because of the importance of this work, a close and critical overview is both timely and desirable. Finally, we are extending a critique of the value of the experimental approach that has been a lively source of debate from the time of Orne (1962) to the recent concerns voiced by Rosenwald (1986). What motivates our interest in this review is the uncritical political currency that such studies have enjoyed during these times of conservative resurgence.

The following pages outline the tradition of aggression contagion studies and their design features. We introduce the specific studies that have been given public prominence, particularly by the Meese Commission. We identify a series of serious weaknesses that should be confronted precisely before these studies are considered as warranting changes in public policy.

## Research Design and Background

The paradigmatic social psychology experiment concerning the effect of aggressive pornography approximates Campbell and Stanley's designation as an example of the 'post-test only control group' design (1966).[2] Subjects are created from a sample, typically of university students in introductory psychology classes. Three groups are created by random assignment. In each of the three groups, subjects are angered by a female confederate who very critically assesses a written assignment prepared by the subjects in what is presented as a learning experiment. Later, each of the groups is exposed to one of three kinds of visual stimuli (neutral, erotic, or aggressive pornography). Finally, subjects are asked to teach the person who earlier had angered them by administering electric shocks for incorrect responses in a bogus learning experiment in which the subjects choose a shock level on a machine from eight keys representing eight levels of graduated shock severity. The level of shock is the measure of aggression. Other designs employ similar procedures for angering subjects (Zillmann, 1984).

Methodologically, the danger of this design, as noted by Gray (1982, pp. 391–3), is that what finally is measured as evidence of aggression is an interaction effect of the stimuli (frustration and type of film) on angered subjects, and the fact that they are first angered may distort the effects of the stimuli considerably from what might be experienced by non-angered subjects. This design does allow for an internally valid comparison of the effects of the three kinds of stimuli on angered subjects. But unless we presume that real world actors are normally angry, interpretations of the effects on non-angered others simply are not defensible.

A factorial research design also is used commonly. In the factorial design, interaction effects can be measured for two or more variables occurring simultaneously. Hence, the effects of different film conditions can be tested separately for male or female retaliatory targets. Alternatively, any other variable could be manipulated at the same time as the film effects. One might complicate this design further by varying the sex of the confederate (male or female), the outcome of the film (positive or negative), the nature of the arousal measurement (physiological or self-report), or the context of the experimental instructions (inhibiting or disinhibiting aggression). In so doing, a complex factorial design with a great many cells is created, thus increasing the difficulty of discerning any pattern in the distribution of cell means. The advantage of the factorial design lies in its capacity to make closer approximations to the real world where multiple simultaneous variables are in operation. Both the post-test only design and the factorial design produce results that are valid for comparative purposes within the groups established for study. In so far as the factorial design is relatively more realistic, it provides a stronger basis for generalization beyond the laboratory, other things being equal. It is, in large part, the seemingly contradictory findings of the many cells of these factorial designs that have troubled researchers seeking a single coherent theory concerning the effects of aggressive pornography.

Pornography studies grow out of aggression research, particularly the research on the effects of media exposure on aggression. The conclusion of this body of research appears to be that media exposure can both facilitate and inhibit aggression. Specifically, new modes of action may be learned by exposure to a model. These modes of action, if practical once, may be retained for reasonably long periods; if a cue situation occurs very similar to the original stimulus, aggression may occur. If exposure occurs within the context of the promise of a reward or positive outcome (i.e., aggression works), it will facilitate aggression. If aggression can be justified, it will be enacted more often, that is, if the exposure is to a situation calling for justifiable aggression similar to the previous condition. On the other hand, if social sanctions and controls are imposed during exposure (i.e., negative evaluation/feedback/instruction), aggression will not be increased. If the outcome is negative (bloody, miserable, painful), aggression may be reduced. If the viewer is exposed to aggressive behaviour that is not justified in the context, inhibition of aggression results (see Baron and Byrne, 1977, pp. 403–52; Goranson, 1970).

The experiments on the effects of erotica, specifically on the aggressive consequences of erotica, are quite consistent with the overall studies. Both inhibitory and facilitative effects have been found (Donnerstein, Donnerstein, and Evans, 1975). Again, many critics feel that the ability to create or facilitate aggression in the laboratory tells us little about factors operating in the real world to produce assault, crimes of violence, or rape (Christensen, 1986; Gross, 1983; Jarvie, 1986, 1987; McKay and Dolff, 1985; Roth, 1982; Soble, 1986; Williams, 1979; Wurtzel and Lometti, 1984).

## Recent Research on Aggression

Two studies lie at the centre of the current debate. The first addresses the separate effects of aggressive and erotic stimuli; the second examines the effect of outcome characteristics on the level of aggression displayed by angry and non-angry men. Both are critical to the current discussion, especially as it concerns censorship.

Donnerstein (1983) sought to examine the independent roles of explicit sexuality and aggression. Male subjects were angered by a male or female confederate and then exposed to one of four films: non-aggressive erotica, aggressive erotica, aggressive non-erotica, or neutral. Self-report data suggest that those exposed to aggressive and aggressive-erotic stimuli found them about equally aggressive. The erotic and the aggressive-erotic stimuli also were found to be equally arousing. The mean shock intensity directed to the confederate in the

Figure 1 Mean Shock Intensity: Four Films × All Subjects Angry (Two Targets)

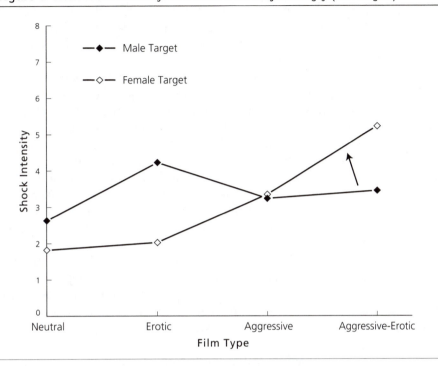

subsequent learning experiment was recorded separately for male and female targets for each of the four conditions.

In terms of design features, all subjects were male in this experiment and all of them were angered before exposure to the stimulus. Important new features of this experiment include the distinctions among stimuli (erotic, aggressive, and aggressive-erotic films) and the use of both male and female confederates. In this design the confederate both angered the subject and was the target of the subject's response.

The line marked by the arrow in Figure 1 represents the heightened effect of the combination of aggression and erotica over aggression by itself, where targets are female. Given a female target, male subjects will display higher levels of shock administration when exposed to sex and violence than when exposed to either violence or sex alone.[3] The lesson drawn from this is that aggressive pornography (as opposed to aggression *per se*) facilitates violence against women. In weighing the relevance of this particular finding and its interpretation, we should not lose sight of one of Donnerstein's observations made elsewhere, especially if we are cognizant of the possible policy implication of these relationships: 'Aggressive behaviour in subjects who have previously been angered has been shown to be increased by exposure to arousing sources such as aggressive-erotic films, physical exercise, drugs, and noise' (1980a, p. 279). And further, Donnerstein observes: 'Films that depict violence against women, even without sexual content, could act as a stimulus for aggressive acts towards women' (p. 286).

The implication of these observations is that a range of arousing stimuli (exercise, noise) have the same qualitative consequence as aggressive erotica and that the aggression may be facilitated without any erotic stimulus whatsoever (Donnerstein and Penrod, 1986). Consequently, extrapolation from aggressive pornography to real world violence against women is of the same order as extrapolating from noise exposure and physical exercise to the same conclusion. In other words, exposure to highly provocative pornography may enhance aggression in those prone to it, just as exposure to annoying noise and tiring exercise may enhance aggression. As we shall see, this observation does not support a social learning model as much as it supports an excitatory transfer explanation.

Donnerstein and Berkowitz (1981) conducted further studies focusing on the *outcome* of the film as well as the arousal of the subjects. It was thought that a violent-erotic film, where the script portrayed victim acquiescence and participation (positive outcome), would facilitate more aggression against confederate targets than a film portraying victim degradation and humiliation (negative outcome).

This study found that for angered subjects the exposure to either kind of aggressive pornography, positive or negative outcome, intensified aggression (see Figure 2). Earlier, Baron (1979) and others had reported otherwise (White, 1979; Zillmann and Sapolsky, 1977). Baron (1974, p. 322), for instance, concluded: 'Exposing angry individuals to sexually arousing stimuli may markedly reduce the strength of their subsequent attack against the individual who provokes them.'

Malamuth and Donnerstein (1982) suggest that these contradictory findings can be explained by methodological/design flaws in the earlier studies. The result of such flaws was, in their view, a serious underestimation of the harm attributable to a particular type of pornography as experienced by a particular viewer under specific conditions. Malamuth and Donnerstein suggest these earlier studies typically did not control for the type of stimulus (erotic vs. aggressive-erotic pornography) or the sex of the target. In what may be seen as a refinement of Baron, they find that for angry males, both positive and negative endings increase aggression against female targets. For non-angry males, only the positive outcome does so. Presumably, the positive outcome film both arouses and disinhibits, and for non-angry men, according to Donnerstein and Berkowitz, this disinhibition is critical to aggressing. Without this disinhibition, non-angry men do not aggress. They must either be angry, in which case they are disinhibited by both endings, or their normal inhibitions must be lifted.

Figure 2 Mean Shock Intensity: Four Films × Angered/Non-angered (Female Targets)

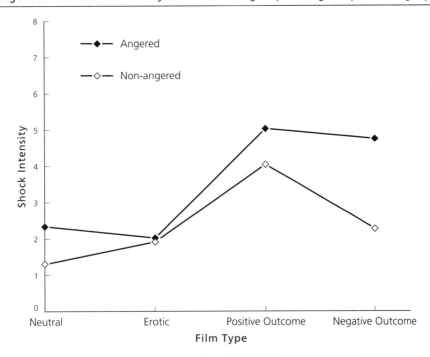

Negative outcome pornography does not disinhibit non-angry men, and they therefore do not aggress.

In earlier work, Berkowitz (1970; 1974) stressed the importance of the subject's identification of the confederate target in the learning experiment with the victim portrayed in the stimulus film. While there may be some importance to this variable, it does not seem to be crucial since, in the later study with Donnerstein, the victim is female in both positive and negative outcome films, but aggression occurs for non-angry males only in the positive outcome instance. Further, the feminists who emphasize the aggressive, assaultive nature of rape also would appear to have little comfort from this study. The negative assaultive feature, which ideologically is depicted as the attraction of rape for males (pornography and rape as backlash), appears to have the opposite valence; for non-angry males it inhibits aggression. This finding is consistent with Barker's analysis of the message of the 'video nasties' which suggests that rape in fiction is not rewarded (1984, pp. 104–18).

What lessons do we draw from these observations? Although the same experts suggest that a link exists between observation and imitation, the linkage is highly qualified, sensitive as it is to certain film types and certain subject states and analogous to aggression promotion in non-sexual conditions (noise, exercise, drugs). As we shall see, the theories designed to interpret the observations cast little light on the subject. In the following sections, we tackle a variety of issues relevant to interpreting the laboratory studies.

## Conflicting Explanations

Several theories have been employed to interpret the experimental observations. The 'arousal model' suggests that 'any dominant response may be "energized" by a state of increased arousal' (Donnerstein and Malamuth, 1982, p. 123). Thus if individuals are predisposed to aggression, increased arousal will activate this predisposition. The angering of subjects in the experiments was designed to incline them to aggress. According to this model, the gender of the target or the victim's reactions to rape (positive or negative outcome) is not expected or predicted to have any impact, and there is still less theoretical rationale to predict different impacts other than by affecting the level of arousal. Since, Donnerstein's work (1984), all pornographic films were equal in the levels of arousal they created (as measured by blood pressure), roughly equal aggressive responses might have been anticipated, but this was not the result. In the Malamuth studies (1984), the positive-outcome violent erotica were more arousing than negative-outcome erotica according to self-report data. Yet only aggressive pornographic stimuli seem to increase aggression (and only against females, not males). In fact, highly arousing but non-aggressive stimuli appear to inhibit aggression against females. Arousing sexual cues under some conditions appears to shift attention away from aggressive responses (Bandura, 1977). Clearly, aggressors, despite the level of arousal, are inhibited by strong social norms that disvalue aggression against females. Thus arousal alone seems insufficient as an explanation for patterns of increases and decreases in aggressiveness as a result of exposure to sexually aggressive material. This confusion over unpredicted results in a simple model calls attention to the existence of as yet unspecified or additional relevant factors. Until these can be described fully, we simply do not have a useful predictive model.

Several researchers stress that the quality of arousal, the valence, is important. Zillmann and Sapolsky (1977) and Baron and Bell (1977) find that aggression by angry men is inhibited by exposure to hard-core or strongly arousing pornography as well as mild or soft-core pornography. According to Baron and Bell (p. 86), aggression may depend on whether the style of the stimulus is, 'tenderness' (aggression inhibiting) or 'wildness' and 'impulsivity' (aggression facilitating). The policy implication of this discovery is not likely to sit well with either conservatives or feminists, since it suggests the justification of soft-core pornography in the name of better gender harmony.

Policy aside, the combination of the arousal model with Bandura's disinhibition model is suggestive. Under this joint model, the norms must be reduced or weakened and the subjects disinhibited before they will aggress. Viewing aggressive pornography is thought to remove inhibitions in two possible ways. Aggressive pornography with positive outcome disinhibits since it is seen to reward violence by pairing it with sexual pleasure. Or alternatively, subjects feel that punishment is justified for lewd behaviour seen on the film and misdirect it to a similar target. Viewing pornography with a negative outcome, it seems, should increase inhibitions and reduce subsequent aggression against females, and this in fact is what occurs with non-angry men. On the other hand, Donnerstein and Berkowitz (1981) believe that angry men are aroused by seeing a female victim suffer and that this predicts increased aggression. A positive outcome will be disinhibiting for the same reason that it will be disinhibiting for non-angry men (the reaction rewards the aggression), and a negative outcome disinhibiting for reasons of identification (the female target is identified with the film victim whose suffering was enjoyed by subjects emotionally predisposed to find it enjoyable).

Most of the models presuppose a disposition to aggression against women that is modified both by the film and by the manipulation of anger. The films stimulate 'intensified aggressive inclinations in both the angered and non-angered men (although more strongly so in the former group) and the depicted positive outcome would lower their restraints against attacking the target' (Donnerstein and Berkowitz, 1981, p. 718). Hence, aggression results from a heightening of aggressive arousal, anger, and a loosening of restraint.

As we observed at the outset, the research designs are questionable since all effects are apt to be interactions between anger and the intervening variable—erotica, noise, exercise, heat, marijuana, or whatever (see Baron and Bell, 1973; Bell and Baron, 1976). This methodological problem seems to have been elevated to a theoretical precept, since it appears that aggressive inclinations are assumed in the theory. The aggressive inclinations that are presumed to underlie the shocking behaviour are only modified, intensified, or inhibited by secondary factors. They are not even studied as a possible gender-related trait in these experiments since all subjects are male, and no grounds exist for differentiating this trait empirically on a gender basis. It might be prudent to ask whether any other assumption might help equally to illuminate the observations since Malamuth and Donnerstein (1982, pp. 123–6) report that the important findings are not explained easily by any of the existing models.

If we examine the shocking intensity for the non-angry positive-outcome aggressive pornography, we find, paradoxically, a relatively high mean (4 out of a possible 8) compared to the other non-angry conditions (see Figure 2). Why does such a stimulus create aggression in non-angry men? Obviously, the assumption of an invariant aggressive disposition, a constant, cannot explain the variation across the stimulus conditions. Donnerstein and Berkowitz say the negative ending does not lift the inhibitions to aggression in non-angry subjects who apparently do not think women subjected to rape should act as though they are enjoying it. If we follow this line of argument, it seems possible that the higher aggression characteristic of the positive outcome group may even be a negative sanction, a punishment for females who are identified with the target for showing that such enjoyment—pretending to enjoy rape (positive outcome)—is noxious. This sex role interpretation suggests that the behaviour is normative and is directed at the reinforcement of sex roles and that it is not founded in biological presuppositions.

We are not arguing that our interpretation is superior to the one advanced but that it may be equally plausible (or indeed, equally implausible). Furthermore, it appears to be consistent with the experimental finding of Baron and Eggleston (1972, p. 321) that under the usual instructions that 'this is a learning experiment', results suggest the 'amount of shock directed by subjects against a confederate was positively related to their expressed desire to help this individual and make the experiment a success.' Thus altruistic motives appear to influence behaviour and, like the spanking of a misbehaving child, these may be misconstrued as aggression. Whether these are real altruistic motives or merely demand characteristics is at this point irrelevant. In either case if they influence behaviour, they do so in the same direction.

This interpretation neither requires the presupposition of any underlying aggressive drive, nor denies that angry respondents may experience experimentally induced retaliatory impulses as augmented by other stimuli (aggressive pornography, noise, drugs, exercise, etc.). The implication of such an interpretation for a public policy regarding censorship is crucial. While the authors of these studies seem predisposed to view the shocking of confederates as an analogue of real world violence directed at innocent female victims and triggered by certain forms of pornography, the results do not sustain such an interpretation. The conduct of non-angry males, even when indicating higher levels of shock intensity, may express altruistic sentiments, in which case censorship on the pretext of third party victimization would be unfounded. Alternatively, if the conduct of angry males exposed to such stimuli is indicative of retaliatory aggression, it is still another question whether the solution lies in control of the intervening variable (pornography, noise, exercise) or the provocation of anger. Obviously, the social and psychological processes underlying these experiments are quite complex, and the significance of the shocking intensities varies with the context. In no case, however, is it readily apparent from these studies that censorship of pornographic stimuli will ensure a reduction in the victimization of women in the real world as we have been led to believe.

Even more importantly, the observations of aggression are not self-evident, and in testing the null hypothesis the experimentalists appear to have little concern for alternative explanations of their data. In this field, the predominant models of disinhibition associated with Bandura, Berkowitz, and Donnerstein contrast sharply with the views of Zillmann (1984), who interprets aggression enhancement as 'excitation transfer'. Zillmann's model would lead to the interpretation of the aggression enhancement of non-aroused males exposed to positive-outcome rape pornography without any references to modelling or cue identification. Zillmann would argue that the positive-outcome film would be highly arousing even in non-angered (i.e., physiologically non-aroused) subjects

(Schachter, 1971, p. 14, describes a similar pattern). Given the opportunity to aggress, the physiology of arousal would boost the aggressive levels without the subjects realizing how involved they were. Hence, the otherwise problematic links between exercise and aversive noise are unproblematic for Zillmann—this is excitatory transfer of the physiological residues from one event transferring to a subsequent overlapping event. In terms of public policy, disinhibition could be altered by giving different lessons in the mass media, but excitatory transfer is a physiological reality: biological noise is not corrected by an act of government. This basic conflict of theoretical interpretations has never been the source of experimental discrimination.

## Measurement Issues

***Aggression.*** Just as there are conflicting theoretical interpretations of the observations, there are conflicting interpretations of what the experimental measures reveal. In *Pornography and Sexual Aggression*, Malamuth and Donnerstein (1984) suggest that their lab effects are proxies for real world rape. But how good are the lab proxies? In most of the designs in this literature, the investigators seek to produce an inclination to aggress by first angering the subject. They then vary the amount of further arousal, finally measuring aggression against a target person. As pointed out earlier, anger is created most often by having the real subject complete an assignment that is graded poorly or harshly by the experimental confederate. But does this produce genuine anger or hurt, stress, or anxiety? After exposure to one of the experimental films, the subject immediately is given the opportunity to shock the confederate within the context of what he is told is a paired learning experiment. The shocks subjects administer are clearly retaliatory in nature and specific to the confederate who insulted the subject. In addition, the retaliation is legitimate within the experimental setting of a learning study where subjects are *instructed to aggress*. Hence, generalization to violent sexual acts of aggression against innocent victims seems unjustified. The retaliation is also immediate: the longest interval between film exposure and opportunity to aggress in the final phase of the experiment is 10 minutes. This is dubbed the long term condition. How generalizable are these findings? Even if the effects discovered in this work are real, it is an open question whether they are enduring. And even if they outlive the 10-minute span, we still do not know what happens in a competitive environment in which there are many stable and changing stimuli around us including the aggressive ones (some, such as the news, may be as arousing as fiction). These limitations suggest the desirability of a design in which both angered and non-angered subjects are retested with the same (or different) target a week or two after the stimulus. In a related study, Zillmann and Bryant (1982; 1984) reported that the retaliatory measures declined after 'massive exposure' to pornography over several weeks.

The laboratory setting is designed to allow maximum control of exposure to the stimulus and to enhance it, by purifying and isolating its effects. In general, more equivocal and weaker relationships and effects might be expected outside the laboratory and after a week or two of duration. So, despite the optimum conditions of laboratory control, Donnerstein and others report what seem to be relatively small effects of pornography exposure despite measuring these immediately. Though statistically higher than the scores of those exposed to neutral or erotic stimuli, the mean scores of those exposed to violent pornography are nonetheless not very impressive in absolute terms (that is, none of the means that are thought to represent high levels of aggression are on the high end of the eight-point scale but occur at the midpoint region). Frequently, in complex factorial designs not all the means are reported, and detailed comparisons of the cells are made impossible (see Donnerstein and Berkowitz, 1981). One might well ask, following Carol Sherif (1980), whether the sorts of means identified in this research constitute valid measures of aggression at all.

**Attitudes and Rape Proclivity.** Malamuth deals more directly than Donnerstein with rape, sexually domineering attitudes, and the prevalence of aggressive pornography. His work, however, raises even more serious methodological questions. Malamuth (1981) developed the Likelihood to Rape Scale (LR). The 'scale' consisted of one item that asks subjects how likely they think they would be to commit rape in the event they could be assured of not being apprehended. Malamuth claims that this single-item scale differentiates accurately and predictively and that it identified approximately 40 per cent of the population of males as potential rapists. This claim is like saying potential bank robbers can be identified by asking people if they would rob a bank if given assurances of complete success. The gap between fantasy and reality in such studies has led some observers to dismiss them categorically.[4]

Incredulity regarding such studies is supported further by the probability of demand characteristics that virtually guarantee that many subjects will answer hypothetically because they believe the researchers want certain types of responses. In order to create two groups with enough cases in each for analysis, Malamuth finds it necessary to consider all those who scored two or higher (on a five-point scale) to be in the 'high' LR category, while only those scoring in the lowest cell were 'low' LR. Sixty-five per cent of respondents put themselves in the lowest cell, 15 per cent in category two, and the remaining 20 per cent in category three, four, or five. The mean overall score must have been quite low but was unreported. Despite the arbitrary cutoff points, most subjects simply do not fall into a high category on this scale, even with the encouragement of demand characteristics.

Since these are laboratory results, far lower effects of the stimuli could be anticipated in real world situations. Moreover, following Malamuth, many more respondents could be expected to fall into the lowest cell of the LR Scale if it were measured in a more realistic way regarding consequences. More realistic questions might include: Would you rape someone if you thought the odds were fifty-fifty that you would be caught and arrested by the police? If the victim were armed with mace and could defend herself? If you were likely to be over-heard? If you were likely to traumatize or injure the victim?

Malamuth contends that the high LR respondents possess discernible person-ality characteristics and value systems. His own study of the proclivity to rape, however, suggests that a significant statistical relationship exists in only one of the three areas predicted, involving just 6 out of the 34 attributional items (see Malamuth and Check, 1981, p. 441). Given the way the data are reported, it is not surprising that rival hypotheses virtually are unexplored in this area.

Finally, there is little empirical evidence to support the argument that the number of aggressive erotic materials is rapidly increasing. Malamuth and Spinner (1980) found 5 per cent of the pictorials in *Playboy* and *Penthouse* to be 'violent' in the highest of the years they examined (and even the extremely low levels exhibited by cartoons entailed for the most part violence against men by women).[5] This topic of sexual violence was also explored by Scott and Cuvelier (1987). They studied *Playboy* magazine over the period 1954 to 1983, and concluded that since 1975 the low levels of aggressive depictions of sex actually have declined. More relevant, there is no experimental study of the effects of mixed erotica in which a small percentage is arguably aggressive while the remainder is not. It seems likely that the mixed stimulus, more akin to the real world experience, would reduce the already low levels of aggressive retaliation found in the laboratory.

***Pornography and Attitude Change.*** Aside from Malamuth's work, the only other major investigation of attitudes is reported by Zillmann and Bryant (1982; 1984). Zillmann and Bryant exposed male and female subjects to 45 minutes of stag films each week for six weeks and measured differences in attitudes compared to subjects without such exposure. They report that the 'massive exposure' resulted in a callousness toward women evidenced by a 'trivialization' of rape and a loss of respect for women. What was the evidence and how was it measured?

Subjects were asked to estimate the prevalence of unusual sexual practices in the population. Those who had been exposed to the dosages of pornography made higher estimates than those exposed to non-erotic fare. Estimates of oral sex approximated those found in Hunt's social survey (1974), leading to the conclusion that 'massive exposure to pornography thus could be said to correct distorted views of sexuality' (Zillmann and Bryant, 1984, p. 133). According to Zillmann and Bryant, this educational function was not found in estimates for group sex, sadomasochism, and bestiality, and they concluded that pornography 'can be said to distort the perception' of sexuality (p. 133). The problem with this conclusion is that it presupposes that subjects are as apt to report bestiality as they are to report oral sex. In all probability, subjects are least likely to report things strongly tabooed, making a comparison of the accuracies of sexual perversions extremely misleading, especially where such taboos remain prominent. Furthermore, if we compare Hunt's survey data with the experimental estimates given by subjects exposed to pornography, contrary to Zillmann and Bryant, the trends are virtually identical; there seems little evidence of 'distortions' of sexuality.

Zillmann and Bryant's 'most astonishing findings' were differentials in the sentences awarded to a rapist in a mock jury study which followed the exposure phase of the research. Subjects were given materials from a rape trial and asked to award a jail sentence to the accused. Those in the exposure group awarded an average sentence of 63.4 months (more than 5 years) versus 119.1 months (almost 10 years) recommended by those in the non-sex film groups. The authors conclude on the basis of this difference that exposure to pornography trivializes rape and leads consumers to treat it as a minor infraction. Several things are disturbing about this conclusion. Sixty-three months, far from being trivial, is a serious and substantial period of confinement. In addition, it is a greater period of incarceration than is actually administered in most rape trials; for instance, in a large Midwestern city, LaFree (1980, p. 846) reports a median sentence of 2.5 years. There appears to be an effect of massive exposure, but there are again several possible interpretations, and they compete favourably with those of the authors. Zillmann and Bryant compare the suggested penalties of those in the neutral and the massive exposure conditions. We could compare the massive exposure as well to real practice, and rather than seeing the problem as explaining the lower levels of punishment awarded by those exposed to massive doses of pornography, see the problem as involving the higher penalties awarded by those in the neutral film condition. Rather than concluding that massive exposure to pornography demystifies sexual deviance and corrects distorted views of rape and rapists, just as pornography was seen to demystify the prevalence of oral sex, Zillmann and Bryant pursue a moralistic route by leaving unexamined, and hence crediting, the non-sex film group's average sentence of almost 10 years. Given this shift back and forth between scientific and retributive standards, and given the greater realism and accuracy of the 5-year estimate, Zillmann and Bryant's conclusions are questionable.

Zillmann and Bryant in this nine-week study employed pornographic films for six weeks of exposure, and then tested for three weeks, but nowhere do they report the dropout levels. If the pornographic stimuli were aversive, we would expect higher levels of attrition in the crucial experimental treatment group. This by itself could create a sampling bias and create significant but artifactual differences across the treatment groups. We shall return to this point shortly.

What about the report of a decline in respect for women? This conclusion was measured by response to a single question: 'Do you support the female liberation movement?' Though those exposed to the massive diet of pornography reported about half the level of support of those not so treated (38 per cent vs. 76 per cent), it seems rather politically and scientifically questionable to conclude that this difference 'presents data that exhibit a loss of faith in women' (Zillmann and Bryant, 1984, p. 134) since we would expect that massive exposure (that is, 45 minutes per week) to fundamentalist Christian sermons would have an identical effect if measured by the same question. The political currency of pornography research appears to determine how the data are interpreted.

The attrition hypothesis also might explain the paradoxical finding that females exposed to films catering to male erotic fantasies also came to lose faith in women. If we are correct about uneven attrition levels across the treatment groups, it is similarly plausible that female attrition levels would outpace male attrition levels. The remaining females would be a self-selected and unrepresentative sample on which to base any extrapolations. This raises larger issues concerning sampling in this area.

## Sampling

As noted by the authors themselves, the subjects of most laboratory experiments are not a representative sample of those to whom we might wish to generalize, and, to the extent that they differ systematically from this population, generalization is not warranted. While this is true of most social psychological lab studies, it is particularly pertinent in pornography research since university students in psychology classes rarely are exposed to aggressive pornography in their own lives and hence are not a very appropriate group to examine for the effects on voluntary consumers of pornography. Zillmann, Bryant, and Carveth (1981) found that their male subjects were alarmed and disturbed by films of sadomasochism and bestiality. If the goal is to generalize to rapists, or would-be rapists, and their responsiveness to pornography, this sample of college students seems an unlikely basis for such a jump.

The studies of the sexual responsiveness of rapists themselves are inconclusive and particularly subject to demand characteristics since rapists, as well as control subjects, are most often studied in treatment centres in the course of rehabilitation programs (Abel, Barlow, Blanchard, and Guild, 1977; Barbaree, Marshall, and Lantheir, 1979; Quinsey, Chaplin, and Varney, 1981). In fact, it seems quite possible that in all studies of sexual arousal of rapists and normal controls, the strongest predictor of arousal level is the experimenter's instructions to control subjects that they will find the erotic subject matter highly stimulating (Quinsey et al., 1981).

The measurement of arousal itself presents many problems. Self-reports, a questionable form of evidence, are often supplemented by measurements of physiological responses, including blood pressure and penile tumescence. Though the self-report and physiological measures most often agree, critics point out that blood pressure readings and penile tumescence are reactive, somewhat controllable, and self-fulfilling (Amoroso and Brown, 1973). For rapists, in addition, there is an enormous sampling problem since most of those convicted of rape and in the treatment programs also are diagnosed as mentally ill or suffering from some other mental debility (Quinsey et al., 1981). They constitute a highly biased sample, one from which generalization would be inappropriate, contrary to the relevance attached to them by experimental psychologists.

In our view, the laboratory studies of pornography simply have not succeeded in establishing relationships that correspond to the real world. Epidemiological, historical, and cross-cultural studies seem to us better vehicles for the discovery of real world patterns regarding pornography.

## Demand Characteristics

In the lab, various demand characteristics give subtle cues to subjects from which a response is constructed, usually one provided inadvertently by the experimenter (Orne, 1962; Rosenthal and Rosnow, 1969; Rosenwald, 1986). Demand characteristics, however, also arise from the limitations or confinement of responses imposed by the design. In the pornography experiments, the only response allowed is by way of shocks administered to the confederate. No other response is allowed (that is, no positive response, no sublimation, no constructive opposition). All shocks are construed as aggression, even though utilized in what the subject is told is a learning experiment where shocks are encouraged to enhance learning. Consequently, subjects are forced into a behaviour they might not select if given a broader range of options. 'In a society in which responses to anger other than aggression are permitted (for example, seduction) aggression need not be the main response of angered men' (Gray, 1982, p. 391), and in fact there is empirical evidence that (for couples participating in the studies) the effect of weekly exposure to hard-core pornography increases intercourse on the evening of the day of exposure (Mann, Berkowitz, Sidman, Starr, and West, 1974). Thus the research design seems to force the issue in a specific direction and toward a specific outcome (with all the professional and ideological attention that emanates from this). Following Gray's view (1982), the key phenomenon is the relationship between provocation and retaliation, not pornography and aggression. Public policy ought to have far more interest in the former than the latter.

Parenthetically, it may be instructive to ponder the policy implications of related aggression studies. Taylor and his colleagues (1976) observed that marijuana in small and large doses (as well as alcohol in small doses) inhibits physical aggression. Were public policy to be made with an eye to these findings, we would justify the legalization of marijuana in the interests of stemming assault and violent aggression. Clearly, it is not wise to attach much importance to the intervening condition at the expense of overlooking the major effect. Apropos of this is Donnerstein's observation that 'without lowered inhibitions, there is no evidence that sexual stimuli affect aggressive behaviour towards women' (1980b, p. 270). The thrust of the studies discussed here is to identify some of the sources of disinhibition (anger, outcome, target gender). And, as we saw, viewing aggressive erotic films with positive outcomes 'could stimulate aggressively disposed men with weak inhibitions to assault available women' (Donnerstein and Berkowitz, 1981, p. 722), especially where the setting is designed specifically to facilitate such a response. Consequently, the public policy options are quite remote.

In fact, one of the most optimistic conclusions of this work is that harmful attitudes toward rape are corrected simply by exposure to the stimuli and debriefing. Contrary to the grave consequences that we might fear arising from the experiments, the researchers do not seem worried that their subjects will become contaminated like the sexual monsters supposedly produced by the real world exposure to pornography (see Gross, 1983). As the researchers are careful to note, debriefing brings to the attention of the male subjects the revelation that women do not enjoy being raped! Hence, the impact of the participation is 'to reduce subjects' acceptance of rape myths'. And while some attitudinal change may follow simply from the transfer of information in the debriefing, 'the combination of exposure to violent pornography that portrays rape myths and the presentation of a debriefing that specifically addresses these myths appears to be most effective in reducing rape myth acceptance' (Malamuth and Donnerstein, 1982, p. 129). Again, if we were to take this discovery at face value, it would not entail censorship but the encouragement of exposure to pornography of all sorts combined with education of the public regarding the facts of rape and assault. Some observers may feel this approximates what is already the case.[6]

## Conclusion

In the real world, pornography occurs in a context. Consumers may not be angry, and effects, if any, are not usually expressed in immediate opportunities to shock a confederate in a learning experiment where punishment has an altruistic foundation and scientific legitimacy. It is a considerable leap from the laboratory to the corner store where men riffle the pages of magazines kept on the top shelf. It is a long step from the laboratory exposure to such stimuli and subsequent aggression to real world sexual and physical abuse. In our view, the relationships discovered in the laboratories are so far removed from the circumstances about which we legitimately are worried and the results so qualified in terms of their equivalence to existing social circumstances as to be politically irrelevant. In addition, the introduction of this type of research into considerations of censorship may even be dangerous since this research seems to underwrite the belief that the censorship of pornography will make the streets safe for women, thus creating a misplaced sense of security. A similar mentality might abolish bridges in the hope of eradicating suicide. Simply because we have the tools to conduct experiments, it does not follow that we will find the answers to all our questions by doing so. To the extent that attention is diverted from other methods and areas of relevant research, this reliance on experiments may even be hazardous to our further understanding of the problem at hand.

It is our contention that the experimental data concerning the harmful effects of aggressive pornography do not demonstrate clearly such effects and that any argument for legislation based on these experimental findings is objectionable. And while further legislation cannot in our view be warranted on the basis of this sort of evidence, it does not follow that we advocate or support aggressive or violent pornography nor that we oppose other arguments, notably moral and ideological, for regulating its production and circulation. Our view is narrowly restricted to the technical adequacy and legislative relevance of the experimental research regarding the harmful effects of exposure.

It seems striking to us that the introduction of every new mass medium (from nineteenth-century police gazettes and turn-of-the-century 'penny dreadfuls' to crime comics and mid-century to today's cable television and videocassettes) has been accompanied by allegations concerning effects on criminality. Visual, mass circulation pornography appears as only the most recent casualty of such respectable fears (Pearson, 1983). This suggests to us that a more productive area of theorizing might consider how the appearance of new media and their fictional subject matter threaten the existing ideological fabric of society and enter public discourse in the guise of concern over threats to public safety. Recurrently, the invention of new mass media have given the working classes and young consumers access to popular forms of entertainment whose sexual and violent themes have engendered misgivings by teachers, politicians, clerics, and other agents of middle-class morality (Gilbert, 1986; McCormack, 1985b). It is this broader contextual and historical background that we would like to see pursued before the contemporary academy in its quest for Walden Three—the rationally ordered society constructed on psychological principles—becomes co-opted by reactionary social and political elements of society in the service of social control (Vance, 1986).

## NOTES

1 Particular attention is given to this new literature in Nelson (1982), Diamond (1980), and Eysenck and Nias (1978). See also Fagan (1984) for a more developed but slanted annotated bibliography prepared by David Scott for a conservative lobby group during the Meese hearings in Washington. Oddly enough, the *Canadian Select Committee of Inquiry Into Pornography and Prostitution* rejected the value of the scientific arguments in a background paper prepared by McKay and Dolff (1985).

2   This design only approximates the criteria for a crucial reason. Campbell and Stanley opt for the design of post-test only over the classic pre-test/post-test control group design because of the likely sensitization effects of the pre-test on the later post-test. These effects interact with the experimental stimulus in such a way that any externally valid generalization concerning the effects of x by itself become questionable. The post-test only design circumvents this problem by avoiding any pre-test. The design variant used by the researchers on aggressive pornography reinstates a sensitization effect by angering the subjects. Ironically, this strategy restores the problem of sensitization that led to Campbell and Stanley's preference for the control group design of post-test only.

3   In the early designs of the classic Milgram experiments, subjects administered shocks without any feedback from the 'learner'. In such cases, conformity was virtually absolute: nearly all subjects administered the maximum levels (Milgram, 1974, p. 22). The subsequent designs (remote feedback, voice feedback, proximity, touch proximity, etc.) introduced more information about the actual plight of the victim that in turn dramatically decreased conformity (see discussion in Mixon, 1972). When we consider the eight-point shock scale of the pornography experiments, it is clear that the conditions of shock administration approximate the Milgram no-feedback condition where maximum severity was observed. We would predict that the introduction of any of the later Milgram feedback conditions, conditions that would presumably make the situation more realistic, would similarly lead to dramatic declines in the levels of shock intensity. Such adjustment would undermine completely the experimental verisimilitude.

4   The Williams committee makes the following observation (1979, pp. 65–6):

> Since criminal and anti-social behaviour cannot itself, for both practical and ethical reasons, be experimentally produced or controlled, the observations must be made on some surrogate or related behaviour, often expressed on a representational object, in some fictional or 'pretend' context. This feature of the work can come close, in some cases, to simply begging the question. The fundamental issue in this field concerns the relations that hold between the reactions aroused in a subject by a represented, artificial, or fantasy scene, and his behaviour in reality. Fantasy and reality, and their relations, are the basic categories of the question. We can only express surprise at the confidence that some investigators have shown in supposing that they can investigate *this* problem through experimental set-ups in which reality is necessarily replaced by fantasy.

5   The violent theme has been an endemic element in pornographic works from the time of de Sade (Davis, 1983). Abraham Kaplan (1955, p. 558) spoke of the 'pornography of violence' in describing the new literary forms of obscenity following World War II (that is, crime comics). Violence is also the leitmotif of the worries expressed in the parliamentary debates in Canada, England, and Australia over obscenity during this time (see Brannigan, 1986). The emergence of themes of violence and sexuality in mass-produced popular literature appears to date to the movies, novels, and comics of the 1930s (see Alloway, 1971; O'Brien, 1981; Roth, 1982).

6   Others regard this conclusion as fantastic: How can stimuli that are made out to be so potent be so easily diffused? Either their potency is overrated, in which case the relevance of the work is grossly exaggerated or the potency is real, in which case experimental participation dangerously socializes the innocent to aggressive conduct. McCormack (1985a) and McKay and Dolff (1985) appear to dismiss the work on this point.

## REFERENCES

Abel, G.G., Barlow, D.H., Blanchard, E., and Guild, D.
1977   The components of rapists' sexual arousal. *Archives of General Psychiatry, 34*, 895–903.

Alloway, L.
1971   *Violent America: The movies 1946–64*. New York: Museum of Modern Art.

Amoroso, D.M., and Brown, M.
1973   Problems in studying the effects of erotic material. *The Journal of Sex Research, 9*, 187–95.

Attorney General's Commission on Pornography
1986, July   *Final Report*. Washington, DC: U.S. Department of Justice.

Bandura, A.
1977   *Social learning theory*. Englewood Cliffs, NJ: Prentice-Hall.

Barbaree, H.E., Marshall, L.W., and Lanthier, R.D.
1979   Deviant sexual arousal in rapists. *Behavior Research and Therapy, 17*, 215–22.

Barker, M. (ed.)
1984   *The video nasties: Freedom and censorship in the media*. London: Pluto Press.

Baron, R.A.
1974   The aggressive inhibiting influence of heightened sexual arousal. *Journal of Personality and Social Psychology, 30*, 318–22.

1979   Heightened sexual arousal and physical aggression: An extension to females. *Journal of Research in Personality, 13*, 91–102.

Baron, R.A., and Bell, P.A.
1973   The effects of heightened sexual arousal on physical aggression. *Proceedings of the American Psychological Association*, 81st Convention, 171–2.

1977   Sexual arousal and aggression by males: Effects of type of erotic stimuli and prior provocation. *Journal of Personality and Social Psychology, 35*, 79–87.

Baron, R.A., and Byrne, D.
1977   *Social psychology: Understanding interaction*. Boston: Allyn and Bacon.

Baron, R.A., and Eggleston, R.J.
1972 Performance of the aggression machine: Motivation to help or harm? *Psychonomic Science, 26,* 321–2.

Becker, H.
1963 *Outsiders.* New York: Free Press.

Bell, P.A., and Baron, R.A.
1976 Aggression and heat: The mediating role of negative affect. *Journal of Applied Social Psychology, 6,* 18–30.

Berkowitz, L.
1970 The contagion of violence: An s-r mediational analysis of some effects of observed aggression. In W.J. Arnold and M.M. Page (eds), *Nebraska Symposium on Motivation* (pp. 95–136). Lincoln: University of Nebraska Press.

1974–81 Some determinants of impulsive aggression: The role of mediated associations with reinforcements for aggression. *Psychological Review, 18* (2), 165–76.

Brannigan, A.
1986 Crimes from comics: The social and political determinants of reform of the Victoria obscenity law 1938–1954. *Australian and New Zealand Journal of Criminology, 19,* 23–42.

Brannigan, A., and Goldenberg, S.
1986 Social science versus jurisprudence in Wagner: The study of pornography, harm, and the law of obscenity in Canada. *Canadian Journal of Sociology, 11* (4), 419–31.

Campbell, D., and Stanley, J.
1966 *Experimental and quasi-experimental designs for research.* Chicago: Rand McNally.

Check, J.V.P., and Malamuth, N.M.
1981, August Can participation in pornography experiments have positive effects? (Paper presented at the annual meeting of the American Psychological Association, Los Angeles.)

Christensen, F.
1986 Sexual callousness re-examined. *Journal of Communication, 36* (1), 174–83.

Commission on Obscenity and Pornography
1970 *The Report of the Commission on Obscenity and Pornography*. Bantam Books.

Davis, M.S.
1983 *Smut: Erotic reality—Obscene ideology*. Chicago: University of Chicago Press.

Diamond, I.
1980 Pornography and repression: A reconsideration. *Signs. A Journal of Women in Culture and Society, 5*, 686–701.

Donnerstein, E.
1980a Pornography and violence against women. *Annals of the New York Academy of Sciences, 347*, 277–88.

1980b Aggressive erotica and violence against women. *Journal of Personality and Social Psychology, 41*, 710–24.

1983 Erotica and human aggression. In R. Geen and E. Donnerstein (eds), *Aggression: Theoretical and empirical reviews* (pp. 127–54). New York: Academic Press.

1984 Pornography: Its effect on violence against women. In N.M. Malamuth and E. Donnerstein (eds), *Pornography and sexual aggression* (pp. 53–81). New York: Academic Press.

Donnerstein, E., and Berkowitz, L.
1981 Victim reaction in aggressive erotic films as a factor in violence against women. *Journal of Personality and Social Psychology, 41*, 710–24.

Donnerstein, E., Donnerstein, M., and Evans, R.
1975 Erotic stimuli and aggression: Facilitation or inhibition? *Journal of Personality and Social Psychology, 32*, 237–44.

Donnerstein, E., and Penrod, S.
1986, December   The question of pornography. *Psychology Today*, pp. 56–9.

Erikson, K.T.
1966 *Wayward puritans: A study in the sociology of deviance*. New York: John Wiley & Sons.

Eysenck, H.J., and Nias, D.K.B.
1978 *Sex, violence and the media*. London: Maurice, Temple, Smith.

Fagan, P. (ed.)
1984  *Pornography: An annotated bibliography*. Washington, DC: Family Policy Insights.

Geis, G.
1974  *One eyed justice: An examination of homosexuality, abortion, prostitution, narcotics, and gambling in the U.S.* New York: Drake Publishing.

Gilbert, J.
1986  *A cycle of outrage, America's reaction to juvenile delinquency in the 1950s*. New York: Oxford University Press.

Goranson, R.A.
1970  Media violence and aggressive behavior: A review of experimental research. In L. Berkowitz (ed.), *Advances in experimental social psychology* (pp. 1–31). New York: Academic Press.

Gray, S.
1982  Exposure to pornography and aggression against women: The case of the angry male. *Social Problems, 29* (4), 387–98.

Gross, L.
1983  Pornography and social science research. *Journal of Communication, 33* (4), 107–14.

Gusfield, J.
1963  *Symbolic crusade*. Urbana: University of Illinois Press.

Hunt, M.
1974  *Sexual behavior in the 1970s*. Chicago: Playboy Press.

Jarvie, I.
1986  *Thinking about society*. Dordrecht, Holland: Reidel.

1987  The sociology of the pornography debate. *Philosophy of the Social Sciences, 17* (2), 82–94.

Kaplan, A.
1955  Obscenity as an aesthetic category. *Law and Contemporary Problems, 20*, 544–59.

1964  *The conduct of inquiry*. San Francisco: Chandler Publishing Company.

La Free, G.
1980 The effect of sexual stratification by race on official reactions to rape. *American Sociological Review, 45*, 842–54.

Linz, D., Turner, C.W., Hesse, B.W., and Penrod, S.D.
1984 Bases of liability for injuries produced by media portrayal of violent pornography. In N.M. Malamuth and E. Donnerstein (eds), *Pornography and sexual aggression* (pp. 277–304). New York: Academic Press.

Malamuth, N.M.
1981 Rape proclivity among males. *Journal of Social Issues, 37*, 138–57.

1984 Aggression against women: Cultural and individual causes. In N.M. Malamuth and E. Donnerstein (eds), *Pornography and sexual aggression* (pp. 19–52). New York: Academic Press.

Malamuth, N.M., and Check, J.V.P.
1981 The effects of mass media exposure on acceptance of violence against women: A field experiment. *Journal of Research in Personality, 15*, 436–46.

Malamuth, N.M., and Donnerstein, E.
1982 The effects of aggressive-pornographic mass media stimuli. *Advances in Experimental Social Psychology, 15*, 103–36.

Malamuth, N.M., and Donnerstein, E. (eds).
1984 *Pornography and sexual aggression*. New York: Academic Press.

Malamuth, N.M., and Spinner, B.A.
1980 A longitudinal content analysis of sexual violence in the best-selling erotic magazines. *The Journal of Sex Research, 16*, 226–37.

Mann, R.D., Berkowitz, L., Sidman, J., Starr S., and West, S.
1974 Satiation of the transient stimulating effect of erotic films. *Journal of Personality and Social Psychology, 30*, 729–35.

McCormack, T.
1985a Making sense of the research on pornography. In V. Burstyn (ed.), *Women against censorship* (pp. 181–205). Toronto: Douglas and McIntyre.

1985b Deregulating the economy and regulating morality: The political economy of censorship. *Studies in Political Economy, 18*, 173–85.

McKay, H.B., and Dolff, D.J.
1985 *The impact of pornography: An analysis of research and summary of findings*. Report 13, Working Papers on Pornography and Prostitution, Ottawa, Ontario: Federal Department of Justice.

Milgram, S.
1974 *Obedience to authority*. New York: Harper & Row.

Mixon, D.
1972 Instead of deception. *Journal for the Theory of Social Behaviour, 2*, 145–77.

Nelson, E.C.
1982 Pornography and sexual aggression. In M. Yaffé and E.C. Nelson (eds), *The influence of pornography on behaviour* (pp. 171–248). New York: Academic Press.

O'Brien, G.
1981 *Hardboiled America: The lurid years of paperbacks*. New York: Van Nostrand Reinhold.

Orne, M.
1962 On the social psychology of the psychological experiment: With particular reference to demand characteristics and their implications. *American Psychologist, 17*, 776–83.

Pearson, G.
1983 *Hooligan: A history of respectable fears*. London: Macmillan.

Penrod, S., and Linz, D.
1984 Using psychological research on violent pornography to inform legal change. In N.M. Malamuth and E. Donnerstein (eds), *Pornography and sexual aggression* (pp. 274–6). New York: Academic Press.

Quinsey, V.L., Chaplin, T.C., and Varney, G.
1981 A comparison of rapists' and non-sex offenders' sexual preferences for mutually consenting sex, rape, and physical abuse of women. *Behavioral Assessment, 3*, 127–35.

Rosenthal, R., and Rosnow, R.S.
1969 *Artifact in behavioral research*. New York: Academic Press.

Rosenwald, G.C.
1986 Why operationalism doesn't go away: Extrascientific incentives of social-psychological research. *Philosophy of the Social Sciences, 16*, 303–30.

Roth, M.
1982  Pornography and society: A psychiatric view. In M. Yaffé and E.C. Nelson (eds), *The influence of pornography on behaviour* (pp. 1–25). New York: Academic Press.

Schachter, S.
1971  *Emotion, obesity and crime*. New York: Academic Press.

Schur, E.M.
1965  *Crimes without victims: Deviant behavior and public policy: Abortion, homosexuality and drug addiction*. Englewood Cliffs, NJ: Prentice-Hall.

Scott, J.E., and Cuvelier, S.J.
1987  Violence in *Playboy* magazine: A longitudinal analysis. *Archives of Sexual Behavior* 16 (4): 279–89.

Sherif, C.W.
1980  Comment on ethical issues in Malamuth, Heim and Feshbach's 'Sexual responsiveness of college students to rape depictions: Inhibitory and disinhibitory effects'. *Journal of Personality and Social Psychology, 38*, 409–12.

Soble, A.
1986  *Pornography*. New Haven, CT: Yale University Press.

Taylor, S.P., Vardaris, R.M., Rawitch, A.B., Gammon, C.G., Granston, J.W., and Lubetkin, A.L.
1976  The effects of alcohol and delta-9-tetrahydrocannabinol on human physical aggression. *Physical Aggressive Behavior, 2*, 153–62.

Vance, C.S.
1986, August   The Meese commission on the road. *The Nation*, pp. 76–82.

White, L.A.
1979  Erotica and aggression: The influence of sexual arousal, positive affect and negative affect on aggressive behaviour. *Journal of Personality and Social Psychology, 37*, 591–601.

Williams, B.
1979  *Report of the committee on obscenity and film censorship*. London: Her Majesty's Stationery Office.

Wurtzel, A., and Lometti, G.
1984  Researching television violence. *Society, 21* (6), 22–30.

Zillmann, D.
1984  *Connections between sex and aggression*. Hillsdale, NJ: Erlbaum.

Zillmann, D., and Bryant, J.
1982  Pornography, sexual callousness, and the trivialization of rape. *Journal of Communication, 32* (4), 10–21.

1984  Effects of massive exposure to pornography. In N.M. Malamuth and E. Donnerstein (eds), *Pornography and sexual aggression* (pp. 115–38). New York: Academic Press.

Zillmann, D., Bryant, J., and Carveth, P.
1981  The effect of erotica featuring sadomasochism and bestiality on motivated intermale aggression. *Personality and Social Psychology Bulletin, 7*, 153–9.

Zillmann, D., and Sapolsky, B.S.
1977  What mediates the effect of mild erotica on annoyance and hostile behavior in males? *Journal of Personality and Social Psychology, 35*, 587–96.

From *Critical Studies in Mass Communication* 4 (1987): 262–83.

# PART II

# Opposing Theoretical Positions
# and the Impact of Social Change

Chapter 1 introduced the two basic orientations or perspectives of sociology—the macro-structural and the micro-interpretive. In explaining human behaviour, all sociologists use the kind of variables specified by one or the other perspective. Chapter 2 discussed the nature of science as it is currently understood, and in combination with chapter 3 it introduced the criteria for scientific studies in sociology. It is now time to treat the various broadly theoretical positions from which sociology is conducted, because such positions often affect our choice of topics and our research is often directed to the eventual resolution of theoretical debates.

Among the first and most basic interests of sociologists are the twin issues of order and change. Some sociologists believe that the bedrock sociological question may be how societies maintain themselves; others tend to focus on the other side of this coin, asking questions about change rather than about the maintaining of order and stability. In addition, a good deal of debate has concerned sociological determinism as opposed to sociological voluntarism. In general, micro-interpretive theorists have tended to emphasize the voluntaristic aspects of behaviour, whereas the social-structural theorists have emphasized the coercive and deterministic aspects of behaviour. This is evident in the micro-interpretive characterization of human beings as 'actors' in contrast with the structuralists' implicit view of human beings are 'pawns' whose behaviour merely responds predictably to external system characteristics and pressures.

In explaining both order and change, the micro-interpretive perspective tends to pose answers in terms of socialization and internalization. Thus, traditional order and stability are a function of proper socialization into the normatively agreed upon rules of the society, whereas deviance is a function of socialization into competing and inappropriate roles. In both areas as well—and perhaps even more often—structuralists have framed their answers in terms of the coercive aspects of the structure of the social system. For them, order is maintained by agents of social control, and change is also structurally induced. In fact, one could develop a four-part table by crossing the foci and the perspectives (see next page).

It should be noted that the macro-structural deterministic view seems to lend itself more easily to explanations of the maintenance of order than of change. Berger's image of concentric circles in which the individual is imprisoned by agents of social control certainly derives from this structural view. By the same token, the micro-interpretive view, with its

Structural and Interpretive Views of Order and Change

|  | Order | Change |
|---|---|---|
| Macro-structural (deterministic view) | Coercive agents of control | Class or other interests in conflict |
| Micro-interpretive (voluntaristic view) | Internalization of culture | Socialization Flexible negotiation of reality Definition of the situation |

imagery of a fragile reality constantly in the process of negotiation and challenge by actors whose definitions of the situation create it, would seem better at explaining variation in behaviour, including deviant behaviour, than why most people behave the same way most of the time. Although most uses of the perspectives fall into these diagonally opposite cells, there are exceptions.

'Order' theorists (that is, those who emphasize stability and maintenance of the system) who approach this issue from a micro-interpretive position have been criticized from within this perspective for overestimating the conservatism of socialization and internalization. Perhaps the best known of these critiques is Dennis Wrong (1961), 'The Over-socialized Conception of Man in Modern Sociology'. Similarly, macro-structural theorists have battled over whether their perspective is inherently conservative. Conflict theorists have taken the position, along with Marxists, that structural theory need not be conservative. The most frequent target of that criticism has been the structural-functional theorists. Some of the latter emphasize an equilibrium-maintenance model of society in which change is rare, inherently disruptive, and difficult to account for sociologically other than as the breakdown in some aspect of the control system. Within such a theoretical model, change will obviously appear as a threat to the stability of the system, and theorists will evaluate change both pessimistically and negatively. But let us examine treatments of change on a more personal level.

Suppose someone were to ask you, as a reader of sociology, to explain the ways in which social change affects people. More specifically, suppose you were asked to forecast the effects of the so-called computer revolution on the nature of work or the effects of changes in the household division of labour on the psychological development of children. These are extremely difficult questions, and you would probably be tempted to avoid simplistic explanations and, if possible, any explanations at all. Still, if the questioner persisted, you might well respond in one of three general ways. A pessimistic response might emphasize the disruptive effects to be expected, perhaps contrasting the 'simpler' past with the complex uncertainties of the present and future. A more optimistic perspective might emphasize the benefits to be expected, mentioning the adaptability of human beings and the 'advances' that past social change has produced for us. Between these extremes, a realistic perspective might well concentrate on the conditions under which, and the categories for whom, positive or negative results actually occur.

Such a division into pessimists, optimists, and middle-of-the-roaders accurately reflects the range of perceiving and interpreting social change in sociology. In general those I shall call the *social-disorganization* theorists have been the pessimists, viewing change primarily as disruptive. Equally generally, those I categorize as *network theorists* have been the middle-of-the-roaders, whereas historically, few social scientists have been what I would consider optimists. Perhaps the development of sociology out of social criticism ensured that only a few among its practitioners would be optimistic.

Chapter 4 introduces the classical typological theorists. Most were pessimists, viewing the emerging modern world from the vantage point of their own upbringing in a more rural, smaller-scale society. Chapter 5 introduces the more modern network theorists. Most of these are contemporary sociologists whose work often emerges from a critique of the typological theorists. Although this is by no means the only or an exhaustive way of thinking about theory in sociology, it is a good starting point, and quite enough for an introductory text.

Having read this part of the book, the reader should have gained an appreciation of the theoretical context of many currently debated points in various substantive areas. Often the same basic points are at issue. Is change disruptive or adaptive? How does the present compare to the past? What have been the effects of various changes that have taken place in the last 200 years? How are these effects actually experienced by groups of people who differ systematically from one another in ways of interest to sociologists? Readers should be able to use these theoretical perspectives, added to what they have learned in part I, to offer competing explanations of various interesting phenomena. Attempts to apply the perspectives in the conduct of actual research as well as a critical examination of a few recurrent research findings form the substance of part III.

# CHAPTER 4

## Setters of the Agenda:
## The Precursors of Modern Sociology

> The despair of the masses is the key to the understanding of fascism. No 'revolt of the mob', no 'triumphs of unscrupulous propaganda', but stark despair caused by the breakdown of the old order and the absence of a new one. . . . Society ceases to be a community of individuals bound together by a common purpose, and becomes a chaotic hubbub of purposeless isolated nomads . . . The average individual cannot bear the utter atomization, the unreality and senselessness, the destruction of all order, of all society, of all rational individual existence through blind, incalculable, senseless forces created as a result of rationalization and mechanization. To banish these new demons has become the paramount objective of European society. (Drucker, [1939] 1985, as quoted in Nisbet, 1970)

All of us have been exposed to the prophets of doom whose subjects may vary but whose line is consistent. These are the experts who rail against our cities, decrying the loss of 'community' and suggesting that urban areas are hotbeds of crime and violence where people live only because they have no alternative. These experts are the ones who tell us that marriage and the family are dying institutions, done in by promiscuity and rampant selfishness. Experts like this believe that modern humanity is the unfortunate product of a technology out of control that is reducing people to mere cogs in the machine—without identity, loyalties, kin, or friends in a hostile environment over which they have quite lost any control.

The pessimistic forecasts of these experts echo the arguments made almost a century ago by a generation of social thinkers who lived at the end of the nineteenth century or in the early twentieth. For the most part they, too, were pessimists confronting a social situation of turmoil and chaos that became known as the period of the 'great transformation' (Polanyi, 1944). In the immediate aftermath of political, urban, and industrial revolutions that destroyed the traditional bases of order in their societies, these social critics looked at the new world emerging and were not convinced that its benefits outweighed its liabilities. They were, in fact, far more conscious of the heavy price they thought had been paid than of any significant gains purchased. Though the individuals differed in many ways, they shared an interest in the lost past and a common reluctance to consider the benefits of change that allows me to categorize them as theorists of social disorganization.

The late nineteenth and early twentieth centuries have long been regarded as a critical period in the formation of modern consciousness. (Hughes, 1958; Coser, 1971; Collins and

Makowsky, 1972; Aron, 1965, 1967). An understanding of this period is crucial if we are to understand the nature and origins of *disorganization* theory. A great many thinkers of that time concentrated on issues central to this book in ways that effectively set the agenda we are still dealing with. Some of these figures, including Freud, Croce, Bergson, and Jung, are not discussed here because they were not primarily sociologists; yet their intellectual struggles inform our current dialogue with history.

For our purposes we are interested primarily in those who shared both a healthy measure of pessimism about the emerging world and an inclination to contrast past and present in sharp dichotomy. This category includes the European sociologists Durkheim, Maine, and Tönnies; and the Americans who, a little later, took up the same theme—Cooley, Redfield, and Parsons. All of these and a good many more, in history, psychology, philosophy, or something quite different, tried to grasp the essence of the change they felt they were undergoing in society. All wrote in a period of intellectual, political, economic, and social turmoil. Each discussed the past they thought they could see disappearing and the future they thought they could make out in the looming shadows. They were the forefathers of the social sciences. It is probably accurate to say as well that their view of the emerging modern society was on balance more pessimistic than hopeful (Ruitenbeek, 1963). To round out the introduction of major early sociological writers, I deal briefly with the work of Weber, Durkheim, and Marx on social change in the larger context.

## DICHOTOMIES DESCRIBING SOCIAL CHANGE

Many of the authors I mentioned devised different dichotomies in an effort to grasp the movement of society from past to present or future. They also hoped to capture, through simplification, the qualitative social change they thought was in process—a change not in degree but in kind, which was permanent and undesirable. Their conceptualizations have enough in common that it makes sense to view their various dichotomies as a syndrome or coherent set of characterizations of this change and the nature of their society as well as the one they were forecasting.

One of their common themes is a change in the structural basis of solidarity or cohesion. A related theme deals with the loss of collective identity or community and its replacement by atomism or individualism. Many more modern authors have been equally impressed with similar trends, and some of these have contributed to literature on alienation in modern life, the arrival and consequences of the mass society (Nisbet, 1953), and the changing nature of identity, family, and religion in the modern world. Indeed the rise of totalitarian and fascist governments in the 1930s and the apparent normlessness and shifting moral quicksand of the 1970s, '80s and '90s have been fruitful ground for modern versions of equally pessimistic views of humankind's loss of contact with, and respect for, humanity. And commentators often view the counterculture—whether the California hippies of the 1960s or more recent intentional communities—as an effort to stem the tides of the future that these authors forecast so long ago. We can even see the popular series of books beginning with *Megatrends* (1982) as a description of some of the more positive counter-trends that may be emerging.

Figure 4.1 Theorists and Their Dichotomies

| *Author* | *Dichotomy* |
|---|---|
| Ferdinand Tönnies (1855–1936) | Gemeinschaft → gesellschaft |
| Emile Durkheim (1858–1917) | Mechanical → organic solidarity |
| Sir Henry Maine (1822–88) | Status → contract |
| Charles Horton Cooley (1864–1929) | Primary → secondary groups, relations |
| Robert Redfield (1897–1958) | Folk → urban |
| Talcott Parsons (1902–79) | Ascription → achievement |
| | Collectivity → self |
| | Particularism → universalism |

Each proposed dichotomy was, then, an attempt to capture the essence of past society, on the one hand, and present or future society, on the other (see Figure 4.1). Each dichotomy suggests that there has been a critical shift in process from one side of the dichotomy to the other and that as a result society will be forever altered and irreparably damaged. Thus the shift is uni-directional, irreversible, and qualitative rather than a mere change in degree in something already present. It is the cost of 'progress'.

## Tönnies: Gemeinschaft versus Gesellschaft

Perhaps the most important dichotomy—since it can be said to subsume the others—is Tönnies's conception of the transition from a gemeinschaft society to a gesellschaft society. Gemeinschaft refers to an intimate, enduring, and usually small-scale social system in which involvement is total, deep, and unqualified. By way of contrast, Tönnies describes the emerging gesellschaft society as transitory, superficial, and more businesslike. Gemeinschaft is private, genuine, and usually rural. By contrast, gesellschaft is public, a mechanical aggregate, and almost always urban. The analysis of the causes and implications of this transformation was Tönnies's life work.

## Durkheim: Mechanical versus Organic Solidarity

Durkheim drew attention to the nature of solidarity or cohesion in the past and in the newly emerging society. He sought to answer the ancient questions: What holds society together? What is the nature of the glue that binds us? What happens when this glue breaks down and the ties erode? Will societies fall apart? Durkheim's dichotomy is between mechanical solidarity and organic solidarity.

Mechanical solidarity was conceptualized as cohesion and community built on a foundation of similarity, an identity that is the product of like experience. Simpler societies were thought to be mechanical in that people were much like one another and each one did the same things as the others. They all shared experiences, attitudes, values, and beliefs. Cohesion was strong, and there was little conflict in such societies because everyone had similar statuses and responsibilities. The modern society Durkheim saw emerging was infinitely more complex. People differed in more ways than they were similar. The division of labour produced a situation quite unprecedented in which people no longer were all hunters, fishermen, craftsmen, and farmers. Only those who were best at farming were farmers, only the best fishermen fished, and so forth. Each person did what was best suited to his abilities. In time people had less and less in common as they became more and more specialized. Thus the division of labour and the specialization characteristic of it increased the differences among society's members and eroded the similarities that had previously provided the stability and glue binding members into a coherent social system.

For Durkheim the basis for the new solidarity or cohesion in society was the interdependence of unlike parts. This was to be a society of specialists held together because of the limitations of specialization. The fisherman could not make shoes; the artisan did not grow her own crops. Each depended on the work of others to satisfy his or her needs. It was a tenuous and fragile cohesion, but it was the shape of the future as Durkheim saw it.

## Maine: Status versus Contract

Sir Henry Maine was a British jurist of the same period as Durkheim who also tried to sum up the shift in human affairs by using a dichotomy. Not surprisingly he pointed to the increasing use of legal contracts to bind people to one another and ensure that obligations would be met. He suggests that in the previous period, then coming to its close, contracts were not necessary since people knew one another well and spent a lifetime in the same circles. In this situation informal sanctions were enough to assure compliance with obligations or responsibilities. For Maine it was apparent that the increasing mobility of the new era made informal controls inadequate and ensured that legal contracts would replace the informal to create and enforce obligations one person had to another.

## Cooley: Primary versus Secondary Groups and Relations

The American Charles Horton Cooley distinguished between the kinds of groups that formed the dominant milieu of one's life in the past as opposed to the emerging future. Each type of group also implied a type of relationship, and again Cooley believed that the dominant type of relationship in the period was changing in a fundamental way. For Cooley the past, the era of his youth but not his later years, was characterized by the predominance of what he called primary groups and primary relationships. His conception is close to Tönnies's, for primary groups are small, intimate, face-to-face groups typified by the family. These were being supplanted, in his view, by secondary groups and relationships. Secondary groups are much like Tönnies's gesellschaft; they are larger, more superficial groups, such as voluntary associations, labour unions, political parties, or relationships in the workplace. The relationships characterizing the primary group are holistic: one knows others with whom one interacts in a multi-dimensional way, a deeper and 'truer' manner; secondary relationships, on the other hand, are specialized, limited to a piece of the person, in a sense, and restricted. An example of a primary relationship is that between parents and children or between siblings. An example of a secondary relationship is that of doctor to patient, or teacher to student. For Cooley the essence of the social change was a change in the quality of relationships and the circumstances in which these occurred. The world was becoming a qualitatively different place and in ways a more unstable place, a faster changing, more risky environment, and a less friendly place, where more responsibility was placed on the individual to make his own way, protecting himself as he went and weighing others carefully as he proceeded.

Let me interrupt the description of these dichotomies briefly to breathe a little more life into these theoretical skeletons by updating Cooley's dichotomy, fleshing it out with current work we can easily trace back to Cooley's concept of primary and secondary relations. I could do the same with any of the other dichotomies, and it might be worthwhile for you to do this yourself since this study of our classic ancestors is meant to be neither hero worship nor respectful acknowledgement of antecedents. These thinkers and their work remain provocative and useful today, and it is this current value that explains their appearance here.

Many modern writers have taken up the implications of Cooley's distinction, and we can find echoes of earlier theorists in much current work on roles and the presentation of self. Thus, for example, Erving Goffman's work on this subject draws attention to how we manage our presentations of our 'selves' to others in order to control the impressions they will form. (See, for example, Goffman, 1959 and 1967.) This idea of 'impression management', the concept of the social world as a manipulated show that is somehow artificial, is a derivation of these early dichotomies. In a primary relationship we 'drop our masks' to show a desire for authenticity, a willingness to accept one another unconditionally, in poverty and in wealth, in bad moods and good, in fact as well as in diplomatic stage-managed 'white lies'. Only in a world of secondary relationships do we realize the possibilities of 'faking it' without being caught. Only if we have to pretend for just a short time and only well enough to pass a superficial test by others who are rarely experts or sceptical of our authenticity can we get away with the dramatic presentation of ourselves as other than our true selves. And these conditions, which are perhaps necessary if we are even to consider arranging ourselves so consciously (and to spawn so many analysts of the phenomenon), are the conditions of the gesellschaft.

It seems clear enough that the temptation to pretend to be someone or something we are not is greater under specific conditions. First, we must believe that altering our persona will be advantageous. In other words, we have to think others will be more impressed with us if we adopt manners, language, or claims to knowledge or experience that we do not, in fact, possess. Second, we must believe that, for one reason or another, we will be able to pretend successfully, that is, without being exposed. This could mean we must believe the audience is naive and will be neither suspicious nor able to judge our claims. It could also mean that we believe we can maintain the pose without, for example, laughing or exceeding our ability to carry it off (by running out of expertise or getting caught in a contradiction or by being introduced to others who are more knowledgeable or sceptical than our original audience). All this depends in part on our assessment of how likely it is we will meet the audience again. If we think the encounter is likely to be short and unimportant, and not one where we could be called to account, we might risk pretending. The secondary relationships of the gesellschaft have at least increased the proportion of relationships that fall into this category.

There is also a risk that what is involved will lead us at some point to be manipulative, not only with our impression, but with both ourselves and others, whom we increasingly view as objects and from whom we are increasingly alienated or distanced. We behave inauthentically, and we may become rather callous about the consequences, for actions have consequences, even if we are not present or held directly responsible for them. The doctor who claims to be a surgeon may never meet a patient again, but surgery is consequential. The quack psychiatrist may do severe damage for which he may not be held responsible. The person who says he will call and would really like to get together but does not do so produces consequences even if not directly touched by them.

This loss of concern for others is a characteristic often alleged to pervade cities, the locale of the gesellschaft. And the strategies adopted to cope in a world of masks and mirrors, where pretence is hard to tell from authenticity, are a problem alleged to be characteristic of modern society. Where even a person's body or the colour of their hair or eyes can be manipulated in the service of impression management—with dyes, contact lenses, face-lifts, implants, and other cosmetic surgery—what are we to believe is real? What indeed is reality?

When we attend large universities and take classes with hundreds of others, none of whom we know, how do we learn what people are really like? When we are anonymous and the likelihood of our being identified is slim, why not vandalize the buildings, spray-paint a car or two, write graffiti on the walls? When no consequences are expected, what constrains our behaviour? When you can get away with so much and remain untouched and unidentified, how is anyone to know you have even been there?

Problems of identity and identity management in a world of strangers are a central implication of this dichotomy treatment. For now, let us end this discussion and return to the dichotomies themselves.

### Redfield: Folk versus Urban

Robert Redfield directs our attention to yet another aspect of the social change he experienced. The world was fast becoming urban. The demographer Kingsley Davis (1965) estimates that as late as 1850 only 2 per cent of the entire world's population lived in cities of more than 100,000 persons. By the end of the twentieth century, perhaps 40 per cent of all people will live in cities of this size. Many more, of course, will live in somewhat smaller cities located in what, only a generation or two ago, were large rural areas. For Redfield this urbanization of society was fundamental, and his dichotomy juxtaposes the contrary lifestyles, expectations, and experiences of folk society in the past with those of the urban society on the near horizon. The qualities of these somewhat contradictory kinds of life are essentially those described by Cooley, Tönnies, Durkheim, and Maine.

### Parsons: Ascription versus Achievement, Collectivity versus Self, Particularism versus Universalism

Several more dichotomies were contributed to this literature by Talcott Parsons. Among these, three overlap and complement those of the other authors considered. For Parsons, the crucial dimension in describing change was that of ascription-achievement. The past was characterized by ascription; the emerging future, by achievement. In the past everyone was severely limited in what they could become by virtue of characteristics over which they had no control—characteristics with which they were born. One was born male or female, and this set straightforward limits on one's possibilities. One was born a serf or a lord, and this, too, set rigid barriers on what the future held. To be the son of a farmer meant that one would be a farmer—the future was prescribed, the roles assigned at birth. There was little or no freedom of choice. The ascribed characteristics of sex, age, religion, and status were the givens that determined what little freedom of choice there was.

By contrast Parsons thought he detected a movement from this emphasis on ascription to an emphasis on achievement—where each person's future was in his own hands with no arbitrary limit on what he could achieve or become. Only talent counted, and one could become anything one could learn or earn. In this world, race, sex, age, or religion were irrelevant. The boss's son did not automatically replace his father. Kinship counted far less than ability and ambition.

We can use the same terms to describe in general the type of criteria most often employed to allocate rewards and opportunities. Thus a society can emphasize ascriptive or achievement criteria. Think, for example, of the classical Indian caste system where opportunities were severely restricted for all by reference to an overwhelmingly important ascribed characteristic—caste. In such an ascriptive society, most decisions about people depend on what a person is, not what the person can do or achieve. In such circumstances it is who you are in ascribed terms that counts, not what you can do. In South Africa under apartheid, the 'master trait' (Hughes, 1945) was race. In such a society, equality of oppor-tunity has a special meaning—equality within the ascribed category—for no one can leave the category.

During the feudal period in Europe or in other feudal systems of stratification, occupa-tion was a given. A child of a serf grew up with only one occupational possibility. No amount of personal ability allowed the child to achieve another occupation.

The change Parsons described as one from systems where ascribed criteria predominate to those where achievement criteria predominate is a change in stratification and related systems of social mobility and its control. Michael Young (1961), for example, has written of 'the rise of the meritocracy'. By this phrase he contrasts the new premises of social mobility with old ones summarized as aristocracy, gerontocracy, plutocracy, or even democ-racy. In the future society Young sees rapidly approaching, only merit will count. No ascribed characteristics will be relevant in allocating opportunities. Neither sex nor race, age nor kinship will make a systematic difference in what one can become. This means such characteristics will no longer be variables significantly related to other variables like income, education, or prestige. Such factors will no longer, according to Young, be capable of explaining any pattern of behaviour. Instead they will be randomly distributed across all categories of the dependent variable and will cease to be meaningful social and sociolog-ical categories. More specifically, age, race, sex, and kinship will not be useful predictors. You will not improve your guess as to whether someone is a doctor or a nurse by knowing their sex. You will not improve your ability to predict a person's income by knowing his race. The only predictor of one's place in society will be ability. Decisions will be based on merit alone, and nothing will be fixed in advance or taken for granted.

Parsons also dealt with collective identity as a crucial dimension along which change took place. In the society of the past, each individual was part of a community; indeed collective identity was far stronger than individual identity. Individual identity was commonly sacrificed in the interests of the collectivity, as exemplified in the phrase 'my country, right or wrong'. Only when ascribed characteristics lose their deterministic power to set limits does collective identity based on those attributes decline and a stronger sense of self-identity grow. It seems as if these two versions of identity—collective and personal—compete, and only if one declines can the other increase. As you might imagine, this raises intriguing problems in situations where a person's collective and individual identities conflict. For Parsons, in any event, modern society was ever more self-oriented and less and less collectivity-oriented. It was more individualistic and less communal.

A third and related dichotomy Parsons pointed to was the nature and scope of society's rules and regulations. In the earlier form of society, rules and decisions were particularistic. They were created for the special cases and not for universal application. In the emerging modern society, rules and laws were intended for universal application, and subsequent decisions were restricted by these rules regardless of any idiosyncratic features. This is closely related to the shift from ascription to achievement. For achievement orientation to become dominant, it had to have advantages. If ascribed characteristics, in fact, limited the success of those who had achieved a great deal and had satisfied the 'rules' for upward mobility, those disqualified from success at birth would not even attempt to earn their way. Indeed, they might seek revolution.

Achievement orientation requires and sustains universalism, and universalism in the making of allocation rules and decisions encourages even women, non-whites, and others with two strikes against them to continue to strive for the success that is, theoretically at least, not denied them. Of course many critics have suggested it is both frustrating and alienating for people who believe they have equal opportunity and that they have met or exceeded the achievement criteria and deserve a reward to find themselves still brought up short by discrimination they were told no longer existed.

## INTEGRATION, PROBLEMS, AND PROSPECTIVE USES

Though all these dichotomies differ in emphasis, they share a common tone. All the social critics see a new order emerging from the old, and all point to areas within it that seem highly problematic and fragile. Some authors are pessimistic in their assessment of this emerging world, though the social scientists were more careful and objective than the philosophers, moralists, and novelists of the transition period. All these authors would likely be in considerable agreement about the shape of both the old and the new social reality. Though each emphasizes a different aspect, the themes are compatible.

It would be well to note here that all these writers to some extent fall prey to a common logical error. They recall or re-create a golden age of community with which to compare the present and future. In so doing they are guilty of a degree of romanticism since their evaluation of the gemeinschaft is rather one-sided. As anyone growing up in a small town knows, gemeinschaft remains stable because social change is not tolerated. Where everyone knows everyone else well, strong sanctions enforce expected behaviour, and change, if possible at all, is difficult. The lure of the city is precisely its vibrant, changing, exciting possibilities. Any large city is a complex society free from the rigidity that accompanies strong, long-standing expectations and social controls. It is true that in moving to the city one loses one's anchors and often finds oneself challenged by the variety of people and behaviour, but this is not necessarily threatening or alienating. It also presents an opportunity for growth and change, that is reinforced by many structural features of the urban context just as such change and growth is discouraged in the small town.

C.W. Mills (1943) wrote a classic analysis of the early American sociologists who dealt with the alleged social problems or 'pathology' of the city. He pointed out that they all shared a perspective in terms of morality and values because of their common origins and location in social structure; this perspective clearly influenced their analyses. In his discussion of this 'professional ideology of the social pathologists' his main point was simply that their views were not so objective as they thought. Like all of us, they were products of their time, and because they came from rural and religious backgrounds they could not appreciate the city's possibilities. The sociologists whose views I have briefly introduced could also be accused of pessimism arising from a bias, that is, their selective recollection of all the good qualities in the passing society in which they came of age.

In a way they could hardly avoid being unfair in the value judgements that are reflected in their dichotomies. The gemeinschaft still calls to us, and many of us would seek such a small-scale utopia. Variously called Eden, Shangri-la, or the like today, it exists only on television and in romantic literature and movies. These early social theorists feared what they did not understand as the door to a new world opened ahead of them; they looked back with fond but biased recollections at the disappearing past.

Even a quick description of these dichotomies demonstrates clearly that they overlap to a considerable degree. They also provide fertile ground for hypotheses and analyses of what implications these changes might have for the institutions that make up our society. Because they overlap, we can think of them as a syndrome or an interrelated set of changes that took place simultaneously during the late nineteenth and early twentieth centuries.

Each dichotomy is an attempt to express the essence of a complicated social upheaval. None of these authors believed their view was complete; the phenomena they sought to grapple with were far too complex. Each sought a distillation, a purification, an exaggeration of the social change they were experiencing. Thus each dichotomy is an oversimplification, what Max Weber would call an 'ideal type'. We cannot claim that any society is wholly ascribed or achieved, for example, but Parsons believed that the emphasis was systematically shifting from ascription to achievement. No society would be composed exclusively of secondary relationships or groups, but these were becoming the predominant form of association, according to Cooley. The same can be said of all these dichotomies. Weber intended the concept of an ideal type to be used as a device for seeing more clearly by paring away the accidental and exaggerating the essential components.

Merely transforming these theoretical dichotomies into empirical assertions provokes other questions. Thus some forms of associations progressively become more common and others less so. What kinds of relationships change first or fastest? Which bases of ascription are most resistant and why? Can you have interdependence without a formal contract to ensure performance? How do people come to think of their identity when ascribed characteristics lose importance? Along which dichotomy do we seem to have progressed farthest in the direction predicted?

In every case the single-headed arrows joining the two extremes are based on the writer's belief that this shift was qualitatively new, fundamental, and hence one-directional. But is it? Is it not possible that what were described as dichotomies would more accurately be viewed as continua? Surely this is implicit when we discuss ideal types and a shift in predominant relationships. In point of fact dichotomous treatment is merely a device to simplify comparison by looking at pure cases toward the end of what is in reality a continuum. Sociologists often contrast black and white, knowing full well that there are countless shades of grey between the extremes.

Can you imagine any circumstances under which society might shift back along any of these continua? For example, is it possible that at some times and in certain places movement reverses direction? Is this so far-fetched when one considers a recession as a period of de-industrialization and when we think of the numbers of people who have dropped out of our industrial system to opt for a simpler life in a rural community? Are there circumstances under which we might imagine society moving back again toward ascription from achievement? Consider recessionary periods when kinship may well become of great importance for determining how scarce rewards and opportunities are allocated among too many equally qualified candidates.

It is possible that the linear uni-directional relationships I have described are, in fact, more varied than suggested. If so, we should reconceptualize the descriptions as change in *variables*, and we might profitably discuss the variation. It is the *extent* of gemeinschaft or *degree* of urbanization we are interested in now, not merely the ideal-type society. We concentrate on the location, circumstances, conditions, and degree, not the fact that we are urban. When we view polar types as locations on a continuum, we are led to ask innumerable questions to pinpoint the position on the continuum for a particular society or part of one at one time under specific conditions. In other words we are beginning to rephrase the original questions to ask, not whether change is complete, but how much and for whom change has occurred and, also more exactly, how these changes are produced. For example, as a result of what exactly does Durkheim suggest that organic solidarity comes about? What specifically is it about a social system that causes the changes these theorists described?

## THE LARGER PICTURE OF SOCIAL CHANGE: DURKHEIM, WEBER, AND MARX

The dichotomies frequently describe the state of the dependent or result variable only. They are not themselves descriptions of the independent or causal variable nor are they specifications of exactly how the causal effects are created. To understand these, one must look beyond simple dichotomies.

Put another way, this suggests we might well adopt a broader view of the question, one in which dichotomies are only a small part.

**Figure 4.2** Some Provisional Conceptualizations of Change

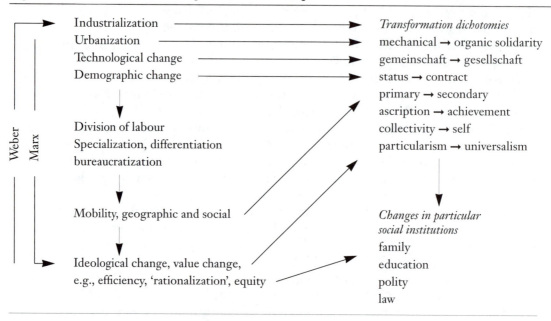

In Figure 4.2 the dichotomies we have so far dealt with occupy only a small part of the area on one side of the figure. The rest of the space contains many phenomena suggested by these same writers as the engines of the social change described in their dichotomies, and some of the intervening variables or processes through which the causal sequence *may* operate. The diagram thus suggests a possible relationship between demographic or population changes and the kind of social change captured in the transformation dichotomies where the latter are treated all together as essentially the dependent variable. In effect I have tried to enlarge the scope of our discussion to consider the sources as well as the effects of social change.

In the process we have opened up new avenues for exploring the relationships among these processes. Putting this last idea another way, it is not yet entirely clear where arrows might join terms in this diagram. Some variables could mediate relationships by intervening or as intervening variables in the chain of causation. Other relationships might well be double-headed or reciprocal, with change in one leading to change in another, thus reinforcing the first trend. Consider the provisional arrows carefully and sceptically. Which make sense, and which do not? How would you join the terms of the diagram? Consider, for example, that for Marx ideology was strictly a by-product of class relations and it was class interests that were the driving force of change, whereas for Weber ideology played a much greater independent role in producing change.

A large body of sociological theory and empirical research deals with the general topic of social change. For example, if industrialization is a key independent or causal variable that leads to many changes by altering the workplace and work relationships, exactly how are its effects created? If urbanization is an engine of social change, exactly how does it facilitate the emergence of gesellschaft? The sources of social change are many and varied (Appelbaum, 1970), but the diagram contains only those commonly considered to be important. Most of the classic theorists dealt with this issue.

## Durkheim: Division of Labour

For Durkheim the increasing division and specialization of labour were fundamental. But where did these changes come from? Perhaps they emerged from the evolutionary rule that systems tend to increase in complexity over time. Durkheim's *Division of Labor in Society* (1893), which sets forth his views in some detail, suggests that what he termed increasing 'moral density' is crucial for determining the nature of social relationships. Moral density is simply the number of people in interaction; so what Durkheim postulates is a basic demographic independent variable leading to change in the nature of solidarity. As societies grow, the number of people interacting increases, and this leads to a division of labour if the society is to manage its resources effectively. This, in turn, suggests another critical factor, the demand for efficiency, or at least effectiveness, in the system. Durkheim's main interest was the effects of such change on solidarity and morality. He proposes that mechanical solidarity is the product of similarity and that the moral code in such a society will be strong, consensually held by all, and represented primarily in criminal laws that are harsh and punitive and that serve to reinforce the moral order. With population growth and the division of labour that allegedly ensues, people diversify to become different from one another and more individuated. Having less in common, they share less and less in the overall consensual morality. Instead their relationships of interdependence become more specialized; adherence to them, or disputes arising from them, require specialized civil law. Since such transformations lead to contract law, the proportion of all law that is civil and contractual rather than criminal changes as societies change. Civil law is not punitive, but restitutive; its purpose is to restore and reinforce obligations rather than to punish. Hence it has less moral force, and the society becomes increasingly fragile since organic solidarity accompanied by restitutive law is weaker than a system of simple mechanical solidarity reinforced by punitive criminal law.

For Durkheim societies would break down under continued pressure. Then traditional agents of socialization and transmission of cultural and social control would cease to apply, leaving individuals in a state of normlessness, or anomie. At this point rules would be confused or non-existent, and the individual would be at a loss as to how to act since so little guidance was available and the old anchors of identity and guideposts for behaviour had grown outmoded. In Durkheim's view the loss of social restraints was a structural phenomenon with the gravest consequences. In his classic book *Suicide* (1897) he analyses self-destruction precisely in relation to this loss of restraint. 'Anomic suicide' is directly related to this loss; another type of suicide, which he calls 'egoistic', reflects complete individuation or the unwillingness of the individual to accept any restraints that once might have held him back from self-destruction. Influenced by the period of the French Revolution, the Dreyfus affair, and the rapid industrialization and urbanization of France, Durkheim wondered whether any stable society would ever again exist.

The kind of division of labour and differentiation central to Durkheim's thought is common to many of the theorists you are likely to come across in various areas. For example, W.F. Ogburn's theory of family change is consistent with Durkheim. Ogburn writes of the family's progressive 'loss of functions' to other new institutions, like schools or homes for the aged, and of the emergence of specialized labour, such as day-care workers and psychiatrists.

With respect to urban sociology, progressive differentiation is again a common theme, as are division of labour and specialized subdivision. Much of the literature on the city deals as well with solidarity and cohesion, and a great deal of it treats the city as the prototype—the clearest instance or foremost example—of the threats and consequences of the breakdown under pressure that Durkheim discussed. Thus we come once more to the social pathologists and their view of social disintegration in the city and its attendant pathological behaviour—rape, murder, violent crimes, mental illness, alcoholism, divorce—an endless litany, the product of the progressive loss of restraints in the individuated and anomic city.

## Weber: Rationalization

Let me now reintroduce another great social thinker who dealt with social change in much of his work. Among other contributions, Max Weber (1864–1920) inspired the study of bureaucracies and the process of bureaucratization in all its ramifications. For Weber bureaucratic arrangements in organizations were a relatively new phenomenon, at least as the predominant organizational form. He asked what a bureaucracy was, where it came from as an organizational form, why it was becoming more common, and what its consequences would be for those who encountered bureaucracies in their lives. More generally he provides us with a theory of social change that concentrates on legitimacy and authority and the bases through which power can be translated into legitimate authority. Weber's main theme is the progressive rationalization of the world we know in all its aspects. Ultimately he suggests that rational-legal arrangements will predominate, though not permanently or without hazard, because they are finally more efficient or rational than any other organizational structure. Demands for efficiency inevitably lead to a bureaucratically administered society. Efficiency is simply not compatible with particularistic and whimsical rules, which fail to provide enough systematic and predictable guidelines. In fact, particularistic rule is almost a contradiction in terms. Still less is efficiency compatible with basing the selection of people for responsible positions in government or industry solely on kinship, ethnicity, sex, or other ascribed characteristics. Efficiency and the maximum rationalization of the system in terms of the best allocation of human energy to positions require that the most able candidate be selected after the widest possible pool of contenders is considered.

Once this notion of the importance of efficiency as a criterion has somehow entered the society, it seemed to Weber that bureaucratic organizations would soon follow. For Weber bureaucracy was the epitome of rationalization. It was a rule-based hierarchical arrangement of 'offices' filled by the most competent people who could be found, all of whom treated their progression through the organization as a career.

Bureaucracies epitomized what Weber called the rational-legal basis of authority in society. One's power was based on competence or ability (rather than on ascribed traits), and this power was circumscribed, or bounded, by a full set of rules. The rules spelled out the power and the obligations of the incumbent so that little room was left for discretion or abuse of power. Indeed bureaucracy as an organizational form minimizes the role of personality in the conduct of the office. For Weber this trend toward a more rational-legal basis for behaviour in society was clear: the future he saw included organizational dominance by bureaucracies rather than by organizations based on blood ties or other ascriptive criteria.

Still Weber recognized the likely flaws of bureaucracies, and his analysis includes two other competing bases of authority. Weber recognized that rational-legal authority was likely to be threatened on occasion by charismatic leaders, whose authority is based on their personalities alone. Their followers obey such people not because of the leader's position or expertise but because of the leader's personal aura. Christ, Gandhi, Buddha, and Hitler are examples of leaders whose success was based on personal magnetism.

Of course charisma is not easy to identify, and some people find particular leaders charismatic while others do not. It is not an easily demonstrated phenomenon, nor is it a stable one. The most serious problem with charismatic leaders is succession. If they are to lead successful organizations or causes—religious, military, or otherwise—they, or someone, must provide for a successor when the leader dies. It is this problem that Weber discusses as the 'routinization of charisma'. If unique personality conveys charisma, how can the organization created by a charismatic leader survive her or his loss? Thus, although charismatic movements or organizations will continue to come into being—though they can never be common—rational-legal organization is a more secure basis for long-lasting effectiveness.

The third basis of authority Weber discusses is traditional authority. This is authority respected by others or defined as legitimate because of history or tradition. To Weber it seems clear that the longer an organization lasts, the more likely it is that its adherents or members will grant the leadership authority on the basis of tradition rather than either charisma or rational-legal rules. This being the case, Weber's analysis of social change oscillates. Some organizations that spring up under charismatic leaders cannot solve the problems of routinization and so they disappear. Other organizations originally based on a rational-legal foundation persist so that the basis of authority shifts to tradition. This tradition may well be challenged eventually by a charismatic opponent or a reminder of the rational-legal origins. A good deal of interesting sociological analysis of organizations chronicles just such histories as sects are transformed into 'churches' and then splintered again into sects and so on.

Despite this constant change, the model of rational-legal bases of action and authority will predominate, Weber feels, because it is somewhat more stable than either competing form and usually more efficient when functioning properly. We need hardly add that it does not always function properly today, when the very term *bureaucratic* conjures up images of red tape and faceless people in three-piece suits hiding behind the rules of their office.

In his discussions of social change, Weber contributed far more than the analysis of legitimacy and the changing foundations of authority. He also argues that ideology is an important independent variable that causes change. Specifically he suggests that the

Protestant ethic of hard work as a means to salvation was partly responsible for the development of the capitalist economic system. In making this argument, Weber was taking issue—as he did on many matters—with the views of Karl Marx, who had argued that ideology or philosophy has no causal power and merely reflects change that is generated elsewhere by the true causal agents. Marx identified these agents as the relationship of people to the means of production.

Weber also took issue with Marx about the nature of stratification systems. Whereas Marx's view was essentially one-dimensional, with all else a function of people's relationship to the means of production, in Weber's view stratification had three dimensions that were related in complex ways in different societies and at different times. For Weber stratification was partly a matter of economic position (Marx's social class), but it also involved a dimension of power that was essentially political and a dimension of status that was a contest for prestige. While stratification involved struggles among organized contenders, this organization took place along several dimensions in addition to Marx's.

To Weber, then, the direction of change was in some ways fairly clear; but change was a permanent feature, and every society would at any time be a changing result of numerous internal conflicts. His view was that only when the sociologist adopts a comparative method and views several societies within a broad historical framework would the main patterns of development come into focus.

## Marx: Class Conflict

The third intellectual giant of this period has already been introduced. Karl Marx (1818–83) is best known as the father of communism and author (with Friedrich Engels) of the *Communist Manifesto*. Marx was a major contributor to political philosophy, economics, and sociology. Though it is difficult to separate those themes in his work, the last is the most important to us here. For Marx ([1848] 1969) 'the history of all hitherto existing society is the history of class struggles'. Marx considered the source of all social change to be conflict—conflict between classes. In turn he defined classes according to people's relationship to the means of production. As these relationships changed over historical time and from society to society, the conflict changed, but conflict was fundamental. As society differentiated and some people came to own the means of production and others became workers who sold their labour to these owners, the basic interests of these two groups moved farther apart. In England and Germany, where Marx lived and wrote during the early years of the Industrial Revolution, it was easy to see firsthand the exploitation characterizing industrial systems. With no child-labour laws, no unions, and little compassion on the part of the factory owners, workers were often ruthlessly exploited and then discarded when no longer as productive as others. Marx, who believed that such exploitation of the multitudes by the few could not persist, devoted his life to the overthrow of such a system and its replacement by a more humane one in which work would not be alienating and no person would be exploited by another.

In most respects Marx's sociology of social class, conflict, the social basis of knowledge, work, and alienation have become standard parts of any current social scientist's perspective.

In fact, Marx's observations on the progressive alienation and powerlessness of the individual are themes taken up in much of the work on organizational sociology, industrial sociology, political and economic sociology, and stratification. His general view of class conflict in urban, differentiated societies is an undercurrent in all treatments of current society. How much conflict is there? How much consensus? How much alienation and in what sense? How can those questions be addressed, and how have they historically been addressed? Is change revolutionary, evolutionary, incremental, planned and administered by people, or is it something technologically determined that is forcing us to adapt to it as best we can? In the analysis of cities, organizations, societies, and identity, such issues become crucial. In our day of rapid technological innovation, it is increasingly urgent that we decide if technology is a powerful force for change beyond our control or a force we can shape in directions we might wish.

## CONCLUSION: THE THREAT AND COST OF OVERGENERALIZATION

Returning finally to the schema of social change at the heart of this discussion, we must note that the relationships among the forces depicted, which we are now prepared to consider as possible independent variables, are indeed complex. In Western societies industrialization and urbanization took place simultaneously, but they need not do so; in other parts of the world we find instances of urban but relatively non-industrial systems and industrialized but relatively non-urban systems. Here we should take our cue from Weber's recommendation that sociology must be comparative and historical.

Many modern and critical sociologists have insisted that we distinguish the consequences of industrialization from those of capitalism. We must also distinguish the effects of urbanization from those of industrialization. Such distinctions are critical in developing and using the sociological perspective. Though we seek universal propositions, we must be extremely conscious of the possibility that our observations are in fact conditional, that is, dependent on other variables of which we may be unaware. Thus American social scientists are frequently accused of overgeneralizing, of assuming that if a regularity or pattern of behaviour shows up in the United States, it will do so everywhere else as well. They are accused of ignoring the importance of the American context in the studies of development, bureaucracy, or the family.

More abstractly, though, a study can be conducted only in a single place, whether a society or a laboratory. This means that what is really a variable—that is, the effect of *variation* in context (national, urban, classroom, social class, laboratory size, type, staff, or whatever)—does not vary for that particular study. In the absence of variation, of course, this 'variable' is a constant that can easily be allowed to fade in importance since it has no demonstrable effect on the dependent variable. Only variables are related to one another in the pattern of behaviour. Context becomes a parameter, and a study done in a unique set of conditions can be incorrectly generalized to other conditions where it might not apply. For example, the effects of educating a large proportion of a country's young people may not be the same in the United States as it would be even in a country as similar as Canada.

Alexander Lockhart (1975) has written an interesting analysis of this phenomenon. He argues that in the United States in the 1950s and 1960s certain social analysts developed the idea that further maturation of the American system could not be achieved by investment in additional capital equipment. Increases in productivity required investment in what they called 'human capital', or educated and skilled people to operate and improve the existing sophisticated equipment. In the aftermath of the first sputnik, the United States renewed its commitment to quality in education and began expanding its programs to train young people.

The ideology of investment in human capital, which was exported around the world, was quickly adopted in Canada. Prominent Canadian politicians and social scientists promoted the view that advanced industrialization and high productivity required highly skilled personnel and that investment in educational expansion would pay off hugely. In response Canada's system of post-secondary education was expanded dramatically in the 1960s.

The predicted boom should have begun in the late 1970s and continued into the late 1990s. Instead, as Edward Harvey (1974) first documented, few jobs are available for these overtrained Canadians, and only the unemployment figures have boomed. In Lockhart's analysis, what happened was that expectations that made sense in a particular place (the United States) were interpreted as universal and applied uncritically and inappropriately in places that were structurally different (Canada). The jobs in management and research and development that absorb so many highly trained Americans do not exist in Canada's branch-plant economy. In short the Americans employed in some of those jobs, in Los Angeles, Chicago, Denver, Houston, or New York, work in the head offices of firms whose subsidiaries are located in Toronto, Vancouver, and Montreal. Americans are employed at jobs that are withdrawn from the Canadian pool as a result of Canada's dependence on the United States. This withdrawal appears on both sides of the ledger, as jobs absorbing trained Americans and as non-existent Canadian jobs for the newly qualified but unemployed Canadians.

To continue the line of the Lockhart argument, it is interesting that we are now well into the process of creating a new ideology to legitimate the reduction of funding in all sectors of social service in Canada (and to a considerable extent in the United States as well). Cutbacks are urged in the interest of 'putting our house in order' and of recognizing that 'we have spent our children's inheritance', in the process, creating false expectations, false aspirations, and a generation that considers itself entitled to a variety of government services. In an earlier day, critics might have called some aspects of the new ideology élitist: now it is just good housekeeping.

The error of overgeneralizing from specific situations or phenomena is easy to make, but it can be serious. Certainly it is one we ought to be leery of making. The classic theorists were probably not so familiar with some of the problems that such overgeneralizations could produce as we are today. Certainly, in their quest for universal patterns, they seldom devoted themselves to the conditional questions that specify circumstances and relevant subpopulations, trends, and counter-trends alike.

## SELECTED QUESTIONS

1. How does your own experience, whether of life in a small town or a big city, fit the models developed by the theorists of this chapter? In what respects does your experience cast doubt on their positions and in what respects confirm it?

2. The concept of *ethnocentrism* refers to judging another culture by the yardstick of one's own culture. Sociologists contrast it with the concept of *sociological relativism*, which refers to the process by which one attempts to describe and assess cultures in their own rights, without assuming that differences from one's own society are marks of inferiority. How were the classic theorists ethnocentric?

3. What do you think are the social-structural implications for the family, for instance, of widespread ideological commitment to 'fairness' or 'equality'? How would family arrangements be changed by such a social commitment?

4. Why is it so crucial that we clearly distinguish the effects of industrial development from those of capitalism?

5. Find two or three examples from current media coverage that seem to embody the kind of pessimistic evaluation of change that the thinkers of this chapter are said to have. How might these accounts be rewritten from a competing perspective or, indeed, can they be?

## ILLUSTRATIVE READING

In the following excerpt from a journal article, Stanley Milgram takes up a theme developed by Georg Simmel (1903) in his essay 'The Metropolis and Mental Life'. The disorganization thesis is evident in the Milgram contribution and in most elements of Simmel's original version. It was Simmel's contention that 'the psychological basis of the metropolitan type of individuality consists in the intensification of nervous stimulation which results from the swift and uninterrupted change of outer and inner stimuli.' (Wolff, 1950: 410) In contrast to small town and rural life, the city bombards us each day with far more stimuli than we can naturally handle. 'Intellectuality is thus seen to preserve subjective life against the overwhelming power of metropolitan life' (413). This idea has many elements, but most are related to what Simmel describes as the 'blasé attitude which has been so unconditionally reserved to the metropolis'. Additional psychological attributes include an attitude and style of behaviour he called 'reserved'. This quality is produced from an element of distrust of people whom we meet so briefly and superficially and is an adaptation to the multitude of stimuli that would otherwise overwhelm us. In Simmel's view this reserve is what makes urbanites appear cold and heartless in the eyes of small-town people.

Simmel's style is provocative and rhetorical; his view of the metropolis primarily negative. Not only is Simmel's view at the foundation of the deterministic theory proposed by

Louis Wirth and elaborated by others, but it also contains the seeds of Fischer's subcultural theory and its network basis. First, though, let us see how Milgram updates and restates Simmel in the following excerpt.

### THE EXPERIENCE OF LIVING IN CITIES: A PSYCHOLOGICAL ANALYSIS

*Stanley Milgram*

> When I first came to New York it seemed like a nightmare. As soon as I got off the train at Grand Central I was caught up in pushing, shoving crowds on 42nd Street. Sometimes people bumped into me without apology; what really frightened me was to see two people literally engaged in combat for possession of a cab. Why were they so rushed? Even drunks on the street were bypassed without a glance. People didn't seem to care about each other at all.

This statement represents a common reaction to a great city, but it does not tell the whole story. Obviously cities have great appeal because of their variety, eventfulness, possibility of choice, and the stimulation of an intense atmosphere that many individuals find a desirable background to their lives. Where face-to-face contacts are important, the city offers unparalleled possibilities. It has been calculated by the Regional Plan Association[1] that in Nassau County, a suburb of New York City, an individual can meet 11,000 others within a 10-minute radius of his office by foot or car. In Newark, a moderate-sized city, he can meet more than 20,000 persons within this radius. But in midtown Manhattan he can meet fully 220,000. So there is an order-of-magnitude increment in the communication possibilities offered by a great city. That is one of the bases of its appeal and, indeed, of its functional necessity. The city provides options that no other social arrangement permits. But there is a negative side also, as we shall see.

Granted that cities are indispensable in complex society, we may still ask what contribution psychology can make to understand the experience of living in them. What theories are relevant? How can we extend our knowledge of the psychological aspects of life in cities through empirical inquiry? If empirical inquiry is possible, along what lines should it proceed? In short, where do we start in constructing urban theory and in laying out lines of research?

Observation is the indispensable starting point. Any observer in the street of midtown Manhattan will see (i) large numbers of people, (ii) a high population density, and (iii) heterogeneity of population. These three factors need to be at the root of any sociopsychological theory of city life, for they condition all aspects of our experience in the metropolis. Louis Wirth,[2] if not the first to point to these factors, is nonetheless the sociologist who relied most heavily on them in his analysis of the city. Yet, for a psychologist, there is something unsatisfactory about Wirth's theoretical variables. Numbers, density, and heterogeneity are demographic facts but they are not yet psychological facts. They are external to the individual. Psychology needs an idea that links the individual's *experience* to the demographic circumstances of urban life.

One link is provided by the concept of overload. This term, drawn from systems analysis, refers to a system's inability to process inputs from the environment because there are too many inputs for the system to cope with, or because successive inputs come so fast that input A cannot be processed when input B is presented. When overload is present, adaptations occur. The system must set priorities and make choices. A may be processed first while B is kept in abeyance, or one input may be sacrificed altogether. City life, as we experience it, constitutes a continuous set of encounters with overload, and of resultant adaptations. Overload characteristically deforms daily life on several levels, impinging on role performance, the evolution of social norms, cognitive functioning, and the use of facilities.

The concept has been implicit in several theories of urban experience. In 1903 George Simmel[3] pointed out that, since urban dwellers come into contact with vast numbers of people each day, they conserve psychic energy by becoming acquainted with a far smaller proportion of people than their rural counterparts do, and by maintaining more superficial relationships even with these acquaintances. Wirth[4] points specifically to 'the superficiality, the anonymity, and the transitory character of urban social relations'.

One adaptive response to overload, therefore, is the allocation of less time to each input. A second adaptive mechanism is disregard of low-priority inputs. Principles of selectivity are formulated such that investment of time and energy are reserved for carefully defined inputs (the urbanite disregards the drunk sick on the street as he purposefully navigates through the crowd). Third, boundaries are redrawn in certain social transactions so that the overloaded system can shift the burden to the other party in the exchange; thus, harried New York bus drivers once made change for customers, but now this responsibility has been shifted to the client, who must have the exact fare ready. Fourth, reception is blocked off prior to entrance into a system; city dwellers increasingly use unlisted telephone numbers to prevent individuals from calling them, and a small but growing number resort to keeping the telephone off the hook to prevent incoming calls. More subtly, a city dweller blocks inputs by assuming an unfriendly countenance, which discourages others from initiating contact. Additionally, social screening devices are interposed between the individual and environmental inputs (in a town of 5000 anyone can drop in to chat with the mayor, but in the metropolis organizational screening devices deflect inputs to other destinations). Fifth, the intensity of inputs is diminished by filtering devices, so that only weak and relatively superficial forms of involvement with others are allowed. Sixth, specialized institutions are created to absorb inputs that would otherwise swamp the individual (welfare departments handle the financial needs of a million individuals in New York City, who would otherwise create an army of mendicants continuously importuning the pedestrian). The interposition of institutions between the individual and the social world, a characteristic of all modern society, and most notably of the large metropolis, has its negative side.

It deprives the individual of a sense of direct contact and spontaneous integration in the life around him. It simultaneously protects and estranges the individual from his social environment.

Many of these adaptive mechanisms apply not only to individuals but to institutional systems as well, as Meier[5] has so brilliantly shown in connection with the library and the stock exchange.

In sum, the observed behaviour of the urbanite in a wide range of situations appears to be determined largely by a variety of adaptations to overload. I now deal with several specific consequences of responses to overload, which make for differences in the tone of city and town.

## Social Responsibility

The principal point of interest for a social psychology of the city is that moral and social involvement with individuals is necessarily restricted. This is a direct and necessary function of excess of input over capacity to process. Such restriction of involvement runs a broad spectrum from refusal to become involved in the needs of another person, even when the person desperately needs assistance, through refusal to do favours, to the simple withdrawal of courtesies (such as offering a lady a seat, or saying 'sorry' when a pedestrian collision occurs). In any transaction more and more details need to be dropped as the total number of units to be processed increases and assaults an instrument of limited processing capacity.

The ultimate adaptation to an over-loaded social environment is to totally disregard the needs, interests, and demands of those whom one does not define as relevant to the satisfaction of personal needs, and to develop highly efficient perceptual means of determining whether an individual falls into the category of friend or stranger. The disparity in the treatment of friends and strangers ought to be greater in cities than in towns; the time allotment and willingness to become involved with those who have no personal claim on one's time is likely to be less in cities than in towns.

## Bystander Intervention in Crises

The most striking deficiencies in social responsibility [occur] in cities in crisis situations, such as the Genovese murder in Queens. In 1964, Catherine Genovese, coming home from a night job in the early hours of an April morning, was stabbed repeatedly, over an extended period of time. Thirty-eight residents of a respectable New York City neighbourhood admit to having witnessed at least a part of the attack, but none went to her aid or called the police until after she was dead. Milgram and Hollander, writing in *The Nation*,[6] analysed the event in these terms:

> Urban friendships and associations are not primarily formed on the basis of physical proximity. A person with numerous close friends in different parts of the city may not know the occupant of an adjacent apartment. This does not mean that

a city dweller has fewer friends than does a villager, or knows fewer persons who will come to his aid; however, it does mean that his allies are not constantly at hand. Miss Genovese required immediate aid from those physically present. There is no evidence that the city had deprived Miss Genovese of human associations, but the friends who might have rushed to her side were miles from the scene of her tragedy.

Further, it is known that her cries for help were not directed to a specific person; they were general. But only individuals can act, and as the cries were not specifically directed, no particular person felt a special responsibility. The crime and the failure of community response seem absurd to us. At the time, it may well have seemed equally absurd to the Kew Gardens residents that not one of the neighbours would have called the police. A collective paralysis may have developed from the belief of each of the witnesses that someone else must surely have taken that obvious step.

Gaertner and Bickman[7] of The City University of New York have extended the bystander studies to an examination of help across ethnic lines. Blacks and whites, with clearly identifiable accents, called strangers (through what the caller represented as an error in telephone dialing), gave them a plausible story of being stranded on an outlying highway without more dimes, and asked the stranger to call a garage. The experimenters found that the white callers had a significantly better chance of obtaining assistance than the black callers. This suggests that ethnic allegiance may well be another means of coping with overload: the city dweller can reduce excessive demands and screen out urban heterogeneity by responding along ethnic lines; overload is made more manageable by limiting the 'span of sympathy'.

In any quantitative characterization of the social texture of city life, a necessary first step is the application of such experimental methods as these to field situations in large cities and small towns. Theorists argue that the indifference shown in the Genovese case would not be found in a small town, but in the absence of solid experimental evidence the question remains an open one.

More than just callousness prevents bystanders from participating in altercations between people. A rule of urban life is respect for other people's emotional and social privacy, perhaps because physical privacy is so hard to achieve. And in situations for which the standards are heterogeneous, it is much harder to know whether taking an active role is unwarranted meddling or an appropriate response to a critical situation. If a husband and wife are quarreling in public, at what point should a bystander step in? On the one hand, the heterogeneity of the city produces substantially greater tolerance about behaviour, dress, and codes of ethics than is generally found in the small town, but this diversity also encourages people to withhold aid for fear of antagonizing the participants or crossing an inappropriate and difficult-to-define line.

Moreover, the frequency of demands present in the city gives rise to norms of non-involvement. There are practical limitations to the Samaritan impulse in a major city. If a citizen attended to every needy person, if he were sensitive to and acted on every altruistic impulse that was evoked in the city, he could scarcely* keep his own affairs in order.

## Willingness to Trust and Assist Strangers

We now move away from crisis situations to less urgent examples of social responsibility. For it is not only in situations of dramatic need but in the ordinary, everyday willingness to lend a hand that the city dweller is said to be deficient relative to his small-town cousin. The comparative method must be used in any empirical examination of this question. A commonplace social situation is staged in an urban setting and in a small town—a situation to which a subject can respond by either extending help or withholding it. The responses in town and city are compared.

One factor in the purported unwillingness of urbanites to be helpful to strangers may well be their heightened sense of physical (and emotional) vulnerability—a feeling that is supported by urban crime statistics. A key test for distinguishing between city and town behaviour, therefore, is determining how city dwellers compare with town dwellers in offering aid that increases their personal vulnerability and requires some trust of strangers. Altman, Levine, Nadien, and Villena[8] of The City University of New York devised a study to compare the behaviours of city and town dwellers in this respect. The criterion used in this study was the willingness of householders to allow strangers to enter their home to use the telephone. The student investigators individually rang doorbells, explained that they had misplaced the address of a friend nearby, and asked to use the phone. The investigators (two males and two females) made 100 requests for entry into homes in the city and 60 requests in the small towns. The results for middle-income housing developments in Manhattan were compared with data for several small towns (Stony Point, Spring Valley, Ramapo, Nyack, New City, and West Clarkstown) in Rockland County, outside of New York City. As Table 1 shows, in all cases there was a sharp increase in the proportion of entries achieved by an experimenter when he phoned from the city to a small town. In the most extreme case the experimenter was five times as likely to gain admission to homes in a small town as to homes in Manhattan. Although the female experimenters had notably greater success both in cities and in towns than the male experimenters had, each of the four students did at least twice as well in towns as in cities. This suggests that the city-town distinction overrides even the predictably greater fear of male strangers than of female ones.

The lower level of helpfulness by city dwellers seems due in part to recognition of the dangers of living in Manhattan, rather than to mere indifference or coldness. It is significant that 75 per cent of all the city respondents received and answered messages by shouting through closed doors and by peering out through peepholes; in the towns, by contrast, about 75 per cent of the respondents opened the door.

Table 1  Percentage of Entries Achieved by Investigators for City and
Town Dwellings (see text)

| | Entries Achieved (%) | |
|---|---|---|
| Experimenter | City* | Small town† |
| Male | | |
| No. 1 | 16 | 40 |
| No. 2 | 12 | 60 |
| Female | | |
| No. 3 | 40 | 87 |
| No. 4 | 40 | 100 |

*Number of requests for entry, 100.
†Number of requests for entry, 60.

Supporting the experimenters' quantitative results was their general observation that the town dwellers were noticeably more friendly and less suspicious than the city dwellers. In seeking to explain the reasons for the greater sense of psychological vulnerability city dwellers feel, above and beyond the differences in crime statistics, Villena points out that, if a crime is committed in a village, a resident of a neighbouring village may not perceive the crime as personally relevant though the geographic distance may be small, whereas a criminal act committed anywhere in the city, though miles from the city-dweller's home is still verbally located within the city; thus, Villena says, 'the inhabitant of the city possesses a larger vulnerable space'.

## Civilities

Even at the most superficial level of involvement—the exercise of everyday civilities—urbanites are reputedly deficient. People bump into each other and often do not apologize. They knock over another person's packages and, as often as not, proceed on their way with a grumpy exclamation instead of an offer of assistance. Such behaviour, which many visitors to great cities find distasteful, is less common, we are told, in smaller communities, where traditional courtesies are more likely to be observed.

In some instances it is not simply that, in the city, traditional courtesies are violated; rather, the cities develop new norms of non-involvement. These are so well defined and so deeply a part of city life that *they* constitute the norms people are reluctant to violate. Men are actually embarrassed to give up a seat on the subway to an old woman; they mumble 'I was getting off anyway', instead of making the gesture in a straightforward and gracious way. These norms develop because everyone realizes that, in situations of high population density, people cannot implicate themselves in each other's affairs, for to do so would create conditions of continual distraction which would frustrate purposeful action.

In discussing the effects of overload I do not imply that at every instant the city dweller is bombarded with an unmanageable number of inputs, and that his responses are determined by the excess of input at any given instant. Rather, adaptation occurs in the form of gradual evolution of norms of behaviour. Norms are evolved in response to frequent discrete experiences of overload; they persist and become generalized modes of responding.

## Overload on Cognitive Capacities: Anonymity

That we respond differently toward those whom we know and those who are strangers to us is a truism. An eager patron aggressively cuts in front of someone in a long movie line to save time only to confront a friend; he then behaves sheepishly. A man is involved in an automobile accident caused by another driver, emerges from his car shouting in rage, then moderates his behaviour on discovering a friend driving the other car. The city dweller, when walking through the midtown streets is in a state of continual anonymity vis-à-vis the other pedestrians.

Anonymity is part of a continuous spectrum ranging from total anonymity to full acquaintance, and it may well be that measurement of the precise degrees of anonymity in cities and towns would help to explain important distinctions between the quality of life in each. Conditions of full acquaintance, for example, offer security and familiarity, but they may also be stifling, because the individual is caught in a web of established relationships. Conditions of complete anonymity, by contrast, provide freedom from routinized social ties, but they may also create feelings of alienation and detachment.

Empirically one could investigate the proportion of activities in which the city dweller or the town dweller is known by others at given times in his daily life, and the proportion of activities in the course of which he interacts with individuals who know him. At his job, for instance, the city dweller may be known to as many people as his rural counterpart. However, when he is not fulfilling his occupational role—say, when merely travelling about the city—the urbanite is doubtless more anonymous than his rural counterpart.

Another direction for empirical study is investigation of the beneficial effects of anonymity. The impersonality of city life breeds its own tolerance for the private lives of the inhabitants. Individuality and even eccentricity, we may assume, can flourish more readily in the metropolis than in the small town. Stigmatized persons may find it easier to lead comfortable lives in the city, free of the constant scrutiny of neighbours. To what degree can this assumed difference between city and town be shown empirically? Judith Waters,[9] at The City University of New York, hypothesized that avowed homosexuals would be more likely to be accepted as tenants in a large city than in small towns, and she dispatched letters from homosexuals and from 'normal' individuals to real estate agents in cities and towns across the country. The results of her study were inconclusive. But the general idea of examining the protective benefits of city life to the stigmatized ought to be pursued.

### Role Behaviour in Cities and Towns

Another product of urban overload is the adjustment in roles made by urbanites in daily interactions. As Wirth has said: 'Urbanites meet one another in highly segmental roles. . . . They are less dependent upon particular persons, and their dependence upon others is confined to a highly fractionalized aspect of the other's round of activity.'[10] This tendency is particularly noticeable in transactions between customers and individuals offering professional or sales services. The owner of a country store has time to become well acquainted with his dozen-or-so daily customers, but the girl at the checkout counter of a busy A & P, serving hundreds of customers a day, barely has time to toss the green stamps into one customer's shopping bag before the next customer confronts her with his pile of groceries.

Meier, in his stimulating analysis of the city,[11] discusses several adaptations a system may make when confronted by inputs that exceed its capacity to process them. Meier argues that, according to the principle of competition for scarce resources, the scope and time of the transaction shrink as customer volume and daily turnover rise. This, in fact, is what is meant by the 'brusque' quality of city life. New standards have developed in cities concerning what levels of services are appropriate in business transactions (see Figure 1).

Figure 1  Changes in the demand for time for a given task when the overall trans-action frequency increases in a social system. (Reprinted with permission from R.L. Meier, *A Communications Theory of Urban Growth*, 1962. Copyright 1962 by the MIT Press.)

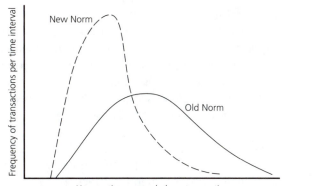

McKenna and Morgenthau,[12] in a seminar at The City University of New York, devised a study (i) to compare the willingness of city dwellers and small-town dwellers to do favours for strangers that entailed expenditure of a small amount of time and slight inconvenience but no personal vulnerability, and (ii) to determine whether the more compartmentalized, transitory relationships of the city would make urban salesgirls less likely than small-town salesgirls to carry out, for strangers, tasks not related to their customary roles.

To test for differences between city dwellers and small-town dwellers, a simple experiment was devised in which persons from both settings were asked (by telephone) to perform increasingly onerous favours for anonymous strangers.

Within the cities (Chicago, New York, and Philadelphia), half the calls were to housewives and the other half to salesgirls in women's apparel shops; the division was the same for the 37 small towns of the study, which were in the same states as the cities. Each experimenter represented herself as a long-distance caller who had, through error, been connected with the respondent by the operator. The experimenter began by asking for simple information about the weather for purposes of travel. Next the experimenter excused herself on some pretext (asking the respondent to 'please hold on'), put the phone down for almost a full minute, and then picked it up again and asked the respondent to provide the phone number of a hotel or motel in her vicinity at which the experimenter might stay during a forthcoming visit. Scores were assigned the subjects on the basis of how helpful they had been. McKenna summarizes her results in this manner:

> People in the city, whether they are engaged in a specific job or not, are less helpful and informative than people in small towns; . . . People at home, regardless of where they live, are less helpful and informative than people working in shops.

However, the absolute level of cooperativeness for urban subjects was found to be quite high, and does not accord with the stereotype of the urbanite as aloof, self-centred, and unwilling to help strangers. The quantitative differences obtained by McKenna and Morgenthau are less great than one might have expected. This again points up the need for extensive empirical research in rural-urban differences, research that goes far beyond that provided in the few illustrative pilot studies presented here. At this point we have very limited objective evidence on differences in the quality of social encounters in city and small town.

But the research needs to be guided by unifying theoretical concepts. As I have tried to demonstrate, the concept of overload helps to explain a wide variety of contrasts between city behaviour and town behaviour: (i) the differences in role enactment (the tendency of urban dwellers to deal with one another in highly segmented, functional terms, and of urban sales personnel to devote limited time and attention to their customers); (ii) the evolution of urban norms quite different from traditional town values (such as the acceptance of non-involvement, impersonality, and aloofness in urban life); (iii) the adaptation of the urban dweller's cognitive processes (his inability to identify most of the people he sees daily, his screening of sensory stimuli, his development of blasé attitudes toward deviant or bizarre behaviour, and his selectivity in responding to human demands); and (iv) the competition for scarce facilities in the city (the subway rush; the fight for taxis; traffic jams; standing in line to await services). I suggest that contrasts between city and rural behaviour probably reflect the responses of similar people to very different situations, rather than intrinsic differences in the personalities of rural and city dwellers. The city is a situation to which individuals respond adaptively.

## REFERENCES AND NOTES

1  *New York Times* (15 June 1969).
2  L. Wirth, *Amer. J. Soc.*, 44, 1 (1938). Wirth's ideas have come under heavy criticism by contemporary city planners, who point out that the city is broken down into neighbourhoods, which fulfill many of the functions of small towns. See, for example, H.J. Gans, *People and Plans: Essays on Urban Problems* and *Solutions* (Basic Books, New York, 1968); J. Jacobs, *The Death and Life of Great American Cities* (Random House, New York, 1961); G.D. Suttles, *The Social Order of the Slum* (University of Chicago Press, Chicago, 1968).
3  G. Simmel, *The Sociology of Georg Simmel*, K.H. Wolff, ed. (Macmillan, New York, 1950) [English translation of G. Simmel, *Die Grossstadte und das Geistesleben Die Grossstadt* (Jansch, Dresden, 1903)].
4  R.L. Meier, *A Communications Theory of Urban Growth* (M.I.T. Press, Cambridge, Mass., 1962).
5  S. Milgram and P. Hollander, *Nation* 25, 602 (1964).
6  B. Latané and J. Darley, *Amer. Sci.* 57, 244 (1969).
7  S. Gaertner and L. Bickman (Graduate Center, The City University of New York), unpublished research.
8  D. Altman, M. Levine, M. Nadien, J. Villena (Graduate Center, The City University of New York), unpublished research.
9  P.G. Zimbardo, paper presented at the Nebraska Symposium on Motivation (1969).
10  J. Waters (Graduate Center, The City University of New York), unpublished research.
11  W. McKenna and S. Morgenthau (Graduate Center, The City University of New York), unpublished research.
12  N. Abuza (Harvard University), 'The Paris-London-New York Questionnaires', unpublished.

# CHAPTER 5

# The Network Perspective:
# A Grounded Alternative to
# Disorganization Perspectives

Instead of looking at the world in terms of *structures*, mainstream sociologists have tended to think in terms of *categories* of social actors who share similar characteristics: 'women', 'the elderly', . . . and so on. Indeed much sociological research in this genre consists of nothing more elaborate than checking to see whether or not actors with one kind of characteristic are more likely than others to have another: 'Do blondes have more fun?'. . . . A better way of looking at things . . . is to view relations as the basic units of social structure and groupings of similarly situated actors as the result. (Wellman and Berkowitz, 1988: 15)

Some people claim they can recognize sociologists by how they answer even the most straightforward of questions. These observers suggest that the sociologist's favourite answer is 'Well, it all depends.' Thus 'Is it going to rain today?' produces the answer 'Well, it all depends on whether the cold front moves in as predicted or not.' 'Do you think I will do well on my sociology exam?' is answered with 'Well, it all depends on whether you've understood the material, can organize your time and your answers, and the like.' Finally 'Is social class a good predictor of political attitudes?' is answered by 'Well, it all depends on how you want to operationalize your terms as well as on other characteristics of your subjects that are confounded with social class.'

Though not everyone expects such cautious answers, they usually concede that the conditions mentioned are relevant and cannot be left out of a useful answer to the questions. Middle-of-the-road sociologists are those who seem most unwilling to give a simple straight answer to questions. For them sociology got into more intellectual trouble as a result of oversimplified and dichotomous thinking than in any other way. Thus they feel answers are rarely true or false; in reality they may depend on who is asking and under what conditions.

One of the best sociologists I have ever known summed up this position in an unforgettable way: 'Never forget that underlying every dichotomy there is a continuum. Real life is never black or white; it is only the shades between.'

Such a statement could well be the credo of the middle-of-the-roaders. It is their goal to identify the things on which the proverbial 'it' all depends! They believe that sociological relationships tend to be conditional, which is to say, dependent on other conditions. Sometimes such conditions strengthen relationships; sometimes they nullify them. Relationships may be true for men but not for women, for the middle class but not the working class, for younger people but not older ones. A theoretical preference for conditional relationships involves at least an implicit suspicion—if not an explicit critique—of the thinking exemplified by the typological thinkers of the previous chapter and their dichotomies.

Although similar critiques and a focus on the conditional nature of relationships are common to all of the middle-of-the-roaders, such common ground does not constitute a theoretical position in its own right. For this we need more. We must find a school of thought that is coherent and constructive rather than merely critical and that offers new insights that in turn generate new and testable hypotheses about the functioning of the social world. Just such a theoretical vantage point is provided by the network theorists.

After reading this chapter, which introduces and illustrates network theory, you should be able to understand and discuss points of contrast between network theory and the kinds of typological disorganization theories presented in chapter 4.

## THE NETWORK APPROACH

In 1957 Elizabeth Bott published a book entitled *Family and Social Network*, written from the network perspective. Since then, network analysis has rapidly become a recognized sub-discipline in sociology with its own specialists, journals, methodologies, and associations. Most important, network analysis is the major systematic and encompassing model opposing the kinds of pessimistic and disintegrative views of the theorists presented in chapter 4.

The principal theoretical premise of network theory is that modern society is not disorganized, nor is it becoming so. On the contrary, though there has been significant change in the fundamental character of society, it is adaptive change in the nature of social order rather than mere disruption of an earlier order with no replacement. Network theory suggests that rather than leaving individuals isolated, anonymous, anomic, and lonely, the changing social order has replaced one set of bonds with another based on a new principle. The old and discarded principle was the sharing of locality; the new principle is the sharing of interests. In the past, society was territorial. Future society will be non-territorial; it will be relational. The same technology described by the classic theorists as one of the solvents of social solidarity, organization, and collectivity has provided us with new ways of relating to others, wherever they may be, and across what were once impermeable boundaries of class, race, and even nations. In this sense the network perspective logically follows earlier paradigms. It represents achievement orientation rather than ascription. Where the classic theorists saw damage to social institutions as a result of mobility and the division of labour, network theorists see structured variation in the opportunity for freedom and individual self-expression and for individuals to achieve what they can with like-minded others.

The differences of orientation largely spring from different analyses of the implications that social change has for social order rather than from a disagreement over independent variables. To network theorists the classic writers were limited by their times and their imaginations. They simply could not envision any basis for social order other than territory or locale. Thus the diminished importance of locale meant, by definition, loss of order. By contrast, network theory postulates the emergence of a new basis for order.

Network theory is what Robert Merton (1949) might have called a 'middle-range' theory. This means that it is grounded in empirical studies of how people actually live their lives among and with others. Thus network theory is generated inductively rather than deductively, built 'up' to propositions from observations rather than deduced from abstract propositions. In this case, network theory emerges, in part—as is often the case with reference to other middle-range theory—precisely from a failure to find in empirical observations the consequences the earlier theorists had predicted. It was created in an attempt to explain the anomalous existence of order where the earlier theorists had predicted chaos. Network theory attempts to provide a theoretical explanation for why the earlier typological theorists' assumption and prediction of disorder were in error. Webber puts it nicely:

> We are passing through a revolution that is unhitching the social process of urbanization from the locationally fixed city and region. . . . Deficiencies of our language and . . . the anachronistic thought-ways we have carried over from the passing era [now create confusion]. We still have no adequate descriptive terms for the emerging social order . . . we seem still to assume that territoriality is a necessary attribute of social systems. . . . The error has been a serious one . . . the influence and significance of geographic distance and geographic place are declining rapidly. (Webber [1968], as quoted in Bernard [1972: 184]).

Here Webber is dealing specifically with old notions of community, neighbourhood, locale, and territory in an urban context. As we have seen in chapter 4, most earlier analysts generally believed that social change equalled social disorganization and, in particular, that urbanization would isolate individuals in an impersonal milieu.

Social disorganization is the main theme of sociology's forefathers. It is illustrated, analysed, or forecast with regard to each social institution: in the disintegration of the family in divorce and the declining importance of marriage; in the anonymity of the urban 'lonely crowd' (Riesman, 1952); in the 'massification' of education with its attendant loss of concern for the student; in the alienation and powerlessness, vulnerability and changeability of individual identity within the confusion of the twentieth century. In each substantive area, social scientists have taken these expectations and transformed them into hypotheses; then each has received considerable testing. The consensus at this time appears to be that these disorganization hypotheses are significantly wanting. This theoretical failure has forced us to search out a theoretical alternative to social disorganization, one consistent with the facts.

## THE ORIGINS OF THE NETWORK APPROACH

Although Bott's is perhaps the most theoretical of the early treatments—and as such has generated a great deal of interest—she was neither the first to undertake network studies, nor was she alone. The empirical work from which the network approach evolved seems to have had four main inspirations: American mass communications research, British social anthropology, urban sociology, and sociometry.[1] In the 1950s the first three of those sources turned up anomalous findings that multiplied rapidly in the course of empirical work on various topics. These built on even earlier findings inconsistent with the disorganization hypotheses. In the late 1950s those findings were integrated into the perspective of network analysis, through the use of methodologies developed earlier in sociometry.

## Mass Communications

In mass communication studies during and after the Second World War, Katz and Lazarsfeld, and Merton tested the idea that the mass media had a direct effect on individuals who were part of a mass audience, that is, unconnected to and unaffected by one another. This idea of a mass audience clearly derives from the disorganization theorists, who suggested that individuals in the modern era were the rootless, anomic, and isolated members of a 'lonely crowd'. In contrast, the empirical research discovered that the messages of the mass media were selected, interpreted, believed, or rejected within an active social context of friends and family, co-workers, peers, and other influential persons. Individuals were not rootless and alone; media had little effect overall and no direct effect at all. A two-step flow of communications took place in which the messages of the mass media were filtered by so-called opinion leaders, who selected, interpreted, and passed on some of what they received to others. Thus the effect of mass media on any individual was in large part seen to be a function of their connections to others; only by analysing the social context and these connections could we understand or predict what information people might actually obtain and how they might define it and react to it. To know simply what message was originally sent was not enough.

## Urban Sociology

Since the 1940s urban sociology had also been accumulating evidence of the vitality of social life in parts of the city where disorganization theory predicted the existence of pathology, alienation, and estranged individuals remote and unconnected to one another. Thus W.F. Whyte (1943) found active organization in what was supposed to be a Boston slum; Young and Wilmott (1957) found a well-organized and relatively satisfying round of life in a lower-class community in London.

## British Social Anthropology

The studies of British social anthropology are perhaps the clearest forerunners of an evolving network approach. John Barnes in Norway, Clyde Mitchell in Africa, and Elizabeth Bott in London were all slowly but systematically putting together a series of accounts of how people organized their lives in various cultures and situations. Their common denominator was a focus that left territory behind and instead explained behaviour in terms of certain structural characteristics of the kinds of connections people had with one another.

## Sociometry

Finally, in the United States from the 1930s, social scientists were interested in mapping the behaviours of individuals in relation to one another within spatial boundaries. Such an emphasis on spatial and relational mapping was consistent with the development of the human ecological models of urban life that Park and Burgess had produced at the University of Chicago. In social psychology a similar idea developed out of Kurt Lewin's interest in field theory, which considered individual behaviour as a product of the lines of force impinging on an individual from others in the 'field'—much as the motion of a billiard ball is affected by others in the field of play. Sociometry researchers usually administered questionnaires, asking respondents who they liked or disliked, whom they wanted to associate with or not, and so on. From the answers, the investigator could draw a sociometric map, or sociogram, representing the number of selections as well as the person by whom they were initiated and whether they were reciprocated. On such maps commonly chosen subjects would appear as sociometric 'stars', and subjects nobody chose would be seen as 'isolates'. These patterns of choice were often related to race, to spatial location in a classroom or office, or to sex, age, or other presumed independent variables. Thus sociograms are a method for collecting data on interaction patterns among individuals and depicting the entire field of those relationships schematically. Methodologically and conceptually, sociometry was an antecedent of network analysis.

## THE PREMISES OF NETWORK ANALYSIS

Network analysis is an empirically grounded model of society that emphasizes a more modern and conditional set of questions than the simplistic and holistic view of its precursors. For whom is the city alienating, and for whom is it not? Who finds modern education impersonal, depersonalizing, and ineffective and under what structural conditions? When do marriages dissolve, and what conditions seem to produce continued commitment? What conditions lead some urban dwellers to experience a significant sense of local community? Under what conditions is education a valuable, intensely personal experience of growth? For whom are marriage and family a central institution?

But it is not the questions it asks that identifies network theory. Rather it is the type of answer provided. To network theorists the answer to each of the questions raised here—and to a great many more—is a structural one. It lies in the 'web of group affiliation', as Simmel (1922) put it long ago, or in the *form* of the set of relationships in which people are involved.

Consider your experience and that of your friends and family. Think of yourself as the centre of a network of people with whom you share some connection, a network of your relatives, for example. Such a network in which you are the centre or anchor is called an egocentric network; of course each person participates in many such networks of relatives, friends, co-workers, neighbours, and the like. In fact each individual is the centre of a unique network and is also a participant (or 'alter') in the networks of others to whom they are linked. Some networks have many participants and others few. In network terminology the *range* of networks varies: that is, some are more extensive than others. In addition networks differ in many other ways. They differ in their importance to their members: some are more *intense* than others. They differ in their *stability* and *durability*. They differ in the *nature of the ties* among participants. Ties can be multi-faceted, multi-purpose, or multi-stranded, or they can be single-purpose or single-stranded. This is network terminology for a distinction that parallels Cooley's between primary relations and secondary relations. Networks can also differ in *density*, which is defined as the proportion of actual connections among members to potential connections if all members were connected to all others.

Though we can describe networks in other ways as well, the basic premise of network theory is that this aspect of variation in *connectedness* to others is a fundamental structural condition that affects many dependent variables that interest us. Most of us these days are well aware of this; indeed, it is common to speak of 'networking' in an effort to use 'connections' with others—to further our job interests, for example. Similarly, 'mentoring' or 'sponsorship' is recommended by consultants as a conscious strategy for using our connections with others—to get into graduate school, to find a spouse, and so on. These days, relationships with others can be pursued through the Internet or the World Wide Web, both of which connote just the kind of image of network connections (with us, the spider, in the centre of the web of connections) that is basic to notions of networks.

Most of the classical social disorganization theorists assumed that the past was a period of high connectedness, when everyone was involved in only small-scale, enduring, and dense networks. They proposed that the solvents of industrialization and urbanization, division of labour and rationalization were dissolving those social bonds, leaving individuals alone and unconnected. But to network theorists that dichotomous treatment of connectedness as either present or absent is misleading. It is also inaccurate to assume a uniformity of experiences. In the past some people belonged to small-scale, enduring, and dense networks; some did not. Today certain people belong to small-scale, enduring, and dense networks; others do not. Many issues are involved here. First, as noted, people are simultaneously involved in many networks of different kinds that serve different purposes, and these networks vary in many ways. Perhaps the nature of our networks has changed, or the proportion of particular kinds of networks may have changed. It is also possible that the numbers of people involved in different kinds of networks have changed.

Second, the consequences for the individual of participation in networks of various kinds are not self-evident. The classical theorists assumed that involvement in small-scale, multi-stranded, enduring networks provided one with identity as well as created a degree of social order. Network theorists have countered with the argument that such networks are coercive and intolerant of change and self-expression.

Third, and perhaps most basic, social-disorganization theorists assumed that modernization meant the loss of all such bonds. Network theorists challenge even this argument, asking again the conditional questions: Who is connected? In what manner and for what purposes? And under what conditions are bonds disrupted, created, or changed?

Since these are empirical questions, the theory that results is far less ambitious and less holistic than those the older theorists of social disorganization proposed. Because of this, one can really only grasp the central tenets of network theory as they are worked out in particular problem areas. This, too, is characteristic of middle-range theories, and it has led to considerable debate about just what a theory is. Even so, let me be clear. Network analysis is structural analysis that falls squarely in the macro-structural perspective discussed earlier. But I can make this much clearer if we return to Bott.

## BOTT'S KEY CONTENTION

Bott's aim was to explain what she called *role segregation* among husbands and wives in London. Role segregation here is the extent to which husbands and wives shared roles jointly or had specialized and non-overlapping roles and responsibilities. Degree of role segregation was Bott's dependent variable—an effect for which she sought the cause. Bott's study was only exploratory, and her sample was rather small. Even today, nearly 40 years later—and after several attempts to test her propositions—it is not clear how much of what she said is either correct or generalizable. Still Bott's study was enormously important theoretically in suggesting what are at least potentially powerful and simple explanations for a wide variety of phenomena. Central to her study was the conviction that 'the immediate social environment of urban families is best considered not as the local area in which they live but rather as the network of actual social relationships they maintain, regardless of whether these are confined to the local area or run beyond its boundaries' (Bott, 1955: 373).

Bott's basic contention was that the connectedness of their network was the key explanatory or independent variable. She suggested a positive relationship between network connectedness and role segregation. In other words, the more close-knit the network, the more role segregation there was. Her independent variable, then, was the connectedness of the network, which could range from relatively close to relatively loose-knit. These two types of networks differ in many significant ways, and role segregation is by no means the only potential dependent variable to which one can relate network connectedness. Figure 5.1 illustrates the ideal typical opposites.

The close-knit network is defined as one in which *A* knows or has contact with *B*, *B* knows or has contact with *C*, and *C* knows or has contact with *A* independently of *B*. In

Figure 5.1 Bott's Network Ideal Types

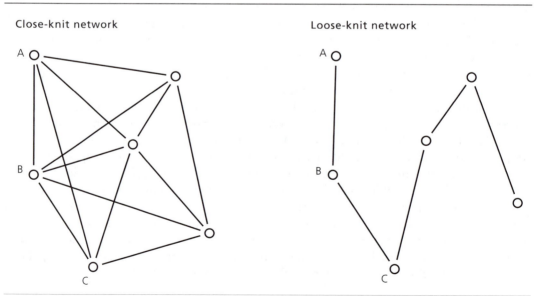

Close-knit network

Loose-knit network

other words—and more simply—one important structural characteristic of the close-knit network is *redundancy*. Many direct and indirect links exist among the network units. In contrast, the loose-knit network is defined as one in which A knows B, and B knows C, but C does not know A. Thus no redundancy shows up in the network, and mediating links are, therefore, of critical importance.

Additional structural features of these network types are of great importance, but let us begin by noting a point of enormous theoretical significance. Although Bott's unit of analysis was the family, it is equally possible to substitute other units of analysis. Thus one could examine kinship networks of nuclear family units, as she does, or friendship networks composed of individuals. One could use institutions as the unit of analysis and examine networks in which these institutions are affiliated, such as the National Collegiate Athletic Association (NCAA) and the National Hockey League (NHL) or academic consortiums such as the University of California or the University of New York. One could even use the provinces of Canada, the states of the United States, or the countries of the world as the units of analysis. Because Bott's analysis is structural, substitution of units should be possible. Propositions concerning the effects of increasing or decreasing connectedness should hold for all structurally similar units of analysis. It is this feature of interchangeability that makes a theoretical model attractive, powerful, and generalizable.

## CONSEQUENCES OR CORRELATES OF VARIATION IN CONNECTEDNESS

Since Bott's work, researchers have related network connectedness to occupational mobility (Katz, 1958; Granovetter, 1973); to the mobilization potential of urban areas threatened with redevelopment (Granovetter, 1973); to the likelihood of feuding among societies described in the anthropological ethnographic literature (Kang, 1976); to the successful existence of political democracy both in organizations and in societies (Lipset et al., 1956; Lipset, 1963); to the mobilization potential of university student bodies; to the creation of collective and individual identities; to nationalism and regionalism; to geographic mobility, emotional support, and well-being; and to the accumulation of venture capital. In all cases the authors base their analysis on what they take to be the implications of differences between close- and loose-knit networks.

Close-knit networks exhibit high levels of redundancy; loose-knit networks are more fragile. Examine Figure 5.1. Let us assume that the unit of analysis is the individual and that, for some purpose, we want to mobilize as much of the network as possible. Let's now assume that a piece of information is dropped into the network at unit A. In other words we tell A that we wish to pass the word that everyone is to get together on Wednesday at the community hall. Now let's further assume that B is ill, out of town, or not accessible. What happens to our attempt to mobilize the network in these two conditions? As you can see, B is a critical link in the loose-knit network, and in her absence—if no other steps are taken to create redundancy—the message will not be passed on at all, and nobody will show up at the hall. In the close-knit network, B's absence is missed but not so much. Many other links exist among all units, so the news will spread quickly, with lots of repetition. That is because each person is linked to many others.

Mobilization is thus far more likely to occur in a close-knit network, other things being equal. The news will get to each person, and additional pressure will result since each person will be told many times and is probably more likely to do what is suggested. Informal peer pressures and sanctions are strong in the more homogeneous close-knit network. Even if B were present in the loose-knit network, and even if the information circulated throughout the network, each person would receive the news from only one or possibly two others not closely linked to his or her social circle. Information would circulate more slowly, and mobilization would probably be less complete since it is easier to turn down one person's request than the same request from everyone you know.

### Urban Renewal

Let me apply this concept to the urban-renewal literature, where I will introduce some additional features (Granovetter, 1973). Sociologists dealing with urban renewal often describe the so-called slums frequently targeted for renewal. Most of these areas are not the disorganized social remnants that outsiders think they are. Usually such areas turn out to be highly organized, familistic, ethnic or racial areas. Within an area of a few blocks several different minority groups might share space, most often in competition for the 'turf' (Suttles 1968). Diagrammatically such an area might look like Figure 5.2.

Each ethnic group will occupy a small area where they exhibit a homogeneous and close-knit network. Several such networks might well exist side by side but entirely unconnected to one another, just as in Robert Park's famous description of the city as a collection of social worlds that touch but do not interpenetrate.

Now let's again suppose a piece of information is introduced—the information that the entire area has been slated for urban renewal—and a neighbourhood mobilization meeting

Figure 5.2 So-called Slums (Units are Families or Households)

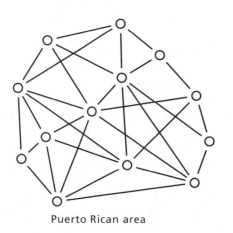

Puerto Rican area

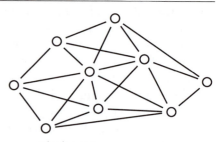

Black area

is to be held at the local hall. Clearly wherever this information originates, it will quickly circulate within a single network and just as clearly it will have no way of entering the adjacent network. The meeting will be well attended by members of one network, which may constitute only a small fraction of the area population. Following this meeting, the development interests will be able to claim that the local public is largely apathetic or that only members of one group have appeared and their views cannot be treated as representative of all local residents. As a result, renewal could proceed without widespread local approval.

Now suppose a redevelopment project were proposed in a predominantly middle-class area like the ones surrounding many university campuses. Some faculty members live there, as do graduate students and a selection of liberal arts and crafts and media people, small businesspeople, and so on from several ethnic and racial backgrounds. This sort of neighbourhood might look more like Figure 5.3. This is a loose-knit network.

Each household has ties outside the area, depicted by the broken lines, and some households are largely unintegrated; one is isolated, and there is a clique of three. Now if this area wanted to mobilize—and assuming that the information entered the main network—what would happen? As before, information would be transmitted slowly, and it would not be repeated often. As a result mobilization would likely involve a smaller percentage of the network members than was the case in the close-knit network. On the other hand, this network encompasses the whole area and crosses socio-economic, ethnic, sex, and racial lines. Mobilization is likely to be more representative of the whole area, and even though a smaller proportion is mobilized, this could be a larger number of people. It may be 90 per cent of one-third of the area population in the first instance, as compared to 40 per cent of 100 per cent of the population in this second instance.

Figure 5.3 Network Configuration of a Predominantly Middle-Class Mixed Area

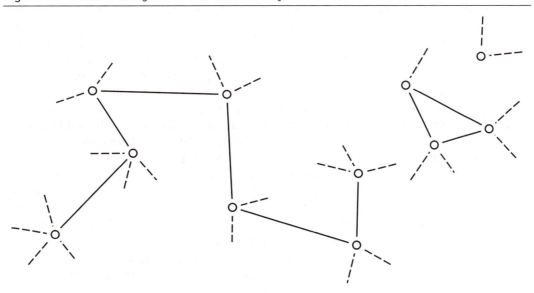

In addition the broken lines represent ties to others outside the local area. Members of the loose-knit network have many of these ties; the members of the close-knit network have few. These ties are important, for they may connect middle-class people to the press, local politicians, commercial interests, urban planners, conservation groups, and others who may be willing to act with the community even though they are not residents. Such ties make successful mobilization more likely in middle-class areas. The absence of just these ties is typical of a strongly locality-based and relatively 'institutionally complete' (Breton, 1964) community, where it is quite possible that the residents do not even speak the language of the surrounding society and are very much an independent enclave. Although such 'urban villages' have their attractions, the literature makes clear that, as Granovetter puts it, there are both 'strengths of weak ties' and 'weaknesses of strong ties'. One such weakness is vulnerability to redevelopment. Let's now examine other patterns of behaviour that vary demonstrably with the nature of the network.

## Social and Geographic Mobility

Both social and geographic mobility appear to be functions of network factors. Sociologists have long been aware of the phenomenon of 'chain migration' for example. MacDonald and MacDonald (1964) argue that this feature as exercised by 'co-ethnics' is structurally responsible for the creation of ethnic neighbourhoods. Chain migration is the use of primary social relationships with previous migrants to learn of new opportunities and to obtain transportation, initial accommodation, and employment. In the common case, one family will arrive in a location and, after a time, will help another family of relatives or co-ethnics to settle in the same neighbourhood.

Jobs at every level from unskilled to professional seem most often to be obtained according to a similar phenomenon involving network connectedness and sponsorship. Rather than reflecting ability or certification alone, jobs appear to be in part a function of whom you know. Thus weak connections to others in a social class higher than one's own are a resource one can use to achieve such social mobility. Though this empirical finding is hardly surprising, one of Parsons's basic dichotomies involves a transition from ascription to achievement orientation. Does this empirical finding mean that Parsons was wrong?

It appears that satisfaction of achievement criteria is a prerequisite for occupational mobility but is far from a sufficient condition. That is, as more people come to share the same qualifications, qualifications alone lose their ability to discriminate beyond their use as a baseline screening device. As more people obtained high-school educations, a university degree became necessary for the same positions. Such upgrading does not correspond to any change in the difficulty of the job; it is due instead to the increasing difficulty of choosing among applicants. Significantly, raising the baseline has the effect of continuing to eliminate those who have been last to acquire minimal certification, and commonly these are the minority groups. Here we seem to have identified the mechanism explaining the workings of 'last hired, first fired'. Whether intentionally or not, such upgrading to select among applicants has the same consequences as discrimination. In this way stratification systems are maintained but at a higher level of achievement (Collins, 1971). What remain crucial are the connections you have, connections that allow you to be selected from a large pool of competitors with the same achievement qualifications.

### Political Democracy, Factions, and Feuds

Social scientists have related political democracy to network connectedness. The theory is that effective and equitable democracy requires a substructure of 'conflicting loyalties' or cross-cutting ties. As S.M. Lipset (1973: 77) puts it:

> The available evidence suggests that the chances for stable democracy are enhanced to the extent that groups and individuals have a number of cross-cutting politically relevant affiliations. To the degree that a significant proportion of the population is pulled among conflicting forces, its members have an interest in reducing the intensity of political conflict. Such groups and individuals also have an interest in protecting the rights of political minorities.

Homogeneous groups with enduring interests are the basis for factions, and factions are serious threats to a democratic system. In power, a faction is often irresponsible to others, since there is little structural pressure to be accommodating. Out of power, a faction might be subjected to abuse as a powerless minority, unconnected to any 'protector'. Factions are far more likely to come into conflict when their alignments are clear and non-overlapping and their constituents are close-knit and homogeneous. Those are also the conditions in which feuding is most likely (Kang, 1976). Structural conditions such as cross-cutting ties of marriage and residence, in which individuals are simultaneously linked weakly to several potentially opposing groups, make feuds or conflicts far less likely among these groups. Mobilization is difficult because the individual belongs to many groups. Conflict is unlikely because individuals would be forced to fight others to whom they are connected. Everyone knows that one solution to the Hatfield-McCoy feud is for a Hatfield to marry a McCoy, though it did not work very well for the Montagues and Capulets in *Romeo and Juliet*.

In Canada the clearest example among several of the structural conditions that produce factions and political unaccountability is surely Quebec. Here we have many lines of differentiation coinciding to produce a relatively stable and homogeneous group that is close-knit internally and only minimally connected beyond its borders. Geographical boundaries coincide with linguistic, religious, legal (Quebec civil law is different from that of the rest of Canada), cultural, and other boundaries. Quebec has often exercised its power to opt out of federal-provincial agreements to which other provinces are a party. Since the 1960s a strong independence movement has evolved, and in the 1970s the provincial government promised to lead Quebec out of the confederation. In 1995, a referendum held in Quebec only narrowly defeated a motion to pursue separation from Canada. Whether this eventually happens or not, it is clear that if a federal government were elected by a majority of the voters in every other province, and if no members of the governing party were elected in Quebec, little means would remain by which Quebec could participate in Canadian politics. This has been the case in western Canada when the federal Liberals have been in power. With no representation within the governing party from western Canada, the region's interests have been ignored at best and more often abused in the interests of central Canadians, whose votes put the Liberals in power. With as much regional inequality in population and interests as Canada has, the very survival of the nation state remains constantly in doubt. Certainly, it is obvious that the network structure is not that of a strongly integrated society.

The Canadian ideology of mosaic, cultural pluralism, or multiculturalism, in so far as it is practised, further reinforces and institutionalizes a substructure that, in network terms, is conducive to weakly connected or unconnected regional and local close-knit networks. This has many implications for assimilation and immigration policy, factionalism, region-alism, stratification, and mobility in Canada. By contrast, the American ideology of the melting pot—again to the extent that it is actually practised—tends to distribute people over territory more widely, creating a single large loose-knit network rather than multiple discrete and relatively close-knit ones. It may in some part be a consequence of this struc-tural difference in links that American national identity seems to override local or regional identities, whereas the opposite seems true in Canada.

## Organizational Democracy

With respect to organizations, Lipset et al. (1956) make this same argument concerning democratic behaviour and factions in their classic *Union Democracy*. Although the condi-tions supporting democracy are complex and numerous, it seems that conflicting or bridging ties are important in protecting minorities from abuse. In other words, in an envi-ronment of constantly shifting coalitions that are issue-specific, any subgroup can find itself a minority at any time. Therefore all have an interest in protecting minority rights. The absence of participation or protection tends to produce high levels of alienation, a high potential for mobilization, and considerable sentiment for separation or revolution. It is ironic that mobilization will tend to be lower in democratic systems, based as they are on relatively weak ties. It is not widespread participation that protects democratic systems; rather it is the structure of participation.

## Stratification and Ethnic Differences in Access to Venture Capital

As one final example of behavioural variation related to variation in network connected-ness, let us consider ethnic stratification, especially the differences in access to resources. Participation in the relevant network means easy and direct access. It means sponsorship, information, and aid. Lack of participation means just the opposite. We can view stratifi-cation in terms of location within or outside of a structure that provides opportunities for mobility and within or outside of a network of others who can help us obtain information about opportunities, if not actually sponsoring mobility.

For instance some groups have easier access to venture capital than others or are better 'connected' than others. Most lending institutions require collateral and various sorts of credit information before making a loan. They prefer customers who are well-established, and have secure jobs, a good record of reliability, and good references (or connections). Put simply, they prefer precisely the kind of customer who needs them least. People without jobs, collateral, references, or a long history of residential and occupational stability will have a harder time getting a loan. In such instances applicants may have to produce a more 'reliable' co-signer, and several applicants may be required to guarantee the loan 'jointly and severally', meaning that each guarantees against default by any other signer. Even so, many people will simply not qualify.

Recent immigrants rarely qualify. Newly-weds just getting started rarely qualify on their own. Ethnic and racial minorities rarely qualify. Such institutions favour the white middle class. Other people are not participants in the network and as such lack sponsors. To be 'disadvantaged' means precisely this when we view stratification from a network perspective.

Given their lack of access to the legitimate and standard means of gaining resource capital, an array of adaptive mechanisms are available to these minorities. The official ideology supports a view that hard work will suffice, that those who do not qualify for assistance must 'pull themselves up by their bootstraps'. The irony of this and like ideologies is obvious, since the ones making this suggestion *have* the help and need it less. But such is stratification. The rules are made by those who already have power, and who tend to legitimate that power and protect the 'haves' from competition. In any event some ethnic minorities and others who do not qualify—including women, by the way—have historically turned to others like themselves to create alternative networks in an effort to put together collective resources from outside the mainstream structure. This is true for newly-weds who borrow from their in-laws for a down payment. It is also true for members of ethnic minorities who borrow for a 'stake'. The same holds for family businesses. And this explains, in part, the ethnic concentrations found in certain industries. Among consciousness-raising groups explicit strategies for creating networks are broadcast, and the new verb *to network* is in vogue in this context.

The stratification system is such that access to easy modes of social mobility is controlled by those with power. These so-called gatekeepers are over-represented in fields like banking, medicine, and law. Their children are more likely than are others to be found in these and similar professions. The children of those less fortunate, on the other hand, are found less often in these professions despite universal education and supposedly equal access to post-secondary training. Private schooling, availability of tutors, letters of recommendation, and other devices are among the partial explanations of the different opportunities for social mobility between the haves and have-nots. Then, of course, there are those who, like the heroes of Horatio Alger, do make it and keep the rest trying (Turner, 1960). Nonetheless, from a network perspective, connections and their use are critical factors in explaining differential achievement.

Ethnic minorities are over-represented in high-risk occupations and those where they are already dominant. Indeed dominance appears to be self-reinforcing. The mechanism for this seems, again, to involve network connections and sponsorship so that opportunities are differentially available, as is knowledge of these as well as the kind of supplementary sponsorship that results in being selected. This appears to be the case at all levels of the system, though mobility—sometimes substantial mobility—does take place. High-risk occupational fields include restaurants, sports, entertainment, and emerging technologies. In these fields there are no gatekeepers. Competition tends to be strong; the capital outlay needed to begin is often very high, and risk of failure is equally high. Here, on the margins, are those groups able and willing to pool their resources in order to gamble on success.

Certain ethnic groups have been able to use kinship and ethnic networks more easily or successfully than others, partly because of the chain migration and institutional completeness already discussed. Where there are multiple ties among members of a group, they are more likely to add to them, but only within the group. If the group has substantial resources, these may be available to an enterprising and ambitious member. If the group controls no discretionary resources, even ambitious members will have to look elsewhere. Social commentators have sometimes offered such a description as a partial explanation of the relative lack of group backing among American blacks, compared, for example, to the extensive use of such resources among Jews, Italians, and Asians. Weak ties can also promote social mobility, as already suggested, and this quite commonly takes place among co-ethnics once some have 'made it'. The geographic and occupational distribution of a group is thus important in many ways, and the presence or absence of links among them is perhaps even more significant.

Organizations also play an important role in ethnic networks. Churches, synagogues, and voluntary organizations like B'nai B'rith or the 'landsmen' associations common in many ethnic communities are crucial as the locus of networks. Such organizations provide a weak link among members who may share nothing else until the tie is somehow activated. If the local organizations are themselves affiliated—regionally, nationally, and even internationally—they are a potent organizational and resource base that members may come to depend on for money, advice, counselling, help in obtaining a job or information, letters of reference, and simple friendship.

Participation in the larger structure of opportunities is a variable and so, too, is participation in smaller alternative adaptive networks. By locating a group in terms of its access to and use of various network structures, we can understand a good deal about its position in the present and future stratification systems of the society.

### A World of Networks and the 'Small World' Experiments

It is its view of the world as sets of networks—some enmeshed in others and some not, some close-knit and some loose—that makes Stanley Milgram's work most instructive. The 'small-world' experiments are a classic demonstration of the truth in the phrase 'it's a small world' (Milgram, 1974). In his major experiment Milgram was able to demonstrate the number of personal links required to connect two randomly chosen people. He asked a random sample of subjects in Omaha to transmit a package of information to a particular stockbroker living in Massachusetts. The crucial rule was that subjects were to use only a personal link to move the package along a chain of personal links ending with the stockbroker. In other words, each respondent was told the target person's name, address, and occupation; if they did not know the target personally, they were to send the package to someone they did know personally who would in turn try to get the information to the target. What was startling in Milgram's experiment was the finding that on average only 5.5 intermediaries were needed to link subject and target personally! Similar studies done internationally have led to fascinating results. For our purposes here it is sufficient to note that some subjects at least participate in loose-knit networks that are capable of linking very different people when mobilized to do so.

## ISSUES INVOLVED IN THE MANIPULATION OF HUMAN BEHAVIOUR

We have now examined, however briefly, a few of the dependent variables related to connectedness. To the extent that one prefers one value of a dependent variable over another—say nationalism over regionalism, or democracy over factionalism, or joint as against segregated role relationships—one might well be inclined to try to identify and then manipulate the independent variables that cause change in the dependent. Thus if you value joint role relationships and if these are associated with loose-knit networks, you might try to loosen network ties. If nationalism is preferred to regionalism, national governments might well implement policies designed to break up close-knit local networks and stimulate more loose-knit national ones. Although the questions involved here are both ethical and practical—and the ethical ones may well be paramount—most scientists would probably agree that the ultimate purpose of science is to give humans control over their environment and the power and knowledge to reshape it. The instances mentioned here may seem relatively benign and self-evident, but the issue of whether or not to actively manipulate the social environment to produce particular changes in the behaviour of others without their knowledge appears more serious if we note that manipulating the relevant independent variable could presumably change the dependent in *either* direction. That is, those who wished to increase factionalism and feuding could also do so to the extent that they had the power to alter connectedness. 'Divide and conquer' is, after all, a venerable and well-established political strategy. Perhaps it is just as well that the social world is so complex that social scientists have to this point had relatively little success in identifying and manipulating the relevant independent variables. But what do you think? If we could alter the environment and thereby alter people's behaviour, would it be morally right to do so?

## CAUSES OF CONNECTEDNESS

It is in analysing the independent variables affecting connectedness that Bott is most suggestive, and knowledge of these independents is what would allow us to alter connectedness and through it the various dependent variables we have identified. Bott relates variation in connectedness to role relationships between husband and wife, but she goes beyond that to specify the structural conditions that, in turn, affect variation in network connectedness. In other words, what was her independent variable becomes her dependent variable as a new series of independents is related to it. Recalling that more recent literature examines a great many other dependent variables and that we can freely substitute other units of analysis for Bott's marital pairs, one could argue that Bott's independent variables ought to have close analogues at every level of parallel network analysis. Perhaps now you can see why Bott's analysis is so exciting; if correct, it would give us the key to many things.

## Economic Interdependence

Bott tells us that the connectedness of the marital networks she described is affected by several major independent variables. The first of these is economic interdependence. The greater the economic interdependence, the more close-knit the network. The converse would presumably also be true: the less economic interdependence, the more loose-knit the network. To Bott economic interdependence means family businesses. Applying this in a broader context suggests that increasing international trade relationships (through NAFTA for instance) and discouraging local or regional trading patterns could also create more loose-knit networks and erode smaller, more close-knit ones. In contrast, tariff walls and restriction of trade would tend to increase local interdependence and make local networks more close-knit. With this in mind, one might read the history of economic relations differently. Free trade and protectionism would have broader implications than commonly assumed.

## Perceived Social Similarity

Bott's second factor is perceived social similarity. This, too, is positively related to network connectedness. The more the local population considers itself to be socially similar, the more close-knit the networks tend to become. In other words, residents of a neighbourhood will tend to be more neighbourly to the extent that they consider themselves to be like, and have things in common with, their neighbours. Neighbourhoods that are segregated, voluntarily or otherwise, by ethnicity, race, age, family composition, or class will tend to develop more close-knit networks than more diverse neighbourhoods. At another level of analysis, we know that enemies are unable to identify with one another; for that reason all programs of inter-cultural exchange and education are based on the premise that perceived social similarity produces identification, interaction, and increasingly close-knit network connectedness.

## Mobility

Migration or mobility breaks down the basis of perceived social similarity to the extent that it brings us into contact with others who are different. For this simple reason, mobility—both geographic and social—is Bott's third feature. Mobility tends to produce loose-knit networks both because we leave old associates behind or weaken ties to them and because mobility means encounters with new associates and the development of new ties, however weak they may be at first. Travel does broaden the mind, and the network, with many important consequences.

Of course, as with the other factors, reality is more complex and varied than these simplified statements make it appear. Travel does not always broaden the mind. It is possible to travel and still be exposed to nothing new, so insulated in a cocoon of McDonald's and Holiday Inns that one sees no foreign culture nor makes any new contacts. It is also possible to be a cosmopolitan of the mind while remaining a geographic local. Some people read widely, continually seeking out new vicarious experiences and enlarging their horizons even though they never leave home. Still, what Bott describes is a general expectation or phenomenon.

## Opportunities for Outside Contacts

Bott's fourth factor is related to these last two, but it is more structural than behavioural. She suggests that opportunities to make contacts outside the local area or network must be present if ties are to become more loose-knit. Again, if there are no such opportunities, a local close-knit network will tend to develop; participants will have no alternative. In this context Breton's (1964) discussion of 'institutionally complete' ethnic communities seems relevant. In such communities, however they originate, one can pass a full round of life within the ethnic enclave. Residents could successfully lead whole lives in a language foreign to the country's majority within what is effectively a transplanted foreign culture, a little piece of Italy or Japan, of Poland, Hungary, or Vietnam. From this example it should be clear that ethnic assimilation can be hastened, delayed, or perhaps even stopped by the structure of networks where the participants are located. Thus, again, we have the potential for melting pot or mosaic. A network interpretation of the concept of 'institutional completeness' follows this chapter to illustrate differences between interpretations of this in network as opposed to the more common ecological or spatial terms.

In this context issues of inequality immediately arise since a central historical question in all such instances concerns the possibility of creating a social structure that embodies the principle of 'separate but equal'. Regardless of whether we are thinking of ethnic segregation in Canada or racial segregation in the United States, regardless of whether policies are consistent with government principles or with general ideology, the evidence appears clear indeed that separation means inequality.

## Ideology

The final factor that Bott dealt with is personal decision or choice. At a different level of analysis, we might term this factor ideology or even politics. Bott concentrates primarily on decisions that have a direct effect on networks but are not selected because of this effect. For example a family could move to a new city as a condition of employment or a promotion. They might also move to a new area because they need more space or so that their children could attend better schools. These moves require family decisions, but rarely do these decisions consciously include evaluation of possible effects on one's social network. None the less, effects do occur because the existing networks are disrupted, though some networks could be maintained in altered form. Telephone calls might, for example, partly replace personal visits. Usually, though, close-knit networks are loosened, as Bott suggests they will be. Again as Bott suggests, people are likely to make new network connections in the new area. The result is, at best, the development of a loose-knit network, often to replace a more close-knit one. In time a new close-knit network might develop, but in the short run mobility is disruptive, and some people can become permanently detached from others who had been important to them.

Network change tends to force people to interact in different ways. Husbands and wives may well do more together, by default, since both have disrupted their old and separate networks. Contact with new acquaintances different from their former friends may tend to produce a degree of tolerance and a new awareness of a range of behaviour that had been unknown.

Decisions to alter networks can be made intentionally as well. Many wives enter or return to the labour force to make new friends, to develop acquaintances outside the narrow circle in their areas, to have conversations with adults other than their husbands on other than family topics. Men and women both often do what they can to connect themselves to others who may be useful to them. More subtly, husbands or wives may introduce new friends to their spouse in the hope that the spouse's attitudes will be influenced by exposure to the new model. Thus women may want their husbands to meet 'John', who is such a good cook or who never brings home his work. Husbands may want their wives to meet 'Joan', who makes all her own clothes or is a lawyer.

At another level of egocentric networks, decisions to alter them could be made to reinforce one's beliefs. Women or men join consciousness-raising groups; members of ethnic minorities join ethnic associations; people join or change political parties. These affiliations are the badges by which others come to know us; they tell us and others who we are.

At still another level, the government of one country could decide that it is becoming too dependent on another. It might break off mutual agreements, try to take unilateral action in a different direction, and otherwise try to loosen the bonds. The same process, of course, occurs between individuals when one or the other wants more 'room'. This has, in fact, given rise to the 'principle of least interest', according to which the party with the least interest in continuing a relationship has the most power within it (Waller and Hill, 1951).

## APPLYING BOTT: CANADIAN-AMERICAN DIFFERENCES IN POST-SECONDARY EDUCATION

Let's try to apply some of Bott's principles of network connectedness to a particular situation in order to illustrate possible applications of her analysis. For this purpose let's again consider Canada and the United States as mosaic and melting pot respectively. I argued earlier that Canada exhibits a somewhat different substructure from that of the United States, one of more networks that are local or regional and close-knit and fewer that are regional or national and loose-knit. We might examine national differences in internal trade patterns or even transportation lines and their use or the use of telephone systems to demonstrate such differences empirically. But let's consider national differences in higher educational systems.

Canada has far fewer institutions of higher education per capita than the United States. Virtually all Canadian colleges and universities are publicly funded in contrast to the large number of privately endowed American schools. This means Canadian schools are more responsible to the provincial governments that support them. Virtually all Canadian post-secondary institutions are located in the largest or second-largest cities of their province; they are rarely rural or in college towns, as is often the case in the United States. The great majority of Canadian undergraduates attend a local university. Both universities and provincial governments have a very local-service-area approach to the student market. This means that most students commute to university; very few universities have a majority of their students living on campus, and most major universities are overwhelmingly local and commuter-oriented, and can afford to remain so since they basically do not have to compete with others for the same students. Aside from fairly obvious implications for innovation, quality, and the college 'press' (overall 'atmosphere' on campus), clear network consequences (and causes) show up.

Students are unlikely to meet students from other parts of the country. In fact they may be more likely to meet foreigners than Canadian students from another region! Most students will even be from the same city, and it is possible to maintain high-school friendships much more easily in such a situation. No Canadian universities draw on a national market for undergraduates. That is in sharp contrast to the emphasis in the United States on going away from home as a rite of passage and the high prestige accorded to the élite schools, which are primarily residential and national in market area.

Those differences have the effect of promoting local or regional ties in Canada and regional or national ones in the United States. As argued earlier, organizations often form the locus of intersecting personal networks. People come together in their use of and membership in organizations. In Canada organizations tend to be more local than in the United States. And with the support of government policy through, for example, the Secretary of State for Multiculturalism, a mosaic social structure is reinforced. Canada has allowed and even encouraged block settlement by ethnic groups of particular areas of land. This policy was not encouraged in the United States. Canada has also encouraged the maintenance of ethnic identities by providing funds and ideological support for organized ethnic groups; ethnic television, radio stations, and newspapers; and, in some cases, religious schools. These mechanisms have been disapproved of in the United States, where the historical ideological emphasis has been on the melting-pot notions of assimilation and loss of ethnicity and where resources have been allocated on a national level more often than on a local one. Clearly, the two governments have manipulated, though not intentionally, most of the factors Bott identifies as causes of variation in network connectedness. In Canada economic interdependence has gone along with territorial concentration to produce local or regional networks and a relatively high level of regional inequality and identity. In the United States mobility has been facilitated and ethnic territorial concentration frowned on. This has promoted loose-knit networks and more national orientations and identity.

## CONCLUSION

Chapter 5 is an abstract theoretical chapter introducing a new way of thinking, that of the network analysts. The kind of typological and dichotomous thinking of the classical precursors of chapter 4 is more familiar to us than is the conditional thinking of the network analysts. And yet, while conditional specification is a basic part of the modern sociological perspective, network analysis involves more than this. The network perspective is an inductively generated attempt to draw lessons that can be applied more widely from the empirical observations of diverse fields. It is 'grounded theory' (Glaser and Strauss, 1967) and theory of the middle range as defined long ago by Merton (1949: 39–72).

Network analysis is an attempt to catch up to a changed social reality and to develop a way of thinking about it that is more sophisticated than earlier models. Let me explain this further. Network analysis is more sophisticated than earlier dichotomous thinking because it deals with variables rather than uniformities or constants. 'Rural' and 'urban', 'ascribed' and 'achieved', and 'gemeinschaft' and 'gesellschaft' are treated, not as clear dichotomies, but as variables that occur in every mixture and are exhibited in degrees. As to my reference about catching up to changes in social reality, network analysts believe that social-scientific conceptualizations of society have lagged behind the real changes wrought by technology. People simply do not relate to one another within the constraints that operated in the past. In earlier days spatial boundaries were social boundaries. This is no longer so; technology has allowed us to interact increasingly without regard to spatial or ecological boundaries. Though this is not the case for everyone equally, it is increasingly so for more and more people, as mentioned earlier in connection with participation in the information super-highway of the Internet and World Wide Web, for example.

The ecological perspective allowed sociologists to analyse the behaviour of groups of people who were in some ways tied or restricted by locale. Today fewer people and fewer interactions are restricted in this manner. The network perspective is broad enough to handle the remaining instances of this kind by reconceptualizing 'groups' as close-knit networks of a local type, networks that do not transcend their local space. In addition this new perspective can handle what the older ecological perspective could not: the increasing number of contacts among people that take place without regard to spatial boundaries. It is in this sense that the network perspective is broader and able to subsume in a meaningful way the useful insights of the older and more spatially limited perspective of the earlier theorists.

The emphasis of the network analysts is on behaviour that interests us, wherever it may occur. The emphasis of the older typological and spatially bounded perspective was on the relationship of behaviour to its locale, or of one behaviour to another. It is this distinction that underlies the difference in conceptualization between a focus on *neighbourhoods* and *neighbouring*. It is this distinction that argues for a shift in attention from a traditional focus on corporate kin groups who occupy joint *households* to a more modern concern with *kin networks independent of households*. This same distinction is central to the debate between those who view identity as a *structure* and those who view it as a *process*.

Perhaps another example can clarify what I know is a difficult point. To a macro-structuralist of the old-fashioned school typical of the social-disorganization perspective, religion refers to an institution, a place, a church, parish, locale, or ministry. The concept of religion thus tends to involve a spatial dimension as a necessary attribute. That is to say that it is difficult to think of religion other than in some manner that is spatially bounded. The social and spatial structures are closely intertwined. In addition, from such a perspective it is also difficult to think of religion as a variable. A church either is or is not. An institution is or is not. A ministry either is or is not. But to network analysts religion refers to behaviour of a particular type, wherever it may occur. It is non-territorial, conditional, and variable. Thus social structure is clearly separable from physical location and physical structure. The church is neither a monumental edifice nor a place; it is an occurrence. The parish is not a locale, but a congregation. To minister means to bring religion to people. It may refer to an electronic ministry of the airwaves; it could mean Billy Graham's crusade from city to city and from Madison Square Garden to a similar facility temporarily rented in another city. It might refer to 'parking-lot churches', the practice of hauling a flatbed truck to a suburban mall and seeking a congregation among the shoppers. Religion could be a street-corner evangelist as well. In any case it is not the edifice, and it is not a spatially delimited activity by definition.

The goal of network analysis is precisely to be able to analyse social structure free from the constraints and limitations of its spatial locale and dimensions. The rationale for network analysis is that this freedom from physical boundaries exists for many people and for many kinds of interactions. The concepts of the network analysts merely reflect more accurately the manner in which real people live their lives under our modern social conditions. From such a perspective, the basic critique of the social-disorganization theorists is that theirs is in many crucial ways simply an outmoded way of grasping and making sense of new social circumstances.

## A Final Caveat

I have not introduced many versions of modern sociological theory in this chapter, any more than the prior chapter introduces and explains all versions and forms of classical sociological theories. To do so would far exceed the scope of an introductory text. I have said that there are many specific theories and kinds of theories in sociology, and the interested student or one who wishes to go much further in the discipline will certainly have to become informed about them. If you choose to study more sociology, you will be exposed to various forms of structural functional theory and conflict theory, to symbolic interactionist theory, and to the many versions of Marxist theory, but this is not the place for such a treatment.

Courses in modern theory should give you some familiarity with ethno-methodological theory and with rational choice theory, with thinkers like Foucault and Habermas, and many others. Again, my orientation is simpler: I just want to give you a broad introduction to the field, not substantively narrow and certainly not comprehensive. I want to raise some questions in your mind and give you a few leads for thinking about them sociologically. It is your sociological imagination I wish to encourage; this is not the time to introduce you to every brand of current theory.

I further assume that your instructor will be introducing substantive theory, if that is their preference, in the areas of their expertise, as you progress. After all, this text is only one of the resources upon which you are expected to draw. I hope you find it useful within such limitations.

## INTEGRATIVE EXERCISE

By now, you have been introduced to the perspectives of sociology, the basic ideas of science, and the particular versions of science endorsed by sociologists of both positivistic and interpretive persuasions. You have also been introduced to what I have called social-disorganization theory and network theory. It is time to put all of this together in a more substantive context. For sociology is not about perspectives, methods, or theory: rather it is fundamentally an applied field, in so far as it asks questions about, and most often seeks explanations for, the behaviour of real people in real situations in the real world, whether that behaviour takes place in religious institutions, in schools, in the urban context, in the family, or in prisons.

That being the case, I would like to ask you at this time to *conduct a literature review* of some part of the substantive literature (by which I mean the empirical literature) in any sub-area of interest to you. It can be a review of recent literature and trends, of the work of the last decade, or of the field from its inception (if you have enough time and energy). It can be a review of one theoretical question or of the kinds of theoretical questions asked over time. In any case, it should be a critical review, the object of which might well be to discover whether, as claimed here, the history of the area can be usefully treated as a dialogue between those who work out of disorganization and network paradigms or perspectives, or between macro-structural and micro-interpretive sociologists. If you were so inclined, you could easily work out a hypothesis to be tested through such a literature review, though this would require careful operationalization of the terms of the hypothesis, and attention to the design of the study.

## Selected Questions

1. In what ways does network analysis stand in opposition to social-disorganization theory? On what specific points do the proponents disagree?

2. What do network analysts allege to be the new basis of social order in the modern world?

3. In what sorts of ways do networks differ from one another and with what consequences?

4. What is the unit of analysis in network theory, and why is this unit of importance?

5. Why are close-knit networks more able to mobilize a high proportion of their participants than loose-knit networks?

6. Why are loose-knit networks said to tolerate more individual identity and self-expression than close-knit networks?

7. According to the network perspective on stratification, what sorts of assets facilitate or inhibit social mobility? What do gatekeepers do, in network terms?

8. Can you analyse your own behaviour as a function of your own network structures?

Notes to the Chapter

1 These are basically the same antecedents discussed in the treatment of social networks in H.M. Choldin, *Cities and Suburbs: An Introduction to Urban Sociology* (New York: McGraw-Hill, 1985), chapter 14. See also L. Bramson, *The Political Context of Sociology* (Princeton, NJ: Princeton University Press, 1961).

## ILLUSTRATIVE READING

The following is an attempt by the authors to illustrate what happens when one translates the older structural and ecological notion of community into one based on a network conception of community as ties. Ideally, you should be able to see how other structural concepts would have to be similarly changed if network analysis were used consistently. More important, if network analysis is a more useful paradigm, you should be able to explain more with it than with the older model. You might well consider some of the examples mentioned at the end of the chapter in this light. How does a network conception of religion alter what we might predict about religious behaviour? How does thinking in terms of kinship relations rather than household structures alter our understanding of the idea and consequences of 'family'?

### SOCIAL NETWORKS AND INSTITUTIONAL COMPLETENESS: FROM TERRITORY TO TIES

*Sheldon Goldenberg*
*Valerie A. Haines*

The concept of institutional completeness plays an important role in the study of ethnic communities in Canadian sociology. Using competing concepts of community as our framework for analysis, we (1) document the shift from an ecological to a network concept of community that occurs in urban and community sociology, (2) demonstrate that the current framing of the concept of institutional completeness rests on an ecological foundation, and (3) argue that shifting to a network concept of community produces a network reframing that extends the utility of the concept of institutional completeness by allowing us to apply it to both territorial and non-territorial communities.

Ever since its introduction in 1964 by Raymond Breton, the concept of 'institutional completeness' has played an important role in the study of ethnic communities in Canadian sociology (Driedger and Church, 1974; Balakrishnan, 1976; 1982; Makabe, 1979; Brym et al., 1985; Pineo, 1988). Yet, despite its popularity, the concept itself and the assumptions which underpin it have not been investigated systematically.[1] To begin to fill this gap, we locate studies of institutional completeness against the backdrop of changing views of the nature of community. After documenting the shift from an ecological to a network conception of community which occurred in community and urban sociology, we (1) establish that the current framing of the concept of institutional completeness rests on an ecological foundation, and then (2) investigate the implications for studying institutional completeness of shifting from an ecological to a network concept of community.

## Competing Conceptions of Community

The concept of community has been the subject of an ongoing debate in the sociological literature (Hillery, 1955; Effrat, 1973; Poplin, 1973; Wellman, 1979; Wellman et al., 1988). In his analysis of competing definitions of community, Hillery (1955: 118) identified three points of convergence among them: social interaction, a geographical area, and a common tie or ties. The best-developed and most influential formulation of this approach to community is found in the writings of the members of the Chicago School of sociology and their followers (cf. Hawley, 1950; Duncan, 1961). According to their ecological conception, communities are clearly discernible, spatially delimited entities with well-defined boundaries (Haines, 1985). Spatial proximity is assumed to be the basis of commonality in outlook and action of community members.[2]

The ecological conception of community was widely accepted at the time that Breton was writing. Even at this time, however, it was not without its critics. Webber's (1963; 1964) concepts of 'community without propinquity' and 'nonplace urban realm' challenged its domain assumption of spatial proximity as the basis of commonality in outlook and action in human communities. This call for a shift from territory to interaction as the defining characteristic of community was reinforced and extended by Martindale and Hanson's (1969) community as a 'systematic unity of life', Tilly's (1973) 'community of interest', Effrat's (1973) 'nonspatial community of limited liability', and, most recently, by the development of network conceptions of community, including Craven and Wellman's (1973) network city, Wellman and Leighton's (1979) network analytic approach to the community question, and Fischer's (1982) personal networks in towns and cities. Most explicit in the case of the network formulations, this approach defines communities 'by links among members rather than by criteria external to the networks, such as geographical mapping' (Craven and Wellman, 1973: 82).

Proponents of the aspatial approach to community do not deny the reality of the place community. But by treating place communities as a special case of community (Webber, 1964; Berry and Kasarda, 1977; Wellman and Leighton, 1979), they avoid the standard ecological assumption that spatial proximity is a sufficient condition for community. Once this assumption is discarded, the spatiality of any community becomes an empirical question (Craven and Wellman, 1973) and the issue of boundary specification becomes a central concern.

## The Ecological Framing of Institutional Completeness

In community and urban sociology, the network approach has been taken seriously. What was once accepted without question by community and urban sociologists as the proper focus for their studies—bounded local areas—must now be defended as a legitimate object of study (cf. Guest and Lee, 1983; Campbell, 1990). But, despite widespread acceptance of the case for aspatial communities, the discussion that follows makes it clear that it has proven difficult to link the network approach to studies of institutional completeness. Like studies of Canadian ethnic communities more generally, most such studies remain firmly grounded in the ecological tradition. In these cases, the ethnic institutions and their participants are studied within geographically defined communities.

In Breton's original formulation, the concept of institutional completeness was used to explain the integration of immigrants in the receiving country; that is, into the community of their own ethnicity, the native/receiving community or other ethnic communities. Integration in all directions is understood to occur through the formation of informal social networks of companionship ties (e.g., visiting friends, meeting socially with co-workers). When an immigrant is 'transplanted from one country to another, he has to reconstruct his interpersonal "field". He will rebuild in a new community a network of personal affiliations' (Breton, 1974: 194). To satisfy other needs like making a living and attending church, immigrants must use existing social institutions. Thus the 'social organization of the communities which the immigrant contacts in the receiving community' is a 'crucial' factor 'bearing on the absorption of immigrants' (Breton, 1964: 193). In the case of the ethnic communities of immigrants, Breton's primary focus, integration is a function of the degree of institutional completeness of these communities: the higher the degree of institutional completeness of an ethnic community, the more institutional services (e.g., religious, educational, political, national, professional, welfare and mutual aid, communication) it can provide for its members and, therefore, the greater 'its capacity to attract the immigrant within its social boundaries' (Breton, 1964: 194). 'Institutional completeness would be at its extreme', then, 'whenever the ethnic community could perform all the services required by its members. Members would never have to make use of native institutions for the satisfaction of any of their needs, such as education, work, food and clothing, medical care, or social assistance' (Breton, 1964: 194).

Breton's strategy for conceptualizing and operationalizing the ethnic composition of immigrants' interpersonal relations moved his analysis of the effects of community characteristics on the integration of immigrants in a network direction. The focus on ties among individuals rather than territory that this approach to the study of integration entails is reinforced by his suggestion that institutional completeness could be treated as the extent to which members 'make use' of ethnic institutions to satisfy their needs (Breton, 1974: 194).[3] But because Breton assumed that the social boundaries of the ethnic communities which he studied were co-terminous with the spatial boundaries of the city of Montreal, he did not exploit these network metaphors. Instead of measuring actors' participation in ethnic institutions wherever it takes place,[4] he measured the degree of institutional completeness of ethnic communities by counting the number of churches, welfare organizations, newspapers, and periodicals which were found in each Montreal-based ethnic community.[5] Breton's conception of ethnic community reproduces the ecological view of the nature of community both in its focus on social relationships within a local area (the city of Montreal) and its lack of concern for the problem of boundary specification.

This ecological conception of ethnic community became a hallmark of subsequent studies of institutional completeness. Like Breton (1964) before them, Driedger and Church (1974) studied institutional completeness within spatially defined communities. But, unlike Breton who randomly sampled census tracts of Montreal, they chose census tracts of the city of Winnipeg that were characterized by particularly high ethnic concentrations. To examine the institutional completeness of these places, they focused on three local services that were available to members of each ethnic group: churches, voluntary organizations, and schools. This focus cleared the way for their demonstration of the importance of residential segregation for the maintenance of institutional completeness and, through this, ethnic solidarity.

This ecological conception of community also underpins Driedger's (1979; 1980) ethnic enclavic perspective on the maintenance of urban ethnic boundaries. Presented as the ethnic equivalents of Gans's urban villages, ethnic enclavic communities develop when 'minorities wish to develop a means of control over a population in a specific area' (Driedger, 1979: 74). They are maintained by the joint operation of ethnic enclavic factors (e.g., residential segregation, institutional completeness, cultural identity, social distance) and social and psychological factors (e.g., ideological vision, historical symbols, charismatic ethnic leadership, social status). For Driedger, then, ethnic enclavity and institutional completeness are logical corollaries of each other.

## Toward a Network Framing of Institutional Completeness

Under its ecological framing, institutional completeness is an attribute of an ethnic community which, by virtue of its ecological grounding, is a place community. Because social network analysts view and classify the various aspects of the social world according to their relationships rather than according to their attributes (Knoke and Kuklinski, 1982), grounding the study of institutional completeness in a network concept of community would shift the focus of attention away from attributes of places to the relations among actors in one or more aspatial networks. And, because the spatiality of communities which are defined in this way is an empirical question, defining their boundaries is of theoretical and practical importance. Actors or nodes for the network must be selected and the types of social relationships to be studied must be specified (Laumann et al., 1983).

In the case of institutional completeness, the appropriate nodes and types of social relations have been identified by ecologically based studies: co-ethnics for the nodes and ethnic education, religious, political, recreational, national, professional, welfare society, and communication affiliations for the social relationships. Instead of counting the number of ethnic institutions in a particular geographical area, the network framing measures levels of participation of co-ethnics in ethnic institutions regardless of their geographical location.[6]

Studies like the one by Driedger and Church (1974) have demonstrated the importance of residential segregation for the maintenance of institutional completeness and, through this, ethnic identity. The network conception of community does not deny the importance of residential segregation in these processes. What it does suggest is that if ethnic communities can be aspatial communities, then residential segregation may be neither necessary nor sufficient for either process. Because individuals can belong to an ethnic community without living in a particular locality, 'residence in an ethnically segregated neighbourhood is one of the least sensitive indicators of a person's ties to an ethnic group' (Reitz, 1980: 117).

Interactions can and do take place within geographically circumscribed areas (e.g., neighbourhoods, census tracts, cities, regions, countries). But not all of the co-ethnics residing in such an area participate in these ethnic institutions nor does any particular local concentration of ethnic institutions preclude participation by co-ethnics who are widely dispersed in space. As Hawley (1950; 1986) in human ecology, Yancey et al. (1976) in the study of ethnicity and Wellman (1979) in the study of the community question have stressed, advances in transportation and communication technologies have 'liberated' community from spatial constraints.[7] Spatial boundaries and social boundaries need not be and frequently are not co-terminous. Once the aspatiality of ethnic communities is recognized, then, non-participation in local ethnic institutions and participation in non-local ethnic institutions become two sides of the same coin. Boissevain's (1971) analysis of the Italian community of Montreal provides a strategic illustration of the former; Bruser Maynard's (1972) work, *Raisins and Almonds*, illustrates the latter.

Building on the element of Breton's work that focused on the participation of individuals in ethnic institutions, Boissevain (1971) viewed the Italian community of Montreal as 'a viable whole, composed of multiple overlapping networks of social relations originating in the fields of kinship, friendship, neighbourhood and the marketplace, which are given a certain territorial unity by the parish structure of the Italian national church' (Boissevain, 1971: 164). It is largely a geographically concentrated community. Most Italians live near relatives, and see a good deal of them on a frequent basis. '57 per cent of the Canadian born (and 52 per cent of the immigrants) in our general sample chose to buy houses in neighbourhoods with which they were already familiar and in which relatives and other Italians lived' (1971: 155). But this means that 43 per cent of the second generation, most of whom grew to adulthood in a community exhibiting high levels of institutional completeness,[8] choose to buy houses elsewhere. This suggests that residential concentration does not necessarily guarantee a strong commitment to the ethnic community and participation in ethnic institutions, although we would be the first to agree with Boissevain that non-local residents can also participate in ethnic services and institutions. Boissevain also notes that only 57 per cent of the Canadian-born attend church services in Italian at least once a year, and 53 per cent of this sample use no Italian at work. This seems to further confirm our contention that at least for some of those living in predominantly Italian neighbourhoods, it is still not the case that spatial proximity assures meaningful participation in ethnic institutional life.

Boissevain's focus on multiple overlapping networks and his conclusion that the Italians of Montreal form a community linking 'people who are geographically separated and who may even belong to different socio-economic classes' (1971: 152) moved his study of ethnic communities in the direction which our network reconceptualization of institutional completeness calls for. His observations that 70 per cent of immigrants and 28 per cent of those born in Canada receive letters from Italy at least once a fortnight and that, for many, both immigration to Canada in the first place and subsequent settlement patterns reflect financial and other help obtained from kin at some considerable distance, are consistent with an aspatial conception of community. But because his focus is 'The Italians of Montreal', Boissevain does not capitalize on the implicit aspatiality of his conception of community. Like Breton before him, he grafts aspatial networks of social relationships onto an ecological foundation.

This description applies equally to Brettell's (1981) comparison of the extent of Portuguese ethnic community formation in Toronto and Paris. Framed by the contrast between a geographical (ecological) conception of community and its network-based counterpart, Brettell (1981: 13) used data on the timing of Portuguese immigration to Toronto and Paris, the numbers of immigrants, their settlement patterns within these cities, their contact with co-ethnics in Toronto and Paris, and the levels of institutional completeness of their ethnic communities in these cities to sustain the conclusion that '"community" in either a geographical sense or an ethnic network sense does not exist for Portuguese immigrants in Paris as it does among Portuguese immigrants in Toronto.' The evidence which Brettell uses to support this conclusion does establish the absence of a geographically based ethnic community in Paris. At the same time, however, it counters her argument for the absence of a network-based community for Portuguese immigrants in Paris, if the aspatiality of a network conception of community is taken seriously. The fact that 'annual religious festivals are celebrated with fellow villagers during the summer visits to Portugal, not on the streets of Paris' (1981: 13), the fact that for Paris immigrants the community of orientation is 'in Portugal itself, in the village they have left' (1981: 13) and the fact that this 'community is sustained by a long distance social network' (1981: 14) through village newspapers sent by village priests; visits with fellow villagers during summer vacations in Portugal; and travel by fellow villagers to Paris for visits or jobs, all point to ties among co-ethnics which span national boundaries and, through them, to community in an ethnic network sense.

The importance of taking the aspatiality of communities seriously is made even clearer in Bruser Maynard's autobiographical *Raisins and Almonds* (1972). This is her account of growing up in various towns in Saskatchewan and Manitoba in the 1920s. Her family was most often the only Jewish family in town. None the less she was able to retain her Jewish identity by virtue of her father's willingness to send away for mail-order Sunday school leaflets from a rabbi in Winnipeg (1972: 20), and through her family's occasional stays with relatives in that city (1972: 66). Other important non-local connections included a subscription to a Jewish newspaper from New York (1972: 163), Sunday in-gatherings of Jewish families from other nearby prairie towns (1972: 29), and even her family's collection of Jewish works of theology and literature (1972: 163). Bruser Maynard's illustrations can easily be supplemented by others that reflect the importance of non-local institutional support for ethnic identity. Maintenance of Jewish identity has been related to taking jobs at remote Jewish summer camps, attendance at religious services on special holidays in a town down the highway, or only when an itinerant rabbi passes through, memberships in national or even international welfare organizations like the B'nai B'rith, or even having Jewish pen-pals in New York or Israel. In all of these cases, the services required to maintain ethnic identity are provided by ethnic institutions which are non-local.

Studies of institutional completeness which are grounded in the ecological conception of community can account for situations where localized social ties comprise a majority of urbanites' social relationships. What shifting to a social network conception of community allows and, in fact, demands is the investigation of the impact of non-local ties on the processes of ethnic identification and assimilation. Localized social interaction does occur but the evidence (Craven and Wellman, 1973; Wellman, 1979; Wellman and Leighton, 1979; Fischer, 1982) suggests that 'such ties, while real and important, comprise a minority of most urbanites' social relationships' (Guest and Lee, 1983: 218). Social ties with co-ethnics can link them to one another across geographical space, maintaining a situation in which ethnicity remains important even without spatial proximity.

## Discussion
Studies of institutional completeness have focused primarily on the implications of co-ethnic affiliations for ethnic identification and assimilation. In its ecological formulation where spatial proximity is key, participation in ethnic institutions presupposes residence in the area in which these institutions are found. This

assumption of the co-terminality of ethnic communities and place communities has been challenged by research using aspatial conceptions of community. Advances in transportation and communication technologies have expanded opportunities for maintaining ethnic identification through ties with geographically dispersed co-ethnics. To adapt Wellman's (1988: 37–8) phrasing, the network framing of institutional completeness confronts head on 'the existence of ramified, spatially dispersed networks of "community ties", even when they do not fit within bounded neighbourhood or kinship solidarities.'

Where networks of community ties do fit within bounded neighbourhoods, the ecological and network conceptions of institutional completeness converge. In these instances, the structure of institutionally complete ethnic enclaves is, as Craven and Wellman (1972: 71) point out, 'reminiscent of the dense "village" networks', networks which they suggest are defined by a proliferation of interactional ties among members that are contained within the boundaries of the village and neighbouring farms. It does not follow, however, that only 'self-contained urban villages' (Wellman, 1979: 1297) are institutionally complete, as the ecological approach suggests.[9] If ethnic communities can be aspatial communities, then institutionally complete communities can assume other network configurations. Linking the study of institutional completeness with the study of social networks not only sensitizes researchers to this possibility but also provides them with the concepts and techniques with which to investigate it.

'Urban villages' or 'ethnic enclaves' can be studied using the network approach. In network terms, such communities exhibit high density, relatively small size, and low diversity, where diversity refers both to geographic range and to heterogeneity of alter's attributes (e.g., religion, sex).[10] Unlike its ecological counterpart, however, the network approach can also handle other network configurations of institutionally complete communities like those illustrated by Brettell's Portuguese and Bruser Maynard's Jews. Size, density, and diversity are not the only network concepts which can be used to characterize the structure of ethnic communities. Institutionally complete communities may also vary across other properties of networks like reachability, anchorage, and composition on the one hand, and features of individual ties like frequency, intensity, multiplexity, and duration on the other. Which measures are most appropriate is an empirical question. By tapping the number and the nature of ties which connect co-ethnics, the network approach can avoid the limitations of the enumerative approach to the measurement of institutional completeness and, at the same time, bring studies of institutional completeness into line with recent developments in community and urban sociology.

## NOTES

1 Discussions of institutional completeness routinely appear in textbook treatments of ethnic communities, but the concept often seems to be ritualistically cited rather than examined. It is not without its critics, however. Roberts and Boldt (1979) and

Baureiss (1981) have criticized the 'enumerative approach' which Breton and others have used to operationalize the concept of institutional completeness. Roberts and Boldt do not deny the value of counting the number of ethnic institutions, but argue that the nature or quality of these institutions must also be considered. Working from a distinction between social organizations (the objects of Breton's enumerative approach) and social institutions, Baureiss extends this critique to suggest that ethnic institutional structure (i.e., kinship, language retention) must also be assessed.

2  Other views of community as a social group with a territorial dimension include Hiller's (1941) community as a local social group, Janowitz's (1952) community of limited liability, and Warren's (1963) functional definition of community.

3  Providing ethnic services and making use of ethnic services are not independent phenomena. A viable ethnic community requires participants; empty schools and churches are presumably not to be considered to be indicators of a high degree of institutional completeness.

4  Using data collected by O'Bryan et al. (1976), Reitz (1980) measures ethnic participation for a sample of respondents from ten ethnic groups and five major Canadian cities. He presents an interesting discussion of institutional completeness which translates the concept into 'institutional strength' and compares members of the various ethnic groups with respect to participation in ethnic institutions. Unfortunately, Reitz cannot tell us where the institutions are with which his respondents are variably connected. It is easy to assume that they are in all cases local institutions, but they need not be so, and it is just this possibility of non-local affiliations with ethnic institutions that is addressed by our network reconceptualization.

5  Even in ecological terms, this operational definition of the relevant community is problematic. Should one use the Montreal metropolitan boundaries of Montreal proper? Should one try to identify the boundaries of ethnic communities within the larger city? Is it relevant how diffused or concentrated ethnic institutions may be within the overall urban area? Driedger and Church (1974) give such issues more attention than is apparent in Breton's original formulation of institutional completeness.

6  Network analysts distinguish between analysis of whole networks and egocentric (personal) networks (Wellman, 1988; Marsden, 1990). Because the whole network approach presupposes closed populations, our network reframing calls for the collection of egocentric network data.

7  Keller (1968: 61) attempts to capture this distinction in her discussion of a 'shift from a neighbouring of *place* to a neighbouring of *taste*'.

8  The social organization of this Italian community includes newspapers printed in Italian, stores in which service people and customers ordinarily speak Italian, workplaces in which supervisors and employees customarily speak Italian, churches in which services are conducted in Italian, and Italian ethnic voluntary organizations and associations. An enumeration of ethnic organizations would result in the classification of this community as relatively high in terms of institutional completeness.

9  Wellman's (1979: 1207) comments on institutional completeness can be read as a variation on this suggestion. 'The argument suggests that primary ties are often dispersed among multiple, sparsely interconnected social networks. These networks, by their very nature, are not "institutionally complete" (Breton, 1964), self-contained "urban villages".'

10  Many network analysts (Burt, 1983; Campbell et al., 1986; Marsden, 1987) treat size, density, and diversity as dimensions of network range.

## REFERENCES

Balakrishnan, B.R.
1976 'Ethnic residential segregation in the metropolitan areas of Canada'. *Canadian Journal of Sociology* 1 (4): 481–98.

1982 'Changing patterns of ethnic residential segregation in the metropolitan areas of Canada'. *Canadian Review of Sociology and Anthropology* 19 (1): 92–110.

Baureiss, Gunter
1981 'Institutional completeness: its use and misuse in ethnic relations research'. *Journal of Ethnic Studies* 9 (2): 101–10.

Berry, Brian J.L., and John D. Kasarda
1977 *Contemporary Urban Ecology*. New York: Macmillan.

Boissevain, Jeremy
1971 'The Italians of Montreal'. In W.E. Mann, ed., *Canada: A Sociological Profile*, pp. 150–65. Toronto: The Copp Clark Publishing Co.

Breton, Raymond
1964 'Institutional completeness of ethnic communities and the personal relations of immigrants'. *American Journal of Sociology* 70 (2): 193–205.

Brettell, Caroline B.
1981 'Is the ethnic community inevitable? A comparison of the settlement patterns of Portuguese immigrants in Toronto and Paris'. *Journal of Ethnic Studies* 9 (3): 1–17.

Brym, Robert J., Michael W. Gillespie, and A.R. Gillis
1985 'Anomie, opportunity, and the density of ethnic ties: another view of Jewish outmarriage in Canada'. *Canadian Review of Sociology and Anthropology* 22 (1): 102–12.

Burt, Ronald S.
1983 'Range'. In Ronald S. Burt and Michael J. Minor, eds, *Applied Network Analysis: A Methodological Introduction*, pp. 176–94. Beverly Hills: Sage Publications.

Campbell, Karen E.
1990 'Networks past: a 1939 Bloomington Neighborhood'. *Social Forces* 69 (1): 139–55.

Campbell, Karen E., Peter V. Marsden, and Jeanne S. Hurlbert
1986 'Social resources and socioeconomic status'. *Social Networks* 8 (1):
       97–117.

Craven, Paul, and Barry Wellman
1973 'The network city'. *Sociological Inquiry* 43 (3–4): 57–88.

Driedger, Leo
1979 'Maintenance of urban ethnic boundaries: the French in St Boniface'. *The
       Sociological Quarterly* 20 (1): 89–108.

1980 'Jewish identity: the maintenance of urban religious and ethnic bound-
       aries'. *Ethnic and Racial Studies* 3 (1): 67–88.

Driedger, Leo, and Glenn Church
1974 'Residential segregation and institutional completeness: a comparison of
       ethnic minorities'. *Canadian Review of Sociology and Anthropology* 11
       (1): 30–52.

Duncan, Otis Dudley
1961 'From social system to ecosystem'. *Sociological Inquiry* 31 (2): 140–9.

Effrat, Marcia Pelly
1973 'Approaches to community: conflicts and complementarities'. *Sociolog-
       ical Inquiry* 43 (3–4): 1–32.

Fischer, Claude S.
1982 *To Dwell Among Friends: Personal Networks in Town and City*. Chicago:
       University of Chicago Press.

Guest, Avery M., and Barrett A. Lee
1983 'The social organization of local areas'. *Urban Affairs Quarterly* 19 (2):
       217–40.

Haines, Valerie A.
1985 'From organicist to relational human ecology'. *Sociological Theory* 3 (1):
       65–74.

Hawley, Amos H.
1950 *Human Ecology: A Theory of Community Structure*. New York: The
       Ronald Press Company.

1986 *Human Ecology: A Theoretical Essay*. Chicago: The University of Chicago
       Press.

Hiller, E.T.
1941  'The community as a social group'. *American Sociological Review* 6 (2): 189–202.

Hillery, George A.
1955  'Definitions of community: areas of agreement'. *Rural Sociology* 20 (2): 111–23.

Janowitz, Morris
1952  *The Community Press in an Urban Setting*. Chicago: University of Chicago Press.

Keller, Suzanne
1968  *The Urban Neighborhood: A Sociological Perspective*. New York: Random House.

Knoke, David, and James H. Kuklinski
1982  *Network Analysis*. Beverly Hills: Sage Publications.

Laumann, Edward O., Peter V. Marsden, and David Prensky
1983  'The boundary specification problem in network analysis'. In Ronald S. Burt and Michael J. Minor, eds, *Applied Network Analysis: A Methodological Introduction*, pp. 18–34. Beverly Hills: Sage Publications.

Makabe, Tomoko
1979  'Ethnic identity scale and social mobility: the case of the Nisei in Toronto'. *Canadian Review of Sociology and Anthropology* 16 (2): 136–46.

Marsden, Peter V.
1987  'Core discussion networks of Americans'. *American Sociological Review* 52 (1): 122–31.

1990  'Network data and measurement'. *Annual Review of Sociology* 16: 435–63.

Martindale, Don, and R. Galen Hanson
1969  *Small town and the Nation: The Conflict of Local and Translocal Forces*. Westport, Connecticut: Greenwood Publishing Corporation.

Maynard, Fredelle Bruser
1972  *Raisins and Almonds*. Toronto: Doubleday.

O'Bryan, G., J.G. Reitz, and O. Kuplowska
1976  *Non-Official Languages: A Study in Canadian Multiculturalism*. Ottawa: Supply and Services Canada.

Pineo, Peter C.
1988 'Socioeconomic status and the concentric zonal structure of Canadian cities'. *Canadian Review of Sociology and Anthropology* 25 (3): 421–38.

Poplin, Dennis E.
1973 *Communities: A Survey of Theories and Methods of Research*. New York: Macmillan.

Reitz, Jeffrey G.
1980 *The Survival of Ethnic Groups*. Toronto: McGraw-Hill Ryerson Ltd.

Roberts, Lance W., and Edward D. Boldt
1979 'Institutional completeness and ethnic assimilation'. *Journal of Ethnic Studies* 7 (2): 103–8.

Tilly, Charles
1973 'Do communities act?' *Sociological Inquiry* 43 (3–4): 209–40.

Warren, Roland L.
1963 *The Community in America*. Chicago: Rand McNally and Company.

Webber, Melvin
1963 'Order in diversity: community without propinquity'. In L. Wingo, ed., *Cities and Space: The Future Use of Urban Land*, pp. 23–54. Baltimore: Johns Hopkins Press.

1964 'The urban place and the nonplace urban realm'. In Melvin M. Webber, ed., *Explorations into Urban Structure*, pp. 79–153. Philadelphia: University of Pennsylvania Press.

Wellman, Barry
1979 'The community question: the intimate networks of East Yorkers'. *American Journal of Sociology* 84 (5): 1201–31.

1988 'Structural analysis: from method and metaphor to theory and substance'. In Barry Wellman and S.D. Berkowitz, eds, *Social Structures: A Network Approach*, pp. 19–61. Cambridge: Cambridge University Press.

Wellman, Barry, and Barry Leighton
1979 'Networks, neighborhoods and communities'. *Urban Affairs Quarterly* 14 (3): 363–90.

Wellman, Barry, Peter J. Carrington, and Alan Hall
1988 'Networks as personal communities'. In Barry Wellman and S.D. Berkowitz, eds, *Social Structures: A Network Approach*, pp. 130–84. Cambridge: Cambridge University Press.

Yancey, William L., Eugene P. Ericksen, and Richard N. Juliani
1976 'Emergent ethnicity: a review and reformulation'. *American Sociological Review* 41 (3): 391–403.

From *Canadian Journal of Sociology* 17 (3) (1992): 301–12.

# Participating in the Discipline

Part III of this text has two purposes. The first—in chapter 6—is to introduce you to the more applied tasks that face every student and practitioner, the most important of which is to translate an interest in a topic into a research project that is feasible, interesting, and useful. It is not enough to understand the perspectives in the abstract, and though methods and theory are essential ingredients of the final product, they are not often that product. Sociology involves the study of substantive topics, using theory, methods, and perspective constructively and usefully. Whereas I claimed at the outset that most introductory texts err in overemphasizing substantive content, I do not want to fall prey to the opposite error of neglecting substance entirely. I am counting on instructors to supplement this workbook with their own selection of substantive areas, again using the contents of this book to enable students to gain a better appreciation of the substantive literature in the discipline. Because the application of the perspectives, methods, and theory introduced here does not come naturally to anyone, I will work through several concrete examples.

The second purpose of part III—in chapter 7—is to invite you to participate actively in the joint and common assessment of claims and in the ensuing debate that characterizes the field, as is your right as well as your responsibility, now that you have been initiated into the ways of thinking sociologically. I have provided materials from two examples of interesting disagreements in the field. I have referred to many more, and again instructors will no doubt choose their own. What is most important is the active participation by students in the assessment of claims to knowledge. Readers of this book should know how to do this and should be eager to try their hand at it; the discipline requires such sceptical and constructive assessment if it is to flourish.

**CHAPTER 6**

# From Problem to Research Paper

This chapter contains a few brief illustrations, drawn from three substantive areas, of how a sociologist might develop a researchable project for a paper. This transformation of a 'topic' into a research paper is one of the most difficult tasks for students (and for many practitioners as well). You should be able to understand each step of the process, as well as the general principles they have in common. This task of developing projects is not nearly as mysterious as it might appear.

I am not here concerned primarily with the actual writing of these projects, but there are many good books that deal principally with this, including M. Northey and L. Tepperman, *Making Sense in the Social Sciences* (Toronto: Oxford University Press, 1986), Sociology Writing Group, *A Guide to Writing Sociology Papers* (New York: St Martin's Press, 1991), H.S. Becker, *Writing for Social Scientists* (Chicago: University of Chicago Press, 1986), and L. Cuba, *A Short Guide to Writing about Social Science* (New York: HarperCollins, 1993). These useful and informative books teach far more than techniques of writing, and I have little hesitation in recommending them to the interested student. None the less, there is no substitute for concrete examples, worked out 'before your very eyes', and it is this that I propose to show you in this chapter.

First, however, I would like to pass on to you an outline I often use in class when I require paper proposals. The first step in considering a project often involves preparing a proposal. It is an extremely useful exercise.

## GUIDELINES FOR PAPER PROPOSALS

A paper proposal should be the skeleton of a finished paper. It is the heart of the paper, lacking only the actual data collection, interpretation, and conclusions. For our purposes, let us suppose that the paper of interest is an *empirical* paper in any substantive field of the discipline. This implies that the proposal must be defensible in its sociological nature and application to the literature in the area. It must deal with a *plausible* and *problematic* topic, and it must be empirical. Furthermore, the guiding hypothesis or proposition suggested should be yours rather than one worked out in class or proposed in the literature. It may be on any topic of interest to you that can be fit within the boundaries of your substantive area. If, having developed your rationale or model, you are in doubt, ask your instructor. You may propose a modified replication, but if you do, you should have a clear rationale for doing so, and a 'twist' of your own to add to the treatment. After all, the idea is that there must be a real problem, in the sense that the result of your hypothesis testing will not be self-evident in advance. There must be equally plausible alternatives or competitors. It is this that makes the study worth doing and the test worth conducting. We do not already know the answer, and it is worthwhile finding out.

The first page or so after the title page, should be the *introduction*. It should clearly state the problem, question, or issue with which your paper will be concerned. It should discuss why this question is worth asking. What is problematic about it? Why would it make a difference if we knew the answer? How is this issue important, both social-scientifically and in terms of any potential practical application? How is it related to broader sociological issues or questions?

After the introduction, and having interested the reader, the next section should be the *literature review*. Here you demonstrate that you have done your homework. The issue or question you are dealing with came from somewhere. Here you trace, critically, its history and antecedents. In doing the literature review, you discuss different methods that have been used in the past to try to come to grips with your issue, detailing their strengths and weaknesses—setting up your eventual treatment in its historical context and demonstrating that, although you are not repeating past studies, you are building on them and are aware of them. The literature review usually concludes with a more refined and sophisticated statement of the problem.

The next couple of pages deal with your *hypothesis* or *expectations*, *model or propositions of interest*, rather than your problem. These propositions or hypotheses are tentative answers to your main question. They give specific details of how you translate the issue into a testable hypothesis of interest to sociologists in this area. You will have to discuss the *operational definitions* of all the terms in your hypothesis that require measurement. You ought also to discuss *rival hypotheses* or relevant qualifications that have occurred to you, and the possible ways of treating these. Your research goal is to test both your main and major rival hypotheses, so as to lend support to your explanation, propositions, or hypotheses by reference to data consistent with them, while simultaneously being able to present data or design that allows you to rule out competing explanations. This section naturally flows into the next.

The next section is *research design*, or a discussion of how you propose actually to conduct the study you have in mind so as to answer the questions you have posed. It tells the reader *what data* you will collect and why those are relevant and adequate for a sensitive test of your hypotheses or model or propositions. If appropriate, it will discuss *sampling* considerations and *instrumentation or measurement*. It answers the questions 'What sort of data would be required to test the hypotheses, and how will those data be collected?' As in other sections, you should be prepared here to demonstrate that you are aware of the choices you are making and problems involved in making trade-offs. You should be trying to anticipate and reply to criticism in advance. Be your own best and most constructive critic. Leave other critical readers no comments to make other than favourable ones.

Defend the choices you make, and do so thoughtfully. If there are options, describe them, as well as your reasons for choosing any particular one.

The last section, which should be perhaps a couple of pages in length, deals with *expectations* for data analysis and describes how you might fit your study back into the literature on the topic. It might well pose additional questions, demonstrating that your paper is not a dead end but that, on the contrary, it stimulates other important, practical, and relevant research. Your goal should be to convince a critic that the study you are proposing is worth doing.

All that is left is the actual collection and analysis of data, and that is fairly mechanical. If you have done everything to this point, you could assign the remaining work to someone else, and anyone should produce basically the same study. If that is not so, you have not provided sufficient detail in the above sections.

Finally, there is a *bibliography* or reference section at the end, which is simply a record of all work you made use of in preparing the proposal. It is a list of articles and books used in the literature review, though it may include other sources, if they were useful, on interviewing or content analysis, for example, or on other areas of literature that seem worthwhile in light of your final discussion section.

The following three examples are intended to show you how various issues might be handled in specific instances. They do not describe proposals, but the processes by which most of the questions raised above might be handled in three different concrete instances.

## FROM PROBLEM TO PAPER: AN EXTENDED EXAMPLE FROM THE SOCIOLOGY OF THE FAMILY

To begin with, a topic does not, by itself, constitute a proposal for a paper, as you have now seen. None the less you would be surprised at the number of times students have asked me whether they can do a paper on divorce, drug use, delinquency, or even gender. A name or concept is not a topic, and a topic is a long way yet from a research design worked out to test some ideas. Topics must be grounded in literature that explains their relevance and sets the context within which they are viewed as problematic. Terms need to be operationalized so they can be examined systematically and tested carefully and rigorously. When you ask if you can do a paper on divorce, the instructor can only reply, 'Maybe, but it depends on how you do it and what you actually want to look at under that rubric.' You need some variables, some hypotheses, a relationship, and first and foremost a question that is sociologically problematic. Those elements do not come out of thin air; you have to go to the library and read about your topic of interest, comparing articles and critically examining them for flaws and contradictions and for issues to which your own paper might in some way contribute. Students are often in far too much hurry to get into the 'field' collecting empirical evidence before they have clearly conceptualized their problem and decided how best to address it. There is an old rule that applies well to such efforts: garbage in, garbage out. Work done at the front end of a project is never wasted, whereas a project that gathers data too early can never recover from that liability. That is why I have emphasized the importance of anticipating problems, objections, and rival hypotheses in advance, early enough to figure out a way of avoiding or handling them while you still can. That and exactly that is the crux of what design in research is all about.

Suppose you wished to examine the question of how mobility affects ties among kin. That interest may be a result of personal concern about whether you will maintain ties with your brother who is going away to university. It may have been produced by reading a novel, the newspaper, or even a sociology book. Your interest is a potential topic for a sociology paper if it meets two criteria. *First, it must be arguably sociological.* Since almost anything can be, that criterion is rarely a problem. To be on the safe side, though, ask yourself if you can put the argument you are considering in terms of common sociological variables and concepts, such as socio-economic status, gender, social structure, culture, or social process. So long as you can, you should be all right, and you probably won't be doing a history or psychology project. Still, you have to demonstrate, and not assume that the topic is appropriately sociological.

*The second criterion—that the topic be 'problematic'*—is both more important and more difficult. The crucial feature of the problematic is uncertainty. Competing answers that are equally plausible indicate a problematic focus. Problematic does not refer to social problems, such as delinquency or drug abuse. It simply suggests that if you can imagine only one possible answer to the question you are asking, it is not problematic and will not make a good project. You will only be describing or illustrating the obvious, and that adds nothing to the knowledge we already possess.

In the case of mobility, both criteria are easily met. Often just how problematic a topic is becomes evident only when you read up on it. And then you can make almost anything problematic by asking how it has changed or how and why it differs from place to place or group to group.

With the effect of mobility on ties among kin, we have satisfied the two requirements, since the subject is certainly both sociological and problematic. It would be somewhat problematic even if our aim were simply to see if we could replicate a past finding at the present time and in a new location. Both the passage of time and change of place introduce new possibilities so that one might not think the same finding equally likely. Thus it would no longer be clear exactly what to expect, and that is precisely what problematic means.

*The researcher's next task is to figure out exactly what to expect the effect to be and to explain why it happens.* To do this you might begin by immersing yourself in the literature to see what others have found to this point and to understand how terms have been defined and measured. In this way, each current piece of research builds on past research.

You might find, for example, that social mobility has to be separated from geographic mobility because they need not occur together and each can have its own effect. As well, the *direction* of mobility might well make a difference to this dependent variable since—in terms of occupational mobility at least—success means upward mobility, and we often interpret stability or downward mobility as failure. In terms of geographic mobility, there might be a major distinction between long- and short-distance mobility, where no discernible effect occurs until a threshold is reached, perhaps at that point where a trip to visit relatives requires a night away from home. In addition, the attitude of the family of orientation may be crucial to both kinds of mobility. If they are supportive and encouraging,

Figure 6.1 Effects of Combination of Parental Attitudes and Mobility Experience on Ties among Kin

| | Mobility Experience | |
|---|---|---|
| Parental Attitude to Mobility | Mobility Takes Place (+) | No Mobility (-) |
| Encouraging (+) | (++) no disruption | (+-) possible disruption |
| Discouraging (-) | (-+) possible disruption | (--) no disruption |

mobility might not be disruptive. If they disapprove, they may consider mobility to be rebellion or deviance, and that rather than the mobility itself may be what disrupts the ties. Methodologically this suggests that variables can be confounded so that we mistakenly interpret mobility as disruptive when in fact the disruption is due to the violation of parental hopes, which is negatively sanctioned by reduced interaction. The possibility that what matters is the combination of parental attitude and actual mobility experience generates the schema of possible outcomes shown in Figure 6.1.

The four-part table is a useful device for the theoretical clarification of logical possibilities. It simplifies by dichotomizing and then simply 'crosses' two variables to create the four logically possible cells. In this case, the table allows us to suggest that mobility is not always disruptive. Where it is consistent with parental attitudes, it may not break ties of kinship. But when it takes place over the objections of the parents, it may be disruptive. Since we need to know both variables if we are to make a prediction, it is clear that the question of the effects of mobility has now become far more problematic.

A literature review will teach us a lot. It will clarify the concepts and alert us to just how problematic and multi-dimensional our idea is. It will also tell us how other investigators have studied various aspects of this question. Not least, it gives us their findings and interpretations, providing us with some understanding of the mechanism or process by which mobility might be thought to affect ties among kin.

Most beginning projects or papers are written at that point, summarizing the steps and stringing together various selections from studies the student agrees with. Most often, negative or anomalous evidence is left out, and the student makes little effort to assess the literature critically or to integrate it systematically. Yet readers at every level can certainly do so, and papers that stop at that point stop far too soon. You do not have to understand sophisticated statistical treatments to do your best to evaluate an empirical paper in light of what you've learned. With some effort, everyone can assess empirical work. Your particular topic emerges from your unique assessment. It is an opportunity to use the literature to answer your questions, even though it was not originally intended to do so. You can re-analyse the studies you have examined; you can critique one study with another; you can suggest alternative interpretations or rival hypotheses; you can try to integrate opposing findings or viewpoints.

If you are engaged in primary research, your work has only begun at this point. You have done what will turn out to be the introduction to your paper. *As a result of the critical literature review, your initial expectations concerning the relationship you are interested in may well have undergone significant revision and considerable narrowing.* In the example at hand, let us say you have now decided to deal with the effects of upward social mobility on the frequency and nature of interaction with parents and siblings. *You can now formulate a specific hypothesis*, proposing, for example, that such mobility has negative effects on interaction. Your hypothesis is still only a statement linking concepts to one another, but it, too, must meet several criteria if you are to be on the safe side. Hypotheses are testable statements of specific relationships between two or more variables. To see if your attempt meets these requirements, ask yourself how it could be tested (and falsified), what the several values of each variable are, and what specific relationship you are expecting. Asking and answering these questions takes you into the next steps, operationalizing the terms and devising a research design. At that point you have a tentative hypothesis.

Remember that the variables must vary. That sounds trite, but one of the commonest errors at the introductory level—and far beyond it—is to construct a research design in such a way that the variables have only single values. For instance a student might want to test the hypothesis that divorces in ethnically mixed marriages are caused by conflicts directly related to ethnic values, for example, over holidays and rituals. The student might interview all the divorced people she can find who were once married to a person of a different ethnic background. She might well find that the most common cause of divorce reported in the interviews is the clash of ethnic values. Does that finding demonstrate that ethnic value conflict causes divorce in cross-ethnic marriages? No, it does not. Several problems arise with this research no matter how good the sampling, no matter how competent the interviewer. The problems are related to research design, the assessment of causality, and the error of making constants out of your variables. The causes of divorce can *never* be discovered if one studies only divorced couples. Perhaps another example will make that point clear.

In an attempt to find the causes of drug addiction by discovering a common denominator among all addicts, many investigators have studied prison inmates who are drug addicts. Some have claimed that personal immaturity is the common denominator; others have discovered an extra chromosome or an addict parent; others have found that each addict earlier smoked marijuana. You have probably read similar studies of the 'causes' of homosexuality, abortion, or whatever. Common-denominator studies do not *ever* prove cause. At most they demonstrate that a correlation exists, but correlation is not causation. All the addicts also drank milk when they were younger, but nobody has as yet seriously argued that milk causes drug addiction!

John Stuart Mill called such a method of proceeding the 'method of agreement'. He argued that it has many deficiencies in demonstrating causality, among them that any correlation could be spurious. Another, more basic deficiency here is that we are not dealing with variables. Since everyone in the sample is an addict we cannot possibly discover another *variable* that distinguishes addicts from non-addicts. Yet that is what we seek. All the addicts smoked marijuana, but that cannot tell us anything about whether non-addicts do or do not smoke marijuana, because our study is confined only to addicts! In the divorce example, the subjects are all divorced. No common denominator, no matter how carefully documented, can explain why they got divorced. We must have variation on this dependent variable. We must compare subjects from continuing cross-ethnic marriages with ones now divorced. Perhaps we will find that an ethnic value clash is common in both classes. In that case it could not be the cause of the divorce. Only if the two groups are similar in every relevant way and the divorced group alone experienced that clash could we argue that it is the cause of divorce. But we must have variation on the dependent variable if we are to get anywhere in explaining the nature of the relationship that interests us.

Your literature review should have convinced you that your question is open and that there are other, not unreasonable causal possibilities. Perhaps primary among them is the possibility, mentioned by Litwak and tested by others, notably Slater (1969): that social mobility, if encouraged, may not disrupt or reduce ties.

*The next step is to operationalize the variables stated in your hypothesis.* Be aware, though, that the 'steps' do not always follow the order given here and certainly do not have to. In practice the steps can occur in every order, and parts of all are involved in each. Real research only looks orderly after the fact when presented to others in the form of *reconstructed logic*.

In any event we now need to decide how to measure upward social mobility and the frequency and nature of interaction. We have already operationally defined 'close kin' by limiting the category to parents and siblings. Again the operationalization stage is closely tied to research design and sampling issues. Indeed the decision to try to operationalize in advance betrays a more quantitative and social-structural approach. A symbolic interactionist might choose to enter the field, once it was selected, with no operationalizations as yet in mind, precisely to see how the actors themselves defined the terms at hand— upward mobility, close kin, and kinds of interaction. But the participant observer will have to produce evidence at some point; if that evidence is to be useful, it will have to have some consistent and clear relationship to the terms of the hypothesis.

Let us suppose we decided to measure upward mobility by asking respondents (or subjects) their present occupation and their father's occupation. We might then locate each occupation on one of the many socio-economic or occupational prestige scales. Next we might decide that a differential of at least 50 points between the two occupations, and in favour of the son, would constitute upward mobility. In making these decisions, we have limited our study to men. We have also limited it to those whose occupations are 50 points removed from one another on a particular scale. We do not treat women, and all those for whom we do not have data on both father and son are dropped. Furthermore mobility is measured at one particular time; therefore career mobility and changes over the lifetime of either subject are lost.

Each of those may be a significant problem, biasing or distorting what we can discover. After reflection, we might try to operationally define the term in another way. No single operational definition would be without its drawbacks. For that reason social scientists usually try to use several overlapping measures for each key term. This is called *triangulation*. In the current example we might gather data on educational backgrounds, family incomes, and occupational prestige. We might also ask the subjects whether they think they have risen above their parents' class. Combining these measures of social mobility, we might argue that we capture more than any single indicator could. Of course how they are to be combined is another tricky issue.

Since most studies use different operational definitions, the reader must assess each study carefully. If you use different measures masquerading as measures of the same term, you may actually get different results. In addition, in your own analysis you must be careful not to interpret what is really only a partial indicator as if it fully captured the meaning of a much broader term.

To continue our example, we need to operationally define what a negative effect would be in terms of interaction with close kin. A crude measure might simply be to count the frequency of family visits over a specific time and suggest that a negative effect would be defined as fewer visits over the same time. But what is a family visit exactly, and how do we know what qualifies as such a visit? Operational definitions are instructions that are supposed to allow others to replicate our findings by duplicating our work. If others cannot duplicate it, it cannot be *replicated*. Perhaps we could ask the subjects a number of questions about the duration of each interaction with close kin, the nature of that interaction (for example, by phone, in your house, at their house), the purpose of the interaction, and the quality of the interaction (for example, was it an interaction with a practical purpose or was it a social interaction?). We could limit ourselves to having them record all those features for a full week. We could also ask the subjects for their judgement or definition of the situation, inquiring simply whether they think they interact a great deal with their close relatives, quite a lot, not much, or hardly at all. There are many other ways that we might elicit what we want to know, and we might find in thinking them over that what we want has changed in the process of carefully considering the measurement possibilities. We may decide, for example, that the negative effect we are interested in is not a quantitative measure at all and that what we really want is the subjects' feelings about the *adequacy* of the interaction levels they experience, whatever they may be objectively.

Suppose we have made those difficult choices. *It is a good idea to restate the conceptual hypothesis now in operational terms*. Doing so virtually tells you how to proceed next since the operational terms tell you what data you will need to obtain in order to test your main hypothesis. In our example we might translate this as follows:

> The higher the differential in sons' and fathers' occupational prestige scores (on the Blau and Duncan scale) in favour of the son, the less frequently will the son interact with members of his family of origin.

If that version of the hypothesis is really what we meant, *we can now try to design research to test it*. If it is no longer what we had in mind, we could try other operational definitions. Each choice about ways of measuring the terms makes a difference in how we can proceed. We could have phrased the hypothesis as follows:

Sons whose occupational prestige scores exceed their fathers' scores by at least 50 points will interact less frequently with their families of origin than other sons.

A third version might interpret the issue a little differently:

Sons whose occupational prestige scores have increased over the last 10 years will interact less frequently with their families of origin than they did 10 years ago.

In design terms we now have several choices. These choices were actually implicit from the beginning. We are hypothesizing that sons experiencing upward mobility interact less frequently with close kin. The question is, less frequently than who? It has been said that all sociology is comparative, and that, at least, is another useful guideline. *Virtually all designs are comparative, either explicitly or implicitly.* In this case we could argue that since we are interested in the effects of upward mobility, we mean 'as compared to their own frequency of interaction before upward mobility took place'. That is in version three of the hypothesis. Our other, and preferable, choice is to interpret the comparison as one involving other people similar to our subjects except that they have either not been upwardly mobile or not been so upwardly mobile. This latter distinction is evident in version one but not in version two. Version two compares two samples (upward and other), and version one treats each variable as continuous (degrees of mobility). But why is version three so quickly disposed of? Simply put, too many things have happened over the 10 years in addition to upward mobility. Each of them could become a plausible rival hypothesis for explaining reduced interaction; and, whether we have said so specifically or not, our hypothesis is really causal. Our implication is that upward mobility is not merely correlated with, but also *causes*, a disruption of kin ties. In the third alternative everyone has aged by 10 years, with many family life-cycle implications. Peoples' needs will have changed, as will their resources. Social norms, too, will have changed. How, then, could we attribute any decrease in interaction we might observe to upward mobility? We would lack a relevant comparative base and have too many plausible rival hypotheses that could not be disposed of in this design. Now, if we compared those sons to others who had not been upwardly mobile in the 10-year period, we would be in business, because both groups would be equivalent in terms of the rival hypotheses. And that would make it impossible to explain differences between them in terms of such factors.

We now have all the main elements necessary for a project in the survey research mode. We are planning to draw, somehow, a sample of subjects and either interview them or give them a questionnaire asking about social mobility experiences and interaction with close relatives. We expect to find that those classified as upwardly mobile (or more mobile) interact less often with close relatives than others who are not classed as upwardly mobile. If we find what we expect, we will interpret it as evidence of the negative causal effects of upward social mobility. But what else might account for such an observation? That is the question that directs us to *consider plausible rival hypotheses.*

Before we collect our data, we want to make sure that we will be able to handle all reasonable objections to our interpretations. We have not specified the mechanism that explains why mobility should have this effect, so it is untested in the research in any more direct manner. Perhaps those who are mobile interact less frequently because they have

Figure 6.2 Mobility Affects Interaction by Altering Availability of Relatives

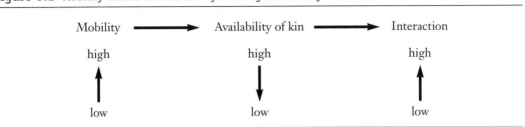

fewer local relatives with whom to interact. That seems likely. We had better ask our subjects how many close kin live in their city or within a day's journey. If we then compare those who have the same number of relatives available and still find a difference in interaction frequencies, our hypothesis will be strengthened. We might find that mobility is related to the number of relatives available and that when we compare the upwardly mobile with the non-upwardly mobile who have equal numbers of available kin, there is no difference in frequency of interaction with them. That is, when they have many (or few) close relatives available, the mobile and the non-mobile do not differ in frequency of interaction with them. In that case we could conclude that the effect of mobility is on the availability of kin rather than on frequency of interaction directly. Schematically, the finding would look like Figure 6.2.

Perhaps those who are mobile are also Asian. Is it possible that the lower frequencies of interaction are attributable to ethnic differences rather than to the effects of upward mobility. If that is plausible, we had better make sure either that we gather information on the subjects' ethnicity or that they are all of the same ethnicity. Without these data we cannot test this rival hypothesis. With it, though, we can compare ethnic groups in terms of interaction frequencies, and we can control for the effects of ethnicity when examining our hypothesis.

We have already illustrated the kinds of analysis that might follow data collection. *The last step is to interpret the data and integrate your findings into the literature.* Let us hope that because your study is a little different from every other study, it will shed new light on the topic you have chosen to investigate.

Finally this interpretation section should not be a dead end. The mark of a good project is that it stretches beyond itself. Important questions raised in it cannot be followed up at the time. These are raised again at the end as points of departure for another research paper that grows out of the first. In this sense one of the hard parts of writing a paper is deciding what to do in it and what must, regretfully, be left out because resources are limited. The research process is never-ending; it is arbitrarily cut off and forced into the constraints of each finite project. Still each project ought to struggle against its confines.

## FROM PROBLEM TO PAPER: AN EXTENDED EXAMPLE FROM URBAN SOCIOLOGY

Suppose you wanted to consider the effect of urbanism on crime—perhaps you were inspired by hearing the news, visiting relatives in a smaller (or bigger) city, or even by reading a sociology text. *The first criterion is that the topic be in some sense sociological.* The test is whether the arguments you are considering make use of sociological terms and concepts. Since urbanism is a social-structural concept, it appears that this criterion can easily be satisfied. Had you been thinking of explaining criminal behaviour with reference to genetic predispositions or psychic drives, it would not so readily be classified as a sociology paper. *The second criterion requires that the issue be 'problematic'*; in other words, there must be other plausible interpretations or answers to the question at hand. In this case you may be considering some version of a hypothesis suggesting a positive relationship between the variables. That would be problematic if, for example, you consider that some structuralists would probably argue that there ought to be no effect because the urban environment is essentially irrelevant to the ways in which people lead their lives. That is, they still interact within small social worlds that are orderly and normative. It could be problematic, as well, if you considered that American cities might display such a pattern, whereas Canadian or British or South American cities might not. Such a possibility could lead you to consider that a positive relationship might well be spurious and that urbanism could be correlated with crime without being its cause. The reason for such a correlation might be racial concentration, poverty, even differential migration, or the existence of subcultures. Alternatively, different cultures could display different relationships. Any such considerations, among others, might be sufficient to satisfy the second criterion.

*The next problem is to decide exactly what you expect the effects to be and to explain why they occur.* As in the family example, the literature review will be most helpful. It provides you with examples of questions others have asked, routes they have followed, false starts already discarded. It saves you time because your research can build on this body of past work.

You might find, for example, that urbanism has been defined in quite different ways and that the choice of any single meaning will make a difference. Urbanism usually refers to size of population, but not always. To Wirth it meant size, density, and heterogeneity. To Simmel and Tönnies, it meant gesellschaft, or a distinctive way of life.

Even a cursory literature review will be enough to show that the dependent variable—crime—is even more complex. A great difference emerges between property crimes and 'crimes without victims' (Schur 1965)—such as gambling, suicide, or prostitution—and crimes against other people. Furthermore, social scientists have noted that official crime statistics are often in error by considerable margins. It is quite possible that differences in reported rates are due more to differences in definitions, reporting procedures, and policing than to differences in the rate of occurrence itself. That makes any comparisons extremely hazardous because it introduces several measurement-based rival hypotheses from which the same observations could have been predicted.

Having reviewed the relevant literature, you will have become aware of a great many issues, strategies, and alternatives. These should be assessed critically, sifted for their value, and, where possible, systematically integrated. Often hypotheses emerge from such efforts, as opposing studies suggest a new hypothesis capable of subsuming contrary findings. Or you might find in the process of organizing the literature that what seems to them to be an important issue has been left out. In that case, too, a new hypothesis could serve to fill this void. The literature is not a record of a research program worked out carefully and in advance by scientists who agree on what to do and how to do it. On the contrary, it is a contradiction-filled record of the kinds of conflicts, both theoretical and empirical, that this book has presented. Any reader can see that very different definitions have sometimes produced contrary findings; every reader can find many studies that seem, even on the face of things, to be weak either in argument or method. It is misleading to pretend that the literature is a coherent and clear record of unambiguous findings properly drawn from well-conducted studies. Only a false sense of the nature of science makes us feel that the literature ought to fit neatly together. As I argue in this book, that is not a reasonable interpretation of the nature of science. Assume rather that scientists disagree and that it is your responsibility to examine their work for yourself to find out what is defensible and what is not. Every reader can do that, though not without effort and not equally well, and everyone can build on past research in conducting a unique study.

In this example let us suppose you have decided to examine the rates of reported crimes against other persons and of property crimes as they correlate with increasing city size. Conceptually the hypothesis might well suggest a positive relationship for urbanism and both crime rates. You could *offer a rationale for these expectations* by arguing that as urbanism increases there is more property available as well as more incentive to steal it. Also, as urbanism increases, people are more and more likely to encounter others who are both unknown and apparently unfriendly. Such rationales begin to provide the 'reasons' for the expected correlations, and they make it clear that the hypothesis is really causal rather than correlational. They also tend to make it evident that each link is really problematic. Indeed a hypothesis becomes interesting and problematic only when it goes beyond the merely correlational. If we stopped at the correlation and tested for it, it would not be problematic, and the paper would come to a dead end with a statement that either the expected correlation existed or did not. The essence of the problematic is alternative explanations. Correlations are either present or absent, strong or weak, positive or negative. When we try to explain *why* they exist, we truly enter the realm of social science.

*The next step is to operationalize our terms.* Here you will have to decide how to measure or empirically identify urbanism and crime. I have suggested that urbanism will be measured by city size in simple population terms. In other words we will rank cities by population. Cross-cultural comparisons will be difficult because the literature review will have informed us that the census definitions of what constitutes a city differ from one society to another. If your link to crime against persons had involved the pathological effects of density, you would be using an interpretive perspective and would need information on the subjects' 'definitions of the situation', because density involves social or cultural definitions rather than any simple structural relationship between size of population and locale.

Suppose further that crime rates are operationalized in terms of officially reported police statistics for these categories. But again such a decision has its drawbacks since the statistics are an indirect record of the actual behaviour you would like to measure. As social phenomena in their own right, the statistics tell us about department definitions, reporting procedures, and the like. Their relationship to actual crime is not straightforward. For these kinds of reasons, some investigators try to get closer to the data they think they really need.

For example they might argue that since most crime is unreported or is redefined in the course of reporting, it would be more direct to conduct a survey asking a sample of residents whether they had experienced either a personal or a property crime within a specified period. Normally a checklist would be provided to tell respondents what kinds of events they ought to report as relevant.

Clearly data from two studies as different as those will quite possibly fail to coincide on some point of importance. For example police rates might well give a lower estimate of crime than would residents' reports in survey research. It is not easy to decide which is a better measurement, but once again there are criteria that every researcher can employ. Operational definitions can be assessed comparatively on two grounds, reliability and validity. Reliability means whether the measurement can be repeated by someone else who can produce the same data classifications as originally found. Reliability thus refers to consistency between investigations or measurements. Our premise is that reliable operational definitions are preferable to those that are not reliable. Validity is also important here. The validity of an operational definition means whether it makes sense or captures the concept of interest to us. Measurements are preferable to the extent that they are more valid than others. For example it is possible to operationally define a 'liberated woman' as one who is more than five feet seven inches tall. Such a measurement would be reliable but of questionable validity. A more useful operational definition might involve a series of questions such as whether they belong to women's groups, read women's magazines, attend women's rallies, are interested in women's liberation issues, and consider themselves to be 'liberated'. The investigator could say that a woman receiving a yes score of four or more on this crude scale would be classified as liberated for purposes of the study. Such a definition could be less reliable, but it is certainly more valid. Ideally we want to maximize both reliability and validity-consistency and truth value.

Suppose you have made these difficult choices. *You are now prepared to restate the conceptual hypothesis in its operationalized version as follows*:

As the population of cities grows, the rates of reported crimes against both property and persons increase.

As before, you must first decide whether this version of the hypothesis is what we really had in mind. Alternatives are always possible. For example, you might be more interested in the effects of the growth of a single city than in the effects of population size in many cities. If so, you might prefer the following version of the hypothesis:

As the population of a particular city increases in size, the rates of reported crimes against property and persons increase.

As before, the different versions of the hypothesis direct you to consider different research designs with which they can be tested. It is important to note that any study will be comparative, since cities are compared, or the same city is compared, at different times. The comparison is what gives you information about your variables as such and spells out the different values of each variable. You may well decide that the second version of the hypothesis is extremely problematic. It is problematic because there are too many plausible rival hypotheses that cannot be dealt with. There are too many because, as the population grows (if it does), many other changes take place, any of which could separately or in combination explain why reported crime rates increase. But since you are looking only at a single city, you cannot deal with these rival hypotheses. That is, you need a control group, but none exists. You need to be able to isolate the independent variable from others to see whether it alone is correlated with changes in the dependent. If you can demonstrate that, you will have the beginnings of a causal argument. As you may remember, demonstrating causality requires association, time priority, non-spuriousness, and rationale. Version two of the hypothesis does not generate data capable of meeting those requirements.

Having opted for the first version of the operational hypothesis, how do you proceed? You will require data on a set of cities of various sizes as well as data on the reported rates of personal and property crime in all these cities. Before gathering the necessary data, though, *you must try to anticipate any rival hypotheses* that might account for the findings you expect, but for other reasons, that is, not because urbanism causes increased crime rates. You might, for example, consider the possibility that as the population grows the police force grows even more. If that is so, it could explain the increase in reported crime as an artifact of the number of police rather than as a result of population growth. Such a possibility indicates that the investigator would be well-advised to gather data on the size of the police force in each city as well. Perhaps as the population grows, the complexity of the population changes so that more ethnic minorities, more poor people, or more potential criminals live in the city. In that case the increases in crime may be caused, not by population growth itself, but by the disproportionate growth in particular segments of the population. This possibility suggests that it would be useful to gather data on each segment of the population as it changes, contributing to the overall population growth. It may even be possible that as cities reach a certain size, organized crime moves in. Whereas some of those variables suggest how crime might be produced by population growth, others suggest how variables other than growth may be responsible.

Each of the examples suggests that you gather more data to illuminate the mechanism or process by which the alleged independent variable affects the dependent. The social scientist's work is not over when the expected correlation is demonstrated.

The last step is to interpret the data analysis and integrate it into the existing literature. Your study is not identical with any other. You must now explain its unique features and tie it into the literature. You might have chosen cities in a different country, province or state or over a different period. You might have measured crime in a slightly different manner. This interpretation documents your attempt to make sense of your data in light of the literature and your hypotheses. Ideally you will be able to add something to what we already know. If you have a successful paper, it will extend beyond itself by suggesting lines of future inquiry. Whether you conclude that your hypothesis is supported or not does not determine whether the paper is a success. We learn from our mistakes. If your data do not confirm your hypothesis, you must go on to revise the hypothesis or to say what you think is going on. Or a paper can be successful if it tells the reader that even an informed and careful investigation can be incorrect and explains the error that others might easily have made but that they will now be spared. In a sense, the best such papers usually end where they began—with a new hypothesis, based on all the research to date, including the newly completed paper, as they again struggle toward a more complete understanding of the phenomenon of interest.

## FROM PROBLEM TO PAPER: AN EXTENDED EXAMPLE CONCERNING IDENTITY

Suppose we wished to examine the relationship between residential segregation and the strength of collective identity. This interest might have arisen from taking a trip through our own or another city, having a conversation with a person of a different ethnic or racial background, or seeing a film about Harlem or the Warsaw ghetto. In order for a question to merit consideration as a paper topic, two criteria must be satisfied: *it must be a sociological topic, and it must be problematic.* To see if it is sociological, we might try to formulate it in sociological terms. In the present case both residential segregation and collective identity are social-structural terms, so no problem arises in this respect. The second requirement is that it be problematic, that is, that there be other plausible ways of conceptualizing the issue or the potential relationships among relevant variables.

In this case we could make the relationship problematic in numerous ways. We might note that voluntary segregation, or segregation by choice, could well have different consequences from forced or mandatory residential segregation. We might note that since we usually study residential segregation by race, and because racial segregation is due in part to income differentials, we do not really separate the various effects of segregation, race, and poverty. We might note that residential segregation is usually part of an overall system of segregation that includes occupational segregation and other forms of discrimination. Finally we could note that though the relationship most frequently examined treats collective identity as the dependent variable, it is possible to treat segregation as the dependent variable and collective identity as the causal or independent variable. Of course, we could as usual also simply argue that at different times and in different societies it is not clear that the same relationship would be expected to hold. Such considerations make it obvious that the issue is indeed problematic.

*The next step is a literature review, in an effort to find out exactly what relationship might be hypothesized and exactly how it might work.* We might learn that the size of the segregated group is an important factor in maintaining a collective identity. We might learn that it is not size so much as resources that are essential. We might be tempted to believe that the group's ideology, or the extent of its visible difference from the majority, is the most important factor regardless of the degree of residential segregation. We will certainly learn that it is a 'messy' subject with many conflicting interpretations and findings, all relevant to the issues of interest to us (Alba and Chamlin, 1983).

Many student papers end at this point, with a classification of the multiple factors found to be related in some way to the strength of collective identity and a conclusion that residential segregation is one of many relevant considerations. Such a paper is common, and the model for it is provided in many textbooks in which the author seems to have taken great pains to eliminate any sense of what was originally most problematic, elusive, and challenging. This kind of retreat or flight from the problem is unnecessary. Of course the world is a complicated place. Of course many factors are relevant to your dependent variable, and of course they are not easy to study systematically. None the less such study is possible to some degree and with some success. We do not want to throw out the baby with the bath water. The fact that we cannot answer all relevant questions does not mean we are paralyzed. We do not seek perfection in our work; we are satisfied to do the best we can. Where we cannot answer questions, we can still ask them and say how they could be dealt with and why an answer would be important. Where we cannot separate the effects of several variables, we can at least note that we recognize the problem and hope that others may solve it.

If we are to carry on with a hypothesis-testing paper, *we must now use our familiarity with the literature to create a conceptual hypothesis*. It must be plausible, problematic rather than trivial, and testable. The easiest hypotheses for most students to handle are modified replications of past research hypotheses. Even here *there must be reasons why you would expect the same results as in the original hypothesis test or different results*. It is in this area of rationale that you will usually find the problematic element. The very idea of a modified replication is to find out whether the altered conditions will affect the outcome. In order to make sense of the results, we must be able to say in advance what is expected and why it is expected.

Let us suppose we hypothesize that *the degree of residential segregation is positively related to the strength of collective identity*. The problematic rationale for such an expectation might be that people who live in close proximity will tend to interact frequently, and the shared territory and interaction will encourage them to identify with one another. Of course this is problematic since reasons abound why it might not work as predicted. The literature review will have told us that where a group is itself highly differentiated, members are less likely to interact and less likely to develop any collective identity. Forced interaction among those who do not like one another does not always lead to collective identity; it may institutionalize hostility. The Hatfields and McCoys were neighbours, as are Protestants and Catholics in Belfast. Such qualifications make it clear that the outcome of any hypothesis testing is indeed in doubt. Furthermore, when there are so many plausible confounding and rival hypotheses, the manner in which we operationalize terms and design our research is of critical importance.

*Turning carefully now to the operationalization of terms*, we will have to deal with residential segregation and the strength of collective identity. *We must decide in each case how to measure the values of each variable*. Residential segregation requires us to examine areas where people live. For a number of areas we will have to discover what proportion of the total population is made up by the group or groups we are speaking of. We have not yet decided whether we are concentrating in this study on racial segregation or on ethnic segregation by income, occupation, or another characteristic. Merely stating the question forces us to reconsider our hypothesis. Do we expect residential segregation to strengthen collective identity on all of these dimensions or only on some of them? What will be the effect of segregation of a population that is homogeneous in all those terms as compared to one that varies on most while sharing a single attribute?

Suppose we decide to examine ethnic residential segregation only. Now we will have to operationalize ethnicity as well, but at least we have a specific dimension or an identifiable target group on which to focus. The choice here is between measuring segregation for a particular ethnic group in different cities and measuring segregation for various ethnic groups in a particular city. This is a research design decision. We might decide to measure ethnic residential segregation by discovering the proportion of the population from each ethnic background in each of a city's census tracts. We might find, for example, that people of Greek origin are concentrated in a single census tract and that fully 85 per cent of them live there. In contrast we might find that people of British origins are so widely distributed through many tracts that only a small fraction live in any one tract. In the latter case we would say that people of Greek origin display more residential segregation than those of British origin.

Or we might choose to compare people of Irish ancestry in Boston and Chicago, selecting these cities because, though they are similar in many relevant ways, we have learned that the Irish are more residentially segregated in Boston. Although I noted that this is basically a research design decision, design and operationalization are closely interwoven. In practice we might find that in ranking by population the tracts in Boston with the most Irish, six tracts account for 75 per cent of the Irish population. In comparison it might take 15 tracts to account for 75 per cent of the Irish population of Chicago. If there were the same number of total tracts in both cities, we might tentatively suggest from those data that the Irish were more residentially segregated in Boston.

Of course it is possible to object to both those operational procedures and devise a new one. As noted in chapter 2, there is less than enthusiastic support in sociology for the repeated use of the same measure of a concept. On the other hand, there are good reasons *for* using the same measure, for replication is the empirical basis of science, and replication requires repeated use of exactly the same design and measurement operations. Yet rather than use operational definitions described in the literature, we could develop new ones, particularly if we have grounds for such a change. That is, we must be prepared to defend our change. In this case we might feel that tract-level data are too far removed from the world of communities and neighbourhoods. We might argue and, even better, demonstrate, that two tracts with the same number of Irish can be quite different in residential segregation at the household level. The fact that a group is widely distributed does not have to mean they are not segregated. The few of them in each tract could live in close proximity, or they might live in opposite ends of the tract. The proper unit of analysis is really much smaller than the city or census tract.

But what of measuring the strength of collective identity? What empirical indicators can we use to measure this concept validly and reliably? Perhaps the simplest way, conceptually, would be to conduct a survey asking the respondents a series of questions, including the following in some form:

1. How strongly would you say that you identify with others in your ethnic group?
2. Do you belong to any organizations that have an ethnic make-up, function, or relationship?
3. Do you contribute to any ethnic charities or other causes?

4. Do you try to teach your children about their ethnic background?
5. If other things were equal, do you think you would sooner hire a person of your own ethnicity than someone else?

These questions would probably be combined to create a scale purporting to measure the strength of collective identity. The more often the respondent said he or she did these things or felt strongly about these issues, the higher the score; the higher the score, the stronger the sense of identity. Each question must be defended. Presumably one would be arguing from a preference for triangulation here.

But a survey might well be far beyond the time, resources, or capabilities of any investigator, even if it did provide the most direct measurement possible. What then could we use? As stated earlier, though direct evidence or measurement is preferable to indirect (because we believe it to be more valid), we often must make do with data one or even two steps removed from what we would like to have. Each step removed produces a gap between what we really need and what we have, and the gap allows for possible distortion or error. As soon as we move from observation of behaviour to reports of behaviour we have reason to question whether substantial error could have been introduced. When we move from actual behaviour to something more indirect linked to that behaviour, the gap is larger, and there are more rival explanations for our observations. Still, even indirect measurement is preferable to no measurement, and there may be ways of overcoming at least some of the alternative explanations of its meaning.

Perhaps we could measure the strength of collective identity at the level of the ethnic group (rather than at the individual level as in the first attempt). We might draw on Breton's (1964) measurement of 'institutional completeness' for this purpose. In comparing ethnic groups, Breton counts the number of ethnic institutions in the community, that is, the number of ethnic schools, newspapers, churches, voluntary organizations, and the like. Ethnic groups that have high total scores are said to be 'higher' in institutional completeness than those with lower scores. Now if we were prepared to argue or assume that high institutional completeness is correlated with a strong sense of collective identity, we might be willing to use institutional completeness as indicating strength of collective identity. Of course an ethnic group could exhibit high institutional completeness only because it is large enough or wealthy enough to do so even though only a few of its members actively participate or identify with the group. So the measure is not completely valid. But then no measurement is perfect.

Our competing operationalizations direct us toward different research designs. We might do our study in a single city with data on several groups or in many cities with data on a single group. We might be doing survey research, or we may be using indirect and secondary data only. These choices would still have to be made, but first we might find it useful to *restate several versions of our hypothesis in its new operationalized terms.*

Here is version one:

As the number of census tracts it requires to account for the total population of each ethnic group in a city diminishes, the average ethnic identity score for respondents will increase.

Version two could be quite different:

The fewer census tracts it requires to account for 75 per cent of the population of a particular ethnic background in various cities, the higher the total number of ethnic institutions serving that group.

In this latter treatment the researcher might decide that, since what is actually measured is institutional completeness, it would be better to alter the hypothesis accordingly. In other words, given the problematic relationship of the indicator to the target concept, and further given that the indicator itself might be closer to the researcher's real interest, there is no need to relate indicator to concept. The altered hypothesis is a revision of the original conceptual hypothesis but one that makes sense and is possible. In a very real sense, which I hope is clear now, every operationalization specifies the hypothesis, usually uniquely. Every research design choice specifies the hypothesis, also usually uniquely. As a result the conceptual hypothesis is never truly tested, and the theory from which it may have been derived can never be directly falsified. It remains untouched; the actual study is quite far removed from it, and therefore it is extremely difficult to move back 'up' from the world of actual data to the theoretical-conceptual realm.

*The first design to be considered is implicit in the first version of the operationalized hypothesis.* It is a survey design in a single city. The investigator will have to create a scale to measure strength of collective identity. The investigator will also have to obtain local census-tract information on the population of each ethnic group in the city and in each tract examined. The survey respondents will have to come from different ethnic backgrounds. They can be surveyed in any convenient location. Quite possibly the survey might involve student respondents in the university; surveys by students and professor often do.

It is clear from this discussion that in this project there are two quite distinct elements to the data gathering. In one, census-tract data have to be examined; in the second a survey must be undertaken. The hypothesis, rationale, and total research design *connect* the two components. Now let's suppose we had the data that we expect. What other explanations might there be for the observed relationship? We ask that question in advance so that we can *gather data on any plausible rival hypotheses* and then have the opportunity to test them as well as our major working hypothesis.

We expect to find that the smaller the number of tracts, the higher the average collective identity score for respondents of that ethnic background. To be sure, such a correlation may be spurious. That is, collective identity may be caused, not by residential segregation, but by some third factor related to both the independent and dependent variable. Perhaps income, migration status (for example, second generation or newcomer), education, visible differences, hostility from others, or in-group ideology is such a factor. Those variables were all referred to in the literature review, and there is ample evidence they are relevant. If they are, in fact, plausible, data will have to be collected on each of them. If we do not collect this information, we will have no basis for attempting to discount these factors. With this information, we can compare various groups that are similar in terms of each factor, seeing whether differences in the dependent variable persist, increase, or diminish. Each outcome will have to be interpreted in light of the competing hypotheses.

The second version of the hypothesis generates quite a different research design. In this case we will have to obtain census data for the same group in several cities, and we will also need data on ethnic institutions in those cities. We can obtain the latter in large part from telephone directories. Or the investigator might decide to correspond with the ethnic associations in each city, asking for a list of local ethnic institutions in the relevant categories. The choice of cities is a significant problem. The more different the cities, the more possible alternative ways of explaining observed differences in collective identity. Again to the extent that the same nominal ethnic group differs from city to city, each of the differences may be part of, or all of, the explanation of any differences in collective identity or institutional completeness.

Such observations suggest that what we might want is a design in which cities are matched, at least roughly, in terms of variables that appear to be relevant, including size, ethnic composition, occupational mix, and the like. As well the ethnic group should be about the same in size, occupational distribution (and hence income and education), and generation of migration. If we could hold all these variables constant in the design, we could have considerable confidence that any differences observed would not be attributable to these constants. If the only factor in which variation showed up was the measure of residential segregation, and the expected differences in institutional completeness did occur, one would have a strong case for arguing the causal link that we hypothesized.

*The last task calls for interpretation of the data that are generated and the integration of your study into the literature.* Limitations of your study should be discussed here, including different choices that you made among problematic alternatives. You might find that, in discussing the limitations of your paper, you are really proposing additional research aimed at overcoming them. You could well end by refining or revising your hypothesis and suggesting that future work that incorporated all the literature, including your study, could begin from where you have left off. As before, if your paper illuminates the road ahead, it will be successful.

## CONCLUSION

Whatever the topic of interest to you, there are some standard practices that will increase the credibility of the claims to knowledge that you wish to make in your paper. This chapter has given you some guidelines for the preparation of successful research papers in sociology. I am confident that if you pay attention to them, both you and your audience will find your study relatively defensible. When you assess studies, your own and others, if you follow the suggestions made here, you will be well on the way to deciding which papers are defensible.

## CHAPTER 7

# Science as a Community Project:
# Taking Your Part in the Ongoing Debate

This chapter has two purposes. First, I want to show you some specific empirical articles drawn from the recent literature of sociology. At this point, you have the tools with which to understand and assess them for yourselves, and it is this I want to encourage. I also want to invite you to take seriously the idea that you are at least a vicarious and potential participant in the debates in the field and that you can appreciate and possibly contribute to those debates.

## SOME INTERESTING DEBATES IN THE FIELD

Perhaps the best-known such debate is between, on the one side, Kingsley Davis and Wilbert Moore and, on the other, Melvin Tumin concerning the causes of stratification. This classic debate between proponents of structural functional and conflict perspectives appears in the *American Sociological Review*. Davis and Moore's initial statement, 'Some Principles of Stratification', appears in vol. 10 (1945) pp. 242–9. Tumin's reply, 'Some Principles of Stratification: A Critical Analysis', appears in vol. 18 (August 1953) pp. 387–93. The 'Reply to Tumin' by Davis (and a paragraph by Moore) appear in the same issue, pp. 394–7, and the final word is Tumin's 'Reply to Kingsley Davis', which appears in vol. 18 (December 1953), pp. 672–3. Even more than 50 years later, this debate is worth reading.

Another debate that scholars have conducted in print concerns the similarities and differences between Canadians and Americans. In that debate, Seymour Martin Lipset, in many books and articles published over more than 30 years, has argued that, for historical reasons, Canadians are generally more conservative than Americans. See, for example, any of the following articles and books by Lipset:

- 'The Value Patterns of Democracy: A Case Study in Comparative Analysis'. *American Sociological Review* 28 (1963): 515–31.

- *The First New Nation* (New York: Basic Books, 1963).

- 'Canada and the United States: A Comparative View'. *Canadian Review of Sociology and Anthropology* 1 (1964): 173–85.

- *Revolution and Counterrevolution* (New York: Basic Books, 1968).

- 'Historical Conditions and National Characteristics'. *Canadian Journal of Sociology* 11 (1986), 2: 113–55.

- *Continental Divide* (New York: Routledge, 1990).

  Lipset's thesis has been hotly contested. See, for example, any of the following:

- T. Truman, 'A Critique of Seymour Martin Lipset's Article, Value Differences, Absolute or Relative: The English-Speaking Democracies'. *Canadian Journal of Political Science* 4 (1971): 497–525.

- S. Arnold, and D. Tigert, 'Canadians and Americans: A Comparative Analysis'. *International Journal of Comparative Sociology*, 15 (1974): 68–83.

- S. Goldenberg, 'Canadian Encouragement of Higher Educational Participation: An Empirical Assessment'. *International Journal of Comparative Sociology*, 17 (1977): 284–99.

- D. Baer, E. Grabb, and W. Johnston, 'The Values of Canadians and Americans: A Critical Analysis and Reassessment'. *Social Forces* 68 (1990), 3: 693–713.

- 'The Values of Canadians and Americans: A Rejoinder'. *Social Forces*, 69 (1) (1990): 273–7.

Another interesting and more methodological debate took place in the pages of the *American Journal of Sociology* in 1988. In it, several well-known scholars disagreed about the interpretation of a study in which they were all involved. By the end the debate became quite nasty and *ad hominem*. See Hans Zeisel, 'Disagreement over the Evaluation of a Controlled Experiment', *American Journal of Sociology*, 88 (2): 378–89, and the reply by P. Rossi, R.A. Berk, and K.J. Lenihan, 'Saying It Wrong with Figures: A Comment on Zeisel', *American Journal of Sociology*, 88 (2): 390–3. This debate ended with 'Hans Zeisel Concludes the Debate', *American Journal of Sociology*, 88 (2): 394–6.

Chapter 3 contains a paper by Brannigan and Goldenberg that takes sides in the debate about the relationship between exposure to pornography and subsequent aggression against women. This is a real debate, in which Donnerstein, Berkowitz, Linz, and others have published many articles arguing that there is such a relationship (and thereby supplying intellectual support to those who would outlaw or censor pornography); others have taken an opposing view. The references at the end of the Brannigan and Goldenberg paper can lead you into this hotly contested area.

Yet another topic of debate is poverty and its causes. A good introduction can be found by juxtaposing the work of Oscar Lewis and that of Charles Valentine. Valentine's (1968) book *Culture and Poverty* is outstanding and makes good reading too.

## FOR YOUR ACTIVE CONSIDERATION

Since it is impossible to include all of the debates in this text, and since they would take us too far afield in any case, I have included only one minor debate composed of a Canadian paper by DeKeseredy and Kelly and the two critiques that followed its publication. You should read the main paper first, try to analyse it yourself, locating it in a theoretical and substantive context, discovering its central questions or hypotheses, examining its research design in light of those issues, assessing the evidence presented by the authors, and evaluating their interpretations of that evidence. At each step, you should be sceptical and constructively critical, considering rival hypotheses or interpretations and examining the paper to see if these have been considered and dealt with.

Having read the paper and done your own critique of it, turn to the works by Fox and Gartner and consider the issues they raise. Do you think the points they make are valid? Are there others you would add? As a hint, let me suggest that you consider the population and the sample used by DeKeseredy. Though the title of the article speaks of its relevance to dating relationships, the sample is of individuals. Can one generalize to the intended population from such a sample? What sorts of design and sampling considerations suggest themselves? Reading the critiques may lead you to read more of the literature in this field: both DeKeseredy and Kelly wrote rejoinders to Fox and Gartner, which appeared in the subsequent issue of the *Canadian Journal of Sociology*. Having read both sides of the issue and the original paper, perhaps you would find it interesting to carry on the debate in class, some of you taking the authors' side and others the side of their critics.

The second main paper I have included is a feminist's attempt to address empirical and methodological issues of feminist analysis in the context of an empirical study of women's decisions regarding child bearing. Like the first paper, it is primarily exploratory and descriptive, rather than hypothesis-testing, though in both there are hypotheses to be drawn from them and implicit hypotheses that are in fact tested in them. I hope that you will read the paper carefully, making note of the substantive and theoretical context into which it seems to fit, finding its central issues or hypotheses, considering the design selected by the author, and sceptically weighing the evidence and interpretations offered. Following this paper is a brief critique of my own; again, I ask you to enter the debate, on either side, as an exercise. Perhaps in this instance it would be profitable to write a rejoinder to my critique, taking the part of the author, or to add your own points to the few I have chosen to emphasize in my short critique.

If you take part in these debates, remember that social scientists are supposed to do their best to remain constructive in their criticisms and impartial in the sense that they do not attack one another personally. Use the criteria you have read in these chapters. Your own analysis and evaluation are legitimate and can be as substantial as any in the literature. The task is not beyond your abilities; simply use your common sense and the tools to which you have now been introduced. And enjoy your active participation in the debates. It is out of just such intellectual exchange and ferment that much excitement and many new ideas eventually emerge. I told you earlier that science is a community project. Doing your part requires your active and considered participation in just such debates. Enjoy them.

## ILLUSTRATIVE READING 1

### THE INCIDENCE AND PREVALENCE OF WOMAN ABUSE IN CANADIAN UNIVERSITY AND COLLEGE DATING RELATIONSHIPS

*Walter DeKeseredy*
*Katharine Kelly*

This paper presents incidence and prevalence data gathered from the first Canadian national representative sample survey on the sexual, physical, and psychological victimization of women in university/college dating relationships. The results, derived from the Conflict Tactics Scale and the Sexual Experiences Survey, reveal that men are more likely to report having engaged in less lethal forms of abuse, and women are more likely to report having been victimized by such behaviour.

Research shows that men who physically assault their spouses do so because their partners have violated, or are perceived as violating, the ideals of familial patriarchy (Dobash and Dobash, 1979; Smith, 1990a; 1993). According to Smith (1990a), relevant themes of this ideology are an insistence upon women's obedience, respect, loyalty, dependency, sexual access, and sexual fidelity. Some scholars contend that many men in college and university dating relationships also espouse a set of attitudes and beliefs supportive of familial patriarchy (Dilorio, 1989; Lamanna and Reidman, 1985; Laner and Thompson, 1982). When their partners either reject or fail to live up to these 'ideals' and 'expectations' (Smith, 1990a), men experience stress which motivates them to abuse women for the purpose of maintaining their dominance and control (DeKeseredy, 1988; DeKeseredy and Schwartz, 1993). While this feminist account of courtship abuse has not yet been directly tested, it is a promising interpretation of the large body of survey data which demonstrates that male-to-female physical, sexual, and psychological assaults are endemic to American university and college dating relationships.[1]

Very few comparable Canadian studies have been conducted. Canadian researchers have focused mainly on the incidence, prevalence, correlates, and causes of male physical and psychological attacks on married, cohabiting, and separated/divorced women (Brinkerhoff and Lupri, 1988; Ellis and Stuckless, 1992; Ellis and Wight, 1987; Ellis et al., 1987; Kennedy and Dutton, 1989; Lupri, 1990; Smith, 1985; 1987; 1988; 1989; 1990a; 1990b; 1991a; 1991b). There are some survey data on the extent of female victimization in post-secondary school dating relationships (Barnes et al., 1991; DeKeseredy, 1988; DeKeseredy et al., 1992; Elliot et al., 1992; Finkelman, 1992); however, these findings are derived only from non-probability samples of university and college students in Ontario, New Brunswick, and western Canada. Table 1 presents these results and the methods used to generate them.

Table 1 Woman Abuse in University/College Dating Surveys

| Survey | Survey Location | Sample Description | Interview Mode | Measure(s) of Abuse | Incidence Rate(s) | Prevalence Rate(s) |
|---|---|---|---|---|---|---|
| DeKeseredy (1988) | Southern Ontario | 308 male university students | Self-administered questionnaires | CTS[a] & 2 modified SES[b] items | 70% reported physical and/or psychological abuse; 69% stated that they engaged in psychological abuse; 12% reported being physically abusive; 2.6% admitted to having been sexually aggressive | Not examined |
| Barnes et al. (1991) | Manitoba | 245 male university students | Self-administered questionnaires | CTS, VBN[c] & CRA[d] Abuse Index | Not examined | 42% reported using violence; 92.6% stated they emotionally abused women |
| DeKeseredy et al. (1992) | Eastern Ontario | 179 female & 106 male university/college students | Self-administered questionnaires | CTS & SES | 13% of the men reported using physical violence; 68% reported psychological abuse; 8% indicated being sexually aggressive. 26% of the females indicated being physically abused; 69% said they were psychologically victimized; 28% stated that they were sexually abused | 18% of the men stated they used physical violence; 75% psychologically abused women; 12% reported acts of sexual assault. 32% of women reported experiencing physical violence; 78% indicated being psychologically attacked; 40% stated they were sexually abused |

**Table 1** Continued

| Survey | Survey Location | Sample Description | Interview Mode | Measure(s) of Abuse | Incidence Rate(s) | Prevalence Rate(s) |
|---|---|---|---|---|---|---|
| Elliot et al. (1992) | University of Alberta | 1,016 under-graduate students (men & women) | Self-administered questionnaires | Modified SES | Not examined | 44% of the students who reported an unwanted sexual experience while registered at the U. of A. stated that the offender was a romantic acquaint-ance & 18% said that the perpetrator was a casual or first date[e] |
| Finkelman (1992) | University of New Brunswick & St Thomas University | 447 under-graduate students (men & women) | Self-administered questionnaires | SES | Approximately 34.4% of the 127 respondents who reported one or more unwanted sexual experiences were victimized by a boyfriend/girlfriend or date[e] | Not examined |

a Conflict Tactics Scale (Straus, 1979).
b Sexual Experiences Survey (Koss and Oros, 1982).
c Violent Behavior Inventory (Domestic Abuse Project, cited in Gondolf, 1985).
d CRA Abuse Index (Stacy and Shupe, 1983).
e Gender variations in victimization are not reported in this study.

Although the surveys in Table 1 support the claim that Canadian female students' lives 'rest upon a continuum of violence' (Stanko, 1990: 85), they do not provide accurate information on how many male-to-female assaults take place in the Canadian post-secondary student population at large. Only random sample surveys can achieve this goal. This study attempts to fill a major research gap by providing estimates of the incidence and prevalence of woman abuse in Canadian university/college dating relationships which are derived from the first national representative sample survey of men and women. Incidence refers here to the percentage of women who stated that they were abused and the percentage of men who indicated that they were abusive in the past twelve months. Prevalence is, since they left high school, the percentage of men who reported having been abusive and the percentage of women who indicated having been abused.

## Method

### Sample Design
Since a critical goal of this research was to yield estimates of woman abuse that are representative of undergraduate and community college students across Canada, a multi-stage, systematic sampling strategy was developed with the assistance of York University's Institute for Social Research (ISR). This sampling plan is described below.[2]

### Regional Breakdown
For the purpose of making regional comparisons, Canada was divided into six strata: Atlantic Canada, including Newfoundland, Prince Edward Island, Nova Scotia, and New Brunswick; Quebec (French-speaking schools); Ontario; the Prairies, consisting of Manitoba, Saskatchewan, and Alberta; British Columbia; and a Language Crossover stratum which included both English-language institutions in Quebec and French-language schools outside of this province (e.g., in Ontario and New Brunswick). The number of schools selected in each area was based on the regional distribution of the Canadian student population as documented by Statistics Canada (1992a; 1992b). Table 2 presents the number of students enrolled in each stratum and Table 3 describes the number of institutions selected in each region (Pollard, 1993).

After the data were collected, the marginal distributions were compared to the distribution in Table 2, and the results were weighted accordingly.[3]

### Selection of Institutions
For each region, the ISR prepared a listing of all universities and colleges that might be included in this study. Universities with fewer than 500 students and colleges with less than 100 students were excluded. Then, random numbers were used to pick schools to participate in this survey, and the selection was based upon each institution's population relative to the overall regional student population.

Table 2 Student Enrolment by Region

|  | Universities | | Colleges | |
|---|---|---|---|---|
|  | N | % | N | % |
| Atlantic Canada | 63,718 | 8.71 | 5,554 | 1.92 |
| Quebec (French) | 162,724 | 22.24 | 109,566 | 37.91 |
| Ontario | 261,996 | 35.81 | 90,339 | 31.25 |
| The Prairies | 117,842 | 16.11 | 30,697 | 10.62 |
| British Columbia | 52,450 | 7.17 | 26,475 | 9.16 |
| Language Crossover | 72,846 | 9.96 | 26,408 | 9.14 |
| Total | 731,576 | 100.00 | 289,039 | 100.00 |

Table 3 Number of Institutions Selected by Region

|  | Universities | Colleges |
|---|---|---|
| Atlantic Canada | 4 | 3 |
| Quebec (French) | 5 | 4 |
| Ontario | 6 | 5 |
| The Prairies | 4 | 3 |
| British Columbia | 4 | 3 |
| Language Crossover | 4 | 3 |
| Total | 27 | 21 |

The sample plan required the selection of 48 institutions (27 universities and 21 community colleges); but four schools were randomly picked twice,[4] and thus a total of 44 institutions were chosen. Additionally, each stratum was over-sampled because we anticipated that several schools would not want to participate due to the sensitive and controversial subject matter, even though both respondents and institutions were guaranteed anonymity and confidentiality. Sixty institutions, for example, refused to participate in Koss et al.'s (1987) comparable study.

Two of the 48 schools originally selected chose not to participate. Administrators at one of these institutions stated that they did not have a policy on research involving human subjects and until one was in place, they would not participate. The other school was simply not amenable to the study.

*Selection of Programs of Study*
Some people believe that the leisure activities of students enrolled in certain programs are characterized by sexist interpersonal dynamics, which in turn lead to woman abuse (Johnson, 1992). On the other hand, some people assert that students who take women's studies courses are less likely to be abusive because they are more sensitized to the negative effects of gender inequality (Schwartz

and Nogrady, 1993). Reliable empirical support for both arguments, however, is not yet available. In order to ascertain whether disciplines vary in their conduciveness to woman abuse, the sample was also stratified by program of study. The ISR assembled this sampling frame by first listing the faculties in each institution and then listing all of the subjects taught within each faculty. The university data are derived from the *1991 Corpus Almanac and Canadian Source Book* (Southam Business Information and Communications Group, 1990). Statistics on community colleges were collected from college calendars.

To select classes within each participating school, a main program of study or faculty was first selected through the use of random numbers, and the probability of selection was directly related to the percentage of students enroled in each faculty. These statistics were compiled from Statistics Canada (1992a; 1992b) sources. Students enroled in larger faculties, such as Arts, had a greater chance of being selected. When a main program of study was picked (e.g., Engineering), all of the subjects taught under this rubric were given random numbers and a particular subject (e.g., Civil Engineering) was chosen.

*Selection of Classes*
The sample was further divided into junior and senior segments in anticipation of different responses from students who attended university or college for various lengths of time. Incoming students were categorized as junior undergraduates and third year undergraduates (second year students in some community colleges) were classified as seniors. Two classes were selected at each institution (four at institutions selected twice), resulting in a grand total of 96 classes. More than 96 classes were selected for sampling and several classes had to be replaced because either they were ineligible or they did not want to participate.

In order to be eligible to participate in this study, university classes had to have enrolments of not less than 35 and college courses were required to have a minimum of 20 students enrolled. Twenty-one classes were replaced because of ineligibility and 17 departments or individual instructors refused an invitation to be included in the survey. One instructor would not allow the investigators to visit his class until January, 1993. Since this would have delayed the completion of the study, his class was excluded from the final study. Thus, we surveyed 95 of the projected 96 classes.

## Arrangements for Data Collection
Before the questionnaires could be administered, in the summer of 1992, the ISR phoned the Chairs of the 96 colleges and university departments that had been randomly selected to participate. During each call, the purpose of the study was made explicit, questions were answered, and the ISR tried to gain initial approval to administer our survey. After the Chairs gave their verbal approval, letters were sent to confirm the details of the data gathering techniques and to determine

the precise location of the class, the time of our visit, and any other details about the distribution of the survey.

The participating institutions were concerned about the ethics of doing this research, and the investigators responded to their demands. In several cases, despite approval from ethical review boards, professors insisted on obtaining the consent of their students before responding to the research team's request to survey their classes.

It should be noted in passing that prior to the distribution of the question-naire, several instructors did not tell their students that the research team was going to visit their class. Others, however, gave their students advance notice and told them about the purpose of the survey. It might be argued that these announcements influenced some students not to participate in this study. For example, instead of answering a questionnaire, several people may have decided to pursue leisure activities or work on various assignments, such as term papers. Additionally, those who have been sexually, physically, or psychologically assaulted may not have attended class because they did not want to be reminded of these painful experiences. There may also have been some students who did not take part because they thought that they did not have much to contribute to the study, especially if they did not experience dating abuse. Unfor-tunately, the precise number of students who did not participate for the above reasons is unknown.

## Data Collection Procedures

In each classroom two questionnaires, one for men and one for women, were distributed. Although both instruments contained some identical items, the wording was changed to ensure that the proper gender was identified as the dating partner. The questionnaires also contained some different items. For example, the women's questionnaire asked about their use of social support services for abused females, and the men's asked about peer support.

The questionnaires were distributed in classrooms for two reasons. First, consistent with Russell (1986), the researchers felt that it was important to be present to offer emotional and informational support (e.g., referral to a women's centre or rape crisis centre) to any respondents who might be traumatized or upset by the subject matter or the recollection of their past experiences. Addi-tionally, the investigators' presence ensures a higher completion rate and encourages respondents to answer all of the questions (DeKeseredy, 1989; Sheatsley, 1983).

Prior to each administration, students were asked to participate in a study on problems in male-female dating relationships. Also made explicit to them was the fact that participation in this survey was strictly voluntary and that any infor-mation they provide would be kept completely confidential. Students were also told that they did not have to answer any question that they did not want to and they could stop filling out the questionnaire at any time. This information was also printed on the cover of the questionnaire which respondents were asked to read prior to beginning.

Following each administration, we provided a debriefing which discussed the reasons for the research, the existing information on the frequency and severity of dating violence, and the role that peers play in the process. All respondents were given a list of local (on- and off-campus) support services for survivors and abusers. Additionally, participants were encouraged to ask us any questions or to discuss the survey with us after completion. These debriefing techniques are similar to those used in Koss et al.'s (1987) national sexual assault study.

## Sample Characteristics

The sample consisted of 3,142 people, including 1,835 women and 2,307 men. Table 4 presents the demographic characteristics of these respondents and Table 5 shows their educational characteristics. As described in Table 4, the median age of female respondents was 20 and the median age of males was 21. Most of the participants identified themselves as either English Canadian or French Canadian, and the majority of them (81.8 per cent of the men and 77.9 per cent of the women) were never married. Table 5 shows, as was anticipated, that most of the participants were junior students and a sizeable portion (42.2 per cent of the women and 26.9 per cent of the men) were enrolled in Arts programs. Approximately 2 per cent of the women were members of sororities and 3 per cent of the men belonged to fraternities.

## Abuse Measures

Any intentional physical, sexual, or psychological assault on a female by a male dating partner was defined as woman abuse. Following Okun (1986) and DeKeseredy and Hinch (1991), the term 'abuse' was chosen over terms such as 'battering' and 'violence' because its connotation addresses the fact that women are victims of a wide range of assaultive behaviours in a variety of social contexts. Indeed, a large body of research shows that male-to-female victimization in intimate relationships is 'multidimensional in nature' (DeKeseredy and Hinch, 1991).

To measure psychological and physical abuse, a modified version of Straus and Gelles' (1986) rendition of the Conflict Tactics Scale (CTS) was used.[5] The CTS consists of at least 18 items and measure three ways of handling interpersonal conflict in intimate relationships: reasoning, verbal aggression, and physical violence. The items are categorized on a continuum with the first ten describing non-violent tactics and the last eight describing violent strategies.

Two new items were added to the CTS. They were employed by Statistics Canada in their pre-test for a national Canadian telephone study on violence against women. These measures are: 'put her (you) down in front of family' and 'accused her (you) of having affairs or flirting with other men'. Previous research

**Table 4** Demographic Characteristics of the Sample

|  | Men (%) | Women (%) |
|---|---|---|
| Age (median) | 21 | 20 |
| *Ethnicity* | | |
| Central American | .2 | .1 |
| Scandinavian | 1.1 | 1.0 |
| French Canadian | 27.0 | 22.4 |
| English Canadian | 46.0 | 47.9 |
| British[a] | 4.3 | 5.5 |
| West European[b] | 2.9 | 3.2 |
| East European[c] | 2.9 | 3.2 |
| South European[d] | 4.9 | 5.5 |
| Far Eastern[e] | 5.0 | 5.3 |
| African[f] | 1.9 | 1.6 |
| Caribbean | 1.0 | 1.6 |
| Middle Eastern[g] | 1.0 | 1.4 |
| Latin American | .3 | .3 |
| Aboriginal | 1.9 | 1.8 |
| Black | .2 | .1 |
| Jewish | .2 | .1 |
| Other | 1.0 | .7 |
| Refugee | 1.7 | .7 |
| Recent immigrant | 4.3 | 3.8 |
| *Marital status* | | |
| Never Married | 81.8 | 77.9 |
| Married | 7.8 | 7.6 |
| Living with an intimate heterosexual partner | 8.4 | 10.5 |
| Separated | .7 | 1.8 |
| Divorced | .8 | 1.9 |
| Widowed | .5 | .3 |

a. Wales, Scotland, N. Ireland, England; b. France, Germany, Holland, etc.; c. Russia, Poland, Baltic States, Hungary, etc.; d. Italy, Spain, Portugal, Greece, etc.; e. Japan, China, India, Hong Kong, etc.; f. North, Central or South; g. Israel, Lebanon, Iraq, etc.

shows that these items are related to physical violence in marital relationships (e.g., Smith, 1990a).

The CTS has been extensively criticized as a simple count of abuse with no sense of context, meaning, or motives for being violent (Breines and Gordon, 1983; DeKeseredy and MacLean, 1990; Dobash et al., 1992). These criticisms are generally in response to some researchers who use sexually symmetrical CTS data to justify their claims that intimate, heterosexual violence is a 'two-way street' and that there is a 'battered man syndrome' (e.g., McNeely and Robinson-Simpson,

Table 5 Educational Characteristics of the Sample

|  | Men (%) | Women (%) |
|---|---|---|
| *Year of study* |  |  |
| First | 39.2 | 42.4 |
| Second | 27.9 | 23.8 |
| Third | 19.3 | 19.6 |
| Fourth | 9.4 | 10.2 |
| Other | 4.0 | 4.0 |
| *Major* |  |  |
| Arts | 29.6 | 42.2 |
| Education | 3.2 | 11.2 |
| Fine Arts | 1.3 | 2.0 |
| Agriculture | 6.1 | 2.9 |
| Engineering | 4.4 | .7 |
| Health | 1.1 | 2.8 |
| Sciences | 13.2 | 9.0 |
| Business | 15.2 | 12.5 |
| Law | 3.8 | 3.0 |
| Trades | 6.5 | 5.8 |
| Service occupation | 1.0 | 3.0 |
| Technology program | 13.0 | 3.3 |
| Don't know | 1.6 | 1.7 |
| Current fraternity member | 3.0 | 0 |
| Past fraternity member | 2.6 | 0 |
| Current sorority member | 0 | 1.6 |
| Past sorority member | 0 | 1.2 |

1987; Steinmetz, 1977–8). While their data do show that women hit men as often as men hit women, these findings do not demonstrate 'sexually symmetrical motivation' (Dobash et al., 1992). For example, as Schwartz and DeKeseredy point out (1993), there has never been any doubt that *some* women strike their partners with the intent to injure. However, research specifically on the context, meanings, and motives of intimate violence shows that most female-to-male assaults are acts of self-defence (Berk et al., 1983; Browne, 1987; DeKeseredy, 1992; Dobash and Dobash, 1988; Dobash et al., 1992; Makepeace, 1986; Saunders, 1986; 1988; 1989; Schwartz and DeKeseredy, 1993).

In response to the above criticisms, also included in our version of the CTS were three questions asking male and female participants to explain why they engaged in dating violence since they left high school. The following measures are modified versions of those developed by Saunders (1988).[6] The responses to them, however, have not yet been analysed:

> On items . . . what percentage of these times overall do you estimate that in doing these actions . . . you were primarily motivated by acting in self-defence, that is protecting yourself from immediate physical harm?
> you were trying to fight back in a situation where you were not the first to use these or similar tactics?
> you used these actions on your dating partners before they actually attacked you or threatened to attack you?

A slightly reworded version of Koss et al.'s (1987) Sexual Experiences Survey (SES) was employed to operationalize various forms of sexual assault. It covers a range of unwanted sexual experiences. Both the CTS and SES are widely used, and they are reliable and valid measures (Koss and Gidycz, 1985; Smith, 1987; Straus et al., 1981). The texts of all of the items used are presented in Tables 6, 7, 8, and 9, and different wording was used for male and female respondents.[8]

## Findings

### The Incidence and Prevalence of Sexual Abuse

The items used in the SES are presented in Tables 6 and 7. These measures range from unwanted sexual contact, to sexual coercion, attempted rape, and rape. In this study, the SES global incidence rate for female victims was 27.8 per cent. Approximately 11 per cent of the males reported having victimized a female dating partner in this way in the past year. The prevalence figures are considerably higher, with 45.1 per cent of the women stating that they had been victimized since leaving high school and 19.5 per cent of the men reporting at least one abusive incident in the same time period. Within the margin of error,[9] except for the male prevalence figure, these results are similar to those reported in the pre-test (DeKeseredy et al., 1992).

Caution, however, must be used in interpreting these figures since they represent a composite of several items which vary in both the amount of violence used and in whether they actually constitute a violation of the *Canadian Criminal Code*. Even so, all the items reflect experiences that many survivors identify as both traumatic and damaging (Kelly, 1988). Furthermore, using the SES allows us to replicate previous work and to compare Canadian results with American data.

It is difficult to compare the incidence findings with other Canadian studies presented in Table 1. For example, though Finkelman (1992) used the same measures and time period, he does not provide data on gender variations in victimization. Instead, he reports the total number of students (both men and women) who were sexually abused. Moreover, for male reports of their behaviour, there are no comparable statistics (that is, figures based on the SES). DeKeseredy (1988) asked men whether they had threatened to use force or actually used force 'to make a woman engage in sexual activities' in the past 12 months. This might have been narrowly defined by respondents to refer to actual or attempted sexual intercourse or to include forced fondling or petting. Because of these problems in interpretation, comparisons are meaningless.

Comparing prevalence findings is also problematic. For example, Elliot et al. (1992) used slightly different measures and combined male and female figures. Methodological differences also make it hard to compare our findings with those produced by Koss et al.'s (1987) national American study. Although these researchers used the same sexual abuse items to determine prevalence rates, they used a broader time period—since age 14.

Despite some methodological differences, the findings presented in Tables 6 and 7 are consistent with Koss et al.'s American national data. They show that male respondents were more likely to report using less severe forms of coercion to get women to engage in sexual activities. These included arguments and pressure, and the use of alcohol. Women's reports concur with male responses in terms of the types of coercion used to engage in sexual activities. There are, however, large gender differences in reporting the incidence of abuse and the reporting gaps widen for the prevalence data.

Interpreting these reporting differences is a complex process. Researchers argue that socially desirable reporting is more common among perpetrators than victims (Arias and Beach, 1987; Dutton and Hemphill, 1992). The greatest differences[10] between men and women were on the most socially undesirable items: sex play, attempted intercourse, and sexual intercourse involving some degree of force. The findings indicate that women were seven to eight times more likely to report these behaviours than men when response differences were standardized using women's figures as the base. This suggests that social desirability is probably shaping responses. However, the response differences on four other items were also large.

On these items women were 6 to 6.5 times more likely to have reported abuse than men. These items included: giving in to sex play or to sexual intercourse due to continual arguments and pressure and attempted sexual intercourse or actual sexual intercourse when you were too drunk or too high to resist. These four items focus on the negotiations between men and women over sexual activity. The differences in reporting rates on these items, most of which are lower in social undesirability, suggest that there may be considerable miscommunication between men and women. The exact nature of this miscommunication cannot be determined from these data. But, given the proposed changes to Canadian laws on consent and sexual assault, they suggest the need for further investigation.

### The Incidence and Prevalence of Physical Abuse

The male physical abuse incidence figure of 13.7 per cent approximates statistics reported in previous Canadian and American incidence studies which used similar methods (DeKeseredy, 1988; DeKeseredy et al., 1992; Makepeace, 1983). Though Table 8 shows that every type of physical violence was used by

**Table 6** Sexual Abuse Incidence Rates

| Type of abuse | Men (N=1,307) | | Women (N=1,835) | |
|---|---|---|---|---|
| | % | N | % | N |
| 1. Have you given in to sex play (fondling, kissing, or petting, but not intercourse) when you didn't want to because you were overwhelmed by a man's continual arguments and pressure? | 7.8 | 95 | 18.2 | 318 |
| 2. Have you engaged in sex play (fondling, kissing, or petting, but not intercourse) when you didn't want to because a man used his position of authority (boss, supervisor, etc.) to make you? | .9 | 10 | 1.3 | 21 |
| 3. Have you had sex play (fondling, kissing, or petting, but not intercourse) when you didn't want to because a man threatened or used some degree of physical force (twisting your arm, holding you down, etc.) to make you? | 1.1 | 13 | 3.3 | 54 |
| 4. Has a man attempted sexual intercourse (getting on top of you, attempting to insert his penis) when you didn't want to by threatening or using some degree of physical force (twisting your arm, holding you down, etc.), but intercourse did not occur? | .6 | 7 | 3.9 | 67 |
| 5. Has a man attempted sexual intercourse (getting on top of you, attempting to insert his penis) when you didn't want to because you were drunk or high, but intercourse did not occur? | 2.5 | 29 | 6.6 | 121 |
| 6. Have you given in to sexual intercourse when you didn't want to because you were overwhelmed by a man's continual arguments and pressure? | 4.8 | 55 | 11.9 | 198 |
| 7. Have you had sexual intercourse when you didn't want to because a man used his position of authority (boss, supervisor, etc.) to make you? | .8 | 9 | .5 | 8 |
| 8. Have you had sexual intercourse when you didn't want to because you were drunk or high? | 2.2 | 25 | 7.6 | 129 |
| 9. Have you had sexual intercourse when you didn't want to because a man threatened or used some degree of physical force (twisting your arm, holding you down, etc.) to make you? | .7 | 8 | 2.0 | 34 |
| 10. Have you engaged in sex acts (anal or oral intercourse or penetration by objects other than the penis) when you didn't want to because a man threatened or used some degree of physical force (twisting your arm, holding you down, etc.) to make you? | .3 | 3 | 1.8 | 29 |

## Table 7 Sexual Abuse Prevalence Rates

| Type of abuse | Men (N=1,307) | | Women (N=1,835) | |
|---|---|---|---|---|
| | % | N | % | N |
| 1. Have you given in to sex play (fondling, kissing, or petting, but not intercourse) when you didn't want to because you were overwhelmed by a man's continual arguments and pressure? | 14.9 | 172 | 31.8 | 553 |
| 2. Have you engaged in sex play (fondling, kissing, or petting, but not intercourse) when you didn't want to because a man used his position of authority (boss, supervisor, etc.) to make you? | 1.8 | 24 | 4.0 | 66 |
| 3. Have you had sex play (fondling, kissing, or petting, but not intercourse) when you didn't want to because a man threatened or used some degree of physical force (twisting your arm, holding you down, etc.) to make you? | 2.2 | 25 | 9.4 | 154 |
| 4. Has a man attempted sexual intercourse (getting on top of you, attempting to insert his penis) when you didn't want to by threatening or using some degree of physical force (twisting your arm, holding you down, etc.), but intercourse did not occur? | 1.6 | 19 | 8.5 | 151 |
| 5. Has a man attempted sexual intercourse (getting on top of you, attempting to insert his penis) when you didn't want to because you were drunk or high, but intercourse did not occur? | 5.5 | 63 | 13.6 | 244 |
| 6. Have you given in to sexual intercourse when you didn't want to because you were overwhelmed by a man's continual arguments and pressure? | 8.3 | 96 | 20.2 | 349 |
| 7. Have you had sexual intercourse when you didn't want to because a man used his position of authority (boss, supervisor, etc.) to make you? | 1.4 | 17 | 1.5 | 24 |
| 8. Have you had sexual intercourse when you didn't want to because you were drunk or high? | 4.7 | 55 | 14.6 | 257 |
| 9. Have you had sexual intercourse when you didn't want to because a man threatened or used some degree of physical force (twisting your arm, holding you down, etc.) to make you? | 1.5 | 18 | 6.6 | 112 |
| 10. Have you engaged in sex acts (anal or oral intercourse or penetration by objects other than the penis) when you didn't want to because a man threatened or used some degree of physical force (twisting your arm, holding you down, etc.) to make you? | 1.4 | 16 | 3.2 | 51 |

Table 8 Psychological and Physical Abuse Incidence Rates

| Type of Abuse | Men (N=1,307) | | Women (N=1,835) | |
|---|---|---|---|---|
| | % | N | % | N |
| *Psychological* | | | | |
| Insults or swearing | 52.7 | 623 | 52.5 | 857 |
| Put her (you) down in front of friends or family | 18.9 | 233 | 30.7 | 491 |
| Accused her (you) of having affairs or flirting with other men | 29.3 | 350 | 37.2 | 614 |
| Did or said something to spite her (you) | 57.7 | 670 | 61.7 | 989 |
| Threatened to hit or throw something at her (you) | 6.1 | 71 | 10.6 | 174 |
| Threw, smashed, or kicked something | 25.4 | 304 | 25.5 | 433 |
| *Physical* | | | | |
| Threw something at her (you) | 3.5 | 40 | 5.1 | 85 |
| Pushed, grabbed, or shoved her (you) | 11.7 | 132 | 19.6 | 319 |
| Slapped her (you) | 2.9 | 30 | 5.5 | 85 |
| Kicked, bit, or hit her (you) with your (his) fist | 1.7 | 16 | 3.9 | 61 |
| Hit or tried to hit her (you) with something | 1.9 | 20 | 3.3 | 54 |
| Beat her (you) up | .9 | 7 | 1.4 | 21 |
| Choked her (you) | 1.0 | 10 | 2.1 | 32 |
| Threatened her (you) with a knife or a gun | .9 | 9 | .5 | 9 |
| Used a knife or a gun on her (you) | 1.0 | 8 | .1 | 2 |

at least one respondent, less lethal forms of assault were reported more often. This is consistent with most of the earlier North American research (Sugarman and Hotaling, 1989). Expectations of socially desirable reporting are further supported when female incidence rates are calculated. These are higher than male figures with 22.3 per cent of the female participants reporting victimization. Again, there are more reports of less lethal forms of abuse, and reporting differences are largest for the most socially undesirable variants of abuse.

Table 9 shows that there are also gender differences in responses to the physical abuse prevalence items. Almost 35 per cent of the women reported having been physically assaulted and 17.8 per cent of the men stated ever having used physical abuse since leaving high school. Both the male and female prevalence figures are similar to the pre-test results (DeKeseredy et al., 1992). But, the male figure is considerably lower than Barnes et al.'s (1991) rate (42 per cent). This inconsistency probably reflects differences between the specific renditions of the CTS employed by the two studies. Barnes et al.'s version included a sexual assault item and several other items were distinct from those used in our modified version.

Tables 8 and 9 include some notable features. For example, on both the incidence and prevalence scales, men were more likely to indicate having used a

Table 9  Psychological and Physical Abuse Prevalence Rates

| Type of Abuse | Men (N=1,307) | | Women (N=1,835) | |
|---|---|---|---|---|
| | % | N | % | N |
| *Psychological* | | | | |
| Insults or swearing | 62.4 | 747 | 65.1 | 1105 |
| Put her (you) down in front of<br>   friends or family | 25.9 | 322 | 44.2 | 742 |
| Accused her (you) of having affairs<br>   or flirting with other men | 40.9 | 495 | 52.6 | 90l |
| Did or said something to spite her (you) | 65.2 | 773 | 72.2 | 1216 |
| Threatened to hit or throw something<br>   at her (you) | 8.0 | 97 | 20.6 | 346 |
| Threw, smashed, or kicked something | 30.6 | 373 | 37.3 | 652 |
| *Physical* | | | | |
| Threw something at her (you) | 4.3 | 50 | 10.6 | 185 |
| Pushed, grabbed, or shoved her (you) | 15.8 | 182 | 31.3 | 529 |
| Slapped her (you) | 4.9 | 53 | 11.1 | 186 |
| Kicked, bit, or hit her (you) with your<br>   (his) fist | 2.8 | 28 | 8.0 | 135 |
| Hit or tried to hit her (you) with something | 2.9 | 33 | 8.0 | 136 |
| Beat her (you) up | 1.0 | 8 | 3.9 | 63 |
| Choked her (you) | 1.0 | 9 | 4.6 | 80 |
| Threatened her (you) with a knife or a gun | .9 | 9 | 2.4 | 41 |
| Used a knife or a gun on her (you) | 1.0 | 9 | .5 | 8 |

weapon than women were to state having been subjected to this form of abuse. Moreover, Table 9 reveals that more men reported threatening a date with a weapon than women reported being threatened. These are considerably socially undesirable acts and men's higher rates of reporting suggest that, not surprisingly, social desirability alone does not account for reporting.

### The Incidence and Prevalence of Psychological Abuse
Similar accounts of psychological abuse were provided by both men and women. For example, the proportion of men who reported having been psychologically abusive is 74.1 per cent and 79.1 per cent of the female respondents indicated having been a victim of such mistreatment. As anticipated, the prevalence figures were higher at 86.2 per cent for women and 80.8 per cent for men.

The male incidence figure is higher than those reported by DeKeseredy (1988) and DeKeseredy et al. (1992). The women's incidence figure is also higher than the DeKeseredy et al. estimate. The male prevalence statistic is about 12 per cent lower than that reported by Barnes et al. (92.6 per cent). This difference probably reflects the use of different measures.

An examination of the psychological abuse items presented in Tables 8 and 9 indicates that there is considerable congruency in reporting. This suggests that there is a perception on the part of abusers that these occurrences are part of the 'common currency' of dating relationships. This is particularly true of insults or swearing, throwing, smashing or kicking something, and doing something to spite a partner. There was less reporting agreement on threatening to throw something at her, putting her down in front of friends and family, and accusing her of having affairs or flirting with other men. These three items are less likely to be equal exchanges and are more likely to be unvaryingly threatening or psychologically damaging.

## Conclusion

Surveys on the extent of woman abuse in Canadian university/college dating relationships are in short supply. The few which have been conducted clearly demonstrate that many women are at great risk of being physically, sexually, and psychologically attacked in courtship. They also intimate that many male dating partners may be attempting to mirror the dynamics of patriarchal marriages in which men have superior power and privilege (DeKeseredy and Schwartz, 1993). However, since the data presented in these studies (see Table 1) are gleaned from non-probability samples, they are only suggestive of the incidence and prevalence of woman abuse in the Canadian post-secondary student population at large. Such data are clearly necessary to 'provide a surer footing than presently exists for the development of social policies and programs needed to ameliorate the problem' (Smith, 1987: 144).

In preparing to conduct this national study, substantial effort was devoted to considering the various measures used by researchers in this field in the past (Kelly and DeKeseredy, 1983). Our intention was to balance the need to replicate previous studies with the necessity of avoiding their methodological problems. The best available measures were selected and where necessary, modifications were made to address known difficulties. One of the major controversies in the woman abuse literature involves the use of composite scales to measure abuse. Such scales include the full range of potentially abusive items, that is psychological, physical, and sexual abuse. Interpreting the data derived from these items is extremely problematic given the range of activities covered. There is, for example, considerable debate about whether certain items in the sub-scales constitute abuse. This paper has presented the abuse figures for sexual, physical, and psychological abuse separately. Consistent with existing research in this area, composite measures (global incidence and prevalence figures) were computed but are not reported here since it is our position that they tend to be so large that they obscure and trivialize the more serious and less controversial abuse figures reported by the respondents.[11]

The results of this nationally representative sample survey provide more accurate and reliable data on the abuse of college and university women by male dating partners. The findings suggest that very serious forms of abuse are quite common in campus dating. A comparison of our global prevalence findings with those reviewed by Sugarman and Hotaling (1989) show that the problem of dating abuse is just as serious in Canada as it is in the US.

Although these figures are high, as is the case with all survey statistics on woman abuse, they should be read as underestimates for the following reasons. First, many people do not report incidents because of fear of reprisal, embarrassment, or because they perceive some acts as too trivial to mention. Second, some people forget abusive experiences, especially if they took place long ago and were relatively 'minor' (Kennedy and Dutton, 1989; Smith, 1987). Third, because of social desirability factors, men are less likely than women to provide reliable accounts of their behaviour. Finally, many women may not want to recall the pain and suffering they endured in their dating relationships (Smith, 1987).

In order to advance a better understanding of woman abuse in post-secondary school dating relationships, and to both prevent and control it, more than just accurate incidence and prevalence data are required. We need to empirically discern the major 'risk markers' (Hotaling and Sugarman, 1986) associated with assaults on female university/college students, such as level of intimacy, ethnicity, and educational status. This type of analysis will provide information on who is at the greatest risk of being abused or of being abusive. Such correlational research will also assist in the development of theories, such as the one offered at the beginning of this article.

Research on the links, if any, between psychological abuse and physical and sexual abuse is also necessary for providing us with more direct interactional warnings. For example, strong correlations between accusations of flirting or having affairs (jealousy) and later physical or sexual abuse could be used to warn people to 'get help' or 'get out' when confronted with such abusive situations.

Another important issue is the possible difference between men and women in their interpretations of consent for sexual activities. As noted above, reporting differences between men and women on the items about sexual negotiations or consent were large and very similar to the gaps between men and women in their reporting of the most socially undesirable activities. These preliminary findings raise important questions of a social and legal nature regarding the interpretations that men and women have of consent within dating relationships. These bear directly on current discussions about whether consent has been given or one partner has simply complied because they felt pressure to do so or were unable to refuse—the 'no means no' debate. Subsequent articles on the national survey will address this and other issues, such as the influence of familial patriarchy on male violence; the context, meanings, and motives assigned to dating violence; the influence of male peer group dynamics on abusive behaviour; and the effectiveness of various social support services for women.

## NOTES

1  See DeKeseredy (1988), DeKeseredy et al. (1993), Koss et al. (1987), Lloyd (1991), Sugarman and Hotaling (1989), and Ward et al. (1991) for comprehensive reviews of these studies.

2 For more detailed information on the sample design, see Pollard (1993).

3 See Pollard (1993) for the precise weighting factors.

4 The selection procedure allowed for the inclusion of schools that were randomly selected more than once.

5 One version of the CTS used in this study was tailored to elicit women's reports of their victimization and the other was designed to elicit men's accounts of their abusive behaviour. The CTS included in the female instrument, for example, was introduced as follows: We are particularly interested in learning more about your dating relationships. No matter how well a dating couple gets along, there are times when they disagree, get annoyed with the other person, or just have spats or fights because they're in a bad mood or tired or for some other reason. They also use many different ways to settle their differences. Below is a list of some things that might have been done to you by your boyfriends and/or dating partners in these circumstances. Please circle the number which best represents your answer in each of the following situations. Please note the items are repeated twice. The first set is for the past 12 months, the second set covers all of your experiences since you left high school. If you are or have been married, please note these questions refer *only to dating relationships*.

6 Two sets of these questions were included in the prevalence section of the CTS. The first set followed the first three violence items, and the other one followed the last six violence items which constitute what Straus et al. (1981) refer to as the 'severe violence index'.

7 For each of these questions, respondents were asked to circle the percentage which best represented their answer.

8 Missing cases are excluded from these tables.

9 There is a 2 per cent margin of error in these results at the 99 per cent level.

10 The gap in reporting was calculated by subtracting the percentage of men who stated that they abused a date from the percentage of women who reported having been abused and then dividing this difference by the percentage of women reporting that type of abuse.

11 The global figures were reported by the press based on a preliminary report to the funding agency and, as expected, a great deal of controversy developed. One consequence of this controversy was that the sexual and physical abuse figures were virtually ignored.

## REFERENCES

Arias, Ileana and S.R.H. Beach
1987 'Validity of self-reports of marital violence'. *Journal of Family Violence* 2: 139–49.

Barnes, Gordon E., Leonard Greenwood, and Reena Sommer
1991 'Courtship violence in a Canadian sample of male college students'. *Family Relations* 40: 37–44.

Berk, Richard A., Sarah Fenstermaker Berk, Donileen Loseke, and David Rauma
1983 'Mutual combat and other family violence myths'. In David Finkelhor, Richard J. Gelles, Gerald T. Hotaling, and Murray A. Straus, eds, *The Dark Side of Families*. Beverly Hills: Sage.

Breines, Winni and Linda Gordon
1983 'The new scholarship on family violence'. *Signs: Journal of Women in Culture and Society* 8: 491–53.

Brinkerhoff, Merlin and Eugen Lupri
1988 'Interspousal violence'. *The Canadian Journal of Sociology* 13: 407–34.

Browne, Angela
1987 *When Battered Women Kill*. New York: Free Press.

DeKeseredy, Walter S.
1988 *Woman Abuse in Dating Relationships: The Role of Male Peer Support*. Toronto: Canadian Scholars' Press.

1989 'Woman abuse in dating relationships: An exploratory study'. *Atlantis: A Women's Studies Journal* 14: 55–62.

1992 'In defence of self-defence: Demystifying female violence against male intimates'. In Ronald Hinch, ed., *Crosscurrents: Debates in Canadian Society*. Toronto: Nelson.

DeKeseredy, Walter S. and Ronald Hinch
1991 *Woman Abuse: Sociological Perspectives*. Toronto: Thompson Educational Publishing.

DeKeseredy, Walter S., Katharine Kelly, and Bente Baklid
1992 'The physical, sexual, and psychological abuse of women in dating relationships: Results from a pre-test for a national study'. Paper presented at the annual meeting of the American Society of Criminology, New Orleans.

DeKeseredy, Walter S. and Brian D. MacLean
1990 'Researching woman abuse in Canada: A left realist critique of the Conflict Tactics Scale'. *Canadian Review of Social Policy* 25: 19–27.

DeKeseredy, Walter S. and Martin D. Schwartz
1993 'Male peer support and woman abuse: An expansion of DeKeseredy's model'. *Sociological Spectrum* 13 (4): 393–414.

DeKeseredy, Walter S., Martin D. Schwartz, and Karen Tait
1993 'Sexual assault and stranger aggression on a Canadian university campus'. *Sex Roles* 28 (5/6): 263–78.

Dilorio, Judith A.
1989 'Being and becoming coupled: The emergence of female subordination in heterosexual relationships'. In Barbara J. Risman and Pepper Schwartz,

eds, *Gender in Intimate Relationships: A Microstructural Approach*. Belmont, CA: Wadsworth.

Dobash, R. Emerson and Russell Dobash
1979 *Violence Against Wives*. New York: Free Press.

1988 'Research as social action: The struggle for battered women'. In Kersti Yllo and Michele Bograd, eds, *Feminist Perspectives on Wife Abuse*. Beverly Hills: Sage.

Dobash, Russell, R. Emerson Dobash, Margo Wilson, and Martin Daly
1992 'The myth of sexual symmetry in marital violence'. *Social Problems* 39: 71–91.

Dutton, Donald G. and K. Hemphill
1992 'Patterns of socially desirable responding among perpetrators and victims of wife assault'. *Violence and Victims* 7: 29–40.

Elliot, Susan, Dave Odynak, and Harvey Krahn
1992 *A Survey of Unwanted Sexual Experiences Among University of Alberta Students*. Research report prepared for the Council on Student Life, University of Alberta. University of Alberta: Population Research Laboratory.

Ellis, Desmond, Judith Ryan, and Alfred Choi
1987 *Lawyers, Mediators and the Quality of Life Among Separated and Divorced Women*. A report prepared for the Laidlaw Foundation. Toronto: The LaMarsh Research Programme on Violence and Conflict Resolution.

Ellis, Desmond and Noreen Stuckless
1992 'Preseparation abuse, marital conflict mediation, and postseparation abuse'. *Mediation Quarterly* 9: 205–25.

Ellis, Desmond and Lori Wight
1987 'Post-separation woman abuse: The contribution of lawyers'. *Victimology* 13: 146–66.

Finkelman, Larry
1992 *Report of the Survey of Unwanted Sexual Experiences Among Students of U.N.B.-F. and S.T.U.* University of New Brunswick: Counselling Services.

Gondolf, Edward W.
1985 *Men Who Batter: An Integrated Approach for Stopping Wife Abuse*. Florida: Learning Publications.

Hotaling, Gerald T. and David B. Sugarman
1986 'An analysis of risk markers and husband to wife violence: The current state of knowledge'. *Violence and Victims* 1: 101–24.

Johnson, Brian D.
1992 'Campus confidential'. *MacLean's* November 9: 43–6.

Kelly, Katharine and Walter S. DeKeseredy
1993 'Developing a Canadian national survey on woman abuse in university and college dating relationships: Methodological, theoretical and political issues'. *Journal of Human Justice*.

Kelly, Liz
1988 *Surviving Sexual Violence*. Minneapolis: University of Minnesota Press.

Kennedy, Leslie W. and Donald G. Dutton
1989 'The incidence of wife assault in Alberta'. *The Canadian Journal of Behaviourial Science* 21: 40–54.

Koss, Mary P. and Christine A. Gidycz
1985 'Sexual experiences survey: Reliability and validity'. *Journal of Consulting and Clinical Psychology* 50: 455–7.

Koss, Mary P., Christine A. Gidycz, and Nadine Wisniewski
1987 'The scope of rape: Incidence and prevalence of sexual aggression and victimization in a national sample of higher education students'. *Journal of Consulting and Clinical Psychology* 55: 162–70.

Koss, Mary P. and Cheryl J. Oros
1982 'Sexual experiences survey: A research instrument investigating sexual aggression and victimization'. *Journal of Consulting and Clinical Psychology* 50: 455–7.

Lamanna, Mary Ann and Agnes C. Riedmann
1985 *Marriages and Families*. Belmont, CA: Wadsworth.

Laner, Mary R. and Jeanine Thompson
1982 'Abuse and aggression in courting couples'. *Deviant Behavior* 3: 229–44.

Lloyd, Sally
1991 'The dark side of courtship: Violence and sexual exploitation'. *Family Relations* 40: 14–20.

Lupri, Eugen
1990 'Male violence in the home'. In C. McKie and K. Thompson, eds, *Canadian Social Trends*. Toronto: Thompson Educational Publishing.

Makepeace, James M.
1983 'Life events stress and courtship violence'. *Family Relations* 32: 101–9.

1986 'Gender differences in courtship victimization'. *Family Relations* 35: 383–8.

McNeely, R.L. and Gloria Robinson-Simpson
1987 'The truth about domestic violence: A falsely framed issue'. *Social Work* 32: 485–90.

Okun, Lewis
1986 *Woman Abuse: Facts Replacing Myths*. Albany: SUNY Press.

Pollard, John
1993 *Male-Female Dating Relationships in Canadian Universities and Colleges: Sample Design, Arrangements for Data Collection and Data Reduction*. Toronto: Institute for Social Research.

Russell, Diana
1986 *The Secret Trauma: Incest in the Lives of Girls and Women*. New York: Basic Books.

Saunders, Daniel G.
1986 'When battered women use violence: Husband abuse or self-defence?' *Violence and Victims* 1: 47–60.

1988 'Wife abuse, husband abuse, or mutual combat? A feminist perspective on the empirical findings'. In Kersti Yllo and Michele Bograd, eds, *Feminist Perspectives on Wife Abuse*. Beverly Hills: Sage.

1989 'Who hits first and who hits most? Evidence for the greater victimization of women in intimate relationships'. Paper presented at the annual meeting of the American Society of Criminology, Reno, Nevada.

Schwartz, Martin D. and Walter S. DeKeseredy
1993 'The return of the "battered husband syndrome" through the typification of women as violent'. *Crime, Law and Social Change* 20 (3): 249–66.

Schwartz, Martin D. and Carrol Ann Nogrady
1993 'Peer support groups and sexual victimization on a college campus'. Unpublished manuscript. Ohio University.

Sheatsley, Paul B.
1983 'Questionnaire construction and item writing'. In Peter H. Rossi, James D. Wright, and Andy B. Anderson, eds, *Handbook of Survey Research*. Toronto: Academic Press.

Smith, Michael D.
1985 *Woman Abuse: The Case for Surveys by Telephone*. The LaMarsh Research Programme on Violence and Conflict Resolution. Report No. 12. Toronto: York University.

1987 'The incidence and prevalence of woman abuse in Toronto'. *Violence and Victims* 2: 173–87.

1988 'Women's fear of violent crime: An exploratory test of a feminist hypothesis'. *Journal of Family Violence* 3: 29–38.

1989 *Woman Abuse in Toronto: Incidence, Prevalence and Sociodemographic Risk Markers*. The LaMarsh Research Programme on Violence and Conflict Resolution. Report No. 18. Toronto: York University.

1990a 'Patriarchal ideology and wife beating: A test of a feminist hypothesis'. *Violence and Victims* 5: 257–73.

1990b 'Sociodemographic risk factors in wife abuse: Results from a survey of Toronto women'. *The Canadian Journal of Sociology* 15: 39–58.

1991a 'Male peer support of wife abuse: An exploratory study'. *Journal of Interpersonal Violence* 6: 512–19.

1991b 'Enhancing the quality of survey research on violence against women'. Paper presented at the annual meeting of the Association for Humanist Sociology, Ottawa.

1993 'Familial ideology and wife abuse'. Unpublished manuscript. North York, Ontario: LaMarsh Research Programme on Violence and Conflict Resolution.

Southam Business Information and Communications Group
1990 *Corpus Almanac and Canadian Source Book*. Toronto: Southam Business Information and Communications Group.

Stacey, William and Anson Shupe
1983 *The Family Secret: Domestic Violence in America*. Boston: Beacon Press.

Stanko, Elizabeth A.
1990 *Everyday Violence: How Women and Men Experience Sexual and Physical Danger*. London: Pandora.

Statistics Canada
1992a *Universities: Enrolment and Degrees 1990*. Catalogue 81–204 Annual. Ottawa: Statistics Canada.

1992b *Community Colleges and Related Institutions: Postsecondary Enrolment and Graduates 1989*. Catalogue 81–222 Annual. Ottawa: Statistics Canada.

Steinmetz, Suzanne K.
1977–8 'The battered husband syndrome'. *Victimology* 3–4: 499–509.

Sugarman, David B. and Gerald T. Hotaling
1989 'Dating violence: Prevalence, context, and risk markers'. In Maureen A. Pirog-Good and Jan E. Stets, eds, *Violence in Dating Relationships: Emerging Social Issues*. New York: Praeger.

Straus, Murray A.
1979 'Measuring intrafamily conflict and violence: The Conflict Tactics (CT) Scales'. *Journal of Marriage and the Family* 41: 75–88.

Straus, Murray A. and Richard J. Gelles
1986 'Societal changes and change in family violence from 1975 to 1985 as revealed by two national surveys'. *Journal of Marriage and the Family* 48: 465–79.

Straus, Murray A., Richard J. Gelles, and Suzanne K. Steinmetz
1981 *Behind Closed Doors: Violence in the American Family*. New York: Anchor Books.

Ward, Sally K., Kathy Chapman, Ellen Cohn, Susan White, and Kirk Williams
1991 'Acquaintance rape and the college social scene'. *Family Relations* 40: 65–71.

From *Canadian Journal of Sociology/Cahiers canadiens de sociologie* 18 (2) (1993): 137–59.

## ILLUSTRATIVE READING 2

### ON VIOLENT MEN AND FEMALE VICTIMS: A COMMENT ON DEKESEREDY AND KELLY

*Bonnie J. Fox*

In collecting representative data on the abuse of women by male dating partners, DeKeseredy and Kelly have done us a service. We have known for some time that it is not rare for men living with women to hurt them seriously, and that it is extremely unusual for women to do so to their male partners. There is little research on more casual relationships, however. Nevertheless, despite the clearly competent sampling and interviewing done by York's Institute for Social Research, I have misgivings about the project after reading this initial summary.

As feminist researchers and educators, working in an environment that is still generally hostile to our analyses, and indifferent to women's particular concerns, it is crucial that we make strong arguments involving claims we can support (although no amount of reason and evidence will persuade everyone). At the same time, as sociologists, our conceptualization of social structure, and our sensitivity to the complexity of the relationship between the individual and society, should lend sophistication to any arguments we make about gender inequality. Thus, long ago, most feminist social science left behind the notion that 'patriarchy' is reducible to powerful men dominating passive, weak women.

This paper is disappointing because it rests implicitly on that argument. Related to this implicit theory are methodological weaknesses that I will try to elaborate. But first a general comment. Devoid of any explicit analysis—statistical or theoretical—the article indicates that DeKeseredy and Kelly assume that the data 'speak for themselves'. That too is a position I thought we had abandoned long ago.

To be fair to these researchers, the issue of violence against women is perhaps the most poorly theorized of all aspects of gender inequality. The argument that men who are powerful victimize women, as a prerogative of their more privileged position and in order to bolster it (by controlling women), is common in the literature. Yet both the empirical research and various feminist insight and arguments suggest a far more complex interpretation.

For instance, the evidence on 'wife battering' indicates that the type of man who is likely to abuse is one who needs to be in control, and one who believes men are entitled to women's services (Dobash and Dobash, 1979; Straus and Gelles, 1990). As well, though, the kind of objective material situation that promotes abuse is one that leaves a man feeling powerless—involving unemployment, perpetual low income, etc. (Straus and Gelles 1990). With respect to sexuality, some writers have discussed the feelings of vulnerability, not potency, evoked by men's desire for women (Hollway, 1983; Kaufman, 1987; Segal, 1990). The point I am trying to make is that the dynamics of violence and abuse are complicated; what is going on is not obvious.

Given that the behaviour in question is so complex, and our understanding so primitive, it is disappointing to see DeKeseredy and Kelly opt for 'global' estimation, of global categories (i.e., 'abuse'), rather than detailed analysis. Their global measures of abuse combine the least with the worst offenses (e.g., rape with an unwanted kiss). Their objective seems to be to support the argument that 'female students' lives rest upon a continuum of violence' by men. Instead, by combining what is debatably abusive with what everyone agrees to be seriously abusive, they stand to trivialize the latter. That 2 per cent of women in

Canadian universities and colleges may be forced into sexual intercourse every year is more obviously significant than the 'global' figures DeKeseredy and Kelly highlight. Not only is forced intercourse different from an unwanted kiss in terms of damage, the questions we need to ask about an unwanted kiss are of a different nature. For example, we are probably much more concerned to determine the meaning attached to the act by both the woman and the man in the case of unwanted 'sex play'; we cannot assume it constitutes abuse, much less intentional abuse.

The argument is, of course, that soft-core abuse leads to hard-core abuse—that we are discussing a continuum. But is there evidence of that? That there are far more instances of the soft-core behaviour than the serious stuff raises the possibility that some men will not move beyond pressure to force. Are there not different types of men, and more generally, wholly different contexts and causal factors behind the use of force than pressure—or, at least, a larger variety of causes and contexts with respect to the latter? We do not know until we investigate.

Similarly, despite their separation of sexual, physical, and psychological forms of abuse, DeKeseredy and Kelly clearly classify them all under the same general category. They all represent 'intentional assault on a female by a male dating partner' ([*Canadian Journal of Sociology*] p. 146). Again, implicit is that the minor abuse (e.g., swearing at someone) is a mild version of the major abuse (e.g., rape). But slippage occurs in other ways: 'intention' refers to one set of possibilities with respect to rape (e.g., inflicting pain, forcing submission, achieving a sense of power, etc.), but likely a very different set of things with respect to a forced kiss (e.g., from desiring sex to wanting to humiliate), or swearing or an accusation of flirting (which are more likely displays of anger, hurt, etc.). In short, it is not clear what 'intentional' means here, when applied to all these phenomena—unless you *assume* that all men aim primarily to use or abuse women.

In the case of 'psychological abuse', DeKeseredy and Kelly's discussion ([*Canadian Journal of Sociology*] pp. 153–5) is less than clear, but it involves reference to 'equal exchanges' between dating partners. It is indeed possible that women are in a less vulnerable position in psychological and verbal battles with men. In other words, this seems a different phenomenon than the other two. But the framework adopted here precludes an exploration of this possibility. This is not to suggest that men are sometimes victims in the ways women can be. It is to suggest that we need to investigate the dynamics of each of these types of aggressive behaviour before we lump them together, and cast women solely in the role of victim—or, at least, passive victim.

A final instance of agglomeration in lieu of disentangling—or analysing—is DeKeseredy and Kelly's frame of reference: dating. Surely 'dating' includes a range of different types of relationships, from serious involvement and commitment to brief encounters between near strangers. Again, my general point is about method: combining what is qualitatively different undercuts any search for understanding.

At minimum, DeKeseredy and Kelly owed themselves and us a look at the statistical relationships in the data they collected: differences between age cohorts, university and college students, fields of study, etc., would at least provide some clues; data on type of relationship, type of man, and both parties' perception of what went on would be more revealing. Are the relationships with key independent variables the same for the different kinds of abuse? Shouldn't DeKeseredy and Kelly have established that before talking of all types of abuse in the same breath? Similarly, that DeKeseredy and Kelly present these figures before looking at their data on why the man used violence/force/pressure is puzzling and supports my sense that they thought the data would speak for themselves, and that all these types of abuse are the same.

In sum, I think that DeKeseredy and Kelly have not shown that 'very serious forms of abuse are quite common in campus dating' ([*Canadian Journal of Sociology*] p. 155). What do they hold to be 'very serious'? Where have they argued that percentages of a particular size indicate commonplace events? Aside from the methodological problems with this article and this project, to suggest the above is politically irresponsible. As many have argued already, conclusions like these instill fear in young women, which serves to control them, rather than to help to empower them. Moreover, weak arguments undercut the campaign to raise people's consciousness.

Clearly women face risks in close relationships with men that men need not fear. But before we can assume that all aggressive and abusive behaviour is of the same nature, and arising from the same sources, we need to investigate. Focus groups and in-depth interviews using various approaches and questions would probably be extremely helpful in developing a sense of how women experience different kinds of incidents, what is going through men's heads, etc. Moreover, different questions need to be asked of men than of women. We need both symmetry and asymmetry in our questioning: we should determine what women do as well as what men do, but because women and men are in different positions we should also ask them different questions, especially about intent or motive (e.g., questions about self-defense are critical for female, but not male, respondents). Most importantly, we need to remember that social science is about asking why, and trying to explain—not counting.

## REFERENCES

Dobash, R. Emerson and Russell Dobash
1979  *Violence Against Wives*. New York: The Free Press.

Hollway, Wendy
1983  'Heterosexual sex: power and desire for the other'. In Sue Cartledge and
      Joanna Ryan, eds, *Sex and Love*. London: The Women's Press.

Kaufman, Michael
1987 'The construction of masculinity and the triad of men's violence'. In Michael Kaufman, ed., *Beyond Patriarchy*. Toronto: Oxford University Press.

Segal, Lynne
1990 *Slow Motion*. London: Virago.

Straus, Murray and Richard Gelles
1990 *Physical Violence in American Families*. New Brunswick, NJ: Transaction Publications.

From *Canadian Journal of Sociology/Cahiers canadiens de sociologie* 18 (3) (1993): 321–4.

# ILLUSTRATIVE READING 3

## STUDYING WOMAN ABUSE:
## A COMMENT ON DeKESEREDY AND KELLY

*Rosemary Gartner*

### Introduction

In the last two decades, violence against women has achieved growing prominence on the public agenda and concomitant attention from academic researchers, in large part due to the work of feminist grass-roots activists and concerned scholars such as DeKeseredy and Kelly (1993). Twenty years ago we knew little about violence against women, except through the incomplete and systematically biased documentation provided by official statistics. Now, thanks to a variety of victimization and self-report survey studies, a more accurate picture of the extent, characteristics, and costs of violence against women can be portrayed. One of the most consistent findings from these studies is that women are at much higher risk of violence, and particularly violence by intimate male partners, than official statistics would lead us to believe.

The research reported by DeKeseredy and Kelly is an effort to contribute to the growing body of work on intimate partner violence against women. Their stated goal is to provide 'estimates of the incidence and prevalence of woman abuse in Canadian university/college dating relationships . . . [through] the first national representative sample survey of men and women' ([*Canadian Journal of Sociology*] p. 138). In this comment, I appraise their analysis from my perspective as a sociologist trained in conventional social science methods (including survey research and techniques of quantitative data analysis), a feminist, and a researcher of violence against women. My conclusion is that, based on both feminist and conventional social science standards, fundamental flaws in the work limit its potential contribution to an understanding or explanation of violence against women.

## Reliability and Validity of the Measures of Woman Abuse

DeKeseredy and Kelly define the focus of their research, woman abuse, as 'any intentional physical, sexual, or psychological assault on a female by a male dating partner' ([*Canadian Journal of Sociology*] p. 146). To capture acts fitting this definition, they use two instruments, both developed and used widely by other researchers: the Conflict Tactics Scales [CTS] (Straus and Gelles, 1986) and the Sexual Experiences Survey [SES] (Koss et al., 1987).[1] Both instruments, they note, are 'reliable and valid measures'. Rather than review in detail the evidence regarding the reliability of these measures, I encourage interested readers to consult evaluations of these instruments by their developers and others (Straus, 1990; Jouriles and O'Leary, 1985; Koss and Gidycz, 1985; Szinovacz, 1983). My reading of this work is that the reliability of the measures varies greatly by the specific comparison made (e.g., intra-individual reliability for reports of victimization or aggression elicited from anonymous surveys vs. face-to-face interviews; intra-couple reliability for reports of victimization vs. reports of aggression; and so forth). Indeed, concerns over the reliability of the CTS have led some researchers to reject its use as a measure of marital violence (Dobash, Dobash, Wilson, and Daly, 1992).

More critical for the work of DeKeseredy and Kelly is the issue of the validity of the two instruments, or whether the SES and CTS measure the concepts DeKeseredy and Kelly intend them to measure. The CTS was designed to measure various conflict resolution techniques in relationships. It is introduced to respondents, as DeKeseredy and Kelly detail, by noting both the normality of disagreements and conflicts between partners in a relationship and the range of different ways disagreements are dealt with. The purpose is to legitimate admissions of even relatively severe forms of aggression and to build toward these through admissions of more common and less harmful conflict tactics. The SES was designed to measure a range of sexual experiences up to and including acts that would be legally judged as sexual assaults. Similar to the CTS, it begins with less coercive acts and builds to more coercive and aggressive acts.

The developers of both instruments consistently have used care in choosing words to describe the behaviours their instruments measure. Because of vagueness and subjectivity, terms such as 'violence', 'assault', or 'abuse' do not appear in either instrument and are used very selectively by the developers in discussing their findings. For example, the series of questions in the CTS about the use of verbal and nonverbal acts that may symbolically hurt the other are combined in the 'Verbal Aggression' scale; the term 'violence' is reserved to refer only to acts that involve the use or threat of physical force. Similarly, Koss distinguishes among the types of sexual experiences tapped by her instrument by labelling them 'unwanted sexual contact', 'sexual coercion', and 'sexual assault' (Koss, Gidycz, and Wisniewski, 1987).

The validity of each instrument, thus, should be judged by how well it measures conflict tactics typically used in relationships (in the case of the CTS) or coercive sexual contacts (in the case of the SES). DeKeseredy and Kelly do not consider this issue; instead, they simply offer the instruments as valid measures of 'woman abuse', as they have defined it. Their assumption is that any one of the items from either instrument is a valid measure of 'abuse', and that each also measures an instance of 'assault' and 'victimization'. (They do, however, explicitly avoid the use of the terms 'battering' and 'violence'.) This assumption underlies their conclusion that 86 per cent of the women in their sample had been 'victims' of 'psychological abuse' and 45 per cent had been 'victims' of 'sexual abuse' since leaving high school.

In considering the validity of these items as measures of woman abuse, let us focus on items from the CTS.[2] Certainly the face validity of questions about a partner's 'spiteful' statements, insults, or swearing as indicators of abuse and assault would be open to question in many people's minds. A rejoinder to this position is that such comments are (1) often experienced as abusive and humiliating by the recipient and (2) part of a continuum of abuse that women experience whereby verbal aggression is frequently associated with more serious and physically harmful acts of aggression.

For a number of feminist and non-feminist scholars, the first point is a central criticism of the CTS: the questions posed in the CTS ignore the meaning of the acts to the persons involved, the sequence of the acts in a wider pattern of interaction, and the context of the acts in a particular relationship. Although DeKeseredy and Kelly acknowledge this criticism, they ignore its implications by asserting that these acts *are* abusive, notwithstanding the motives of the 'abuser' or the interpretation of the 'abused'. In so doing, they violate a fundamental principle of feminist research: listening to women's (and men's) subjective interpretations of their experiences. Apparently, their judgement, as researchers, as to what constitutes abuse is more vital than judgements based on the lived experiences of their respondents.

The second point—that such forms of verbal aggression are part of a continuum of woman abuse and related to physical violence—is undermined by the consistent finding of gender symmetry in the use of verbal aggression, as measured by the CTS and similar instruments. Unlike DeKeseredy and Kelly, most researchers using the CTS ask *both* females and males about being users as well as targets of these verbal conflict tactics.[3] According to this research, women and men are about equally likely to use verbal aggression (Stets and Henderson, 1991; Laner and Thompson, 1982).[4] Furthermore, when asked about perpetrating physical forms of aggression, women and men report similar levels of aggression (Stets and Henderson, 1991; Sugarman and Hotaling, 1989).[5] Data showing similar levels of verbal and physical aggression by males and females raise at least two problems for DeKeseredy and Kelly's purposes. If we grant the validity of the CTS as a measure of abuse, we must acknowledge that men are subject to a variety of forms and high levels of abuse from their female partners. If, however, we challenge the CTS-based finding of gender symmetry in abuse by citing evidence of gender asymmetry from the most reliable data on violence available—homicide statistics[6]—we must question the criterion validity of the aggression measures from the CTS. In other words, similar levels of verbal and physical aggression in the CTS self-reports of females and males do not square with very different levels of serious criminal violence by males and females against their intimate partners (Dobash et al., 1992).[7]

Based on these concerns, my conclusion is that the CTS and the SES are not valid measures of 'woman abuse' as defined by DeKeseredy and Kelly. Either instrument, as a whole, may be a valid measure of conflict tactics or sexual experiences as defined by their developers, but that issue is best left for (and has been addressed by) others. Furthermore, either instrument may include items that could constitute part of an instrument to measure 'woman abuse', as defined by DeKeseredy and Kelly. Justifying the choice of items would, however, require both more empirical examination of the measurement properties of the instrument and more theoretical grounding. Validity can only be judged in the context of a theoretical network that surrounds the concept of interest and has to be assessed indirectly against a pattern of external evidence. Neither of these criteria is met by DeKeseredy and Kelly.

## Sampling and Non-Response Bias

As noted above, the major goal of DeKeseredy and Kelly's study is to conduct a survey on the extent of woman abuse using a nationally representative sample of university and college students. Although there have been many surveys of Canadian college students using the CTS, SES, and other instruments, as DeKeseredy and Kelly point out, conclusions from these surveys are greatly limited by their sampling frames. To minimize these problems, their study relies on an elaborate and sophisticated sampling design.

Whether the sampling design accomplished its goal is, however, impossible to determine. First, no statistics on the characteristics of the Canadian university and college student population are provided for comparison with the characteristics of the sample (with the exception of regional distribution). We do not know, then, how well the sample represents the population. Second, even assuming a reasonably representative sample, it is unlikely that the students who actually responded to the survey are representative of this population. Of the 3,142 respondents to the survey, 1,835 (58 per cent) were female and 1,307 (42 per cent) were male. According to government estimates, however, the gender distribution of the university and college student population is approximately equal. The most likely explanation for the unequal gender distribution of respondents is dispropor-tionate selection out of the survey by male students. However, DeKeseredy and Kelly provide no information on this or any other characteristic of the non-respon-dents—including their numbers—that would allow us to verify this explanation.

Let us assume that the total sample was, indeed, approximately equal in its gender distribution. If selection out of the survey (whether by males or females) was random, it will not affect estimates of the incidence or prevalence of abuse. However, if selection was systematic, as the unequal gender distribution suggests, these estimates will be biased. With information on non-respondents, one could estimate the effects of non-response bias on the results. Without this information, we simply do not know how non-response bias affects the esti-mates of incidence and prevalence. It is plausible that persons who are perpe-trators of aggression will be more likely to select themselves out, which would explain the underrepresentation of males among respondents. This would produce a downward bias on estimates of the incidence and prevalence of abuse. The effects of non-response on estimates of victimization are much more difficult to predict. As DeKeseredy and Kelly imply, women's experiences of and attitudes toward abuse are likely to affect their willingness to respond to ques-tions about abuse (and their definitions of abuse) in complex ways. Without information on non-respondents, we can only speculate about the direction of bias in the estimates.[8]

## Discussion and Conclusion

These criticisms of the research of DeKeseredy and Kelly may be seen by some as narrow, technical concerns of a conventional social scientist who lacks empathy for and understanding of the extent and severity of woman abuse. It might be argued that, regardless of potential errors in DeKeseredy and Kelly's estimates of the incidence and prevalence of woman abuse, the finding that a high proportion of female college students reports experiencing verbal, physical, or sexual aggression from their dating partners is *prima facie* evidence of the importance of woman abuse as a social problem and provides important infor-mation and justification for social action.

I would disagree with both claims. First, as to my perspective, violence against women concerns me greatly; my purpose in studying it (Gartner, Baker, and Pampel, 1990; Gartner and McCarthy, 1991; Crawford and Gartner, 1992) is to gain greater understanding in order to prevent it. Second, I view the findings of DeKeseredy and Kelly's research not as, at worst, benignly inaccurate, but as distracting and detracting from the search for understanding, explanation, and prevention of violence against women.

First, consider whether their research contributes to an understanding or expla-nation of violence between intimate partners. Such violence is, by definition, a feature of relationships, of interactions between at least two people. Sociologists have long argued that violence cannot be adequately understood as simply a characteristic of individuals. Yet the DeKeseredy and Kelly survey individualizes the phenomenon of woman abuse, divorces it from its context in relationships where both parties can potentially exercise power, domination, and control. Where women are only and always the victims and men only and always the offenders, no insights can be gained into how the dynamics of relationships produce violence—and violence that has more lethal consequences for women than for men. Without information on how both men and women define and perceive verbal aggression from their partners, no insights can be gained into why men more often than women see this verbal aggression as justification for severe physical attacks on their partners. Surveys such as DeKeseredy and Kelly's, then, do not allow us to address critical questions such as: Why, given apparent gender symmetry in verbal and minor forms of physical aggression, is there gender asymmetry in serious physical and sexual violence? What distinguishes relationships in which only verbal aggression is used from those in which verbal aggression is accompanied by physical and sexual aggression? Why do we find differences in men's reports of their acts of aggression and women's reports of their victimization?

Finally, consider whether DeKeseredy and Kelly's research contributes to more effective public policy to prevent woman abuse. The implication of their study is that most women, even those who are well-educated, will be victims of woman abuse in their lives. What does this mean for the allocation of inevitably limited resources to the prevention of violence against woman? Should we support increased spending on programs for intervention into 'abusive' relationships, as defined by DeKeseredy and Kelly? My point is a simple and perhaps obvious one: defining abuse as broadly as do DeKeseredy and Kelly trivializes the very serious and life-threatening forms of abuse that many women suffer. Moreover, the conclusion that abuse is widely spread throughout society, affecting women at all class levels, is technically correct. But it ignores the well-documented fact that life-threatening and lethal abuse are disproportionately experienced by women who are economically disadvantaged. The possibility that findings of 'widespread woman abuse' will divert attention and resources away from women at high risk of severe violence from their partners distresses me, as a feminist and a social scientist.

## NOTES

1 The CTS was modified for this study by omitting the series of questions on reasoning as a conflict resolution technique and by adding two questions to the series used to measure 'verbal aggression' in the CTS. The wording of the SES has also been modified slightly from Koss et al.'s original version.

2 Some of these points could be illustrated using the SES. Again, it is important to stress that the developer of the SES does not use the terms 'abuse' or 'assault' in referring to reports of 'giving in to sex play [or sexual intercourse] when you didn't

want to because you were overwhelmed by a man's continual arguments and pressure'. Koss classifies these as instances of 'sexual coercion', not 'assault' or 'abuse'.

3  This is consistent with the design of the CTS as an instrument to measure conflict as a characteristic of relationships, not as an instrument to measure victimization as a characteristic of women and offending as a characteristic of men. DeKeseredy and Kelly's procedure of only asking women about things done to them and only asking men about things they do is thus inconsistent with the purposes of the CTS. Furthermore, it also implies that women are only passive objects, only men are active subjects, and aggression is gender-specific behaviour; these implications fly in the face of empirical reality and many feminist perspectives on gender and aggression.

4  Some surveys find women are more likely than men to use verbal aggression, though this gender difference is typically small.

5  Some research on dating couples also finds that a higher proportion of men than women report sexual pressure by their partners, including pressuring them to have sex and getting angry if refused (Rouse, Breen, and Howell, 1988).

6  Data from Statistics Canada on homicides by intimate partners in Canada show that men outnumber women as offenders by over three to one.

7  The criterion validity of the CTS-derived estimates of physical aggression is problematic on a second dimension. DeKeseredy and Kelly note that their estimates of the incidence of male physical abuse are similar to estimates obtained in research in the US. Data showing that the rate of spousal homicides is much higher in the US than in Canada question the predictive validity of the CTS physical abuse measure.

8  An uncontrolled variation in the survey procedures could provide an indirect (if far less than ideal) way to gain some information on selection out of the survey. As DeKeseredy and Kelly note, some instructors gave their students advance warning about the survey while some did not. A comparison of the characteristics and responses of respondents from classes given advance warning with those not given advance warning could suggest ways in which non-response might bias the estimates.

## REFERENCES

Crawford, Maria and Rosemary Gartner
1992  *Woman Killing: Intimate Femicide in Ontario, 1974–1990*. Final report for the Ontario Women's Directorate and Ministry of Community and Social Services. Toronto: Women We Honour Action Committee.

Dobash, Russell P., R. Emerson Dobash, Margo Wilson, and Martin Daly
1992  'The myth of sexual symmetry in marital violence'. *Social Problems* 39: 71–91.

Gartner, Rosemary, Kathryn Baker, and Fred C. Pampel
1990  'Gender stratification and the gender gap in homicide victimization'. *Social Problems* 37: 593–612.

Gartner, Rosemary and Bill McCarthy
1991  'The social distribution of femicide in urban Canada, 1921–1988'. *Law and Society Review* 25: 287–312.

Jouriles, Ernest N. and K. Daniel O'Leary
1985 'Interspousal reliability of reports of marital violence'. *Journal of Clinical and Consulting Psychology* 53: 419–21.

Koss, Mary P. and Christine A. Gidycz
1985 'Sexual Experiences Survey: Reliability and Validity'. *Journal of Consulting and Clinical Psychology* 53: 422–3.

Koss, Mary P., Christine A. Gidycz, and Nadine Wisniewski
1987 'The scope of rape: Incidence and prevalence of sexual aggression and victimization in a national sample of higher education students'. *Journal of Consulting and Clinical Psychology* 55: 162–70.

Laner, Mary R. and Jeanine Thompson
1982 'Abuse and aggression in courting couples'. *Deviant Behavior* 3: 229–44.

Rouse, Linda P., Richard Breen, and Marilyn Howell
1988 'Abuse in intimate relationships: A comparison of married and dating couples'. *Journal of Interpersonal Violence* 3: 414–29.

Stets, Jan E. and Debra A. Henderson
1991 'Contextual factors surrounding conflict resolution while dating: Results from a national study'. *Family Relations* 40: 29–36.

Straus, Murray A.
1990 'The Conflict Tactics Scales and its critics: An evaluation and new data on validity and reliability'. In M.A. Straus and R.J. Gelles, eds, *Physical Violence in American Families*, pp. 49–73. New Brunswick, NJ: Transaction Publications.

Szinovacz, Maximiliane E.
1983 'Using couple data as a methodological tool: The case of marital violence'. *Journal of Marriage and the Family* 45: 633–44.

From *Canadian Journal of Sociology/Cahiers canadiens de sociologie* 18 (3) (1993); 313–20.

## ILLUSTRATIVE READING 4

### RE-THINKING WHAT WE DO AND HOW WE DO IT: A STUDY OF REPRODUCTIVE DECISIONS

*Dawn Currie*

This paper examines the current impasse which feminism has created by promoting methodology as an end in itself. Stanley and Wise (1983), in particular, argue that feminist consciousness is a 'way of doing feminist research' which must reject a masculinist structure-orientation. Challenging their claim that feminist research cannot and should not 'go beyond' the realm of personal experience, the author discusses her current research on reproductive decision-making which highlights the necessity of transcending the strictly personal worlds of women. The author argues that debates about 'masculine scientific' versus 'feminist personal' methodologies are better understood in the context of testing established theory through logico-deductive research as opposed to the discovery of grounded theory (Glaser and Strauss, 1967) through an inductive approach. From this perspective, debates concern the practical rather than the political correctness of our choices.

All is not well with the state of feminist research. As McCormack (1987) claims, feminism has created a crisis for our thinking about research and appropriate methodology. She relates this crisis to our discovery that there are two versions of truth: patriarchy's view from outside the lives of women and feminism's inside view grounded in women's lived experiences of oppression. Expressed as a choice between 'scientifically objective' and 'experientially subjective' ways of doing research, feminism has come down upon the side of the latter. Indeed, what has differentiated 'feminist' research from 'malestream' social science is the privileged position which it accords to consciousness. Rejecting objective scientific 'facts', feminism begins instead with the perceived world so that experience rather than scientific 'knowledge' is authority.

With others (Reinharz, 1979, 1983; Oakley, 1981), Stanley and Wise (1983) identify the problem of traditional social science as a separation between the subjective and objective which they claim leads to a denial of the subjectivity of women's experiences by accepting only 'objective' ways of knowing. Stanley and Wise argue that two fundamental insights of the Women's Liberation Movement which have been forgotten can provide us with a way of knowing and learning about the world which overcomes this false distinction. The first is feminism's acceptance of personal experience as valid. The second is a claim that the distinction between 'objective' and 'subjective' is false, arising from a masculine experience of the world. They argue that the traditional male emphasis has been on objectifying experiences and 'getting away from' the personal into some transcendental realm of 'knowledge' and 'truth'. In this way feelings are removed from our experiences of the world as these experiences become objects of scientific study. This process of objectification results in depersonalized 'truths' about the way in which systems, structures, and institutions are the source of our oppression. It allows us to hide behind collectivisms rather than take responsibility for the fact that 'only people oppress people' (Stanley and Wise, 1983: 106–7). In the final analysis, Stanley and Wise argue that current trends in feminist theory and research have betrayed the fundamental feminist claim that 'the personal is political' by continuing a traditional 'structure orientation' rather than developing a 'people orientation'. In order to develop such a method, they draw upon their personal experiences of oppression as lesbians to argue that ideas about how 'structures' impose themselves through 'socializing' various 'internalized' behaviours and attitudes are, quite simply, irrelevant (Stanley and Wise, 1983: 80). Because they believe that the individual's experience should form the basis of both theory and practice, they insist that:

> There is no 'going beyond' the personal, that chimera of contemporary feminist theory. To talk about 'going beyond' is to posit a false distinction between experience and between structure and process (ibid., 1983: 83).

Stanley and Wise maintain that the original contribution of feminism to the social sciences is the proposal that women's experiences constitute a different view of reality and a different way of making sense of the world. They suggest that 'feminist consciousness' forms an untapped store of knowledge about the world which can be an epistemological foundation for new theories.

I agree with many of their arguments; in particular, that '*each* of us have [sic] to find out the nature of our own oppression in order to fight these' and that 'the nature and dimensions of these differ according to our different lives'. I also agree that feminist theory should not become 'expert's theory', rejecting other women's experiences which don't correspond by calling them inadequate or falsely conscious. However, I disagree with the notion that structures and institutions are not oppressive forces and that they are constructed entirely out of everyday life. I find their rejection of an objective study of social institutions and structures dangerous.[1] In particular, conceptualizing our research choices as between masculinist scientific objectivity and feminine intuitive subjectivity—outsider versus insider views—is a no-win situation. The purpose of this paper is to engage in a bit of feminist self-criticism about a new orthodoxy which threatens to promote feminist methodology as an end in itself. The vehicle for this discussion is my current research on reproductive decision-making which brought me face-to-face with the limitations of both mainstream and feminist research perspectives. This paper will discuss these limitations, indicate research choices made during the current study, and illustrate the consequences of the approach developed for theorizing about women's reproductive choices. While not claiming to solve all the dilemmas of such an ambitious project, the results of this case study raise a number of questions about how we currently think about what we do as feminists and how we do it.

### Something Old, Something New, Something Borrowed . . . A 'Re-marriage'?

From another perspective, the competition between 'outsider versus insider' or 'structural versus personal' views reflects epistemological debates concerning the usefulness of logico-deductive versus inductive research. The emphasis in mainstream sociology is currently the verification of established theory through logico-deductive research which has been linked in North America with the growth of rigorous quantitative research. Adopting this approach means that we attempt to deduce theoretically the 'origin' of women's oppression from outside women's lives and inside established theories. In her criticism of the domestic labour debate for doing precisely this, Vogel (1983) points out that, although the oppression of women can be analysed with the guidance of a theoretical framework, the origin of women's oppression is itself not deducible theoretically. While she argues that this question is an historical rather than a theoretical one, others note the futility of such a task given that most 'established' theory explicitly excludes issues of gender.

The limitations of a strictly logico-deductive approach were one of the first problems I faced in the study of reproductive decision-making. In particular, I wanted to know how women decide about having or not having children in order to assess the feminist goal of 'freely chosen motherhood'. While the traditional literature on fertility is vast and indeed begins 'where women are', it does not offer much direction. A number of theories about decision-making borrow heavily from classical economic theory. Beginning from the utilitarian assumption that individuals maximize the utility of their choices through rational assessment of alternatives, this literature offers a 'cost-benefit' model of decision-making, represented in Figure 1. A 'cost-benefit' analysis suggests that individuals perceive alternative courses of action, develop preferences for options, and upon that basis choose one line of action as preferable. In terms of children, the benefits are largely psychological satisfactions, while the costs are both monetary and non-economic. Overall, traditional models suggest that decision-making proceeds through an orderly series of 'stages', each requiring the cognitive assessment of personal preferences compared with given alternatives in order to maximize the utility of reproductive behaviour. The 'problem' for women today, reflected in declining rate of fertility, is the expansion of alternatives so that a number of 'choices' compete with motherhood—the most obvious one being career.

Feminist writers adopting this approach (see Fabe and Wikler, 1979; Gerson, 1985; O'Donnell, 1985) argue that women's decisions for or against motherhood and for or against work ties develop out of a negotiated process of balancing the opportunities and incentives in one sphere against the constraints of the other. Noting that women may experience difficulties in their decision-making, this experience is portrayed as primarily an 'approach-avoidance' conflict. Russell and Fitzgibbons (1982) claim that this type of conflict is an inevitable consequence of expectations that are 'in transition':

> The concept that a female can grow up to be a fulfilled and whole woman, independent of motherhood, has emerged and is expanding. Both the positive and negative aspects of motherhood are being examined. Women are becoming aware that they have the choice to have children, but with this awareness comes the pain of decision (1982: 46).

Figure 1  Reproductive Decision Making as a 'Cost-Benefit' Analysis, Showing Indecision and Contraceptive Risk-taking

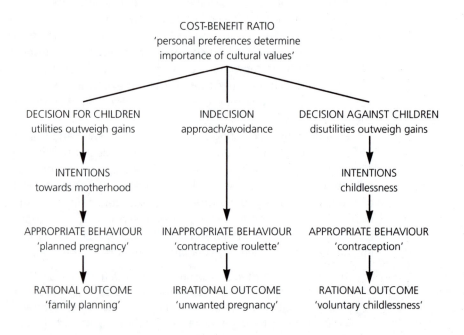

PERCEPTION OF OPTIONS
'awareness of choice'
childed vs. childless

ASSIGNMENT OF VALUES TO OPTIONS
'cultural values of children'
Costs vs. Benefits

COSTS
- expenditures on housing, feeding, schooling, etc.
- foregone income of mother
- foregone career advancement of mother
- loss of freedom
- worry about a child

BENEFITS
- fulfillment of adult status
- expansion of self
- establishment of primary group affiliation
- stimulation/relief everyday routine
- power/control over another's life

COST-BENEFIT RATIO
'personal preferences determine importance of cultural values'

DECISION FOR CHILDREN
utilities outweigh gains

INDECISION
approach/avoidance

DECISION AGAINST CHILDREN
disutilities outweigh gains

INTENTIONS
towards motherhood

INTENTIONS
childlessness

APPROPRIATE BEHAVIOUR
'planned pregnancy'

INAPPROPRIATE BEHAVIOUR
'contraceptive roulette'

APPROPRIATE BEHAVIOUR
'contraception'

RATIONAL OUTCOME
'family planning'

IRRATIONAL OUTCOME
'unwanted pregnancy'

RATIONAL OUTCOME
'voluntary childlessness'

## Feminist Re-discovery of Grounded Theory:
## A Study of Deferred Childbearing

Smith (1981: 2) argues that due to an androcentric bias within our discipline, as feminists and sociologists we must begin to reconstruct sociology from the standpoint of women. Methodologically, this requires that we treat women's worlds as 'problematic'. From this perspective our research directs attention to sets of questions which may not have been posed by malestream science or to sets of puzzles which do not yet exist but which are 'latent' in the actualities of experienced worlds (Smith, 1981). Therefore we must start from the experienced worlds of women. However, as Glaser and Strauss (1967: 6) argue, the task of the sociologist is more than fact-finding or description: it is the development of sociological explanations from data. In particular, Glaser and Strauss emphasize the value of 'grounded theory'—theory that emerges from systematically obtained and analysed data. They compare this method to the logico-deductive approach of normal science. In contrast to deduction, the discovery of grounded theory demands that the hypotheses and concepts are not only drawn from the data, but that they are worked out during the course of research. In this way, *generating the explanation cannot be separated from the process of conducting research*. The method which Glaser and Strauss find useful for the generation of theory is the general method of comparative analysis through the systematic choice and study of comparison groups. The task is not to provide a 'perfect' description of a phenomenon (an impossible task at best), but to develop a theory that accounts for much of the relevant behaviour. This requires the generation of general categories and an exploration of their properties as the guide to theoretical explanation (Glaser and Strauss, 1967: 30). Both categories and their properties are indicated by the data (and are not the data themselves). Overall, Glaser and Strauss emphasize *theory as a process*; that is, theory as an ever developing entity rather than a perfect product. Of interest to the project at hand is what Glaser and Strauss (1967: 32) identify as substantive theory: an elaborated and systematic explanation developed from a substantive, or empirical, area of sociological inquiry. Substantive theory falls between theories of the 'middle range' as minor working hypotheses of everyday life and the 'all-inclusive' grand theories of sociology.

According to Glaser and Strauss (1967: 38), the type of categories which should be generated during data collection has two related features. Firstly, the concepts should be *analytic*—sufficiently generalized to designate characteristics of concrete entities, not the entities themselves. They should also be *sensitizing*—yield a 'meaningful' picture, abetted by references which enable one to grasp the reference in terms of experience. The purpose of data collection is the generation of hypotheses which concern suggested relations between the categories. At this point the researcher is no longer a passive receiver of impressions, but begins to verify these hypotheses through comparisons of groups. It is this aspect of the 'real life' character of the field work which Glaser and Strauss emphasize. From this *in vivo* accumulation of inter-relationships, the core of the theory emerges. Furthermore, the 'unstructured' nature of the investigation acknowledges that researchers are likely to develop insights about theoretical issues during data collection, and furthermore that the researcher can make the most of them through systematic comparative analysis. Like Kuhn (1970), Glaser and Strauss note that informed 'hunches' are often the prelude to major scientific discoveries, although retrospective accounts of the process of research often obscure this point. The source of these hunches is the sensitive insights gained via the researcher's intimate association with—rather than distance from—the data. Furthermore, Glaser and Strauss (1967: 252) add that crucial insights may come from *the researcher's personal experiences prior to or outside the research*.

## The Study

The material for this paper comes from a broader project in which I interviewed 76 women about their postponement or rejection of motherhood.[2] The sample contained women who were over 30 years of age and either unchilded, pregnant, or new mothers. Data were collected through unstructured personal interviews which were tape-recorded and lasted for one or two hours. Central to the field work was a process of discovering new themes from the experiences of women themselves, rather than one of asking research subjects to respond to categories deducted from established theory.[3] By including women at varying stages in the decision-making process, this study differs from previous research on contraceptive risk-taking which focuses more narrowly upon the 'risk-takers'—respondents who have experienced an 'unwanted' pregnancy. Broadening the approach in this way has two distinct advantages. It allows us to examine risk-taking as a *characteristic of reproductive decision making rather than as a characteristic of the women themselves*. It *reduces the limitations inherent in strictly retrospective studies*. During the fieldwork a number of women discussed risk-taking as their current contraceptive practice. While this may not eliminate entirely an element of rationalization, it does eliminate re-interpretation which may occur if this practice is explored retrospectively in the light of pregnancy.

This research further differs from previous studies in the categorization of data. Unlike Gerson (1985) and others, this project did not classify respondents upon the basis of reproductive outcome (as childed versus unchilded). Rather, based upon women's experiences, respondents were categorized according to the self-report of their *decision status*. The initial—and to begin, obvious—categories were simply 'decided' and 'undecided'. During interviews further categories became apparent. Decided women described themselves as either 'for' or 'against' motherhood, and either as early deciders, those who decided after much difficulty, or those who re-decided. Similarly, undecided women described themselves as putting off the decision, not ready to decide, or unable to decide.

Significantly, while the majority of childed women were those who had decided for motherhood, two women who had decided against motherhood and many more women who reported themselves as unable to decide were childed, indicating the importance of these distinctions for analysis of women's control over reproduction. The properties of decision making suggested by women's accounts included ambivalence, conflict, and indecision. The task of data analysis, therefore, is an explication of relationships between these properties, as well as relationships between these properties and decision status.

### Experiences of Decision Making: 'If you look at it rationally, there's no good reason to have a child'

Given the diversity of their reproductive status, there was a wide variation in the extent to which women felt that their reproductive history included conscious deliberation. Looking back over her life, this 38-year-old television director described herself as 'childless by default':

> To say I've made up my mind would indicate that I at some point said 'Am I or not?' and then said 'yes' or 'no'. I think that what has happened is that I've arrived at age 38 not having had children, but having at various points wanted them, but not having them for various reasons. And not having them by 38, and being single and heavily into career, it's highly unlikely that I will. So, . . . my childlessness is a matter of default rather than anything else. I just arrived at it.

It was far more usual, however, for respondents to have expended a great deal of time and energy deliberating about motherhood. Some women discussed a decision which resembles the conscious and goal-oriented behaviour typified by traditional approaches as 'rational' decision making:

> There are a lot of things that I want to do which I couldn't afford to do if I had children. I do actually enjoy working and I don't feel particularly that I'd want to have a child and farm it out with child-minders. I wouldn't mind it so much if there was a nanny who was a constant sort of person, but I couldn't afford to do that so it's not a possibility . . . And again, I quite like travelling, and things like going to the theatre. Really, I suppose, a lot of the things are financial. On the salaries we earn, I don't think that we would be able to do those sorts of things and then have children. For example, we'd have to sell our house if I got pregnant now . . . I do feel I've made my own decision as far as I'm concerned. I have made up my mind that I do not want to have children.

Despite a great deal of 'thinking' about motherhood, however, a number of women were unable to reach a decision. Undecided women represent a significant portion of this sample (22.4 per cent) and include both unchilded and childed women. Similar to respondents in O'Donnell's (1985) study, a number of women reported that they 'just fell pregnant'. The story of this 37-year-old graphic designer is typical of a number of women who 'never really decided':

> Well, if you'd asked me *then*, I would have said, 'I've made no decision. It was a very crazy fluke—here I am pregnant!' But looking back now, uhm, I think what I did was get sloppier and sloppier, and just waited until the decision was made for me . . . I started to say quite often, 'Oh, it's safe, don't worry', which I had *never* done before.

Similarly, 37-year-old Carol found herself in what she called a 'very interesting situation' at the time of her interview:

> I'm letting fate—which is a word I don't like to use—let it happen. . . . The use of contraception has just gone into a total decline, basically. . . . I think I can relate to women who say that it would be easier to just wake up and find yourself pregnant. To be suddenly in a situation where it's not even discussed—if we'd had this interview last year, I never would have dreamt that I'd be doing what I'm doing at the moment, which is not being careful and 'going with the flow', if you like. (laughs) It's a curious time for me, really.

One new mother summarized rather well what many more women were saying:

> I don't think I could think of any 'reasons' for going ahead with motherhood, really. I've always maintained actually that if it were a rational decision there is no really good reason to have a child. It costs you money, so it's not financially advantageous. It restricts your freedom. It's damaging to your career. If you look at it *rationally*, there's no good reason.

Beginning from women's experiences rather than from theoretical models, how can we explain women's decisions? Unable to make 'rational' decisions, did these women merely make 'emotional' ones, as Russell and Fitzgibbons (1982: 51) claim? More importantly, why were some women able to make conscious choices while other women were not? Finally, how might the answers to these questions relate to 'contraceptive roulette'? As a group, these women were 'reproductively advantaged' in that they occupied the upper social classes, faced overall stable employment prospects, and almost universally described their personal relations as providing the 'opportunity' for both fertility regulation and parenthood. Within this fairly homogeneous group, were the differences in women's experiences and decisions merely idiosyncratic, as suggested by O'Donnell (1985)? The remainder of this paper will explore these questions.

### The Right Time for Motherhood: 'There doesn't seem to be a right time to have children'

Similar to previous research, most of the women in this study (67 per cent) demonstrated an ambivalent attitude towards motherhood during interviews. Some women used the term ambivalent to describe themselves:

> I was feeling so ambivalent that I decided that I would have a baby, or not have a baby, depending on how he felt.

Most women expressed their attitude in other ways, however:

I think that the conclusion which I have reached for myself for the moment is, if Calvin very much wanted it I would, but I don't want to enough myself, so it would have to be a joint venture. (undecided)

Table 1 summarizes the major themes about motherhood which underscore the ambivalence of respondents. Within this study, ambivalence is not defined as merely recognizing simultaneously negative and positive aspects of motherhood as cost-benefit approaches imply, but as an attitude which finds neither

**Table 1** Motherhood Themes

| Positive Themes | No. | % |
|---|---|---|
| 1. A baby/child would be enjoyable or rewarding | 18 | 27.7 |
| 2. Motherhood would add a new dimension to life | 13 | 20.0 |
| 3. A baby would enhance a marriage or partnership | 11 | 16.9 |
| 4. Motherhood involves you in a 'larger' project | 9 | 13.9 |
| 5. Pregnancy/motherhood would be fulfilling in a physical/sexual way | 5 | 8.0 |
| *Total | 56 | |
| % of all themes | | 16.9 |

| Negative Themes | No. | % |
|---|---|---|
| 1. Motherhood would conflict with waged employment or impede career | 48 | 73.9 |
| 2. Parenthood/motherhood means being 'tied down' | 44 | 67.7 |
| 3. A baby would place a strain on relationship with partner or threaten relationship with partner | 27 | 41.5 |
| 4. Economic costs are prohibitive or threaten lifestyle | 25 | 38.5 |
| 5. Women end up with all or most of the responsibility for childcare/domestic labour | 23 | 35.4 |
| 6. Women lose their identities as individuals and assume an identity as 'mother' or 'housewife' | 21 | 32.3 |
| 7. Childcare labour is difficult because it is demanding or monotonous | 19 | 29.2 |
| 8. Respondent might feel 'trapped' or claustrophobic | 12 | 18.5 |
| 9. Childcare labour is socially isolating | 11 | 16.9 |
| 10. Motherhood means that women become economically dependent | 9 | 13.5 |
| 11. Respondent feels incapable of becoming a mother or unable to put in enough time or effort | 9 | 13.5 |
| 12. The thought of childbirth is off-setting | 8 | 12.3 |
| 13. Pregnancy/motherhood is physically exhausting | 8 | 12.3 |
| 14. Society generally is very anti-child or anti-mother | 7 | 10.8 |
| 15. Respondent worries about postnatal depression | 5 | 7.7 |
| *Total | 276 | |
| % of all themes | | 83.1 |

Notes: Based on 65 interviews these are unprompted in the sense that the repondent was not presented with categories but open-ended questions about what they imagined that motherhood would be like for them, etc.

* More than one theme was mentioned per interview.

Table 2 The 'Right Time' for Motherhood, Factors

|  | No.* | %** |
|---|---|---|
| 1. Career/Employment Security | 21 | 56.8 |
| 2. Suitable Relationship | 20 | 54.1 |
| 3. Financial Security | 17 | 45.9 |
| 4. Accommodations Suitable | 11 | 29.7 |
| 5. Personal Maturity | 6 | 16.2 |
| 6. Miscellaneous | 2 | 5.4 |

Base *N*: 37 interviews

\* more than one factor contributed to the 'right time'

\*\* percentage of respondents mentioning this factor

sets of factors in themselves a satisfactory or compelling basis upon which to make a decision. Few women could discuss concrete 'reasons' for their decision. Instead of discussing 'why' they would or would not want children, or even 'whether or not' they wanted children, regardless of their decision status most respondents referred to whether or not was a 'right time' for motherhood. A 32-year-old musician, for example, claimed that she had been unable to reach a decision after almost two years of deliberation and as a result was experiencing a great deal of personal conflict. She opened her interview:

> I'm finding it difficult to make a decision. I've put it off and put it off because of financial instability and partly because of my career—I'm frightened about getting out of the swim and then getting back in again. There doesn't seem to be a *right* time to have children.

Similarly, a 30-year-old dental assistant who was pregnant at the time of the interview recalled her decision making:

> I was starting to be very practical—looking at the pros and cons of 'Do I really want a baby now that we've both agreed this is the *right time*?'

Overall, undecided women talked about the 'right time' looking ahead into the future, while many who had reached decisions discussed why it had been the 'right time' for them when they did decide. In total, 37 respondents (or 55 per cent) either discussed their decisions in terms of a right time or indicated that their decision making was grounded upon the notion of a right time. Table 2 summarizes the responses which these women provided when queried about 'what would make it the right time'.

From Table 2, four major themes emerge as respondents discussed their notions of 'right time'. The establishment of their career or of job security was an important factor in 57 per cent of the cases. This reflects the fact that most women reported that they would continue their careers or employment, so that when contemplating motherhood they worried about their work commitments. Although legal maternity leave offered to protect most employed women during their withdrawal from the workplace, this absence was seen as placing them at a disadvantage when it came to career advancement. A 36-year-old bank manager recognized the impossibility of satisfactorily resolving her career demands:

> I must confess, the more ambitious one becomes the greater the danger of saying 'Well, I'd just like to do *this*', 'I'd just like to get this appointment under my belt', and 'I think that this would establish me'. If you're not careful, it just rolls on and on. So it is really trying to decide when is the best time, and of course you very quickly realize that there isn't a best time . . . No time is the right time. All you can do is avoid the worst time.

The second theme mentioned as a component of the 'right time' was the establishment of a 'suitable relationship'. Despite variations in how individual respondents described a relationship as 'suitable', universally it implied the presence of a supportive partner. For women expecting to continue employment, this translated into more than financial or emotional support—it meant a partner who would be actively involved in childcare responsibilities:

> I would find it very difficult to take less than 50% from a man. I would get *very* irritated by any less. And that frightens me, because it could very easily destroy a relationship. (30-year-old solicitor, undecided)

Given that patterns of childcare have changed very little despite two decades of feminist struggles (Martin and Roberts, 1984; Oakley, 1979), respondents recognized that when 'push came to shove', it was most likely that the final responsibility for a child would be theirs:

> When it comes down to it, I think as a woman I would feel that it was my responsibility, regardless of all the thinking I've done about it. It's considered the woman's area. . . . The worry is that the man will just do it when it suits him, you know, which seems to be the paternal contribution to a traditional relationship. Women continually throughout their lives take the responsibilities and make sure that things get done when there are children. (32-year-old secretary, decided against motherhood)

A significant number of women indicated that disputes about the sharing of domestic labour were already an area of conflict with partners and that they therefore worried that domestic conflict would be aggravated if a baby was added to their household. Sandra, the bank manager, had been married for nine years and described her domestic situation as conflict-ridden:

> We have talked about this because it is a recurring problem. It comes up time and time again. And I have tried to make it abundantly clear that it's going to have to be a joint responsibility and that I see the whole thing in terms of *parenthood*, and not in terms of motherhood. Now, how that works out in practice is open to debate. . . . But based on what I know already about him and his responses, I

obviously have to feel that I can't expect a lot—I even have to agitate to get lawns cut, and that sort of thing. So I don't think I'm under any illusion at all on that score.

At the time of interview Sandra had decided to 'go for motherhood'. She indicated that she had resolved her 'domestic dilemma' by planning to purchase childcare labour. Like many other women who discussed purchased domestic or childcare labour, however, she did not find this an entirely satisfactory resolution. In the extreme, some women found this dilemma irresolvable and therefore discussed their decision as opting for either motherhood or career. Francine, a 32-year-old advertising consultant who had been married for eight years, called this the ultimate deciding factor:

I have to be realistic about it. It's no good seeing potholes and just heading for them unrealistically. . . . I know he won't give in. I don't think there would be much point in me having a child hoping that he would suddenly become a doting father. . . . I think that the only way around this is just to avoid it, you know.

The third major theme regarding the 'right time' was financial security. Because the notion of 'affording children' includes a lifestyle component, it cannot be discussed in absolute terms. For many women the notion of affording a child is tied in with discussions about work commitments because parenthood would make their employment more necessary. For Margaret, a 35-year-old artist, financial considerations were primary:

I spend a lot of time trying to think what it would be like to have a child. I think about it on the *practical* level. First of all, financially coping with a child. (unchilded, conflict and indecision for two years)

For some who had decided for motherhood, financial security dictated how long they had to wait:

I actually thought that it was the right time for the past few years. Four years ago we talked about it and decided then that we would like to start a family, but we were then thinking about two years ahead. . . . I wasn't very happy about it but I could see the practical side of it. We had a flat, and it could be that in a few years we could save enough for a house.

While the above respondent was able to 'plan and save' for motherhood, this was not always possible. Rosemarie, a 35-year-old secretary who had been married for ten years, argued that an irresolvable dilemma was posed by the fact that financially she would be unable to give up her job:

In the end I don't see that—we've worked hard for ten years, and to have to sell one's house—that to me is wrong. And then I think, (sigh) if we don't have some money so that I can give the child pleasure, then there's no point having them— do you see? There's a sort of twisted problem.

. . . But I—not *like* to work, I *have* to work, yes I have to work. . . . I thought 'there must be some way of doing it'. So I tried to find out places where I could find out about nannies and all this sort of thing, you know. But then I started to think, 'What if we have the child and then I didn't want to go back?' Say I didn't want to go back to work but I *had* to—what would happen in a situation like that?

. . . And you start feeling a little bit of guilt about leaving the child with someone else. . . . In a way, I'm not satisfied working and leaving somebody else with a child when I'm *just* a secretary. (unchilded, undecided with conflict)

In the final analysis, Rosemarie felt that the notion of the 'right time' was not relevant to her situation. She summarized her current position:

I feel I have to make up my mind definitely before I'm 38, yes? . . . I really have to make up my mind either way. Uhm, (pause). It frightens me. . . . I think if I were pregnant, then we'd have to sit down and just *do* something.

Within the context of an unprompted interview, over half of the respondents referred to the 'right time' as the focus of discussions. Clearly, within the context of these interviews the notion of '*time*' is a euphemism in that it did not refer to age and, in most cases, did not refer to an identifiable point in the respondent's life. Rather, the term 'time' refers to a *configuration of material circumstances*. From Table 2 we have seen that the material conditions referred to were career/employment security, shared parenting, adequate finances, and suitable housing. Women in this study felt that they must be prepared to personally manage these *practicalities* of motherhood before they were 'ready to decide'.

This 42-year-old psychologist indicated how her initial ambivalence towards motherhood was resolved once the practicalities of motherhood could be seen as manageable within the context of her daily life:

You can still have those fantasies about being trapped in a bungalow with children and sinking into a depression. But I know now that has no reality because it isn't how my life is, due to my finances and my relationship with Richard. (childed, decided for motherhood)

In this way, being 'ready' to decide means that initial worries have been dissolved, as indicated by Table 3. Although respondents were likely to discuss their readiness as a personal characteristic, namely 'maturity', Table 3 illustrates how readiness corresponds to a configuration of material circumstances within which the personally problematic aspects of motherhood do not appear inevitable. Women could visualize how they might juggle work/career demands, domestic schedules, financial commitments, etc., in order to establish motherhood as a *viable* alternative.

While ambivalence is rooted in women's thinking about motherhood, this discussion shows how it reflects what Rich (1977) identifies as the contradictory dimensions of motherhood. On the one hand, mothering is a relational

Table 3 How the 'Right Time' Resolves Ambivalence so that Women Feel 'Ready to Decide'

| Worries about Motherhood | What Would Make It the 'Right Time' |
|---|---|
| 1. Motherhood would be difficult to combine career/employment | Career is established |
| 2. Respondent would feel 'tied down' | Respondent feels 'ready' to be tied down |
| 3. Baby would place a strain on relationship | Relationship is stable/partner is suitable |
| 4. Financial costs/housing | Financial security has been achieved/'nest' is ready |
| 5. Sexual division of labour | Respondent can afford to purchase childcare/partner willing to be involved |

experience. Rich argues that the biologically determined relationships of mothering universally include those between mother and child; mother and father; women as mothers to society. In this study, respondents identified the relational dimension as the potentially rewarding aspect of motherhood. On the other hand, mothering acquires an institutional form which is culturally and historically specific. Rich argues that the specificity of motherhood in a patriarchal society has ghettoized and degraded the female potential. Characteristic of capitalist society, motherhood as a social role requires enforced heterosexuality, economic dependency, isolation, primacy of the infant's needs to its biological mother. In this study, it is the institutional aspects which render motherhood personally problematic. Women rejected the historically specific or concrete form of motherhood, while regarding as desirable its inherently relational dimension. Given, therefore, the contradictory nature of motherhood as promising simultaneously fulfillment and self-abnegation, it is not surprising that ambivalence is characteristic of the decision-making process. Furthermore, although achievement of the 'right time' has meaning only within the context of individual lives, it requires the manipulation of processes beyond the control of individual women. What does this mean for women's decision-making and their 'choices'?

## Decision Making Re-visited: Rhetorical Questions about Motherhood

Despite expanded opportunities for education and waged employment, a number of writers have documented the persistence of a 'motherhood mandate' (Veveers, 1980; Busfield and Paddon, 1977; Russo, 1979; Blake, 1975). In the final analysis, motherhood remains an important (if not primary) source of identity for the cohort of women in this study. For this reason, women's discussions of their expectations started from the perspective of motherhood rather than 'non-motherhood', so that undecided women as well as women who had decided against motherhood raised questions about the motherhood potential. In fact, very often women 'just assumed' that they would have a family 'some day'. This does not mean that women do not make decisions, however. Rather, it means that decisions begin from the position of considering motherhood. Colleen, a 30-year-old solicitor, indicated that she had not decided about motherhood and that she was putting off the decision until she was 35 because she did not feel 'ready to decide'. This did not mean that she was not thinking about motherhood, however. On the contrary, since reaching 30 she had become more aware of the 'practicalities' of having children and spent a great deal of time imagining whether and how motherhood might fit into the context of her day-to-day life:

> Certainly for the last five years or so I've been more aware of the practicalities of having children, how much it involves. . . . It literally seems to be a question of either you give up work or manage in some way, which involves getting all sorts of other things sorted out. So that you've got the support structure or, you know, the externals that you need to worry about set up.

Colleen discussed in detail the type of management to which she referred:

> For *me* it would be important not to feel that I'm running around in circles all the time, while also having the money to make the management aspect easier so that you could run a car, have a relatively nice house, have a washing machine—all quite simple things, but one has to have a certain standard of living to be able to maintain those things. . . . It is a matter of thinking more concretely about details like the day-to-day care arrangements.

For Colleen these arrangements included the purchase of a house with another woman on the 'understanding' that one or both of them might have a baby. Yet she stated very clearly that she had not reached a decision.

Like Colleen, during interviews women explored personal worries about the practicalities of motherhood. Dialogues with different women about their decisions were similar in that each contained a repertoire of rhetorical questions about the ways in which motherhood would change (or not change) the respondent's life. Deciding about children is not a single question, therefore, but involves a series of interrelated questions, summarized in Table 4. Not surprisingly, these questions deal with factors identified by women as central to the 'right time'. Women's questions concerned whether or not they would continue working, and if so whether maternity leave was feasible, what arrangements would be available for childcare that would be both acceptable and affordable, how a baby might alter domestic relationships, what impact maternity would have on their standard of living, and so on. *Although the questions raised were personal ones, they addressed 'structural' or social process: the organization of waged employment, the sexual division of childcare labour, the privatized costs of reproduction.* Only after the respondent could conceptualize whether and how these practical questions could be answered did she feel that external

**Table 4** Rhetorical Questions Asked by 67 Women

1. *Career Questions*

    Would I continue working?
    - No: Will I be bored/isolated at home?
        Could I cope financially?
        Will I become boring to my husband/partner?
    - Yes: What childcare is available? Can I afford it?
        Will I feel guilty going back to work?
        Will maternity leave be a problem?
        Would I tell my boss about my intentions?
        How will my co-workers react?
        Will motherhood be detrimental to my career/employment?
        Would I be able to cope with motherhood and employment?
        When would be the best time at work?

2. *Relationship Questions*

    How does my partner feel about fatherhood?
    How does he feel about motherhood?
    Would my partner be supportive/do his 'share'?
    Will there be disputes about domestic labour?
    Would my partner find me less interesting/attractive?
    Are we likely to argue about parenting?
    Will we have enough time for the two of us?
    Will my partner be jealous of the baby?

3. *Financial Questions*

    Can I/we affford a baby now? Or in the future?
    How will my/our standard of living change?

4. *Personal Questions*

    Do I like babies/children?
    Can I cope with motherhood?
    Will I resent the baby if there are problems?
    Am I ready for the responsibility?
    Will I become depressed?

constraints had been eliminated or managed so that decision making could be based upon considerations of a different nature: whether or not she actually liked children.

Overall, deciding about motherhood involved the conceptualization of potential strategies which would enable the respondent to cope with the practicalities of motherhood. These strategies varied in the degree to which they were able to address satisfactorily the interrelated concerns, however. The development of strategies depended first upon individual access to, or ownership of, necessary resources. For example, a woman can only 'choose' a domestic career if her or (more likely) her husband's resources allow it. Similarly, she can 'decide' to hire a nanny only if living arrangements and income render it a real option. For this reason, these types of strategies represent *individualized or personal solutions to structural processes*. The nature and demands of the workplace are determined by economic processes beyond the manipulation of individual actors. Women's continued responsibility for childcare is maintained through a complex set of processes which perpetuate the sexual division of domestic labour. The privatized costs of reproduction are the consequence of market processes. It is the impact of these processes upon the daily lives of respondents which dominate their decisions about motherhood. Figure 2 schematically summarizes an interrelated set of decisions which constitute, for women, a decision about motherhood.

In contrast to cost-benefit models of decision making, Figure 2 illustrates how decision making as an irresolvable dilemma for some women is rooted in the material context of motherhood and not just in their 'thinking' about mother-hood. Although some women may be able to achieve a degree of control over structural processes which resolves their ambivalence, others described the circular nature of decision-making dilemmas. Rosemarie, the 35-year-old secretary, has been unable to decide after two years of deliberation:

> There's a sort of twisted problem. I suppose if (pause) if I was married to someone who had lots of money, I could stay home and give the child the things I would want to give a child. Then I probably would. But I *have* to work, financially I have to work . . .

> Another thing I feel guilty about is that, to me, a secretary is not a good job. I would never say this to anyone who is a secretary, but to me it is not. In a way, I'm not justified working and leaving a child with someone else when I'm just a secretary. If I did a career that had some sort of purpose, like a teacher, or something, then I wouldn't feel so guilty. But being just a secretary, in the back of my mind, I don't think it justifies going back to work, although I *would*—do you see? . . . I think about it so much lately that it's becoming—I don't know, I'm becoming paranoid about it.

From the situations of women like Rosemarie, the outcome of a 'rational' assessment of their situation is indecision accompanied by personal conflict. Overall, one third of the women in this sample described their decision making as a period of personal duress which, for some, precipitated a 'crisis' in their personal lives. Like Rosemarie, many more women described the guilt which accompanied their decision making. Ironically, this guilt seemed to place women in a no-win situation, because women wanting children argued that their motivations were selfish:

> I suppose for me motherhood (pause), I suppose it's a *selfish* thing to some extent. (decided for, childed)

At the same time, women wanting to remain childless were likely to describe their motives similarly:

Figure 2 Reproductive Decision Making as Personal Solutions to Structural Dilemmas, Showing Indecision and Conflict

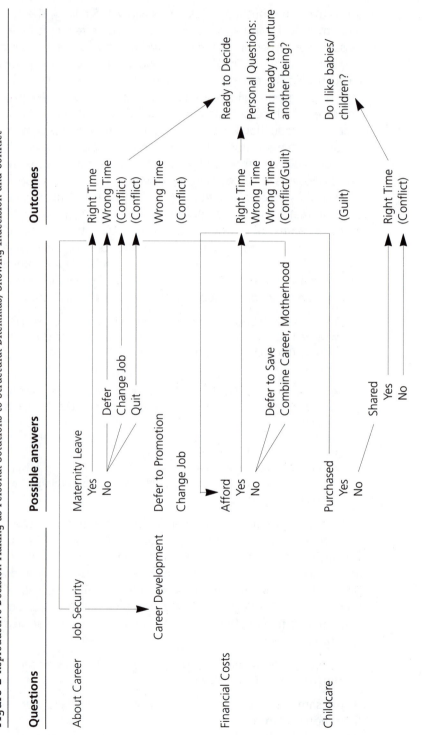

> Perhaps we're being very selfish about it. But then, on the other hand, why not? I would rather face up to the fact that I'm being selfish now than to find out too late I couldn't cope. (unchilded)

Clearly, conflict and guilt cannot be explained as a consequence of which choices women make. *Conflict and guilt develop during and as a consequence of making choices.* In this study, these experiences stem from the internalization by women of the structural contradictions of motherhood. Although rooted in the 'consciousness' of respondents, conflict and guilt result from personal struggles which arise when the social institution of motherhood places women in antagonistic relationships in their personal lives—particularly between themselves and the workplace or themselves and their domestic partners. For many women, their 'choices' appear as impossible alternatives. At the same time, the rhetoric of 'reproductive freedom' obscures the way in which women internalize structural antagonisms as personal ones. The notion of 'right time' is important, therefore, because it highlights this process of individualization. With few exceptions, women referred to the biographical context of decision making rather than to social processes.

By discussing their experiences in a biographical context of 'time' rather than a social one of 'process', women's own decision making often remained inexplicable even to themselves. This 36-year-old mother explained her own decision making: 'I was 35, my IUD fell out. I thought that was a sign.' Upon further query, however, she indicated a number of factors which made this moment the 'right time' to consider motherhood:

> Well, it was just—you know, my partner wasn't desperately keen before, and I was also not quite sure, and so on. So it hadn't really come up until that happened. And then I thought 'Well, yes. I think this might not be—I'll just see what happens' sort of thing. 'I can handle it now, financially and career-wise'. I was settled and stable.

In like manner, a number of women who had experienced a protracted period of indecision characterized by ambivalence developed idiosyncratic explanations for their behaviour. Although discussing their moment of decision in terms of mystical or biological forces, however, corresponding to their stories were identifiable changes in their material circumstances.

Given the biographical context within which motherhood is assessed, for some women the 'right time' never comes. From this perspective, *contraceptive risk-taking has new significance for it is characterized as a consequence of powerlessness rather than 'inappropriate' cost-benefit assessments*, as traditional approaches imply. Women in this study faced the often impossible task of developing personal strategies to resolve structurally generated problems. While risk-taking does not bring control over structural processes, it re-locates the contradictions by bringing them within the realm of personal activity. Once within the context of the respondent's personal life, these contradictions become accessible to personal activity, as illustrated by Rosemarie's story:

> If I were just pregnant, that would be it. That would mean that I wouldn't have all this thinking about it, yes? . . . I think it would be if I were pregnant, than we'd have to sit down and just do something.

A decision to 'just let things happen' is not an unarticulated decision in favour of motherhood, however. A number of women reported terminating pregnancies which resulted from risk-taking behaviour. This 37-year-old geologist discusses her 'unplanned' pregnancy which resulted from risk-taking:

> We never planned either way . . . [when pregnant] I think we were both quite excited. But while being pleased and excited, it didn't mean that we were going to go through with it. We just decided that we'd have to think about it.

While 'unplanned' pregnancies impart an immediacy to decision making, if processes which made motherhood problematic in the first place remain, these pregnancies were then evaluated as 'unwanted'. Women thus discussed unwanted pregnancies as occurring at the 'wrong time'.[4] *Unplanned pregnancies through risk-taking behaviour are not the result of irrational thinking or behaving, however. Paradoxically, they result from women attempting to resolve rationally their personal dilemmas within an irrational framework of impossible choices.*

## Summary and Discussion
Although the context of reproductive decision making is dominated by pronatalist attitudes and expectations, traditional approaches of cost-benefit analyses obscure this by portraying 'alternatives' as carrying personal rather than cultural priority. In the current research, however, virtually all women discussed motherhood because women conceptualize their future in terms of this potential. When considering their future in terms of motherhood, they described the day-to-day practicalities of adding children to their lives. Within the context of their daily lives, motherhood was seen as 'problematic'. The source of their personal problems was identified as the nature of waged employment, the sexual division of domestic labour, and the financial costs of children. Although appearing as 'private troubles' within individual biographies, however, these problems stem from social structure—the organization of the workplace and of the family as a social institution rather than a set of personal relations. While writers in the tradition of Russell and Fitzgibbons (1982) claim that the awareness of choice inevitably will be accompanied by the pain of decision, we have seen this 'pain' stems from the personalization of responsibility for problems generated by structural process. The notion of 'right time' for motherhood reflects this personalization. Although we have understood in this discussion that the 'right time' refers to a configuration of material conditions not always amenable to individual control, to the women interviewed it implied that the problems of motherhood could be solved through their own judicious planning. In Table 4, the

'right time' represents a moment when motherhood can be conceptualized as a viable alternative. With the external demands of employment, domestic schedules, etc. rendered manageable, decision making concerns personal preferences for children. Because this moment resolves initial ambivalence about motherhood, women described it as being 'ready to decide'. As we have seen, however, being 'ready' to decide is an individual and not a social responsibility, so that 'freely chosen motherhood' is, likewise, an individual and not a social responsibility.

Taking a 'structural' approach, writers like Fabe and Wikler (1979), Gerson (1985), and others argue that women's choices relate to the competing alternative commitments to work and family:

> Women's decision for and against motherhood and for or against committed work ties develop out of a negotiated process whereby they confront and respond to constraints and opportunities, often unanticipated, encountered over the course of their lives (Gerson, 1985: 213).

From this analysis of structural coercion, reproductive freedom is portrayed as alternatively expanding opportunities and removing constraints for women. In contrast, this current study illustrates that *solutions to 'opportunities and constraints' are individually negotiated. It is the privatization of alternatives which must be addressed in order to transcend a movement for 'liberation' which incorporates an ideology of personal responsibility shared by a current moral backlash.*

In conclusion, this study does more than add to our understanding of decision making by giving visibility to women's experiences. It challenges established theory by recognizing how the normal practice of social science research obscures the structural roots of women's oppression through the development of paradigms which portray decisions as the outcome of entirely cognitive assessments. As we have seen, feminist approaches which begin from the experiences of women as a rejection of established theory often perpetuate this process by emphasizing women's accounts as self-evident explanations. Contrary to the claims of Stanley and Wise, *this study illustrates the necessity to transcend the purely personal worlds of women.* For women in this study, the personalization of reproductive decision making is the process which rendered it oppressive.

Returning to the issues raised at the beginning of this paper, when thinking about 'what we do' and 'how we do it', the current state of our discipline requires that we begin from the experienced worlds of women. In this way, we want to 'discover grounded theory' so that we do indeed begin from the consciousness or subjective worlds of women. However, women's consciousness of their world cannot be mistaken for a developed explanation, as some writers imply. In the current study, women often assigned a biological 'imperative' to their decision making:

> I'm not sure why, but the emotional and hormonal thing must be closely linked. . . . Yes, those sort of emotional things probably coincided with the menstrual cycle—peaks of being 'maternal' were emerging and showing themselves.

I did not accept these explanations for women's behaviours, however. Although the research begins by 'experiencing the experiences' of women, a process through which my consciousness as researcher was altered—my task included 'explaining the explanations' of women—a process whereby the consciousness of the researched might be raised in order to change the material basis for the experiences of decision making. In sum, the subjective component of feminist research is a dialectical process which includes much more than simply adopting an experientially-based perspective and leads us necessarily to questions about social process, or 'structure'. *Against feminist approaches which portray the separation of the personal and the structural as a false distinction, this research suggests that what we need is not a research choice between 'structure' or 'people', but rather ways of conceptualizing relationships between the two.* As shown here, this is not the accomplishment of choosing between 'subjective' and 'objective' analyses.

Returning to the 'insider' versus 'outsider' view, the dilemma posed for feminist research is not the 'correctness' of choosing either as the proper vantage point. Rather, feminism is a challenge to the necessity of this type of choice. Beginning from the standpoint of women, our goal includes the expansion of knowledge through the development of feminist theory. If our 'feminist' knowledge is to remain as processual and open-ended as Glaser and Strauss advocate, it will be necessary to test our theories through a logico-deductive approach in order to expand, revise, or reject our knowledge as *this knowledge is used to transform its very basis*. For this reason, in feminist research we need flexibility in how we think about what we want to achieve. Surely this requires that we re-think adherence to a static way of doing 'feminist research' reflected in debates about the correct choice of method.

## Notes

1 This discussion is more adequately expanded in Currie and Kazi (1987: 77–98).
2 These women lived within easy access of London during the winter of 1984–5. Subjects were recruited through referral and various methods of solicitation. Not surprisingly, this sample is all white, primarily heterosexual women in [occupational] Class III Non-manual and above. The ways in which the experiences of this group resemble those of other women can be established only through further research.
3 Remembering that responses are unprompted, percentages are more significant than may be initially apparent. Undoubtedly, if women had responded to fixed categories most percentages would be much greater.
4 Similar to the concept of 'right time', the notion of 'wrong time' reflects the way in which respondents personalized the responsibility for timing pregnancy. When queried, the 'wrong time', not surprisingly, reflects the absence of factors which

make the time 'right'. Because the factors again are structural processes beyond individual control, we can see that the notion of 'unwanted' pregnancy is socially constructed and historically specific. Women did not recognize this as so, however, and as a consequence experienced a great deal of conflict and guilt about pregnancies which came 'at the wrong time'.

## REFERENCES

Blake, Judith
1975 'Coercive Pronatalism and American Population Policy'. Pp. 346–69 in Kammeyer (ed.), *Population Studies: Selected Essays and Research*. Chicago: Rand McNally.

Bouma, Gary D., and Wilma J. Bouma
1975 *Fertility Control: Canada's Lively Social Problem*. Don Mills, Ont.: Longmans Canada Limited.

Busfield, Joan, and Michael Paddon
1977 *Thinking About Children: Sociology and Fertility in Post-war England*. Cambridge: Cambridge University Press.

Currie, Dawn, and Hamida Kazi
1987 'Academic Feminism and the Process of De-radicalization: Re-examining the Issues'. *Feminist Review* 25 (Spring).

Fabe, Marilyn, and Norma Wikler
1979 *Up Against the Clock: Career Women Speak on The Choice to Have Children*. Berkeley: Warner Books.

Gerson, Kathleen
1985 *Hard Choices: How Women Decide About Work, Career, and Motherhood*. Berkeley: University of California Press.

Glaser, Barney G., and Anselm L. Strauss
1967 *The Discovery of Grounded Theory: Strategies for Qualitative Research*. Chicago: Aldine Publishing Company.

Kuhn, Thomas
1970 *The Structure of Scientific Revolutions*. Chicago: University of Chicago Press.

Luker, Kristin
1975 *Taking Chances: Abortion and Women's Decisions Not to Contracept*. Los Angeles: University of California Press.

Martin, Jean, and Ceridwen Roberts
1984  *Women and Employment: A Lifetime Perspective*. London: Her Majesty's Stationary Office.

McCormack, Thelma
1987  'Feminism and the New Crisis in Methodology'. A paper presented at a conference on the Effects of Feminist Approaches on Research Methodologies. Sponsored by the Calgary Institute for the Humanities, University of Calgary. January 22–24, 1987. Calgary, Alberta.

Oakley, Ann
1979  *From Here to Maternity: Becoming a Mother.* Harmondsworth, Middlesex: Penguin Books Limited.

1981  'Interviewing Women: a contradiction in terms'. Pp. 30–61 in H. Roberts (ed.), *Doing Feminist Research*. London: Routledge and Kegan Paul Limited.

O'Donnell, Lydia N.
1985  *The Unheralded Majority: Contemporary Women as Mothers*. Massachusetts: D.C. Heath and Company.

Reinharz, Shulamit
1979  *On Becoming A Social Scientist: From Survey Research and Participant Observation to Experiential Analysis*. San Francisco: Jossey-Bass.

1983  'Experiential Analysis: A Contribution to Feminist Research'. Pp. 162–92 in G. Bowles, and R. Klein (eds), *Theories of Women's Studies*. London: Routledge and Routledge.

Rich, Adrienne
1977  *Of Women Born: Motherhood as Experience and Institution*. London: Virago Press.

Russell, Anne, and Patricia Fitzgibbons
1982  *Career and Conflict: A Woman's Guide to Making Life Choices*. New Jersey: Prentice-Hall, Incorporated.

Russo, N.F.
1979  'Overview: sex roles, fertility, and the motherhood mandate'. *Psychology of Women Quarterly* 4: 7–15.

Smith, Dorothy E.
1981  'The Experienced World as Problematic: A Feminist Method'. The Twelfth Annual Sorokin Lecture at the University of Saskatchewan, Saskatoon, January 28, 1981.

Stanley, Liz, and Sue Wise
1983 *Breaking Out: Feminist Consciousness and Feminist Research*. London: Routledge and Kegan Paul.

Sugarman, Leonie
1985 'Dilemmas of the Childbearing Decision'. *The Journal of The British Association for Counselling*, 51 (February).

Veveers, Jean E.
1980 *Childless By Choice*. Toronto: Butterworth and Company.

Vogel, Lise
1983 *Marxism and the Oppression of Women: Toward a Unitary Theory*. New Jersey: Rutgers University Press.

From *Canadian Review of Sociology and Anthropology* 25 (2) (1988): 231–53.

## CRITIQUE OF CURRIE'S 'RE-THINKING WHAT WE DO'

Currie begins by announcing that her article (and her version of feminist sociology) seeks to transcend the strictly personal worlds of women, in contrast to the radical vision of interpretive feminist sociology represented by Stanley and Wise (1983: 83) in which 'there is no going beyond the personal'. Thus, the task she sets herself is to demonstrate the possibility and utility of conducting a version of feminist sociology in which the investigator begins with the lived experience of 'female' actors but tries to move beyond their experience. This battle between those who would limit sociology to thickly descriptive personal accounts and those who would try to develop generic insights that subsume and transcend those descriptions is as old as the social sciences and remains a live issue today. Currie explicitly sets her paper in this context, reiterating at the end that her 'task included "explaining the explanations" of women'.

In her introduction, she tells us that this study was conducted qualitatively (or inductively—seeking to move towards more general and abstract statements from empirical observations) in an effort to discover grounded theory. She also tells us that the materials used come from a broader project in which she interviewed 76 women about their postponement or rejection of motherhood. (A footnote informs us that the women lived near London during the winter of 1984–5, were recruited or solicited in some manner and were all white, primarily heterosexual, and in [occupational] Class III Non-manual and above. We are told that the question of their representativeness awaits further replication. That position is quite common among qualitative researchers, in distinction to the confidence in generalizability that positivistic researchers have based on their sampling protocols.) Data were collected through unstructured personal interviews one or two hours in length, and the respondents were categorized according to self-report of their decision status with respect to having children. The initial categories were simply 'decided' and 'undecided'. Subsequently, further categories became apparent as decided women described themselves as either 'for' or 'against' motherhood and as early deciders, those who decided after much difficulty, or those who changed their minds. Similarly, undecided women described themselves variously as putting off the decision, not ready to decide, or unable to decide. The women's accounts included ambivalence, conflict, and indecision.

Currie contrasts her orientation to more positivistic literature, which tends to be based on a theoretical cost-benefit model that suggests that the choice made (for or against motherhood) reflects the assessment of relative costs and benefits and that the 'problem' for women today is that many choices now compete with motherhood, thus explaining the declining rate of fertility.

Currie tells us that a significant proportion of this sample (22.4 per cent) consists of undecided women and that the category includes both unchilded and childed women.[1] Though her percentage calculation makes little apparent sense, the designation of this category as that which is of interest will produce a significantly different analysis because most positivistic research would presumably have begun by searching for differences in the experiences of mothers and non-mothers, treating motherhood status rather than decision status as the dependent variable. In other words, since the two categories (motherhood and decision-making status) do not overlap perfectly, we will in fact be explaining different things, and the phenomenon of interest to her has in fact emerged as it should in interpretive analysis, from the responses of the actors themselves.

The issue now is to explain variation in their decision status, which is what we might well expect to see Currie develop. Why were some women able to make conscious choices whereas other women were not? Did the former make emotional and idiosyncratic decisions, or is there a logic and a pattern to them? How might the answers to such questions bear on the idea of 'contraceptive roulette'? This last issue appears to have emerged from the accounts given her by subjects who 'never really decided' but 'let it happen'.

We are told that '67 per cent of the women in this study demonstrated an ambivalent attitude towards motherhood during interviews',[2] where ambivalence refers to their sense that there is no compelling basis on which to make a decision in either direction. Table 1 provides both positive and negative themes spoken of by women without prompting by the interviewer. We are not told, though, as one might have expected to be, how the themes relate to the categorization of the women with respect to their decision status. In other words, we are not given any clear operational definitions of the variables or reasons why an indicator is assigned the meaning it is. Currie tells us that few women could discuss concrete reasons for their decision and that instead they referred to whether or not there was a right time for motherhood. Table 2 identifies six categories of the 'right time for motherhood' factors as described by the 37 women who discussed their situation in this manner. The first three of these are then illustrated from the interviews themselves, as is standard practice in much qualitative research. Currie then suggests, for no discernible reason, that the notion of time refers to 'a configuration of material circumstances' rather than to age or an identifiable point in the respondent's life. She suggests that the women felt 'they had to personally manage these practicalities before they were ready to decide'.

That would seem to make it clear that these 37 women were undecided and that issues relating to the 'right time' are their explanations for their decision status, but she resists this simple interpretation of the data.

In her critical attempt to move beyond the respondents' own explanations, Currie admits that, as seen in Table 3, right-hand column, 'respondents were likely to discuss their readiness as a personal characteristic, namely "maturity"' (factor 5 of Table 2), but again, rather than accept their statements at face value, she argues in opposition that readiness is a configuration of material circumstances. In the subsequent brief section, she goes on to argue that 'in this study, it is the institutional aspects which render motherhood personally problematic'. So far as I can see, she gives no explanation for choosing to disbelieve her subjects at this point and no evidence whatsoever in support of her contention that institutional aspects explain their difficulty in deciding about motherhood. On the contrary, it is clear that this explanation does not arise from their statements, and in fact is in opposition to their own explanations.

Currie goes on to expand upon her explanation for the ambivalence (of these 37 subjects) that appears to have become her central issue (rather than explaining the decision status of all the women in her study). In choosing this strategy, she loses her dependent variable and is forced into a common-denominator study instead—a form that, though quite common, is an inadequate basis for establishing a causal relationship since there is no dependent variable as such. (For further explanation, see the illustrative reading on hypotheses and variables in chapter 2.) She describes the conflict and guilt that often characterize the statements of these women and suggests that those experiences are a result of being caught between impossible alternatives. As she approaches her conclusion, she claims that in this context '*contraceptive risk-taking has new significance for it is characterized as a consequence of powerlessness rather than inappropriate cost-benefit assessments. . . . Unplanned pregnancies through risk-taking behaviour are not the result of irrational thinking or behaving, however. Paradoxically, they result from women attempting to resolve rationally their personal dilemmas within an irrational framework of impossible choices.*' I would argue that this case remains, quite simply, unsubstantiated.

This article is very vulnerable to both methodological and substantive criticism. Still, it is a useful example of an ambitious kind of qualitative research informed by feminist thinking of a particular type. There is no point served in exhaustively criticizing it here; in any case every reader should be able to suggest additional criticisms to those I have sketched out. Indeed, you might well want to spend some time in a tutorial discussing the paper and this critique of it.

The first and least serious criticism is statistical. Currie presents statistical analysis of tables with no regard for the numbers of cases on which the percentages are calculated, and in such a manner as to make it impossible to understand her calculations. This is irritating at least, and provides sufficient reason to warrant close examination of her data, which unfortunately, are not provided in enough detail to allay my suspicions.

Second, in explaining the explanations of the actors, which is her announced intent, Currie has to choose when to give weight to their own explanations and when to ignore, deny, or reinterpret them. What is crucial is that there is no explanation of how she made that decision. For example, Currie tells us that, though the women 'were likely to discuss their readiness as a personal characteristic, namely maturity', she chooses to disregard and contradict their explanation and analyse their indecision as a reflection of institutional arrangements and material conditions. What rationale is there for this, and how convincing is it? Surely even for feminist researchers operating in the mode of grounded theory construction, there is some obligation to provide evidence for their claims and rationales for their expectations. In their absence the sceptical reader has little reason to be less sceptical.

What is perhaps even more serious is that Currie fails to exercise much sociological imagination, treating her subjects' ambivalence as a unique feature of the contradictions involving motherhood in our society. In fact, however, there are many situations in which we have to make decisions without sufficient knowledge of relevant factors to compel one or another decision. Thus, one might perhaps profitably ask how the strategies of these women differ from the strategies and experiences of people contemplating early retirement, marriage, a career choice, or suicide. It seems to me that for her women and for those in any of the above situations, one choice is somehow to force fate to decide for you, over-coming the ambiguities and unknowables of an attempt to weigh costs and benefits. Thus, the women who simply can't decide may *decide* to let chance force the issue; and the choice is not unlike that by which a student who can't decide whether to go to law school or grad-uate school or which to go to, might send applications to many of both in the hope that only one will accept him or her.

Far from 'challenging established theory by recognizing how the normal practice of social science research obscures the structural roots of women's oppression through the development of paradigms which portray decisions as the outcomes of entirely cognitive assessments', such a revised analysis, more closely based on what her respondents say, and taking their words at face value, would be entirely compatible with the cost-benefit and rational-choice model Currie earlier criticizes. Certainly it appears that to emphasize the 'structural roots of women's oppression' is to read a great deal too much into what they say, with no corroboration or independent evidence that her position is supportable. At least so it seems to me. But you are free to disagree.

Finally, as noted, in the course of her analysis Currie seems to lose her dependent vari-able, which I take to be decision-making status, and to focus instead on that category of women who experience ambiguity, seeking to explain the source of their feeling. She finds that source in the institutional arrangements in our society regarding motherhood. Unfor-tunately at this point she appears to be guilty of trying to explain a constant (since all are ambivalent) by reference to another constant (since the institutional arrangements affect all of them), and that simply does not work. Science involves hypotheses or statements of specific relationships between variables, with variation in an independent variable system-atically related to (and therefore potentially affecting or even causing) variation in the dependent variable. That suggests quite a different line of analysis from the one pursued here, and I think it might have been more fruitful.

## CONCLUSION

It was my purpose in this final chapter to give you an opportunity, a challenge, and an invitation. The opportunity was to take part, at least vicariously, in some of the debates that characterize the discipline, and by so doing to learn to appreciate the give and take of intellectual disagreement. The challenge is to employ what you have learned to participate more actively in the assessment of some contentious articles published in recent years in Canadian sociology. The invitation is to realize that this book is only the merest introduction to the study of sociology. I have tried to pass on to you some sense of what the discipline looks like, how one might use it, and to what end. I have tried to give you a sense of what the sociological imagination looks like and what it can illuminate. If you find this book useful, I hope you will accept my invitation to look into the field more seriously.

## NOTES TO THE CHAPTER

1 Talk about misplaced precision! Currie calculates and reports what seem to be precise percentages in many tables in which such a calculation makes no sense at all. If in this instance N = 76, 22.4 per cent would be about 17 women.

2 It is unclear again where this number comes from, for Table 1 is based on 65 interviews whereas there were 76 in 'the broader project' from which the material in this paper is derived. If the total N is 76, 67 per cent would be 51 women, and if 65, 67 per cent would be 43.55 women. There is no explanation of why only 65 interviews are used.

# Postscript

This has been a challenging book to write and to rewrite. l have considered it a wonderful opportunity to invite those who are interested to try to understand and use the sociological perspective and to assess what it illuminates. That has been my guiding orientation throughout. It is this orientation to *using* and *assessing* that I have tried to capture in the title *Thinking Sociologically*. It is these related practical skills that I have sought to illustrate and teach.

If I have succeeded in interesting you in sociology, you may choose to consider a great many questions and go on to study as many substantive courses, but in all of them your skill in using the perspective and evaluating what it illuminates will be crucial. Though the 'facts' have a sometimes disconcerting way of changing, they must always be subject to your critical assessment. Perhaps that is the most noteworthy aspect of the orientation I mean this book to emphasize: you are not merely a passive spectator in the process of your introduction to sociology. Rather you are the key participant, and you have the responsibility to participate knowledgeably and skillfully. I realize you will reply that at this level you do not have the knowledge to participate. l have quite often been told by students that my standards are too high and that they do not, after all, intend to become 'professional sociologists'! I object vehemently, saddened that our educational system has managed to convince so many capable students that they are unable to think for themselves, that the only role for which they are suited is that of a sponge, soaking up what is offered and squeezing it out at examination time. Such a view of students and their abilities is demeaning, and it is a terrible indictment of our system that students themselves are willing to accept such a definition of the situation. Sociology students might well reflect on the implications of such a system as well as its possible causes and consequences.

You can certainly think, and you will never know enough to be confident that you know everything of relevance to the case you are asked to assess. That is as true of me as of you. It is equally true for all of us. But since we live in a world of imperfect knowledge, we must make decisions despite our limitations. I refuse to allow my own students to opt out so easily. You can participate, and you must participate if your education is to be meaningful and useful to you. In addition, since science itself is a 'community project', we need active and critical participation. I believe that when you enrol in a university or even pick up a book like this to read in other circumstances, you make a tacit bargain to participate in this way. Surely that is the meaning of the degrees and grades you seek. They tell others that you are able to participate usefully in these areas. You have the intelligence and the ability. Until now you may have been asked or encouraged to use them only rarely, but if this book has succeeded, you have both been challenged to participate and taught the skills necessary for productive participation.

Those readers who have been provoked, encouraged, and excited by this book will find that I am asking them to think for themselves, ask critical questions, and consider disagreeing with the experts. They find that fun, and so it should be. Sociology is not characterized by right answers, at least not by any that are right simply because the instructor or the book or an article says so. That is not to say, as some students mistakenly think, that all opinions are equally legitimate and correct and that everybody has a right to their opinion. In fact I am not interested in opinions at all. Sociology deals with evidence, and it is conclusions that are warranted by the evidence that concern us. Indeed as prospective scientists, you now know that the process by which you come to conclusions is always far more important than the conclusions themselves. Science rests on your ability to be an open-minded sceptic, demanding of yourself and others that they be prepared to defend their claims to know. In these circumstances no one has the 'right' to hold an opinion if it is not defensible.

If you are now prepared to regard evidence critically and actively rather than uncritically and passively, then I have in some part succeeded. If you cannot now read the newspaper or watch a commercial without rival interpretations and critical comments coming unbidden to mind, then I have met with some success. If you go to your next class and are tempted to object to the arguments made by your teacher, text, or classmates, then this book has partly succeeded. If you cannot any longer stand idly by as others make claims that seem to be without foundation, then I have also partly succeeded. Perhaps now you understand more fully why I believe that teaching is a subversive activity. Most important, if you have taken the next step beyond mere negative criticism and cynicism to creative thought, then I have succeeded. For it is only at this point that you become a participant in science and not a carping outsider. If you offer constructive criticism, if you are prepared to present alternative explanations that better meet your own requirements for evidence— then I have truly succeeded, and so have you.

Though I believe the sociological perspective is a valuable one, I do not expect all readers to become sociologists, nor do I address myself to them in the hope of converting them. My hopes are more grand than that you merely learn some sociology. I want to 'jump-start' your brains again, brains that our system skillfully manages to put to sleep but that were once, and can again be, lively, questioning, and active. I want you to participate with enthusiasm in your own education but to temper that enthusiasm with a commitment to evidence and the careful consideration of alternatives. I want you to realize that theory, methods, and subject matter are thoroughly intertwined and inseparable—and to act accordingly. I want you to understand both that science is tentative and why it must always be so.

I raise many questions in this book, far more questions than answers. That too is what I take to be part of the process of *learning to learn*, which is what I have been most interested in here. Reality contains more questions than answers. What I hope I have accomplished here is to have taught you that questions are important, that asking them can be fun, that how they are asked determines how and whether they can be answered, and that we learn primarily from our attempts to solve these problems, whether our attempts succeed or not.

# Bibliography

Adams, B.

1967a Occupational position, mobility and the kin of orientation. *American Sociological Review* 32: 364–77.

1967b Interaction theory and the social network. *Sociometry* 30: 64–78.

1970 Isolation, function and beyond: American kinship in the 1960's. *Journal of Marriage and the Family* 32: 364–77.

Adorno, T.W., et al.

1950 *The Authoritarian Personality*, New York: Harper & Row.

Aiken, M.

1964 Kinship in an urban community. Ph.D. dissertation, University of Michigan.

Aiken, M., and R. Alford

1967 Community structure and innovation: the case of urban renewal. *American Sociological Review* 35: 650–64.

Aiken, M., and D. Goldberg

1969 Social mobility and kinship: a reexamination of the hypothesis. *American Anthropologist* 71: 261–70.

Alba, R., and M. Chamlin

1983 A preliminary examination of ethnic identification among whites. *American Sociological Review* 48: 240–7.

Appelbaum, R.

1970 *Theories of Social Change*, Chicago: Markham.

Aron, R.

1965, 1967 *Main Currents in Sociological Thought*, 2 vols, New York: Basic Books.

Axelrod, M.

1956 Urban structure and social participation. *American Sociological Review* 21: 13–18.

Axelrod, M., and H. Sharp
1956 Mutual aid among relatives in an urban population, pp. 433–9 in R. Freedman et al. *Principles of Sociology*, New York: Holt, Rinehart and Winston.

Barnes, J.
1954 Class and committees in a Norwegian island parish. *Human Relations* 7: 39–58.

Becker, H.S., Jr.
1963 *Outsiders: Studies in the Sociology of Deviance*, New York: Free Press.

Berger, P.L.
1963 *An Invitation to Sociology: A Humanistic Perspective*, Garden City, NY: Doubleday, Anchor Books.

Bell, C., and H. Newby
1971 *Community Studies*, London: George Allen and Unwin.

Bennett, J., and L. Depres
1960 Kinship and instrumental activities: a theoretical inquiry. *American Anthropologist* 62: 254–67.

Bernard, J.
1972 *The Future of Marriage*, New York: Bantam.

1973 *The Sociology of Community*, Glenview, Ill.: Scott Foresman.

Bott, E.
1955 Urban families: conjugal roles and social networks. *Human Relations* 8 (4): 345–84.
1957 *Family and Social Network*, London: Tavistock Institute.

Boyd, M., and E.T. Pryor
1990 Young adults living in their parents' homes, pp. 188–91 in C. McKie and K. Thompson (eds), *Canadian Social Trends*, Toronto: Thompson Educational Publishing.

Bramson, L.
1961 *The Political Context of Sociology*, Princeton, NJ: Princeton University Press.

Brannigan, A., and S. Goldenberg
1987 The study of aggressive pornography: The vicissitudes of relevance. *Critical Studies in Mass Communication* 4: 262–83.

Breton, R.
1964 Institutional completeness of ethnic communities and the personal relations of immigrants. *American Journal of Sociology* 70: 193–205.

Burgess, E.
1925   The growth of the city: an introduction to a research project, in R.E. Park and R.W. Burgess, *The City*, Chicago: University of Chicago Press.

Campbell, D.
1969   Prospective: artifact and control, chapter 8 in R. Rosenthal and R. Rosnow (eds), *Artifact in Behavioral Research*, New York: Academic.

Campbell, D.T., and J.C. Stanley
1963   *Experimental and Quasi-Experimental Designs for Research*, Chicago: Rand McNally.

Charon, J.M.
1985   *Symbolic Interactionism: An introduction, An interpretation, An integration*, 2nd edn, Englewood Cliffs, NJ: Prentice-Hall.

Collins, R.
1971   Functional and conflict theories of educational stratification. *American Sociological Review* 36: 1002–19.

Collins, R., and M. Makowsky
1972   *The Discovery of Society*, 2nd edn, New York: Random House.

Cook, T.D., and D.T. Campbell
1979   *Quasi-Experimentation*, Boston: Houghton Mifflin.

Cooley, C.H.
1922   *Human Nature and the Social Order*, rev. edn, New York: Scribner's.

Coser, L. (ed.)
1965   *Georg Simmel*, Englewood Cliffs, NJ: Prentice-Hall.

1971   *Masters of Sociological Thought: Ideas in Historical and Social Context*, New York: Harcourt, Brace, Jovanovich.

Cottrell, W.F.
1951   Death by dieselization: a case study in the reaction to technological change. *American Sociological Review* 16: 358–65.

Cox, K.
1982   Housing tenure and neighborhood activism. *Urban Affairs Quarterly* 18: 107–29.

Craven, P., and B. Wellman
1973   *The Network City*, Toronto: University of Toronto Centre for Urban and Community Studies.

Crenson, M.
1978   Social networks and political processes in urban neighborhoods. *American Journal of Political Science* 22: 578–94.

Currie, D.
1988   Re-thinking what we do and how we do it: a study of reproductive decisions. *Canadian Review of Sociology and Anthropology* 25 (2): 231–53.

Darroch, A.G., and W.G. Marston
1971   The social class basis of ethnic residential segregation: The Canadian case. *American Journal of Sociology* 77: 491–510.

Davis, F.J. (ed.)
1979   *Understanding Minority-Dominant Relations*, Arlington Heights, Ill.: AHM.

Davis, K.
1965   The urbanization of the human population, pp. 3–24 in *Cities*, New York: Scientific American.

DeKeseredy, W., and K. Kelly
1993   The incidence and prevalence of woman abuse in Canadian university and college dating relationships. *Canadian Journal of Sociology* 18 (2): 137–59.

Deutscher, I.
1973   *What We Say/What We Do*, Glenview, Ill.: Scott Foresman.

Drucker, P.
[1939] 1985   *The End of Economic Man*, Ann Arbor: University Microfilms International.

Durkheim, E.
[1893] 1964   *The Division of Labor in Society*, trans. J.S. Spaulding and G. Simpson, Glencoe, Ill.: Free Press.

[1897] 1951   *Suicide*, trans. J.S. Spaulding and G. Simpson, Glencoe, Ill.: Free Press.

Duvall, E.
1976   *Family Development*, Philadelphia: Lippincott.

Felson, R.
1981   Social sources of information in the development of the self. *Sociological Quarterly* 22: 69–79.

Fox, B.J.
1993   On violent men and female victims: A comment on DeKeseredy and Kelly. *Canadian Journal of Sociology* 18 (3): 321–4.

Furstenberg, F.
1966   Industrialization and the American family: A look backward. *American Sociological Review* 31: 326–37.

Gans, H.
1962   Urbanism and suburbanism as ways of life, pp. 625–48 in A.M. Rose (ed.), *Human Behavior and Social Process*, Boston: Houghton Mifflin.

1962   *The Urban Villagers*, New York: Free Press.

Gartner, R.
1993   Studying woman abuse: A comment on DeKeseredy and Kelly. *Canadian Journal of Sociology* 18 (3): 313–20.

Gibson, G.
1972   Kin family network: overheralded structure in past conceptualizations of family functioning. *Journal of Marriage and the Family* 34: 13–23.

Glaser, B., and A. Strauss
1967   *The Discovery of Grounded Theory*, Chicago: Aldine.

Glazer, M.
1972   *The Research Adventure*, New York: Random House.

Glazer, N., and D.P. Moynihan
1963   *Beyond the Melting Pot: The Negroes, Puerto Ricans, Jews, Italians, and Irish of New York City*, Cambridge, Mass.: MIT Press.

Glick, P.
1955   The life cycle of the family. *Journal of Marriage and the Family* 17: 3–10.

Goffman, E.
1959   *The Presentation of Self in Everyday Life*, Garden City, NY: Doubleday, Anchor Books.

1967   *Interaction Ritual: Essays on Face to Face Behavior*, Garden City, NY: Doubleday, Anchor Books.

Gold, R.L.
1958   Roles in sociological field observations. *Social Forces* 36: 217–23.

Goldenberg, S.
1977   Kinship and ethnicity viewed as adaptive responses to location in the opportunity structure. *Journal of Comparative Family Studies* 8: 149–64.

1985   An empirical test of Bott's network hypotheses based on analysis of ethnographic atlas data. *Behavior Science Research* 19: 127–59.

1993   On distinguishing variables from values and hypotheses from statements of association. *Teaching Sociology*, 21 (1): 100–4.

Goldenberg, S., and V. Haines
1992   Social networks and institutional completeness: from territory to ties. *Canadian Journal of Sociology*, 17 (3): 301–12.

Golding, W.
1954   *Lord of the Flies*, London: Faber and Faber.

Gordon, M., and H. Downing
1978   A multivariate test of the Bott hypothesis in an urban Irish setting. *Journal of Marriage and the Family* 40: 585–95.

Granovetter, M.S.
1973   The strength of weak ties. *American Journal of Sociology* 78 (1): 360–80.

Hammond, P. (ed.)
1968   *Sociologists at Work*, Garden City, NY: Doubleday, Anchor Books.

Harvey, E.
1974   *Educational Systems and the Labour Market*, Don Mills, Ont.: Longman.

Heberle, R.
1960   The normative element in neighborhood relations. *Pacific Sociological Review* 3: 3–11.

Heller, C. (ed.)
1969   *Structural Social Inequality*, New York: Macmillan.

Hoffer, E.
1951   *The True Believer*, New York: Harper & Row.

Hughes, E.C.
1945   Dilemmas and contradictions of status. *American Journal of Sociology* 50: 353–9.

Hughes, H.S.
1958   *Consciousness and Society: The Reorientation of European Social Thought, 1890–1930*, New York: Random House.

Hunter, A.
1975   The loss of community: an empirical test through replication. *American Sociological Review* 40: 537–52.

Kadustrin, C.
1983   Mental health and the interpersonal environment: a reexamination of some effects of social structure on mental health. *American Sociological Review* 48: 188–98.

Kang, G.E.
1976   Conflicting loyalties theory: a cross-cultural test. *Ethnology* 15: 201–9.

Kaplan, A.
1964   *The Conduct of Inquiry*, San Francisco: Chandler.

Katz, E., and P. Lazarsfeld
1955   *Personal Influence*, Glencoe, Ill.: Free Press.

Katz, F.
1958   Occupational contact networks. *Social Forces* 37: 252–8.

Keller, S.
1968   *The Urban Neighborhood*, New York: Random House.

Kim, I.
1981   *The New Urban Immigrants: The Korean Community in New York*, Princeton, NJ: Princeton University Press.

Kohn, M., and C. Schooler
1982   Job conditions and personality: a longitudinal assessment of their reciprocal effects. *American Journal of Sociology* 87: 1257–86.

Kuhn, M.H., and T.S. McPartland
1954   An empirical investigation of self attitudes. *American Sociological Review* 19: 68–76.

Labovitz, S., and R. Hagedorn
1981   *Introduction to Social Research*, 3rd edn, New York: McGraw-Hill.

LaPiere, R.T.
1934   Attitudes and actions. *Social Forces* 13: 35, 230–7.

Leslie, L., and K. Grady
1985   Changes in mothers' social networks and social support following divorce. *Journal of Marriage and the Family* 47: 663–73.

Lewin, K.
1951   *Field Theory in Social Science*, New York: Harper & Row.

Lieberson, S.
1987   *Making It Count*, Berkeley: University of California Press.

Lipset, S.M.
1965   Revolution and counterrevolution: The United States and Canada. In T. Ford (ed.), *The Revolutionary Theme in Contemporary America*, Lexington: University of Kentucky. Also in W.E. Mann (ed.), *Canada: A Sociological Profile*, Toronto: Copp Clark, 1971, 24–36.

1963   *Political Man*, Garden City, NY: Doubleday, Anchor Books.

Lipset, S.M. et al.
1956   *Union Democracy*, Garden City, NY: Doubleday, Anchor Books.

Litwak, E.
1960a  Geographical mobility and extended family cohesion. *American Sociological Review* 25: 385–94.

1960b  Occupational mobility and extended family cohesion. *American Sociological Review* 25: 9–21.

Lockhart, A.
1975   Future failure: The unanticipated consequences of educational planning, pp. 182–207 in R.M. Pike and E. Zureik (eds), *Socialization and Values in Canadian Society*, vol. 2, Toronto: McClelland & Stewart.

Lofland, J.
1976   *Doing Social Life*, New York: John Wiley & Sons.

MacDonald, J.S., and L.D. MacDonald
1964   Chain migration, ethnic neighborhood formation and social networks. *Milbank Memorial Fund Quarterly* 42: 82–97.

Madge, J.
1965   *The Tools of Social Science*, Garden City, NY: Doubleday Anchor Books.

Marx, K.
[1859] 1975   *Critique of Political Economy*, New York: International.

Marx, K., and F. Engels
[1848] 1947   *The Communist Manifesto*, R. Pascal (ed.), New York: International.

McCall, G., and J.L. Simmons
1966   *Identities and Interactions*, New York: Free Press.

Mead, G.H.
1934 *Mind, Self and Society*, Chicago: University of Chicago Press.

Merton, R.K.
1949 On sociological theories of the middle range. Pp. 39–72 in *On Theoretical Sociology*, New York: Free Press.

1957 Patterns of influence: local and cosmopolitan influentials. Chapter 12 in *Social Theory and Social Structure*, Glencoe, Ill.: Free Press.

Milgram, S.
1970a Interdisciplinary thinking and the small world problem. Chapter 6 in M. Sherif and C.W. Sherif (eds), *Interdisciplinary Relationships in the Social Sciences*, Chicago: Aldine.

1970b The experience of living in cities: a psychological analysis. *Science* 167. Reprinted in J. Helmer and N.A. Eddington (eds), *Urbanman: The Psychology of Urban Survival*, New York: Free Press, 1973: 1–12.

1974 *Obedience to Authority*, New York: Harper & Row.

Mill, J.S.
1965 Pp. 52–74 in J. Madge, *The Tools of Social Science*, Garden City, NY: Doubleday, Anchor Books.

Mills, C.W.
1943 The professional ideology of social pathologists. *American Journal of Sociology* 49: 165–80.

Mitchell, J.C.
1969 *Social Networks in Urban Situations*, Manchester: Manchester University Press.

Miyamoto, F., and S. Dornbusch
1956 A test of the interaction hypothesis of self conception. *American Journal of Sociology* 61: 399–403.

Moreno, J.L.
1945 *Sociometric Measurement of Social Configurations*, New York: Beacon House.

Mulkay, M.
1979 *Science and the Sociology of Knowledge*, London: George Allen and Unwin.

Naisbitt, J.
1982 *Megatrends*, New York: Warner Books.

Nann, R.
1975   Relocation of Vancouver's Chinatown residents under urban renewal. *Journal of Sociology and Social Welfare* 3: 125–30.

Newman, W.M.
1973   *American Pluralism: A Study of Minority Groups and Social Theory*, New York: Harper & Row.

Nisbet, R.A.
1953   *The Quest for Community*, Oxford: Oxford University Press.

1970   *Tradition and Revolt*, New York: Random House (Vintage Books).

Novak, M.
1972   *The Rise of the Unmeltable Ethnics: Politics and Culture in the Seventies*, New York: Macmillan.

Park, R.E.
1915   The city: suggestions for the investigation of human behavior in the urban environment. *American Journal of Sociology* 20: 577–612.

1928   Human migration and the marginal man. *American Journal of Sociology* 33: 881–93.

Parsons, T.
1943   The kinship system of the contemporary United States. *American Anthropologist* 45: 22–38.

Parsons, T., and R.F. Bales
1955   *Family, Socialization and Interaction Process*, Glencoe, Ill.: Free Press.

Phillips, D.
1971   *Knowledge from what? Theories and methods in social research.* Chicago: Rand McNally.

Polanyi, K.
1944   *The Great Transformation*, Boston: Beacon.

Postman, N., and C. Weingartner
1969   *Teaching as a Subversive Activity*, New York: Delacorte.

Redfield, R.
1947   The folk society. *American Journal of Sociology* 52: 293–308.

Riesman, D.
1952   *The Lonely Crowd*, New Haven: Yale University Press.

Robinson, W.S.
1950 Ecological correlations and the behavior of individuals. *American Sociological Review* 15: 351–7.

Rodman, H.
1967 Marital power in France, Greece, Yugoslavia, and the United States: a cross-national discussion. *Journal of Marriage and the Family*, 29 (2): 320–5. Reprinted in I. Reiss (ed.), *Readings on the Family System*, Holt, Rinehart and Winston, 1972: 270–5.

Ruitenbeek, H.M.
1963 *Varieties of Classic Social Theory*, New York: E.P. Dutton.

Schnaiberg, A., and S. Goldenberg
1989 From empty nest to crowded nest: The dynamics of incompletely-launched young adults. *Social Problems*, 36 (3): 251–8.

Shibutani, T.
1955 Reference groups as perspectives. *American Journal of Sociology* 60: 562–9.

Simmel, G.
1922 *The Web of Group Affiliations*. Trans. R. Bendix; reprinted in Simmel, 1955.

1955 *Conflict and the Web of Group Affiliations*. Trans. K. Wolff and R. Bendix, New York: Free Press.

1903 The metropolis and mental life. Pp. 409–24 in K. Wolff, 1950.

Slater, M.
1969 My son, the doctor: aspects of mobility among American Jews. *American Sociological Review* 34: 359–73.

Stanley, L., and S. Wise
1983 *Breaking Out: Feminist Consciousness and Feminist Research*, London: Routledge and Kegan Paul.

Sussman, M.
1953 The help pattern in the middle class family. *American Sociological Review* 18: 22–8.

Sussman, M., and L. Burchinal
1962 Kin family network: unheralded structure in current conceptualizations of the family. *Journal of Marriage and Family Living* 24: 320–32.

Suttles, G.
1968 *The Social Order of the Slum*, Chicago: University of Chicago Press.

Thomas, W.I.
1923   *The Unadjusted Girl*, Boston: Little, Brown.

Thomas, W.I., and D. Thomas
1928   *The Child in America*, New York: Knopf.

Thoits, P.
1983   Multiple identities and psychological well-being: a reformulation and test of the social isolation hypothesis. *American Sociological Review* 48: 174–87.

Turner, R.
1960   Sponsored and contest mobility and the school system. *American Sociological Review* 25: 855–67.

Valentine, C.
1968   *Culture and Poverty*, Chicago: University of Chicago Press.

Waller, W., and R. Hill
1951   *The Family*, New York: Holt, Rinehart and Winston.

Warren, R.B., and D.I. Warren
1977   *The Neighborhood Organizer's Handbook*, Notre Dame, Ind.: University of Notre Dame Press.

Webber, M.
1968   The post-city age. *Daedalus*, Fall: 1092–94.

Wellman, B.
1979   The community question: the intimate networks of East Yorkers. *American Journal of Sociology* 84: 1201–31.

Wellman, B., and S.D. Berkowitz, eds.
1988   *Social Structures*, New York: Cambridge University Press.

Whyte, W.F.
[1943] 1981   *Street Corner Society*, 3rd edn, Chicago: University of Chicago Press.

Wirth, L.
1938   Urbanism as a way of life. *American Journal of Sociology* 44: 1–24.

Wolff, K.
1950   *The Sociology of Georg Simmel*. Trans. K. Wolff, New York: Free Press.

Wrong, D.
1961   The oversocialized conception of man in modern sociology. *American Sociological Review* 26.

Yancey, W., E. Ericksen, and R. Juliani
1976   Emergent ethnicity: a review and reformulation. *American Sociological Review* 41: 391-403.

Young, M.
1961   *The Rise of the Meritocracy*, Baltimore, Md.: Penguin.

Young, M., and P. Wilmott
1957   *Family and Kinship in East London*, London: Routledge.

# Index

*Italic* page numbers indicate a reading.